Scarlett Johansson

Happy Birthday, Scarlett Johansson caricature (courtesy David Cowles, 2012).

Scarlett Johansson
The Life and Films

Kim R. Holston *and*
Warren Hope

McFarland & Company, Inc., Publishers
Jefferson, North Carolina

ALSO OF INTEREST BY KIM R. HOLSTON AND FROM MCFARLAND

Science Fiction, Fantasy and Horror Film Sequels, Series and Remakes: An Illustrated Filmography with Plot Synopses and Critical Commentary, Volume I (1997; paperback 2016);
Science Fiction, Fantasy and Horror Film Sequels, Series and Remakes: An Illustrated Filmography, Volume II, 1996–2016 (2018); *Movie Roadshows: A History and Filmography of Reserved-Seat Limited Showings, 1911–1973* (2013); *Susan Hayward: Her Films and Life* (2002; paperback 2009); *The Marching Band Handbook: Competitions, Instruments, Clinics, Fundraising, Publicity, Uniforms, Accessories, Trophies, Drum Corps, Twirling, Color Guard, Indoor Guard, Music, Travel, Directories, Bibliographies, Index*, 3d ed. (2004)

BY WARREN HOPE AND KIM HOLSTON AND FROM MCFARLAND
The Shakespeare Controversy: An Analysis of the Authorship Theories, 2d ed. (2009)

ISBN (print) 978-1-4766-7307-3
ISBN (ebook) 978-1-4766-4250-5

LIBRARY OF CONGRESS AND BRITISH LIBRARY
CATALOGUING DATA ARE AVAILABLE

Library of Congress Control Number 2021022080

© 2021 Kim R. Holston and Warren Hope. All rights reserved

No part of this book may be reproduced or transmitted in any form or by any means, electronic or mechanical, including photocopying or recording, or by any information storage and retrieval system, without permission in writing from the publisher.

Front cover image: Scarlett Johansson (as Jordan Two Delta/Sarah Jordan)
The Island, 2005 (Warner Bros./Photofest)

Printed in the United States of America

*McFarland & Company, Inc., Publishers
Box 611, Jefferson, North Carolina 28640
www.mcfarlandpub.com*

Table of Contents

Acknowledgments	vii
Chronology	ix
Prologue by Kim Holston	1
Introduction	3
1. Childhood	9
2. Child Actress	13
3. Adult Breakthrough: *Lost in Translation* (2003)	41
4. Working, Part 1	49
5. Woody Allen's Muse?	78
6. Working, Part 2	92
7. She Plays Big: The Marvel Universe	118
8. Working, Part 3	140
9. Her Own Unique Oeuvre	172
Epilogue	198
Appendix 1. "Film Odyssey: Scarlett Johansson Gets Under Our Skin" by Robert Castle	201
Appendix 2. Non-Screen Credits	204
Filmography	205
Chapter Notes	217
Bibliography	229
Index	237

"Another thing he taught me was not to nod my head when I am acting. This infuriates him. 'Remember to be definite,' he said, 'moving your head is indefinite. Only make a move when it means something.'"
—Dawn Addams, "My Life as Chaplin's Leading Lady," *Films and Filming*, August 1957

"Johansson is willing to do *less* to let the camera come to her. 'You have to take the time to have a thought,' she says, 'and that always allows for certain moments of silence.' Like those screen beauties of the '40s and '50s, she implies worlds but usually shows very little."
—Joseph Hooper, "Scarlett Fever," *Elle*, November 2007

"In her short career Scarlett Johansson has played so many roles and embraced so much human variety that it can prove hard to characterize her. She has operated beyond the limits of one persona, and she has not, as Marilyn Monroe or Audrey Hepburn once did, come to mean one complex thing, to make up one strongly delineated way of being in the world. From her many parts, however, one may tease out a particular thread that sheds more light than any comparable star's career could on the contemporary meaning of the film star, and by extension of the contemporary idea of the person."
—Michael Newton, *Show People: A History of the Film Star*, 2019

Acknowledgments

For help of various kinds or for taking an interest in our work on this book, the authors wish to thank Robert Castle, Stephen A. Miller, Heather Reese, Tom Winchester, Mary Magana, Emily Cackowski, Matt Brutosky, Theresa Dutko, James Berardinelli, Keith Smith, Bree Lankford, Rosemary Madrigale, Carol Welch, Ellen Youngdahl, Stephanie Sharon, Jessica Williams, Megan Sullivan, Natalie Griffith of *Sight & Sound*, artist Peter Cowles, photographer Dave Gatley, and Nancy Holston.

Chronology

November 22, 1984—Scarlett Ingrid Johansson born in New York City
1994—Film debut in *North*
1996—Independent Spirit Award nomination for Best Female Lead in *Manny & Lo*
November 8, 1998—Wins *The Hollywood Reporter* Best Young Actress in a Drama Film (*The Horse Whisperer*) award
2002—Graduates Professional Children's School
2002—*Screen World 2002* includes as a "Promising Personality of 2001"
2003—60th Annual Venice Film Festival Upstream Prize for Best Actress, *Lost in Translation*
February 15, 2004—Accepts BAFTA Award for Best Actress for *Lost in Translation*
2004—Golden Globe Award nominations for Best Performance (Actress) in a Motion Picture—Drama for *Girl with a Pearl Earring* and Best Performance (Actress) in a Motion Picture—Musical or Comedy for *Lost in Translation*
2004—Poses for famed photographer Annie Leibovitz at Chateau Marmont, West Hollywood
2004—Golden Globe Award nomination for Best Performance (Actress) in a Motion Picture—Drama for *A Love Song for Bobby Long*
2004—Hosts Pussycat Dolls at Viper Room, West Hollywood
2005—Golden Globe Award nomination for *Match Point*
January 10, 2006—Guest on *The Late Show* with David Letterman
March 2006—Poses nude with Keira Knightley on *Vanity Fair* cover
2006—Hosts *Saturday Night Live* (also 2007, 2010, 2015, 2017)
2006—FHM readers rank "Sexiest Woman Alive" in its 100 Sexiest Women in the World supplement
October 25, 2006—Stars in video accompanying Bob Dylan's "When the Deal Goes Down"
November 2006—*Esquire* Ranks "Sexiest Woman Alive"
2007—Represents Louis Vuitton fashion handbags
February 2007—Appears with Justin Timberlake in music video "What Goes Around … Comes Around"
February 2007—Receives Harvard Hasty Pudding Woman of the Year award
March 2007—Named "Smoothest Celebrity of the Year" (female) by Nad's Hair Removal
March 2007—Ranked "Sex Star of the Year" by *Playboy*
March 2008—In *Vanity Fair*'s big Hollywood issue Johansson and Javier Bardem pose as Grace Kelly and James Stewart, respectively, in a tribute to Hitchcock's 1954 classic, *Rear Window*.

Chronology

May 4, 2008—On TV's *The Simpsons* (Season 19, Episode 18) Woody Allen says he's thinking of adopting Scarlett Johansson

May 16, 2008—Releases "Anywhere I Lay My Head" album of Tom Waits songs

September 27, 2008—Marries actor Ryan Reynolds (divorced 2010)

December 11, 2008—Co-hosts with Michael Caine the 15th Nobel Peace Prize Concert for Martti Ahtisaari in Oslo, Norway

December 17, 2008—Blows nose into bag on Jay Leno's *The Tonight Show*, snot to be auctioned for charity on eBay

September 15, 2009—Releases *Break Up* album with Peter Yorn

2010—Tony Award for Best Performance by a Featured Actress in a Play for *A View from the Bridge* revival

December 2010—*GQ*'s "Babe of the Year"

2011—Private photos of various female celebrities, including Johansson, hacked

February 4, 2012—Receives Best International Actress award at the Golden Camera Awards in Berlin, Germany

May 2, 2012—Receives star on Hollywood Walk of Fame

September 7, 2012—Speaks at Democratic National Convention in support of Barack Obama

September 22–December 30, 2012—Chateau Marmont photograph by Annie Leibovitz part of Wexner Center for the Arts exhibit in Columbus, Ohio

January 17, 2013—Plays Maggie on Broadway in *Cat on a Hot Tin Roof* revival

November 2013—*Esquire* Ranks "Sexiest Woman Alive" for 2nd time

November 2013—Appears with Matthew McConaughey in *The One Street of Dreams*, director Martin Scorsese's video/TV commercial for Dolce and Gabbana

2013—Provides computer voice Samantha in *Her*

April 2014—Appears as the *Under the Skin* alien on cover of *Sight & Sound*

July 25–27, 2014—*Lucy* wins the weekend with $44 million take

September 4, 2014—Gives birth to Rose Dorothy

October 1, 2014—Marries French journalist Romain Dauriac (divorced 2017)

December 5, 2014—Sings New Order's "Bizarre Love Triangle" at *Vice Magazine*'s 20th Anniversary party at Brooklyn Navy Yard

February 2015—*Total Film* ranks her "Woman of the Year"

February 23, 2015—At 87th Academy Award show introduces *The Sound of Music* 50th Anniversary tribute by Lady Gaga; smooched by John Travolta on Red Carpet

April 12, 2015—Along with other *Avengers: Age of Ultron* cast members, presents Robert Downey, Jr., with the Generation Award at MTV Movie Awards, for which she was nominated for Best Actress in *Lucy*

April 13, 2015—Joined Robert Downey, Jr., Chris Evans, Chris Hemsworth, Jeremy Renner and Mark Ruffalo to promote *The Avengers: Age of Ultron* on *Jimmy Kimmel Show*

April 27, 2015—Guest on *The Late Show with David Letterman*

May 2, 2015—Hosts *Saturday Night Live* for 4th time

June 24, 2015—On CBS TV's *Big Brother* premiere; contestant Meg mocks herself by saying Scarlett Johansson could play her in a film

July 30, 2015—Madame Tussauds New York unveils Scarlett Johansson figure

September 9, 2015—First female guest on *The Late Show with Stephen Colbert*

2016—Hong Kong man creates Scarlett Johansson robot

December 5, 2016—Travels with Chris Evans for Chairman's USO Holiday Tour to Turkey, Qatar, and Afghanistan
January 21, 2017—Speaks up for Planned Parenthood at Women's March on Washington
February 26, 2017—Presents Best Song award at 89th Academy Awards show
March 11, 2017—Joins Five Timer Club hosting *Saturday Night Live*
April 5–7, 2017—Guest at Women in the World Summit in New York City
June 11, 2017—Tony Awards Presenter
Autumn, 2017—Appears on PBS' TV series *Finding Your Roots*
November 6, 2017—Helps organize and participates in *Our Town* reading in Atlanta for Puerto Rico hurricane relief
April 23, 2018—Attends *The Avengers: Infinity War* world premiere in Los Angeles
April 24, 2018—Joins Robert Downey, Jr., Chris Evans, Chris Hemsworth, Jeremy Renner and Mark Ruffalo on *Jimmy Kimmel Live* to promote *The Avengers: Infinity War*
May 7, 2018—Attends 2018 Met Gala in New York City
September 17, 2018—Attends Emmy Awards
November 11, 2018—Wins *E! People's Choice Award* as Female Movie Star of 2018
November 15, 2018—Attends American Museum of Natural History 2018 Gala
2018—*This is What Democracy Looks Like* short (about the two Women's Marches)
April 8, 2019—Appears on *Jimmy Kimmel Live* with other cast members to promote forthcoming premiere of *Avengers: Endgame*
May 19, 2019—Engagement to Colin Jost announced
April 10, 2019—Attends *Avengers: Endgame* world premiere in London
December 9, 2019—Golden Globes: Nominated for Best Performance by an Actress in a Motion Picture—Drama (*Marriage Story*)
December 11, 2019—Screen Actors Guild: Nominated for Outstanding Performance by a Female Actor in a Leading Role (*Marriage Story*) and Outstanding Performance by a Female Actor in a Supporting Role (*Jojo Rabbit*)
December 14, 2019—Hosts *Saturday Night Live* for 6th time
January 7, 2020—British Academy of Film and Television Arts: Nominated for Best Actress in a Leading Role (*Marriage Story*) and Best Actress in a Supporting Role (*Jojo Rabbit*)
January 13, 2020—Academy of Motion Picture Arts and Sciences: Nominated for Best Performance by an Actress in a Leading Role (*Marriage Story*) and Best Performance by an Actress in a Supporting Role (*Jojo Rabbit*)
Spring 2020—Appears as Black Widow on covers of *Empire* and *Total Film*
October 2020—Marries Colin Jost

Prologue

by Kim Holston

In mid–April 2014 I scanned the web and local newspapers for the announcement of the opening of the intriguingly titled film *Under the Skin*. The poster, Scarlett Johansson's enigmatic visage surrounded by what seemed like stars, was at least as compelling and mysterious as the title. What little I'd read, namely that Johansson was *the* star of this Jonathan Glazer science fiction film, promised something special but as days passed there was no indication that the film would open anywhere in Delaware, southern New Jersey or the Philadelphia metropolitan area. I became uneasy. What if we missed it? Warren Hope and I had made rendezvous for every Johansson picture during the previous decade, undertaking somewhat heroic efforts to find *The Spirit* at the AMC Marple 10 in Springfield, Pennsylvania, and *Hitchcock* at the Bala Theatre in Bala Cynwyd, Pennsylvania, when these movies failed to show at our preferred meeting place, the Regal Edgmont Square 10 between Newtown Square and West Chester, Pennsylvania. We had to keep the string alive.

So began the phoning of theaters most likely to carry what was coming to be identified as an "art film." People at the Bala, the Bryn Mawr Film Institute and the Colonial in Phoenixville had not even heard of *Under the Skin* but said it seemed up their alley. Nevertheless, my gut told us that if Holston and Hope did not venture beyond their normal bailiwick we would fail to see this film in a theater. As it transpired, between Washington, D.C., and New York City, Philly's Ritz East and, of all places, the Neshaminy Mall's AMC Neshaminy 24 northwest of the city were the only venues showing it. The die was cast. On Wednesday, April 30, I left my home in Delaware and met Hope in Pennsylvania. Braving rising waters from torrential downpours we drove into Philly. There were perhaps twenty people attending that 2 p.m. showing at the Ritz. In the lobby, the ticket taker cum concessionaire told us that older folks thought the movie was "too weird" but that the younger crowd loved it. We were prepared to love it and did so, and we'd kept our record intact.

Introduction

"I think I have a nice face shape and a nice profile."
—Scarlett Johansson to Jane Gordon, "Of Course I've
Got a Big Ego—and All Actors Think They're
THE ONE," *Daily Mail*, December 21, 2013

In the mid–2000s, Philadelphia's WIP Sports Radio hosts Angelo Cataldi and Al Morganti pondered the identity of the most beautiful Hollywood star of the moment. Angelina Jolie's name came up and Morganti added, "And that Swede." He meant Scarlett Johansson, whose father is Danish.

What put Johansson in the upper echelon of stunning were not just her big eyes, excellent profile, and "that mouth of hers that is set in a perpetual, charming moue."[1] It was the curvy figure at odds with so very many film stars of recent decades but totally in keeping with such Hollywood icons as Marilyn Monroe and Kim Novak.[2] Additionally, Johansson had the husky voice allowing her to join the ranks of Lauren Bacall, Novak and Kathleen Turner.

No one, it seems, has recognized that facially she bears some resemblance to Jean Seberg. (See, for instance, photos in *Screen World 1959* of Seberg in 1958's *Bonjour Tristesse*, *Screen World 1964* of 1963's *In the French Style*, and *Screen World 1965* of 1964's *Lilith*.) With Novak, Johansson shared the art of stillness, which in Novak's instance was called iciness—and considered a negative trait.[3] Johansson has employed this attribute to create with excellent effect the oeuvre of "the other," the alien. (See Chapter 9: "Her Own Unique Oeuvre.")

As her acting career advanced—complemented by her position as a prime fashionista, social activist, and spokesmodel—Johansson appeared on the red carpet at film premieres and charity fashion events.[4] She hawked her films on TV talk shows. Still, Johansson generally eschewed most of the celebrity grind. She shielded herself, and later her child, from the paparazzi. "She poses for fans at a premiere or on the street but draws the line at being interrupted in a restaurant. She says she works hard to keep her private life private."[5]

Certainly, being a fashion-plate was not all roses. In 2006 Johansson said dolling up for red carpet affairs was hard work and pointed to the Academy Awards: "It was 'frantic and surreal' and on the red carpet you were shoved willy-nilly."[6] Still, she liked "the facade of glamour ... and the performance it entailed.... It's important for people to buy into that idea."[7]

In 2007 she told an interviewer that the red carpet required giving "it the sprinkle of stardust it deserves." She'd pick a concept, like Harlow or Bacall, find the appropriate designer, a Roland Mouret or a Tara Subkoff, for instance, to provide a modern slant.[8]

Scarlett Johansson at Metropolitan Museum of Art Costume Institute Benefit Gala, New York, NY, May 7, 2018 (Sky Cinema/Shutterstock.com).

Like the late British-based horror film icon Ingrid Pitt, Johansson is "strong-featured": a face writ large with big eyes and a strong nose. Also like Pitt, she is "full figured" in an era of androgynous female thespians. In short, despite her height—she told Barbara Walters that on a good day she was 5'4",[9] Johansson had gravitas from the day she showed herself on screen as an adult in *Lost in Translation*. That appearance caused *Rolling Stone* critic Peter Travers to rhapsodize that Johansson was possessed "of smashing loveliness and subtle grace."[10]

Johansson's looks naturally secured her product endorsement gigs. In her early maturity she became the spokesperson for L'Oreal and Reebok.[11] Curiously, the ads for Dolce & Gabana seem only to appear in U.S. magazines, not on TV.

In 2009 she represented Moët & Chandon champagne.[12]

In 2011 promotional videos for the bubbly famous since 1743 were filmed at Jean-Remy Moët's French chalet in Trianon and designed to highlight, according to Moët & Chandon's President and CEO Daniel Lalonde, "a return to the immutable elegance and glamour that are inherent to both Moët and Scarlett...."[13]

Johansson protested her "objectification/sexualization" by the media, yet as a fashionista and product endorser, she posed innumerable times in sexy attire, or sometimes no attire as she and Keira Knightley did for the March 2006 *Vanity Fair* cover. She *is* sexy.

Johansson's emergence as the screen's paramount "other," which we examine in Chapter 9, has been occasionally noted by interviewers and critics. For instance, in 2014 her profession as a film star and related career as a model and spokesperson combined with her avocation as an activist was well distilled by Jimmy So of *The Daily Beast*, who concluded that "she's the current reincarnation of Hollywood glamour, of persona whipped into myth, celebrity, and impenetrable gloss. She is the alien life form too good at seduction."[14]

As for her career path, after *Lost in Translation* Johansson was on the road to full-fledged stardom—and respect as an actress, especially by those with whom she worked. The trajectory is fascinating. Early on she was nominated for awards. In 2003, BAFTA (British Academy of Film and Television Arts) nominated her as Best Actress in both *Lost in Translation* and *Girl with a Pearl Earring*, and she won for the former. She shared the lead in such films as *The Perfect Score*, *A Love Song for Bobby Long*, and *The Other Boleyn Girl*. She was not much more than eye candy in *The Prestige*, but she was totally serious about her career and focused on the work. Woody Allen used her to great effect in *Match Point* (2005) and would subsequently employ her in two other movies. To the moderate chagrin of both, she was labeled his muse.

Her mother, Melanie Sloan, was her agent until 2009. Her roles took a decided upswing after that. Back in the days when Johansson was beginning to make her mark, the Internet Movie Database listed the *Gladiator* clone *Amazon* on her future schedule. It was aborted. Edith Wharton's 1913 novel *The Custom of the Country* was foreseen as an 8-episode TV production but, as of this writing, has come to nought. A filmization of Truman Capote's novel *Summer Crossing* directed by Johansson seems always "in development." She was to play Betsy Balcombe, the 13-year-old who befriended Napoleon in 1815 when he was sequestered on St. Helena. Johansson said she felt a kinship with the character. Universal/Focus expressed interest, but it didn't pan out.

Having conducted mini-theatricals around her house as a child, and despite the hard work that acting involves, Johansson has always found joy in moviemaking. "A movie set for a kid is the most incredible thing ever. You're getting all the attention you crave—especially me, I was such an attention whore back then—but it was just magical. It still is."[15]

She told an interviewer in January 2012 that in those early days of stardom she took roles commensurate with her looks. "Why not? You're 19, and you're feeling fabulous and young.... It's nice for people to think you're attractive.... But I was never, like, a model or anything. I think because I wasn't 90 pounds and 6 feet tall.... I was suddenly this 'bombshell' and 'hourglass' and all those things, but I never wanted to make my career off that."[16]

Busy was Johansson's byword. She had six films released between October 2013 and August 2014. She played a Jersey girl in *Don Jon*, a computer program in *Her*, reprised her *Iron Man 2* (2010) superheroine but mortal Natasha Romanoff, aka Black Widow in *Captain America: The Winter Soldier*, portrayed a mysterious alien from somewhere preying on Scottish men in *Under the Skin*, became a computer program or something like it in *Lucy*, and did Jon Favreau a favor by appearing briefly as a restaurant hostess in the comedy-drama *Chef*. It was quite a spate of different characters, with *Captain America* and *Lucy* action blockbusters and *Under the Skin* akin to an edgy and cerebral Kubrickian science fiction masterpiece.

Soon afterward she continued playing the ultimate martial arts expert Black Widow in the Marvel Universe movies. She also provided the voices for the snake Kaa in *The Jungle Book*, the hedgehog rocker in *Sing*, and a dog in *Isle of Dogs*.

For the most part Johansson succeeded in overcoming the "she's too pretty" label that rebuffs beauties from being taken seriously and thus getting plum roles. Nevertheless, a film she really wanted but failed to get was the English-language version of *The Girl with the Dragon Tattoo* (2011). Many auditioned, but Rooney Mara got the nod. In her 2017 interview with Howard Stern, Johansson responded to the rumor that she was considered "too beautiful" for the role of the character Lisbeth Salander. She couldn't convince director David Fincher she could be, in his words, "totally uncaring" of herself. She told him, "I will, I can be that person." His response: "No you can't."[17]

Intentionally or not, Johansson created her own oeuvre.[18] She excelled as "the other." Stillness and silence were characteristics of some of these characters, and it was evident early on and in her breakthrough role in *Lost in Translation*, where she was both still and an outsider.

Johansson's unique features and demeanor fit to a T for filmmakers creating "the other." Beginning in 2006, Johansson became attached to films that questioned our humanity and foresaw a future of robotically and/or genetically modified people. As a clone in *The Island*, a computer program's voice that became sentient in *Her*, an alien who consumed men and slowly questioned her raison d'être in *Under the Skin*, an American student abroad transmogrified into the ultimate computer program in *Lucy*, and the cyborg major in *Ghost in the Shell*, Johansson became the alternative to a card-carrying, organic human. Add to these films her outings as Black Widow, a mortal who consorted and fought beside scientifically enhanced beings who for all intents and purposes were immortal: the likes of Captain America, Hulk, and Thor.

We perceive special attributes beyond Johansson's looks that make her unique: stillness and silence. We are not alone. As the reader will learn, a few perspicacious critics have made a similar observation, but generally this attribute is not even recognized, much less heralded. In sum, Johansson is an actress and movie star, social activist, and fashionista.[19] A woman of extraordinary mien. We will not see her like again.

A Note on Format

While this is a mostly chronological examination of Scarlett Johansson's career and films, we veer off on three occasions to assess the movies with common threads: the three Woody Allen efforts, Black Widow and the Marvel Cinematic Universe, and the oeuvre in which Johansson essays "the other": the clone, the computer operating system, the alien, the reluctant drug mule who merges with the universe, and the cyborg.

To avoid nitpicking, note that the release dates of some of Johansson's films pose a mild problem in that some of them played at a film festival in one year before getting a general or sometimes limited (*A Good Woman*, *Under the Skin*) release the following year. Problematic release dates are noted in the Commentary.

Each film begins with a plot synopsis, followed by extracts from contemporary reviews, commentary that includes behind-the-scenes information, and our analysis.

1

Childhood

> On YouTube one can watch her reading for a part at age nine, "and the self-consciousness is frightening; ... she seems like a child impersonating a child..."
> —Anthony Lane, "Her Again," *New Yorker*, March 24, 2014

The future famous movie star and increasingly well-regarded thespian of both stage and screen, Scarlett Ingrid Johansson was born in New York City on November 22, 1984. Her mother was New Yorker Melanie Sloan, her father Karsten Johansson, Danish-born but part Swedish by virtue of his paternal grandfather. She has a twin brother, Hunter, and an older sister, Vanessa, and brother, Adrian, plus Christian, a half-brother from her father's first marriage.

In a 2016 interview for the inflight magazine *Scandinavian Traveler* Johansson said the only Danish words she knew were *Jeg elsker dig* (I love you). "My parents always used Danish as a secret language, so we kids wouldn't understand what they were talking about." Ejner and Hedda Bainkamp Johansson were her grandparents. Ejner's Swedish father was known as Axel Robert Johansson. His wife was Danish. Johansson said her Danish granddad "was a well-known cultural personality. And my great-grandfather came from Sweden. Hence the name Johansson...." Johansson holds both U.S. and Danish passports. "I really feel that Scandinavia is part of my heritage."[1]

When she was 32, Johansson learned that much of her mother's side of the family—Ashkenazi Jews from Eastern Europe—lost their lives during World War II, some in extermination camps, others in the Warsaw Ghetto. She was visibly shaken when this was revealed to her by historian Henry Louis Gates, Jr., on the TV series *Finding Your Roots*. On a happier note, she was very surprised to learn that her Danish father's lineage could be traced to Sweden. In fact, the Swedish line has a coat of arms from 1689. She told Gates that as a child, her father proclaimed her a Viking princess. More curiously, perhaps, is that her father's father had a degree in art, was a critic, and directed films. This astounded Johansson, who'd never met that grandfather. Her father had broken ties with him after his mother died and Ejner remarried.[2]

Asked about her mother's influence, Johansson said she never felt pressure to do anything. "I don't watch teen movies, so I never really wanted to do that." But as far back as she could remember she wanted to act. She was a ham, singing and dancing and dreaming of Broadway. Her mother showed her her own favorite movies.[3] These included musicals, 70s political thrillers, and films directed by Elia Kazan and John Cassavetes. "I've got to say, there's nothing quite like watching *Network* as a 9-year-old," said Johansson.[4]

She'd previously told an interviewer that she and her siblings were grounded in reality, which helped them deal with their parents' divorce when she was thirteen. "There was never any strangeness about custody.... They were very civilized about the whole thing, thank God."[5]

In 2005 her interviewer was told that the tabloids made up nasty stories about her relationship with her mother. "She's an incredible businesswoman, a very strong woman." Naturally she "does drive me nuts sometimes."[6]

Of the classic movie stars Johansson has referenced, Lauren Bacall she admired and Marilyn Monroe she loved, but her favorite was Rosalind Russell. *Auntie Mame* was among her favorite films. Russell reminded her of her maternal grandmother. "My grandmother is an atheist and was a supporter of socialism and other things that have always been a bit taboo."[7]

Meet Me in St. Louis might be her favorite film, but *Willy Wonka and the Chocolate Factory* has also been put forth as number one.[8] Of more modern movies, she loves *Moonstruck* and *Crossing Delancey*.[9]

Johansson revealed that other than her sister, she had no mentor as a child, but she did want "to be like Judy Garland in *Meet Me in St. Louis*. She had both a fragility and a strength that I was in total awe of. Other than my mother, I think she was the picture of femininity to me."[10]

Johansson has always been enamored of her hometown, whose denizens according to her were straightforward and could identify bullshit. Her fashion sense she attributed to residing in the Big Apple.[11] She grew up in Greenwich Village, attended public school on 11th Street, and felt a real sense of community. In Sheridan Square she played around

Scarlett Johansson, mother Melanie (right), and grandmother at Walk of Fame ceremony, Hollywood, May 1, 2012 (Dfree/Shutterstock.com).

the George Segal sculpture of gay couples, and on Christopher Street she'd sneak into bars.[12] A decade later Johansson reiterated her commitment to being a city girl: "It seems wonderful to be raised in a natural setting, but I wouldn't know how to do it. A big city would always draw me back."[13] She had vivid memories of growing up on Washington below 14th Street in a development of brick buildings in the '90s, "owning the street." As "a major ham," she'd "improvise and do weird vocal exercises." She took acting, singing and tap dancing classes.[14] "I didn't have any nicknames growing up, though I've heard I'm called Scar-Jo, which I loathe. It sounds like a bad hip-hop name!"[15]

The elementary school she and her twin brother Hunter attended was P.S. 41., aka Greenwich Village School. Later she attended and in 2002 graduated from Professional Children's School in Upper Manhattan. The latter had been founded in 1914 to serve students in dance and theater but provided a curriculum that included such traditional subjects as English, science, mathematics, languages, and social sciences. She attended the Lee Strasberg Institute for four years and seemed to remember being "ten when the rest of the class could have been eighteen."[16] She did Strasberg on weekends.[17] Johansson had plenty of high school chums and did attend three proms. Of the latter she said, "It was never fun." She failed to get into NYU's film school.[18]

Johansson debuted professionally with Ethan Hawke in *Sophistry*, a 1993 off-Broadway production.[19] Her role was too small to be noticed by the *New York Times*, but the play was given passing marks.[20]

Johansson tried to break into showbiz via commercials. She and her siblings read for a talent agency, but her older brother was the only one given the green light, and he wasn't that keen on the notion. "Nobody was that interested, including my mom," recalled Johansson, who said she was "totally devastated." Nonetheless, she kept at it.[21]

Her throaty voice was a problem. Did she have a sore throat? According to Atchison, film casting directors appreciated that voice, however. In 2013 she recalled her commercial audition fiascos. She remembered sounding "like a whiskey-drinking, chain-smoking fool" when she was nine.[22]

Johansson told *Cosmopolitan* in 2008 that she was born to perform: "I never struggled with trying to figure out what it was I wanted to do or what made the sparks go for me. I always had that huge *laaa* aspect to me." Waving jazz hands, she added, "I was one of those kids."[23]

"Johansson's demeanor—onscreen and off—is almost uncannily self-possessed, as though she didn't so much cast off childish, girlie notions as never have them in the first place."[24] Her mother was strict about her work hours and made sure she attended school each day.[25] "I had a big imagination," said Johansson, recalling in 2015 those disastrous commercial auditions and how she cried in the subway. Her mother said she could give it up. The daughter was adamant. "Waiting for the B train, I had my come-to-Jesus moment."[26]

Growing up did have its difficulties. "I was on public assistance until I was, probably, a teenager.... We struggled until I became financially independent of my parents."[27] Her fraternal twin brother Hunter said the family's modest "background gave them the ability to empathize with other people." He added that this empathy and understanding of human experience "makes Scarlett a great actor."[28]

By the time of *The Horse Whisperer* (1998), Johansson learned that she could "manipulate this thing that I'm doing.'" Acting "was something you could craft."[29] In 2014 Johansson told *Vanity Fair* she "realized I could still own my own performance, that it was mine to present however I wanted to."[30] Craft it she did, and in her best films, from *Manny & Lo* to *Under the Skin*, she would employ stillness and silence to create a unique screen persona.

In 2013, after the release of *Her* and the compliments given Johansson concerning her unseen but supremely captivating computer operating system Samantha, she was asked if she could imagine receiving an Academy Award nomination for a silent movie? She said having a dearth of dialogue would give her "greater freedom to interpret my performance." A silent movie would be right up her street, and she referred to the dialogue-light *Girl with a Pearl Earring* and *Under the Skin* as examples of the "opportunity to use a kind of nuance that just comes from the expressions in your eyes."[31]

2

Child Actress

> "I learned early on how to manipulate my emotions.... As far back as I can remember, I've been hyper-aware of human behavior and able to mimic it somehow. That's why I can do what I do."
> —Scarlett Johansson to Chip Brown,
> "The Smart Bomb," *Elle*, January 2006

Like Natalie Wood, who became a raving beauty and famous actress, Scarlett Johansson was not a child star, rather a child actress. This allowed her to avoid the paparazzi and ride under the radar of the celebrity machine during her youth. Contributing to this was the fact that many of her early films were independent productions that did not receive wide release (*An American Rhapsody*) or, like her first movie (*North*) were excoriated and sank from view.

North (1994)

Eleven-year-old North (Elijah Wood) is a star student, a topnotch athlete, and a mean interpreter of Tevye in his school's production of *Fiddler on the Roof*. However, North's parents (Julia Louis-Dreyfus, Jason Alexander) are oblivious to his merits. Depressed, North ensconces himself in his special thinking place, a comfy chair in a department store and engages the man playing the Easter Bunny (Bruce Willis) in conversation. Afterward he tells his journalistic classmate Winchell (Matthew McCurley) that he needs new, more appreciative parents. Winchell deems this a capital idea and assists North by publishing a broadside and otherwise making the world cognizant of North's plan. North begins his journey, auditioning parents from Texas to Hawaii, from Alaska to China, from Zaire to Paris. The last family he visits comes closest to his dreams. Mr. Nelson (John Ritter) is a pediatrician who lives in an iconic New York City suburban house with picket fence, a wife (Faith Ford), a son North's age (Jesse Zeigler), and younger sister Laura (Johansson). Yet North is dissatisfied and discovers that his true parents want him back. Overcoming obstacles put in his path by erstwhile chum Winchell, he reunites with his folks at his thinking place. However, Winchell's assassin (Jon Lovitz) is there, too, and fires his pistol. North then wakes up and the Easter Bunny takes him home. Was it all a dream? Perhaps not. He fingers the silver dollar with the hole in it given him by Gabby (Bruce Willis), the cowboy who looks amazingly like the Easter Bunny and many another character who helped him on his way.

Bottom: Jesse Zeigler (left), Elijah Wood and Scarlett Johansson; top: John Ritter and Faith Ford, *North* (Castle Rock Entertainment/Columbia, 1994).

Reviews

The *New York Times* was mildly positive. *North* was "a playful modern fable..." that didn't always jell "but much of it is clever in amusingly unpredictable ways." Elijah Wood "is currently the most natural, confident child actor of his generation, but he's not always an ideal straight man." Alan Arkin provided "extra energy." There was a good deal for children to enjoy.[1] On the other hand, Roger Ebert was scathing, deeming the film "one of the most unpleasant, contrived, artificial, cloying experiences I've had at the movies. To call it manipulative would be inaccurate; it has an ambition to manipulate, but fails." Wood and director Reiner couldn't salvage it.[2]

Commentary

In her film debut as the cheery Laura, Johansson plays football in the backyard and board games with the family inside. She tells North she's happy to have two big brothers. The credits list her as Scarlett Johanssen, not Johansson.

Johansson acknowledged becoming emotional remembering that she knew by nature what to do that first day on the set. It could have been fate. "I just love everything about making movies."[3] Another goal was to represent a fashion house and to acquire, like a $15,000 Chanel suit. So if becoming a star would net her that prize...[4]

Analysis

North may not deserve to be "hated" but it begins to fall apart in the second half. As usual in so very many modern comedies (if that's what this is), criminality rears its ugly head as Winchell conspires with Arthur Belt (Jon Lovitz) to have North assassinated. Of course, if it's a dream…. Even if it's become a cliché, there is at least one funny scene: North sitting between his potential Parisian parents-to-be watching TV where every channel features a Jerry Lewis movie.

Director Reiner's Amish folk are caricatures and the landscape is distinctly not "Pennsylvania Dutch," rather some wheaty farmland looking more like golden California hills than the green of such Pennsylvania counties as Berks, Lancaster and Lebanon. (Amish farmers did appear in Nevada in 1955's *Violent Saturday*.)

Just Cause (1995)

Harvard-educated attorney become advocate for abolishing the death penalty, Paul Armstrong (Sean Connery) is cajoled by Evangeline Brown (Ruby Dee) into investigating her grandson Bobby Earl Ferguson's (Blair Underwood) presumed murder of a young girl in Florida. Taking his wife Laurie (Kate Capshaw) and young daughter Katie (Johansson) to visit his wife's parents (Hope Lange, Kevin McCarthy) in the Sunshine State, Armstrong proceeds to antagonize the residents of Ochopee, especially Sheriff Tanny Brown (Laurence Fishburne), under whose aegis Bobby Earl was coerced into confessing to the murder. Armstrong learns from Bobby Earl that another inmate of his prison, Blair Sullivan (Ed Harris), a notorious serial killer, confessed to him that he committed the murder. When Armstrong uses Sullivan's directions to locate the murder weapon in the swamp, Tanny has no choice but to help free Bobby Earl. However, it was a set-up. Called to the prison, Armstrong is directed to Sullivan's parents' home and finds them dead. Back in the prison, Armstrong is told that "they" have instituted a plan. Bobby Earl had actually murdered the young girl. Before Armstrong can glean more information, Sullivan is electrocuted. Armstrong rushes to his hotel only to see Bobby Earl driving away with Laurie and Katie. Tanny had been tracking Bobby Earl but his deputy had been killed. Now he and Armstrong race after Bobby Earl and locate his isolated swamp hideout. Set upon by the fugitive, Tanny is wounded. Bobby Earl grabs Katie but Tanny reappears and helps Armstrong, who stabs the murderer and watches him sink into the swamp as alligators latch onto his body.

Reviews

The *Los Angeles Times* found it slow moving in every place but the bogs, a "mishmash of moments from *Cape Fear* and *In the Heat of the Night* by way of *Strangers on a Train*."[5] The *New York Times* said it "lacks all sense of lifelike detail." Direction was "utterly out of sync with its subject matter. All the actors are immaculately barbered, whether they are in the groves of academe or on death row." Laurence Fishburne gave the movie "its only real mystery and excitement." In the detective Tanny Brown he "creates a tricky, elusive figure who stands in sharp contrast to the film's stolid, one-note characters."[6]

Analysis

Despite the negative reviews, *Just Cause* is entertaining enough and the revelation of Bobby Earl's actual guilt not immediately apparent, possibly because of Blair Underwood's ingratiating performance. It does have a fair share of dopey moves, however. Tanny telling Armstrong they must split up when they approach Bobby Earl's house must inspire moans in any veteran moviegoer of crime and the science fiction and horror genres. Nothing good comes of separation in these scenarios. Although the locale is different, Johansson might have stepped across the studio lot from her family in *North* into this.

Manny & Lo (1996)

On the run from their foster home, Laurel, aka Lo (Aleksa Palladino), and her younger sister Manny (Johansson) take up residence in unoccupied dwellings until Lo finds she's pregnant. Stumbling on a secluded cabin, they make it their home and kidnap store clerk Elaine (Mary Kay Place), who they suspect knows something about birthing babies. Her legs shackled, she has nowhere to go and eventually empathizes with the girls, especially Manny. The owner of the house appears, and Elaine makes him hostage to herself by knocking him over the head and securing him in the barn. An exasperated Lo confronts Elaine: "Have you ever heard of a hostage who took her own goddamn hostage?" Eventually the man breaks free and the girls take to the road again and with Elaine's help Lo's baby is born. All three then continue their road trip together.

Reviews

The *New York Times* called it a "lovely tale." It was "told with the utmost warmth and clarity...." Johansson and compatriot Palladino were "exceptionally assured...." The

Scarlett Johansson (left) and Aleksa Palladino, *Manny & Lo*, Pope Productions, 1996. VHS Marketing Campaign (UK) copyright Paramount Pictures, 1998.

film was constructed "gently toward a fable's happy ending."[7] Roger Ebert thought the film "serious about its characters, but with sidelong glances at the absurdity of the situation...." It eschewed melodrama for character.[8] *Reelviews* described it as "a wonderfully-textured comic fantasy about family life." Like Roger Ebert, it commended the film for "the quiet, character-driven scenes...." Aleksa Palladino and Mary Kay Place were excellent, but Johansson stood out. It was easy to believe Johansson's Manny was a real person, not an actress.[9] *SFGate* said, "The film's style finds its best expression in the stillness of young Scarlett Johansson, who plays Manny. Finding poised child actors is difficult enough, but Johansson's peaceful aura, which takes in everything with equanimity, is something special. If she can get through puberty with that aura undisturbed, she could become an important actress."[10]

In 2014 *The New Yorker* looked back, observing that the younger Manny watches the world, "wondering what's to be had from it—not what harm it might inflict on her.... That is the Johansson look, already potent and unnerving."[11]

Commentary

Manny & Lo debuted at the Sundance Film Festival in January 1996. Its U.S. general release was in July. Johansson received an Independent Spirit Award nomination for Best Female Lead but lost to Francis McDormand for *Fargo*.

What struck one 2004 interviewer about Johansson was "That low, froggy hush of a voice" plus "the utter lack of pretense in her performance."[12]

Analysis

In *Manny & Lo*, Scarlett Johansson achieves her peak performance as a child actor. Her combination of innocence and maturity, gravity and lightness, seem to have made her perfect for the part of Manny, the younger of two sisters of the title roles. More to the point, perhaps, is that Manny's role is the central one—not only the biggest part but also the part that provides the film's point of view. The picture begins and ends with her voice raising a question that gives the whole film its perspective and a dreamlike quality. "Did you ever dream about someone before you met them in life?"

The movie seems determined to be made from a combination of Hollywood clichés. It is a road picture, a coming-of-age movie, and a buddy movie. What turns these clichés inside out is gender: the film consists almost exclusively of female roles—men are absent or "the baddies," policemen as threatening authority figures, a homeowner who disrupts the makeshift family the sisters established with Elaine, played exceptionally well by Mary Kay Place, the mother replacement the girls kidnapped, by asserting his right of private property, and the absent fathers—the father of Manny and Lo and the father of the baby Lo is carrying. In an odd way, pregnancy and parenthood are the dominant themes of this movie that was accurately described by Caryn James in the *New York Times* as a "warm, fabulously unsentimental comedy about two sisters on their own...."[13]

What makes this movie a comedy is neither jokes nor pratfalls, but the old tradition that a comedy should end with a wedding (see also *Rough Night*), a wedding as a festive symbol of fertility. In the same way, tragedies traditionally end with death, with funerals marking the end rather than the beginning of life. It is a commentary on our age that the "wedding" with which this comedy ends is the birth of a baby girl to an unwed mother outdoors with the new mother's younger sister on hand as a witness and a woman they kidnapped acting as midwife. The birth is celebrated when this "family" piles into its old station wagon and drives into the future.

The trigger for this film's plot is the death of the mother of the sisters—an event that took place before the film starts. The sisters had been placed in foster homes, but Lo, the older sister, flees her foster home, obtains an old station wagon, and "frees" Manny from her different foster family. It's clear Manny did not especially want to be freed; she half-heartedly speaks up for her foster family, but it is also clear that she wants to please her sister and so goes along with her wishes. This maturity and sense of responsibility displayed by the younger sister is typical of why Johansson is so good in the part. There is nothing mawkish in either her weak defense of the status quo or in her willingness to join her sister's rebellion. She assumes the role of the older—the wiser, the more mature, the more responsible—sister naturally, simply by putting her sister's needs and wishes above her own. It is the precocity that seems to be one of Scarlett Johansson's gifts that enables her to walk the tightrope of this young character without losing her balance.

If the death of the mother is the film's trigger, Lo's becoming an expectant mother in a rather offhand way is its primary complication. Rather than just having two orphan sisters on the road, dodging the authorities and making their way through the no-man's land of contemporary America, they now have to deal with a birth and establishing a home for yet another child. This plight drives them to inadvertently find a replacement mother by kidnapping Elaine, a childless woman who works in a store that sells baby supplies. She is so knowledgeable and competent that she gives potential customers the kind of sage advice that loses sales for her niece, the store's owner who is more than willing to put sales above truth. This is a good example of the film's attitude toward contemporary life. It gently exposes the generalized falsification that dominates the age and links it to the distribution of commodities that did not even exist in an earlier period but now assume the role of necessities. Aunt Elaine's concern for the children of her customers is a kind of equivalent for Manny's concern for Lo. In both cases, a social sense of responsibility takes priority over individualistic wishes.

This juggling of roles is suggested in a nuanced way. Under the tutelage of Elaine, Manny and Lo become Amanda and Laurel, growing into the names they were given at birth, names that had been lost in the nicknames they must have assumed through their birth mother. The seating arrangements in the station wagon also reflect the shifting roles of the three main characters. At the beginning, Lo is driving and Manny is in the back seat. Eventually Lo drives and Manny and Elaine are both in the back seat. Lo decides to jettison Elaine and drops her off. She is unable to proceed far without her, though, and goes into labor. At this point Johansson as Manny really takes control by assuming additional responsibility. She climbs over the seat, puts the station wagon in reverse, and backs up until she locates Elaine, thus allowing her sister to safely give birth. An additional nice touch is that she is guided by Elaine by following the "listen to your baby" device that the sisters had used to monitor Elaine when she was their prisoner.

The movie's plot constitutes a psychic family reunion, hence its dream-like quality. Before the credits a question is raised; after the credits is the answer. "Did you ever dream of someone before you met them in life?" The answer is Elaine, the replacement mother, who in the end drives the family with its new addition in the station wagon into the future.

Manny and Lo is where Johansson is noticed as a talent. It's her first significant role and film, one that is to be included in her "best of" efforts.

If Lucy Fell (1996)

Artist and art teacher for children like Emily (Johansson), Joe MacGonaughill (Eric Schaeffer) and psychologist Lucy Ackerman (Sarah Jessica Parker) share a New York brownstone apartment. Once upon a time they made a pact to commit suicide by leaping from the Brooklyn Bridge if neither had met their soulmate by the forthcoming May 28. Will they stick to the deal?

Lucy is currently intrigued by Bwick Elias (Ben Stiller), a somewhat goofy artist, while Joe is astounded that after five years yearning and spying on neighbor Jane (Elle Macpherson) he's got a date with her. Yet Joe and Lucy are not fully at ease with their new potential soulmates. In truth, they are not simpatico. Lucy understands this as Emily appears in the doorway and says, "Bingo!" May 28: Joe heads for the bridge but Lucy rushes after him. Realizing they are eminently compatible, they renege on their pact.

Reviews

The *New York Times* found the film a "coy, smart-alecky comedy...." The denouement was "predictable from its first frame."[14] *Video Movie Guide 1997* called it an "annoying, witless comedy...."[15] *Magill's Cinema Annual 1997* complained that *If Lucy Fell* had none of the earmarks of what it purported to be: a romantic comedy. It was not funny.[16]

Commentary

If Lucy Fell was a March 1996 release. In 2013, Cody Clarke posted his analysis of director Schaeffer's oeuvre. It was complimentary and for *If Lucy Fell* mentioned Johansson as "a kid, but displays pretty good chops."[17]

Analysis

In *If Lucy Fell* Johansson plays a child named Emily according to the cast list although the name does not seem to be used in the film. She is one of a number of kids who take art classes from Joe, a painter and the male lead played by Eric Schaeffer, the roommate

Scarlett Johansson, *If Lucy Fell* (MPCA/TriStar, 1996).

and eventual love interest of the Lucy of the title, the psychologist played by Sarah Jessica Parker. Schaeffer also directs and takes some of the blame or credit for the story. The movie's described as a screwball comedy and hangs on a formulaic plot of the type that might work as a screwball comedy—roommates unhappy with their respective love lives revive a pact first formed in college to kill themselves on Lucy's thirtieth birthday if they haven't by then found happiness. In the interim, Lucy agrees to go out with every man who asks her on a date and Joe agrees to talk to Jane, played by Elle Macpherson, a neighbor he has spent the last five years watching and dreaming about and saving himself for. What keeps this plot from producing a rollicking romp is the script. Odd even outrageous things happen to the characters but they remain unfunny. Worse, the characters seem all but incapable of saying things that are funny. The result is a screwball comedy with few laughs.

Johansson's role is not insignificant. She appears to be the largest child in the class and is also precocious in the sense that she seems very aware of what is going on with the adults around her and tends to observe them with a sly, knowing smile. She becomes the go between for Bwick Elias, the satiric caricature of a ridiculous but successful avantgarde artist played by Ben Stiller, with Lucy. She translates Stiller's inarticulate statements into understandable sentences. In addition, when Stiller phones Lucy the call is received by Emily on her portable phone—suggesting that he can speak to Lucy only through her. Emily also seems to be a neighbor or the daughter of a neighbor and friend of Lucy. When the movie heads toward its intended resolution with Lucy and Joe meeting on the Brooklyn Bridge to declare their respective love for each other rather than jumping, Emily is present to reinforce the importance of the pivotal scene. Lucy alone in her apartment finds herself thinking of her roommate as a potential life mate for the first time. When she says the name Joe aloud, Emily appears in the doorway and says, "Bingo! That will be twenty-five cents." Earlier in the film, Lucy gave advice to the school kids and charged them small amounts. This reversal of roles is a nod in the direction of the idea that the instincts of kids are of more value than the ludicrous views of adults when it comes to matters of the heart. The child actor's role is a speaking part with some symbolic oomph that she carries off well because of her poise and credible knowingness. In a movie that is extremely short on real feeling, and authenticity, she provides something of a relief. It's no surprise that Eric Schaeffer cast her in his next film, *Fall*.

Fall (1997)

Taxi driver Michael Shiver (Eric Schaeffer) picks up supermodel Sarah Easton (Amanda de Cadenet) and during the ride asks her to dinner. She declines and when stumbling upon him outside a restaurant fears he's stalking her. He isn't, merely dining with women friends. Although Sarah tells Michael she has no intention of leaving her husband Philippe (Rudolf Martin), who is in Europe, Michael intrigues her and they begin an affair. On one of their dates they attend a church service where one of Michael's female friends is using performance art as her thesis on the way to Episcopalian priesthood. A young girl (Johansson) in the "cast" seems a bit frightened by the ceremony.

Sarah visits her husband in Spain, and Michael sends a thousand roses to her room. Rudolf has himself had an affair, but the couple remain committed. Nevertheless, back in the States, Sarah and Michael rendezvous, with Michael humorously posing Plans A through D for their future. Sarah can't understand why he drives a cab and argues that he can't understand her high-powered life. He admits to having written a best-selling novel a decade previously but not finding fulfillment in the notoriety that followed. Nevertheless, Sarah gives up on the relationship and flies to Philippe in Paris. Michael follows and observes Sarah and Philippe exiting the Hotel Regina into the maelstrom of fame. She spots him but puts her finger to her lips. He returns to New York resigned to his fate while Sarah finds Michael's book in a package delivered to her hotel room. Insert: "to the celebration of all slain hope" As the end credits begin, a couple resembling Michael and Sarah are seen walking through a park.

Reviews

The *New York Times* called it a "narcissistic stab at romantic comedy...." Although the dialogue was uninhibited and Manhattan's Upper West Side well photographed, overall it tilted toward the "vain and smug."[18] *Magill's Cinema Annual 1998* said it was "yet another vanity project that allows the narcissistic actor the opportunity to surround himself with beautiful women who cannot help but fall...." Dramatic tension was in short supply. It "is a remarkably self-indulgent project for someone who, to date, has accomplished so little."[19] Leonard Maltin called it puerile and, "Any resemblance between these characters and actual human beings is strictly coincidental."[20]

Commentary

There are those, or at least one, personage who argues that filmmaker Schaeffer's characters are actual human beings and considers Schaeffer a brilliant filmmaker who knows he's ridiculous but who is honest and creates for himself not a three-, but a four-dimensional character.[21]

Fall was a June 1997 release.

Analysis

Fall is a poor man's *9½ Weeks* (1986) and might reasonably be entitled *Two Months Max*. Eric Schaeffer again directs and plays the male lead. He is not rapidly disillusioned by his dream girl of a supermodel as in *If Lucy Fell* but instead becomes involved in an affair marked by sexual obsession with some kinky twists. Schaeffer plays a New York cab driver who ten years earlier wrote a best-selling novel named *Michael* and Amanda de Cadenet plays the married supermodel, Sarah, who climbs into the backseat of his cab, setting off the action that follows. Johansson's part comes as a result of one of Michael's two female friends producing a piece of performance art in lieu of a dissertation as part of her education to become an Episcopalian priest. Johansson appears in the cast as "Little Girl" and seems to be a potential human sacrifice in the friend's satiric play. Amid preaching about the need for resurrection and a woman in a straight jacket shouting about eating a human heart, she speaks her single line, "I'm scared," and with a look and a sound that are completely believable. If someone wished to search for symbolism, it might be possible to argue that the Little Girl's blonde hair and full lips are meant to suggest a young version of Sarah the supermodel but in a film of this kind it is probably just as well not to push things too far. The action of the picture is framed by Michael waking up in his room with a shelf full of memorabilia of popular culture from his own childhood—a shelf dominated by a snow globe of the Lone Ranger and a balloon happy face. This framing seems to confess that all that came in the middle—the affair—was basically a fantasy that has changed nothing. This air of unreality runs throughout the movie and it is in this way that it is a poor man's version of *9 ½ Weeks*. Roger Ebert came to the defense of that erotic drama by arguing that the performances of Mickey Rourke and Kim Bassinger made their characters believable, credible.[22] Eric Schaeffer and Amanda de Cadenet were unable to do the same in *Fall*.

Home Alone 3 (1997)

Foiled in their attempt to steal a missile guidance microchip, four agents realize the Parisian bag they must retrieve has made its way to a Chicago suburb. They know the block but don't know which house contains the model car in which they've secreted the item. While they stake out the block and begin invading each house during the day when the suburbanites are at work or school, they fail to realize that Alex Pruitt (Alex Linz) is watching them through his telescope. Alex had contracted chicken pox and is home from school. To her regret, his mother Karen had bustled off to work for an hour or so and left him alone.

Alex can't convince the police that he's on to something shady so takes it upon himself to foil interlopers via homemade booby traps. He is vindicated. Even his brother and sister (Johansson) applaud him.

Review

For a third in a series, this breaks the mold of being terrible. In short, it is not close to being painful to watch. In fact, Roger Ebert liked it better than the first (*Home Alone*, 1990), a smash hit. He even recommended it—for children, "not to grownups unless they are having a very silly day." He found the rationale for leaving Alex home better than in the first outing. He liked Alex Linz immensely and thought the booby traps funnier.[23]

Commentary

Home Alone 3 was released in December 1997. Johansson would play off Linz again two years later in *My Brother the Pig*.

Analysis

The progenitor film *Home Alone* (1990) was a gigantic success written and produced by director John Hughes and directed by Chris Columbus. It involved the travails of young Kevin McCallister (Macaulay Culkin), inadvertently left behind in his suburban Chicago home when his family rushes off on a Christmas vacation.

Despite Roger Ebert's positive review, *Home Alone 3* is generally regarded as a turkey. It did make money. Johansson had more on-screen time to harass and be harassed by her brother than she did in her Eric Schaeffer outings.

The Horse Whisperer (1998)

In the country outside New York City, young Grace MacLean (Johansson) and her friend Judith (Kate Bosworth) take a morning horseback ride, but on an icy hill their mounts slide into the road and the path of an oncoming tractor-trailer. Judith and her horse Gulliver are killed. Grace loses the lower portion of her right leg, and her horse Pilgrim is so maimed that the vet thinks it best to put him down.

Grace's mother Annie (Kristin Scott Thomas), a high-powered New York City editor, nixes euthanasia and drives both Grace and Pilgrim across country to Montana to see Tom Booker (Robert Redford), a so-called "horse whisperer." Initially skeptical, when he meets the disabled Grace and sees the traumatized and mangled Pilgrim he elects to give it a go.

During the therapy, Tom and Annie fall in love. Eventually, as both Annie and her husband Robert look on, Grace mounts Pilgrim. Both horse and rider are reborn. As much as she wants to stay with Tom, Annie realizes she must return to New York and her husband.

Reviews

The *New York Times* commended Redford for ignoring the soapy aspects of the book and "found his own visually eloquent way to turn the potboiler into a panorama...."[24] Roger Ebert considered it a soap opera dignified by "a magnificence in his [Redford's] treatment...."[25] Reelviews.net praised Johansson as having delivered an Academy

Scarlett Johansson and Robert Redford, *The Horse Whisperer* (Touchstone, 1998).

Award-worthy performance. She was compared to Christina Ricci and Natalie Portman as an exemplary actress, using subtle expression changes and body language to excellent effect.[26] *The Washington Post* called the film a "tastefully understated, morally upright adaptation…" of the novel. Redford's translation of Evans' novel to the screen was akin to what Clint Eastwood had done with *The Bridges of Madison County*. There were shortcomings to be sure, e.g., over-length, anticlimactic, but it was "a grown-up film…" that "explores its ambitious themes and dysfunctional relationships with thoughtfulness and sincerity."[27]

Commentary

The Horse Whisperer was Nicholas Evans's first novel, a tremendous bestseller.

Johansson said of her character: "Grace is a very sensitive character. She's fragile and you have to be careful not to take her sarcastic humor as mean. She's from New York and she's very quick. She's smart but hurt deeply. This film is about people building relationships with each other and trying to heal a variety of wounds. It's about people who are kind of renewing themselves, renewing their souls."[28] Johansson imagined a person who'd lost a body part would never get over it, "and I had to develop that from the dramatic part of myself." An 18-year-old boy showed Johansson how to deal with her prosthetic leg, and the makeup artist Gary Liddiard would alert her to faux pas, like swinging her leg.[29] Director and star Redford assisted her to "find my place in a scene, since we would sometimes shoot out of sequence. He would retell parts of the story, to help me guide my emotions."[30]

Analysis

Pilgrim and Grace are appropriate names for the central allegorical figures in a spiritual journey even if they refer to a horse and a girl. The movie opens with the girl, Grace (Johansson), waking up in a kind of paradise—a farm that is quiet, peaceful, and with the sun shining—where she goes horseback riding on Pilgrim with a friend, Judith (Kate Bosworth). What launches the spiritual journey is an accident or, more precisely, two accidents—one between the two horses and riders and the other involving a tractor trailer, a loud, mechanical vehicle that seems completely out of place and seems to arrive out of nowhere. In a way, it arrives from the life of Grace's mother, Annie MacLean (Kristin Scott Thomas), who starts the same day by running through the streets of Manhattan, eating a hurried breakfast alone, and arriving at work as the driven editor of a magazine entitled *Cover*. There she barks orders, makes rapid decisions, and threatens to bring a libel suit against someone over the objections of a voice on a phone.

The inter-splicing of scenes from these two separate and very different lives suggests from the beginning that the mother-daughter relationship will be central to the film's plot. It is the accidents that leave Judith dead and Grace and Pilgrim severely injured that bring the two lives together at a hospital and the spiritual journey begins there. Annie finds herself unable to make a decision and refuses to follow the recommendation "to put Pilgrim down." She also learns that a part of Grace's leg must be amputated. The physical and psychic damage done to Pilgrim and Grace as the result of a literal fall lead to the quest for salvation, healing of a kind that will achieve a new wholeness represented by Grace once again riding Pilgrim.

The audience sees next to nothing of the initial healing process. Pilgrim is slow to heal and remains angry and hostile, rearing up when anyone tries to approach him. Grace tries returning to school on two crutches but refuses to continue after less than a day. Her mother encourages her to continue and asks, "What's your next class?" "Gym" is the bitter response that ends the discussion. Scarlett Johansson plays a withdrawn, sullen, angry teen very well and her mother responds in a characteristic way, by doing research in an attempt to find someone who can help Pilgrim. Grace's father, Robert MacLean (Sam Neill), seems to accept that the help provided by doctors, physical therapists, and a psychiatrist is all that can be done and he wants to carry on with their lives, hoping that things will come right in time. Annie's unwillingness to accept that what is offered is all that is possible shows the admirable side of her demanding nature. It is also what leads her to learn about Tom Booker, the title character, played by the movie's director, Robert Redford.

An attempt by Annie to convince Booker over the phone to fly east to look at Pilgrim and consider what can be done is a complete failure based on misunderstanding. Rather than give up, Annie ultimately concludes that taking Grace and Pilgrim to where Booker is, in Montana, is the right thing to do. The trip itself seems Quixotic at best, difficult and with no results at all guaranteed. Still, something in Annie is instinctively drawn to do it. Nonetheless, this physical journey runs parallel to the spiritual journey that is the basis of the film—from east to west, from city to country, from crowded highways filled with threatening tractor-trailers to open spaces where horses are at home. The trip if anything drives mother and daughter further apart. Grace sits in a backseat wearing earphones to listen to music, a way to isolate herself from her mother. Annie suggests she use the radio instead—an invitation to sit closer together and share the music—but Grace rejects the suggestion, irritated she had to remove an earphone to hear the suggestion. Annie decides to stop and see the national memorial to the Battle of the Little Bighorn only to find the site of Custer's Last Stand is closed. Grace does not even climb out of the car.

There is a suggestion of the mythic about the character of the horse whisperer too, someone who understands horses and calms them by gentleness who is a figure associated with Native Americans and the original bond between humanity and horses. As played by Redford, Booker often doesn't even whisper but simply stands or squats and stares. He nonetheless early shows that he understands people as well as horses. When he visits Grace and her mother at their motel to have a first look at Pilgrim, he finds Annie in another room on the phone with her office in New York and Grace sitting mesmerized in front of a TV that is showing an old movie. This scene conveys in an understated way that the electronic media connect people with others who are not present while isolating them from the people who are present.

Grace makes clear that coming to Montana is her mother's idea and she doesn't want to be involved. After seeing Pilgrim, Booker says he can only help if Grace is willing to take part and he insists on the girl answering for herself. "There isn't much else to do around here," she says. Booker declares, "That's not good enough. I can't help you," and walks away. "What do I have to do?" Grace calls, Johansson giving the question real urgency, a credible cry from the heart, as if she suddenly realizes she's been tossed a lifeline and she needs to grab it. This brief exchange establishes the basis for the all-important relationship between Booker and Grace.

Roger Ebert, who gave this film a mere three stars, arguing that Redford's magnificent directing gave dignity to what is basically a soap opera, argues that the relationship between Redford and Johansson makes the film. He seems not to have realized that Johansson's range was in part responsible for the quality of that relationship.

Booker suggests that Grace start to earn her keep by helping with the horses, carrying buckets of water and providing food for them. This offhand suggestion accomplishes a couple of things. It starts to overcome the self-pity that is associated with feeling useless. The work actually strengthens Grace, helping her to go from a crutch to the use of a cane to getting around on her prosthetic limb. She also starts to become accustomed to being around horses again too and horses that are dependent on her. Taking on a responsibility and fulfilling it gives her a sense of self-respect and a renewed sense that she is trustworthy. Johansson pulls off this series of transitions in a way that seems natural yet believable. She also portrays an early teen who is observant and thoughtful, capable of making the most of the relationship with Booker.

One pivotal scene takes place when they walk to a pickup truck and Booker suggests that Grace drive. "I can't drive," she says. "No time like the present to start," he says, handing her the key. She gets things off to a jerky start by giving the engine too much gas, but soon he's guided her to a straight road, she looks nervous but willing to steer, and he pulls his hat down over his eyes as if he does not need to watch what she's doing. It is a small scene but one that captures in an unsentimental way the mutual trust that's being established between them.

Unlike the characters in the film, the audience witnessed the accidents that propelled this journey. Grace has apparently not described it to anyone. Booker tells her that knowing exactly what happened would help him work with Pilgrim, but says that Grace should take her own time about describing it to him. One day she feels not only willing but compelled to describe it to Booker in a way that makes clear she suffers guilt as well as grief over Judith's death and also a fear of Pilgrim's behavior, the way he had reared up. Booker briefly makes two points: "You did nothing wrong. It could have happened to anyone. It could have happened to me." and "You know what I think? I think that damned horse loved you so much he tried to protect you." These statements leave Grace smiling through her tears. Here again Johansson's performance is a balancing act that never falls either into the sentimental or the melodramatic. The performance is marked by naturalness and credibility.

This combination of naturalness and credibility is perhaps drawn on most when she mounts Pilgrim and rides him around the corral, going from uncertainty and hesitation to real pleasure conveyed by a smile reminiscent of the one she wore the morning when the film began before the accidents occurred. This entire spiritual journey has been framed by the growing love affair between Booker and Annie, but that seems secondary to the healing of Pilgrim and Grace no doubt in part because of the chemistry that seems to have been established between Redford and Johansson as actors.

Banter with David Letterman

The Horse Whisperer premiered on May 15, 1998, and on May 20 the 13-year-old Johansson was the first guest on CBS-TV's *Late Show with David Letterman*. It was a funny and informative episode in which Johansson more than held her own with the veteran talk show host, talking about her previous films, riding, photographing the Big Sky Country, and Robert Redford.

Johansson told Letterman she'd been in the business for five years, and they joked about that being a while in "Scarlett years."

She said that when she was three she told her mother she "had a fire in my brain to act...." Letterman suggested that kids could be petty about another's success, but Johansson said her chums had been supportive. Letterman replied, "Well good, that probably says something lovely about you. It's probably because you're a nice, decent person that they behave in kind." Johansson replied, "Well that's debatable, but, you know."

Johansson revealed that she'd fibbed to Robert Redford about being familiar with horses and joked about calling Redford "Booey." Letterman pretended that Redford was an old codger who needed to be photographed through leaves.

Letterman quizzed her on Montana and said he'd be going out there soon because "I realized I'm a cowboy." Johansson told Letterman to steer clear of the plagues, meaning mosquitoes and locusts. Letterman responded, "I'm a cowboy. I can handle that crap."

Eight years later Johansson reflected, "I didn't know until *The Horse Whisperer* what was authentic and what wasn't.... I just knew how I felt, and I just reacted. I was a kid. It's probably the best way to act because it's completely instinctive. I think every actor is always trying to get back to some kind of original innocence."[31]

Johansson had great respect for co-star and director Robert Redford who "allowed me to discover every emotional place I needed to be."[32] Further, "I don't think I've ever been so carefully directed by someone. Things always work out for the (right) reason. My career took a different turn."[33] Redford famously called her "13 going on 30."[34]

In 2009 she told an interviewer that while watching the film she found herself painfully awkward.[35]

My Brother the Pig (1999)

Thirteen-year-old Kathy Caldwell (Johansson) is awakened courtesy of her younger brother George (Nick Fuoco), who tied his pet white rat to her leg. Kathy's father Richard (Judge Reinhold) mollifies her by recalling how thrilled she was when her baby brother was brought home. She will have nothing of this and rues the fact that her parents are taking time off from family life for a romantic vacation in France. She, George and his friend Freud (Alex Linz) are left in the care of coed housekeeper Matilda (Eva Mendes, here as Mendez, who would appear in the future Johansson film, *The Spirit*). Via a voodoo-like process, George is turned into a pig, and Matilda poses a solution which involves a drive to a small Mexican town where her grandmother concocts a potion. During a full moon shining through a rocky crevasse resembling a giant wolf head, George returns to his human form except for the fact that there's a curled pig's tail on his back that Kathy notices when they get home on the same day as their parents.

Review

Dove said the adventure was "filled with fun and excitement. Scarlett Johansson does a great job in playing the self-centered teenage girl that is being bothered by a pesky little brother."[36]

Commentary

Johansson's mother, Melanie (Sloan) Johansson, was mentioned first in the "Special Thanks" portion of the credits.

According to the Internet Movie Database (IMDB), the film had a Japanese video premiere on September 9, 1999, a U.S. film premiere on September 10, and a TV premiere on November 25, 2002.

Analysis

My Brother the Pig is mildly entertaining but strains credulity. Not, as might be assumed, by the story itself. Well, not too much. Not the transformation into a pig, rather the Mexican town butcher going on a rampage and brandishing a cleaver as he chases Kathy and her friends around town. That was over the top and contrived to introduce more action. As Kathy, Johansson is suitably exasperated by her kid brother's shenanigans and shows promise for the future.

An American Rhapsody (2001)

Mid–20th century Hungary, under the postwar Stalinist thumb: Fearing imprisonment or worse, Peter (Tony Goldwyn), Margit (Nastassja Kinski) and their older daughter Maria (Klaudia Szabo) flee into Austria.

Left to right, top: Judge Reinhold, Scarlett Johansson, Romy Walthall (Windsor) and Eva Mendez (Mendes); bottom: Nick Fuoco and Alex D. Linz, *My Brother the Pig* (Unapix Productions/Brimstone Entertainment, 1999).

Their infant daughter Suzanne (Raffaella Bansagi) is left behind with Margit's grandmother Helen (Agi Banfalvy), presumably temporarily.

Justly fearing she will be imprisoned for helping Peter and Margit escape, Helen deposits the child with Jeno (Balazs Galko) and Teri (Zsuzsa Czinkoczi), a couple living in the countryside. Finally, when Suzanne (Kelly Endresz-Banlaki) is six years old the Red Cross facilitates her flight to California, where Peter works in the airline rather than the publishing industry he'd hoped to enter. Suzanne seems to think she's on vacation and won't call Margit "Mama," rather "Lady." Understanding Suzanne's unhappiness, Peter makes a deal. When she's older he will buy her a ticket to Hungary. That day approaches after Margit, fearing the teenage Suzanne (Johansson) is on the wrong track, locks her in her room and bars the window.

Peter returns from a business trip and Suzanne calmly tells him it's time for him to honor his promise. She meets her adoptive parents in Budapest, where they live in public

Left to right: Nastassja Kinski, Scarlett Johansson, Tony Goldwyn, and producer Colleen Camp at Hollywood Film Festival premiere of *An American Rhapsody* (Fireworks Pictures, Seven Arts Pictures) at Paramount Studios, August 3, 2001 (Depositphotos.com).

Scarlett Johansson, *An American Rhapsody* (Fireworks Pictures, Seven Arts Pictures, 2001).

housing because their farmstead was confiscated by Communist bigwigs. To their alarm, she insists on seeing her grandmother, who reveals that Margit's father was killed by a drunken Russian soldier at the end of the war and that Margit was pinned to the floor beneath her dying father. Helen tells her granddaughter she, Suzanne, knows what she must do. Suzanne returns to her biological family in California, apparently realizing Hungary, still a totalitarian state, is not what she imagined. She obviously now empathizes with her mother.

Reviews

The *New York Times* thought the narration suggested writer-director Eva Gardos based the film on personal experience. Unlike Elia Kazan's *America, America* (1963), it "does not seem to have been subsidized by the State Department." It was not a tribute to a land of opportunity, rather a tale of an interrupted childhood "replaced by something artificial and grotesque." It was a modest film in which most events rang true.[37] Roger Ebert thought it demonstrated "the way unhealthy states create unhealthy citizens...." Reminding the reader how good Johansson was in *Ghost World* (shown at the Seattle International Film Festival in June), Ebert says her character Suzanne wants to be "a California girl and have fun, fun, fun, and her mother treats her like a bomb about to explode." The character was not "a colorful victim" but an ordinary adolescent retreating "into secrecy and passive hostility.... Suzanne is not meant to be a rebel with or without a cause, but more like the bystander in a sad historical accident."[38]

Magill's Cinema Annual 2002 said the characters "pace themselves as they endure the film's emotional riptide...." Reminding the reader of Johansson's characters in *Ghost World* and *The Horse Whisperer*, the young actress stretched "her talents a bit further here while also learning how to speak Hungarian." Kinski gave a "riveting performance as the overprotective mother..." while Tony Goldwyn brought "warmth and compassion..." as the overworked dad. For the most part sentimentality was eschewed. The film could have been longer.[39]

Commentary

An American Rhapsody played at a film festival in Nantucket in June 2001. In August it had a limited U.S. release. It won the 1998 grand prize from the Hartley-Merrill International Screenwriting Competition.

The film opens with a profile of Johansson and her voice providing a sense of the movie's subject matter and point of view: "In the summer of 1965, I was 15, and my life was already falling apart, so I went back to Hungary." The movie we are told all but immediately is "based on a true story" and at the end of the movie we learn it is dedicated to "My mother and father." The story the movie tells is the story of Eva Gardos, its writer and director, and this probably does much to explain both its strengths and weaknesses.

Analysis

In a way it is a miracle that *An American Rhapsody* ever came to be made. Early in her career, Eva Gardos worked as a production assistant on Francis Ford Coppola's *Apocalypse Now* and met Colleen Camp on the set of that film. Gardos told her the story of her coming to the West from Hungary after having been left there when her parents and older sister escaped from the Communist regime. She was encouraged to write a script and try to tell her story to a large audience through film. Camp did not only encourage Gardos but also took a small part in the movie and became a producer herself in addition to raising funds for it from others. The result is an independent film shot in two countries in 34 days and on a small budget. It was not a big success at the box office or critically. It is often described as having received "mixed reviews"—a kind of damnation through faint praise.

The problem with the movie seems to spring from its script. Gardos admits that she found it easier to write the bits of the story she did not personally witness—the escape by her parents and sister, for instance, negotiating with human traffickers, crossing the border into Austria under barbed wire fences and the watchful eyes of armed guards, and so on. She seems to have lacked the requisite distance from the events in her own life or at least some of them to describe them in ways that are credible and interesting without either becoming slightly sentimental or trying to attach too much importance to them by connecting them directly to the history of the Cold War. For instance, the black-and-white file footage of Hungarians marching with banners of Stalin seem a slightly heavy-handed way to compare life in a totalitarian state with the Technicolor life in Los Angeles. What might well have been a small, lyrical and personal movie seems to have become partially lost in an attempt to make it something more ambitious.

On the other hand, there are a number of good performances in the movie, especially that of Johansson. She virtually begins and ends the movie and as the opening voice-over makes clear she provides its point of view. The fact that it is a first-person narrative emphasizes the personal and lyrical quality in it that should no doubt have remained dominant and consistent. Johansson is very believable as a troubled teen. Her hostility is mainly aimed at her mother, well played by Nastassja Kinski. She objects to her mother's claims of having endured much in the past, demands to know why she was left behind when the others left their native land, feels a continuing loyalty to her adoptive parents and the idyllic if not Edenic life she lived with them in the country, and rebels by drinking, smoking, riding in convertibles, and openly defying her mother to be with her boyfriend. The result of this behavior is for her mother to attempt to make a prison of her daughter's bedroom—putting bars on the window and a lock on the door after she sneaked out through a window and stayed out all night. In a neat way, the American home becomes a totalitarian jail, making Communist Budapest a possible attractive alternative by comparison. Just as the mother as a young woman escaped a kind of prison for freedom, so the daughter is willing to fight for freedom—to the extent that she tries to force the door of her bedroom by firing rounds from a pump action rifle into it. It's this crisis that is resolved by Suzanne, the daughter, traveling to Budapest to visit her biological grandmother, her mother's mother, and her adoptive parents.

Reviewers tended to neglect the crucial role of the grandmother in the movie. Suzanne's parents had in fact arranged for traffickers to take her to join them in Austria, but when the woman who was to facilitate the escape said she drugged the infants and carried them across the border in a sack the grandmother could not bring herself to let the child go. Soon after she had Suzanne placed with a childless couple in the countryside, the grandmother was jailed herself as punishment for her daughter's and son-in-law's escape and the substantial, upper middle-class home in which she lived was confiscated by the State and divided into apartments. Learning these details from her grandmother as well as learning that her grandfather had been shot dead when he intervened with a drunken Russian soldier who had made sexual advances to her mother in a café—a part of the story about which her mother had been silent—helped reconcile her to her biological family and her adopted country.

Johansson is good at gradually learning about her past without hysterics or any sense of the kind of dramatic epiphany that would strain the credibility of the audience. She seems thoughtful and able to absorb a good deal in a quiet, watchful way. Suzanne never declares what she will do or what she has decided about her future. Instead, she asks her grandmother what she should do and the grandmother simply responds, "I think you know." She is then able to tell her adopted parents about her decision and flies back to California where she is met by and reconciled with her mother.

If critics were not especially generous to *An American Rhapsody*, some of them clearly thought highly of Johansson's performance. Kenneth Turan, for instance, wrote in the *Los Angeles Times*, "Critical to this [keeping 'mawkishness mostly at bay'] is the confident, straight-ahead performance of Scarlett Johansson as the film's teenage protagonist, Suzanne. With impressive credits that include *Manny and Lo*, *The Horse Whisperer*, *Ghost World*, and the Coen brothers' upcoming *The Man Who Wasn't There*, Johansson is rapidly becoming one of the top screen actresses, and her piercing, unfussy work here shows exactly why."[40]

Ghost World (2001)

Best friends Enid (Thora Birch) and Rebecca (Johansson) welcome high school graduation but have no immediate plans for college or anything else. They might get jobs at the end of the summer.

Enid befriends Seymour (Steve Buscemi), a self-described dork with a world-class

Scarlett Johansson (left) and Thora Birch, *Ghost World* (United Artists, 2001).

collection of jazz and blues LPs. Although Enid acts as matchmaker for Seymour, she eventually sleeps with him.

As the summer runs out, Rebecca gets a job at an upscale coffee shop. She and Enid have grown apart although she finally agrees that Enid can move in with her. Enid has second thoughts after watching the dude on the abandoned bus stop bench actually step onto a bus. She packs her valise and waits for the return of the bus, which carries her off to…?

Reviews

The *New York Times* called it "the best depiction of teenage eccentricity since *Rushmore*…" and "its question-mark ending reminded me of *The Graduate*." The cast brought "Mr. Clowes's sad world of loneliness and disaffection to vivid comic life."[41] Roger Ebert said, "I wanted to hug this movie." It gave the audience "specific, original, believable, lovable characters, and meanders with them through their inconsolable days, never losing its sense of humor."[42] *Time* described it as the teen comedy "genre's cleansing, toxic-antidote.…" One of the reasons the two leads, Birch and Johansson, had been chosen was because they were not over 18. That left Christina Ricci out. Johansson had "been playing wise children for almost half her life" (*Manny & Lo*, *The Horse Whisperer*). In *Ghost World* she was "Enid's more passive ally. 'Rebecca's head is screwed on right,' Johansson notes, 'but Enid's is sort of floating around.'"[43] *Magill's Cinema Annual 2002* was mostly positive but found fault with Enid's transformation near the end, when audience empathy might dissipate. However, Thora Birch "redeems many of these faults," fully fleshing out her character. As Becky, Johansson "handles her part with understated effectiveness; she has a raspy voice, cloudy eyes, and a sometimes fixed stare, as if being only a step away from a coma or a nap. Life just isn't very interesting for Becky, but she will manage somehow."[44]

Commentary

Ghost World was released between July and September 2001. Johansson said she thought she was 14 when the script came to her and that Thora Birch was already signed on for Enid. She admired Birch, slightly older but a spokesperson for her generation. Johansson wasn't keen on doing a slasher movie or "anything that was just not cool." That was her criteria, and *Ghost World* was "written in my language.…" Her own "monotonous take on life seemed to work really well with the flavor of the film."[45]

Director Zwigoff said the studio wanted Rebecca to be played by anybody but Johansson and noted in 2017 the irony that Johansson's prestige was such that she had the power to greenlight movies.[46]

Foretelling Billy Bob Thornton's comments in the special features of *The Man Who Wasn't There*, *Ghost World* producer Liane Halfon said, "Scarlett was super self-assured."[47]

Analysis

Ghost World is primarily a vehicle for Thora Birch, who plays Enid, a high school student whose graduation is temporarily put on hold because she needs to take a summer art class, taught by the laughably wonderful Illeana Douglas. This academic hiccup upsets the plans Enid had made with her best friend, Rebecca, played by Johansson. They were both misfits in high school who kept their vulnerabilities under control by an energetic use of irony, satire, and sarcasm, putting all around them down as a way to keep potential disappointment at bay. They roll their eyes and raise their eyebrows as classmates talk about colleges and majors and careers. They are out of step and happy to be that way and plan to stay that way. Their modest scheme for the future is to obtain jobs and rent an apartment together. Rebecca pursues this plan in a surprisingly dogged and ambitious way while Enid stays sidetracked with hilarious antics in her summer art class.

The division between the two friends widens when what starts as a cruel trick played on a lonely eccentric man portrayed memorably by Steve Buscemi turns into a kind of romance for Enid. Rebecca works in a Starbucks-like coffee shop and goes apartment hunting while spending less and less time with Enid. Enid, despite half-hearted efforts, does little to forward the plan of getting a job and sharing the apartment Rebecca found and strongly desires. Johansson becomes an identifiable foil for Birch. She really is able and eager to become part of the world as it is while Enid's "maladjustment" is far greater—or far healthier—depending on what you think of the world as it is. Enid seems to have an artist hidden inside her while Rebecca becomes something of a yuppie before our eyes. In the end, Enid is able to continue with neither Rebecca nor Seymour (Buscemi). She finds a wistful ending by disappearing on a bus on a route that has been discontinued—either a suggestion of a way of going forward by making renewed contact with the past or potentially an imaginative indication that she has no way forward and literally disappears into a ghost world. Rebecca on the other hand, showing ambition, impatience, and a good deal of cruelty clearly has a future among the living.

Terry Zwigoff, the director of the wonderful *Crumb*, co-wrote this film with David Clowes based on Clowes's graphic novel of the same name. The look of the film and the performances to some extent suggest the sense of exaggeration that tends to be part of the comic book world. Nonetheless the film causes thought on the part of viewers in addition to providing them with a good deal of fun. Birch and Johansson both seem well cast as comrades in arms who find they are forced to go separate ways after colliding with what passes for the adult world.

The Man Who Wasn't There (2001)

> "You don't see people like her very often, like the young teen actresses usually don't look like her or act like her, or anything. She's kind of her own thing. It's great."
> —Commentary by Billy Bob Thornton,
> *The Man Who Wasn't There*, DVD, USA Films, 2002

A small town in postwar America. Malaise permeates the psyche of Ed Crane (Billy Bob Thornton), a reluctant barber tired of the constant gabbing of shop owner and brother-in-law Frank (Michael Badalucco). When Creighton Tolliver (Jon Polito) passes through town, Ed puts up $10,000 in this entrepreneur's dry-cleaning scheme. This money is acquired by anonymously blackmailing Nirdlingers store owner Big Dave (James Gandolfini) the boss of Ed's wife Doris (Frances McDormand), with whom he's having an affair. Big Dave thinks that Tolliver is at the heart of the blackmail scheme. At the store by night, Big Dave tells Ed about the blackmail plot he discovered when beating Tolliver. During the confrontation Ed fatally stabs Big Dave in the jugular with a cigar knife. Doris is implicated, and at the urging of his friend Walter Abundas (Richard Jenkins), whose teenage daughter "Birdy" (Johansson) Ed admires for her piano expertise, Ed hires big-time Sacramento lawyer Freddy Riedenschneider (Tony Shalhoub). Before the trial, however, Doris hangs herself. Ed proposes to Birdy that he become a kind of manager and takes her to a San Francisco impresario of note only to learn that Birdy, while proficient, has no true talent. In fact, on the way back to town, Birdy harbors little desire to enter the musical field. She might become a veterinarian. She tells Ed he's an enthusiast, appreciates his consideration, and attempts to show her gratitude with oral sex. Aghast, Ed crashes the car. Neither he nor Birdy are killed but in the hospital, Ed is confronted by detectives who arrest him for Tolliver's murder. They'd found Ed's investment contract on the body and thought that Ed used Doris to embezzle the money. According to them, Tolliver found out and confronted Ed, who killed him. Riedenschneider is called back but things go awry, starting with an attack on Ed by Frank. Ed is sentenced to death by electric chair. From the jail, Ed sees a UFO, which Big Dave's wife (Katherine Borowitz) had told him about after her husband's demise. Awaiting electrocution, Ed muses on the possibility of meeting Doris in the afterlife.

Billy Bob Thornton and Scarlett Johansson, *The Man Who Wasn't There* **(Good Machine/Gramercy Pictures, 2001).**

Reviews

The *New York Times* compared it to *Mulholland Drive*, whose director David Lynch shared with the Coens the director's prize at Cannes. Like him, they'd "used the noir idiom to fashion a haunting, beautifully made movie that refers to nothing outside itself and that disperses like a vapor as soon as it's over." The cast, including Johansson "are all terrific."[48] *The Atlantic* thought it "among the very best-looking of all their [the Coens] films." However, it veered off course halfway through, with the episode in which Crane ingratiates himself with Birdy seemingly connected to "a different, and notably more contemporary, film, especially in the final sequence in which she explicitly offers him oral sex."[49] Roger Ebert liked it better the second time around. Whereas at Cannes he found it too leisurely and heard French critic Michel Ciment say, "A 90-minute film that plays for two hours," subsequent viewings revealed its virtues. It was in fact a "voluptuous feast."[50]

Commentary

This was released in October 2001 and is number 11 in the filmography of iconoclastic and Academy Award–winning writer-directors Ethan and Joel Coen. On the DVD, the Coens and Billy Bob Thornton agreed that Johansson intimidated them a little. Unlike most people, she had no self-doubt. She was extraordinary, had confidence and could "project a kind of wholesome innocence."[51]

Johansson admired the Coens at work because they and their crew were so well organized. "It was really just the ideal way to make a movie. I would love to work with them again sometime."[52] Johansson would get her wish when she landed a second role in the Coen universe as the glamour-puss Hollywood star in 2016's *Hail, Caesar!*

Analysis

Johansson plays a relatively small but extremely important role in this Coen brothers' homage to film noir of the post–World War II years because the character she plays, Birdy Abundas, has a small but important part in the life of Ed Crane, the film's narrator and title character, portrayed by Billy Bob Thornton. Johansson plays a high school student who lives with her father, Walter Abundas (Richard Jenkins), a lawyer, and plays the piano—especially Romantic piano sonatas by Beethoven. The sound of these sonatas makes up much of the film's music, suggesting the pervasive nature of her presence even when she is not on screen. She plays the part with what seems for her a natural mixture of innocence and precocity, youth and maturity, that allows her to become a symbol of life abundant, of both vitality and possibility, for Crane.

Crane is early established as a forgettable person—silent, introverted, passive. He cuts the hair of Creighton Tolliver, a con man who apparently seeks financing for a dry-cleaning venture, in the afternoon, but the man fails to recall Crane when they meet again later in the day. When Crane thinks he is introducing himself to Birdy, on the other hand, she assures him, "Oh, I know you, Mr. Crane. I used to come to the barbershop with my father." Crane's reaction to Tolliver's forgetting him was disappointment if not hurt. Birdy dismisses Crane's apology for failing to remember her, "You can't be expected to remember every skinny kid who comes to the barbershop with her father."

She is, of course, no longer a "skinny kid," but an attractive teenager Crane has been drawn to because she's playing the piano in the music department of Nirdlingers Department Store, the store where Crane's wife Doris, played by Frances McDormand, works as a bookkeeper.

Birdy and Crane have both left a party that is being thrown in the store to celebrate the forthcoming opening of Big Dave Brewster's Annex. Crane says the music is pretty and asks if Birdy made it up. She becomes immediately instructive without being at all condescending—telling Crane about Beethoven's deafness and stating that although the composer wrote the music he never heard it or, at least, never heard it in the usual way. This conversation serves to raise a theme that is important in the movie, the relationship between the reality of the imagination and the reality of the actual world. Birdy's withdrawal from the party to make music, her appearance, and her knowledge make her appear to Crane as a symbol of the artist and the life of the imagination. Their relationship develops as a result of Crane's daydream of helping Birdy become a concert pianist and serve as her manager—an imaginative alternative to his life as a second barber in the shop of his brother-in-law.

When Birdy takes part in a concert at the high school, Crane attends and seeks her out afterwards to congratulate her. She is with a boy from the school and she introduces her friend to Mr. Crane. Birdy is modest in response to Crane's praise and the whole interaction grows awkward. The school kids are a potential couple and Crane's presence is as odd man out, the man who should not be there, perhaps, but is.

Nonetheless, after Crane's wife Doris is arrested for the murder of Big Dave Brewster, her boss and lover, memorably played by James Gandolfini, who was actually killed by Crane, the barber develops the habit of spending evenings at Birdy's home even when her father is away, pursuing his hobby of tracing his family's ancestry. It's on one of these occasions that Crane, in Birdy's bedroom, tells her he'd like to take her to San Francisco to play the piano for a famous teacher there who could help her become a concert pianist. Birdy is not immediately enthusiastic about the idea, admitting she is not at all sure she wants a career as a pianist, but finally agrees.

Two of the most antithetical male characters to Crane, Big Dave Brewster and Frank, at two different times in the film, aggressively ask Crane, "What kind of man are you?" In a way, this is the fundamental question the film poses to those who watch it. Birdy provides the answer or, at least, an answer, as Crane drives her home after the famous music teacher says she is a nice girl who can play the piano correctly but lacks the soul of a musician.

Crane wants to dismiss the teacher's opinion and try to find someone else who will take Birdy on and launch her musical career. Birdy says she's not sure she wants a career and if she did she thinks she'd like to be a veterinarian. She asks Crane, "Do you know what you are? You're an enthusiast." If there's one thing most of the characters who knew Crane thought he was not it was an enthusiast. He's been portrayed as not only silent but also asexual—he is shocked by and rejects Creighton Tolliver's offer of a homosexual encounter and he confesses to the Medical Examiner when he is told that Doris was pregnant when the state was to take her life for a crime she did not commit that he and his wife had not performed the sexual act for years. Birdy does not only recognize Crane, a kind of bird, as an enthusiast but she also regrets not playing the piano better because that would have pleased him. She decides to please him in another way. She moves close to him in the front seat of the car, kisses his cheek, places her hand on his thigh, and proceeds to perform fellatio or at least tries to. Crane responds with, "Heavens to Betsy, Birdy" and crashes the car.

Birdy, we learn when Crane asks about her, broke her clavicle, a collarbone, in the accident, and we never see her again. Crane is in far worse physical condition, but is met by police detectives who inform him he is charged with the murder of Creighton Tolliver, a crime committed by Big Dave Brewster, the man Crane actually killed.

Crane is tried, found guilty, and in the end we learn that he has written his story at a nickel a word for a men's magazine, the pulp forerunner of film noir, while on death row. In a way, the relationship between Crane and Birdy reflects the realism of even a young woman as compared to the fantasies of even an older man. Perhaps because raised by her father alone and, as a result, early admitted to the all male world of the barbershop, Birdy was psychologically prone to be drawn to an older man. In any case, Crane's attempt to blackmail Big Dave so he could invest in Tolliver's dry cleaning scheme, like his dream of a life with Birdy as manager of her musical career, shows his romanticism, his lack of realism. Beethoven's piano sonatas provide the appropriate accompaniment to this examination of a difference between women and men.

Eight Legged Freaks (2002)

Black sheep Chris McCormick (David Arquette) returns to his hometown of Posterity, Arizona, and finds the citizenry pressed by the mayor to accept a mining company buyout. This is not the only issue affecting the community. After a drum of toxic waste falls into a stream, infected crickets are consumed by spiders in the home-made desert "museum" of Joshua Taft (Tom Noonan) and mutate, growing to monstrous proportions. This development supersedes Sheriff Samantha Parker's (Kari Wuhrer) immediate issues with her willful teenage daughter Ashley (Johansson). The arachnids have made a mineshaft their prime habitation and begin to assault the community at large. Taking refuge in the Prosperity Mall, the survivors make their way into underground tunnels after Chris tries to use his phone to alert distant authorities. He concocts a scheme to blow up the methane-infused shafts, and as Sam starts the generator with a taser proffered by Ashley, incinerates the spiders and escapes to admit his love for Sam.

Reviews

Roger Ebert enjoyed "laughs, thrills, wit and scary monsters...." Like *Critters* (1986) it kidded itself and got away with it. Johansson initially seemed "superfluous..." but became "indispensable in scenes involving a stun gun and, of course, lots of spiders."[53] *TheFrightFile*, by contrast—or not getting the tone—said the film neglected characterization and bemoaned the fact that a Joe Dante or Tim Burton hadn't been its director. "Scarlett Johansson, possessing such talent in 2001's *Ghost World* and *The Man Who Wasn't There*, is relegated to the thoroughly disposable role...."[54]

Analysis

Johansson does have a pivotal role, tasering her boyfriend when he gets too fresh, telling her mom where Wade absconded to, and producing the stun gun again to charge up the generator. There are some quite disturbing scenes of spiders attacking humans.

2. Child Actress

Scarlett Johansson (top left), French promotional card for *Eight Legged Freaks* (Warner Bros., 2002).

Where does *Eight Legged Freaks* fall in the giant spider/bug subgenre of the Science Fiction, Fantasy and Horror genre? Like *Matinee* (1993), is it a homage to *Tarantula* (1955), *The Incredible Shrinking Man* (1957), *Earth vs. the Spider* (1958), *Kingdom of the Spiders* (1977)?

Johansson, at age 16, was here transitioning into what filmgoers and critics will soon label a bombshell and "the sexiest woman in the world," a star and actress who hearkened back to the classic and glamorous Hollywood of the pre- and war years in which Lana Turner and Rita Hayworth held sway as sex symbol icons.

As the years passed, Johansson's body would, as one pundit observed, become the object of intense scrutiny.[55] It may be that this was caused by years of less than full-figured actresses gaining cache, founded in the mid- and late sixties by British model Twiggy and U.S. actress Mia Farrow. Johansson was unique by comparison.

3

Adult Breakthrough

Lost in Translation (2003)

"Stardom would come upon her, and with it the unknowability that both tempts and eludes the public's craving to know more."
—Anthony Lane, "Her Again: The Unstoppable Scarlett Johansson," *New Yorker*, March 24, 2014

"Johansson was surely born to listen on screen, her features reacting instantly to Murray's quirky anecdotes."
—Paul Julian Smith, "Tokyo Drifters," *Sight & Sound*, January 2004

While a young woman (Johansson) sleeps high above a modern metropolis, American movie star Bob Harris (Bill Murray) arrives by night at the same Tokyo hotel. During his cab ride into town he'd seemed perplexed by the garish, dreamlike neon images permeating the urban center. Making nice with his innumerable hosts but wishing to sleep—which he finds difficult throughout his stay—Bob sits sedately on his bed.

The woman Bob will shortly meet is Charlotte, the young woman who'd slept or at least rested above the city as Bob arrived. Her husband John (Giovanni Ribisi) is a photographer on assignment that leaves him little time for his wife. In an elevator Bob makes eye contact with Charlotte.

Taken to a studio for a commercial promoting Suntory whiskey, Bob finds it a grueling experience. The director speaks no English, and the translator is only marginally better.

Charlotte, meanwhile, visits a temple and later on the phone to friend Lauren says, "I didn't feel anything." Lauren needs to stop the conversation for a moment and when she comes back on the line Charlotte says all is okay. But it isn't and she mumbles that she doesn't know who she married. After hanging up she begins crying.

In the hotel's nightclub, Bob and Charlotte spot each other again. She sends over a drink.

Later Charlotte and John accidentally run into the ebullient but shallow actress Kelly (Anna Faris) in the hotel hallway.

Next day Charlotte is shown how to arrange flowers the Japanese way. Later she takes a bath, then lies in bed watching TV. Like Bob, who in his room is also awake and watching TV, she finds it difficult to sleep.

In the nightclub Charlotte finds herself sitting next to Bob. She doesn't know what to order and he says, "For relaxing times, make it Suntory time." Bob tells her he's taking a break from his wife, forgot his son's birthday, and is there to endorse Suntory for $2 million. He's been married for 25 years, Charlotte for two. She'd graduated the previous spring with a degree in philosophy. "I wish I could sleep," she says.

Next day Bob goes to the pool while Charlotte observes players at an arcade. In the evening John and Charlotte visit the nightclub with Kelly and her chums. Charlotte sees

Japanese Chirashi mini-poster for *Lost in Translation* (Focus Features, 2003).

Bill Murray and Scarlett Johansson, *Lost in Translation* (Focus Features, 2003).

Bob who tells her he's planning a prison break. Bob accompanies Charlotte to meet her mostly Japanese friends.

After a night on the town, Bob carries a sleeping Charlotte to her room and returns to his. Next day he discovers that Charlotte had bumped her toe, tells her it looks dead, and takes her to a hospital.

Later, both reclining on his bed, Charlotte says she doesn't know what she's supposed to be. Bob says she'll figure it out and adds that children are the most delightful people one can ever meet.

That evening Charlotte knocks on Bob's door and asks him to come with her and some friends, but he can't and she hears the reason: the chanteuse is in the room, having spent the night in Bob's bed. Charlotte and Bob have a tense lunch and don't regain their rapport until they meet outside during a fire alarm. She learns that he's leaving the next day, but in the nightclub he says he doesn't want to go. "Then don't. Stay here with me," she responds.

Next morning, Bob leaves a message on Charlotte's phone, trying to be funny by saying she still has his jacket, that she stole it.

Charlotte appears in the lobby—with his jacket. They part.

In his limo Bob spots Charlotte walking on the street and leaps out. "Hey, you." They embrace and he whispers something into her ear. She seems to understand. He returns to the cab. Fadeout.

Reviews

Reelviews called Johansson "luminous" and a match for Murray. Their rapport greatly exceeded typical "screen chemistry.[1]

New York said director Coppola had discovered "a metaphor for modern alienation that is so mundane it's funny," transforming "the dark night of the soul into one big cryptlike luxury hotel." Johansson's character was special, not a typical "snuggle-bunny," rather "a performer who plays a young woman with smarts and substance."[2]

The Associated Press said director Sofia Coppola had emerged further from her father Francis Ford Coppola's shadow, demonstrating an "observant eye for detail and ability to evoke mood...." Murray may have done his best work, matched by Johansson "who continues to show a maturity beyond her years...." And, "Johansson, at 18, is young enough to be his daughter, yet she seems so comfortable in her own skin and possesses such poise and insight, she's easily his equal."[3]

SFGate called it "gorgeous..." and "A delicate, beautifully observed study of impossible romance...."

Scarlett Johansson, *Lost in Translation* (Focus Features, 2003).

Nothing was imposed or overstated. Director Coppola's "languid style" allowed the actors to demonstrate their shine. Bill Murray "has never been this touching...." Johansson, who'd been "so impressive in *Manny and Lo* and *Ghost World*, is in some ways Murray's mirror, in other ways his opposite. While Murray suggests a man who's crumbling inside and out—and yet retaining a childlike goofiness—Johansson endows Charlotte with a skepticism and world-weariness that seem at odds with her youthful radiance."[4]

Boxoffice said director "Coppola manages to transcend all the usual romantic clichés...." Murray and Johansson inspired awe by creating "the kind of on-screen chemistry that rarely graces American cinemas without the intermediary of subtitles. It's been years since Murray has been this funny or this affecting, and he has certainly never been this understated. Johansson is equally impressive, measuring Murray scene for scene with a canny blend of soulful sadness and cunning confidence."[5]

Elle complimented her cliche-free and fresh performance based a good deal "on an unself-conscious sexiness that is equally a function of the intelligence behind her slightly dreamy-looking eyes as it is of her petite but sumptuously curvy body."[6]

Commentary

In an interview just after its New York City premiere on September 9, 2003, Coppola said that she wanted Johansson for the part of Charlotte because of the quality she had shown as a child in *Manny & Lo*.[7] A decade after the film's release Coppola was queried about the influence of *Lost in Translation*, especially on millennials. She spoke of living in Tokyo in her 20s and including many true things in the film. Bill Murray was a catch. As for Johansson, "I loved her low voice." Coppola was asked about the famous early shot when the audience sees Johansson lying in bed in her underwear. It was inspired by painter John Kacere's images of other girls in lingerie. The shoot was a short and tough one, with language and cultural issues. The budget was low and they didn't have permits to shoot on the street. They'd just film until told to move on. The Park Hyatt hotel restricted the shoot to early morning so as not to bother guests. "We were always sneaking around the hotel. But now I've heard they have *Lost in Translation* tours there." Asked about the final farewell, Coppola said she remained supportive of Murray's comment that "it's between them!" And, "It was always meant to be this tender goodbye where they both knew that they had touched each other in some way."[8]

In 2014 *The New Yorker* recalled how this film made Johansson a star: A quarter of an hour in "a breathtaking closeup of her face, as she applied lipstick...."[9]

Also in 2014, *The Daily Beast* began its critique of *Under the Skin* with a retrospective tribute to Johansson in *Lost in Translation*, beginning with an admonition for men to arrive on time because "The first thing we see is Scarlett Johansson's rear end, laid sideways on a bed, the full, unhindered view of it only just sheathed, hurtfully, by the thinnest pink underpants known to man, in an overt act of provocation against man."[10]

The only negative comments about the film related to a supposed critique of Japanese society. To counter that and see how close the film came to the truth, see the "Mission to Tokyo" chapter in Anthony Bourdain's 2000 expose, *Kitchen Confidential*. Chef Bourdain viewed the city and its denizens much like this film's characters, and not negatively. Upon reflection, we can recognize here the original outrage over Johansson—or anyone not from a foreign culture—doing anything that could even remotely be construed as anti-multicultural. This issue would be kicked up again in *Ghost in the Shell* when Johansson had the temerity to play an Asian. Sofia Coppola's comments about Japan in her 2003 Charlie Rose interview also put the lie to any such criticism.[11]

In her book, *Film and Female Consciousness*, Lucy Bolton devoted a chapter to *Lost in Translation*. She compared it to Billy Wilder's 1955 classic comedy, *The Seven Year Itch*, in particular Marilyn Monroe's "The Girl." Both films' male leads were middle-aged and married. The male and female leads were thrust together unexpectedly and transformed, but neither film featured a "quest for love."[12] Comparison could also be made a la Monroe as Johansson "has frequently appeared to imitate Monroe off-screen, wearing tight-fitting, vintage dresses which accentuate her curvaceous body, with platinum waved hair and glossy red lips."[13]

Bolton recognized the stillness and silence of Johansson's persona, noting that when she frequents an amusement parlor her observations are unspoken, and we don't know what she's feeling. Verbal information is eschewed in favor of her visual perspective via shot/reverse shots. Despite her character's silence, the audience uses its sensory knowledge to see what she sees.[14] But when Charlotte visits the temple, "Her reactions ... are unspoken and difficult to read."[15] "In other scenes, Charlotte sits on the window-sill, or lies in the bath, contemplating the vista of the city below. In these contemplative scenes, the emphasis is on her gaze: her state of undress is not designed to be seen by anyone else, as she is alone in her room."[16]

Predictive of her future style, silence and stillness, "Much of Charlotte's screen-time is spent silently wandering around Tokyo, exploring the city and observing its inhabitants: in the amusement arcade, the temple, and the hotel." Observing a wedding party, "She makes little effort to converse."[17] After karaoke, Charlotte and Bob have a smoke in the hall—in silence.[18]

In this and in the forthcoming *Girl with a Pearl Earring*, "her sexuality has been conspicuous for its restraint; she's a master of unspoken ardor."[19]

In *Sight & Sound*, Paul Julian Smith wrote, "And Johansson, a fitting muse to Vermeer in Peter Webber's *Girl with a Pearl Earring* (2003), shows that beyond her beauty (and pink pants) she can convincingly pass for a philosophy graduate, a role few Hollywood starlets could carry off."[20]

Although she'd garnered some attention for her independent outings *Manny & Lo* and *Ghost World*, and the major film *The Horse Whisperer*, it was here in her first adult role that Johansson created a stir and signaled the birth of a new star: when the camera closed in on the sleeping Charlotte (Johansson), back to the camera, wearing a sweater and panties. When she awoke and her eighteen-year-old face and figure were seen, it was a revelation. This creature was not androgynous and obviously no victim of an eating disorder. This put her at odds with many other film actresses of the era.

In 2004 Johansson explained how *Lost in Translation* transformed her life and would presumably help her make more exceptional, people-pleasing movies. She didn't mind that her fame would facilitate dinner reservations but "the most important thing to me is the actual work."[21]

There was another mild controversy during awards season. A journalist was perplexed that neither Murray nor Coppola mentioned Johansson at the Golden Globes and Academy Awards. It was curious "why they would so pointedly ignore the superb performance of an actress whose contribution was as integral to the ineffable magic of this movie as either of theirs. But if Johansson was stung by the neglect, she didn't show it."[22]

Asked about this omission a couple years later, Johansson denied being miffed that she wasn't mentioned during Coppola's Academy Award acceptance speech for best screenplay. Sofia was accepting for writing and Murray had written a significant amount of it. "Sofia came up to me afterward and said, 'Oh, I'm such an ass, I forgot!' I was like, 'It's OK; it doesn't bother me.' If she was accepting for directing, then it probably would have bothered me. But, um, it didn't."[23]

Johansson told an interviewer that her solo scenes were considerably improvised. She said she and director Coppola "never really spoke about the character." She did not like directors who asked what she was thinking about in a take. "I'm not going to tell you what I'm thinking about; that's for me."[24]

Yet she did a director like Coppola who "knew what direction she wanted the character to go." She could recognize subtleties in Johansson's performance that "I didn't even realize were happening...." [25]

Coppola was asked if there were lines in the script for the audience to hear from Murray at the finale. She loved Murray's reply to that question: "It's between lovers." Coppola added, "I wrote some stuff but I wasn't happy with it. There was dialogue but it was really sparse. Ultimately I liked it better that you don't hear it, that you can put in what you want them to say. You wish he'd say, 'I had a great time with you and you're great,' but instead he says, 'I left my jacket.' That's what people do."[26]

Fourteen years later Johansson told Howard Stern, "Nobody knew that it would be so profound." She said it was initially difficult for her and Bill Murray to relate to one another but when the cameras rolled, they were simpatico.[27]

Analysis

Johansson's ability to display innocence, maturity, and intelligence all at once probably best conveys the power of her stillness. As a result, she is capable of being the center of attention while alone and doing and saying nothing.

Charlotte is a twenty-two-year-old recent Yale graduate, a philosophy major, who has been married for two years to John (Giovanni Ribisi), a photographer who is in Tokyo to take pictures of a rock and roll band. Charlotte is there to keep him company. He is too busy with his work and eventually tells an actress named Kelly (Anna Faris) who is a friend and a fan of his photography that he has little need for or interest in his wife's company. Their conditions seemed to be summed up by John's ability to sleep soundly and snore while Charlotte suffers from insomnia.[28]

Their relationship seems to be reflected in John's ritualistic saying "love you" when he leaves her to go to work and she never uses the same words back. The result is that Charlotte is not only at a loose end but, it is soon apparent, lonely, unhappy, and unsure of her marriage. It is no doubt significant that Charlotte and John have no last names. Their identity as a married couple is incomplete.

She becomes a silent person in a hotel room, looking out of a high window at a glittering modern section of the city of Tokyo. Or she wears earphones to listen to a guru's tape about the soul's search for purpose in life. Or she sits on the Bullet Train on the way to Kyoto, looking out a window that reflects her own face, wearing earphones, while passing a snow-capped Mount Fuji. In time, these shots serve to define her mental state and become supplemented by her scenes with Bob Harris (Bill Murray). While this performance could have easily become a cliché, a self-indulgent portrait of an educated, well-off young American who is "trying to find herself," instead Johansson's playfulness and seriousness, her sensuality and intelligence, make it a portrait of an interesting individual.

After a famous opening shot of Johansson's glorious body parts covered with only underwear, what could understandably be mistaken for a view of Fuji, the film opens and closes with Bob Harris's arrival and departure. He travels by cab through Tokyo from the airport to the hotel at night, clearly tired, and sees a large picture of himself in a whiskey ad and rubs his eyes as if he doubts his own image. The film ends after his final parting from Charlotte with him in a cab in the daytime going to the airport. What happens between this arrival and departure is the story of a remarkable relationship between a man and a woman who are married to other people.

Marriage is the main subject of the movie. At one point, John and Charlotte are in their hotel room. John packs up his gear to go to work while Charlotte puts on what appears to be a comically long scarf she has apparently been knitting—a potential symbol of the way she has been trying to pass the time. "Do you think this is done?" she asks. John gives her a look of incomprehension and admits, "I don't know." While the question she asks clearly refers to the scarf there is the suggestion that it could also be asking about their relationship, their marriage. Later, when she takes the train to Kyoto she is wearing the scarf, symbolically carrying her questions about the marriage with her. While in Kyoto she stumbles across a wedding party of Japanese in traditional dress. The groom holds an ornamental umbrella over himself and his bride and she gently places her hand in his as they climb the steps of a temple. Charlotte witnesses this couple in silence but there is a stark contrast between this traditional, religious ceremony and the marriage she is a part of. There are no speeches, no life-changing moments, no long distance calls to either John or Bob, but merely watching, serving as a witness, and that is enough.

Robert Frost said poetry is what is lost in translation. There is something of the magic of poetry at work in *Lost in Translation*. This idea that understatement—or an image rather than a statement—is enough seems to have grown out of the limitations that were necessary parts of the way the movie was made. It had a low budget—$4 million reportedly. It was shot in less than a month, often making the most of street scenes in Tokyo or the empty corridors of the hotel at night. Shooting began before Bill Murray was firmly lined up even though the director has said she had written the part of Bob Harris for him and would not have been able to make the film without him. The separation between Harris and Charlotte that first emerges when they see each other in an elevator otherwise filled with Japanese people and eventually dissolves as they meet and talk in the bar of the hotel is the portrait of two lonely people far from home falling into more-than-friendship that is at once restrained and heightened by their avoidance of the sex act. The limitations that were overcome to make the film are equivalent to the kind of tightening that causes a flower to bloom. Johansson and Murray made the most of Sofia Coppola's Academy Award–winning script.

4

Working, Part 1

"Work is the one thing I can do. It's constant; it's the one thing I can count on."
—Chip Brown, "The Smart Bomb," *Elle*, January 2006

"I wasn't very self-conscious. I never know what my face is doing."
—Doug Atchison, "Girl with the Golden Touch,"
MovieMaker, Winter 2004

Girl with a Pearl Earring (2004)

Delft, Holland: 1665. Griet's family sends her to the home of the painter Johannes Vermeer to be a maid. Vermeer (Colin Firth) has a family but not a happy one and he is dependent on patrons, notably Van Ruijven (Tom Wilkinson), to make ends meet. During the course of her employment, Griet, although working in the shadows, catches the eye of her rather reclusive and slow working employer, who senses some sort of kinship with her. He shows her how to mix pigments before putting on hold his family portrait of the Ruijven clan in order to paint Griet. His portrait distresses Vermeer's wife Catharina (Essie Davis), especially as it features Catharina's pearl, and Griet is let go. She soon receives a token: the scarf she wore for the painting plus the pearl earrings.

Reviews

The *New York Times* review was also an analysis, a necessarily brief biography of Vermeer, and a tracking of the film's preproduction and making. The film "captures the mood of a mid–17th-century Delft household as reflected in Dutch genre paintings. And it skillfully evokes the light, color, silence and intimacy that characterize Vermeer's works." Also, "The film is remarkably silent...." Johansson was the film's center. "17 when the film was

Scarlett Johansson, *Girl with a Pearl Earring* (Archer Street Productions, 2003).

made, she also looks the part, not only in her costumes but also with her large eyes, peach skin and full lips, all suggesting both innocence and sexual awakening." She was not the original choice for Griet. Kate Hudson pulled out and Ralph Fiennes as Vermeer and director Mike Newell followed. In the new iteration, director Peter Webber interviewed a raft of actresses between 16 and 24 years old. Webber said, "one worked ... Scarlett Johansson."[1]

On December 12, the *Times* had another review, this one uncomplimentary: "Ms. Johansson is photographed so that her skin is as opalescent as her earring, but the movie is opaque. It is an earnest, obvious melodrama with no soul, filled with the longing silences that come after a sigh." Still, it was "a dexterous and absorbing visual re-creation of the lighting and the look that Vermeer achieved in his work...."[2]

People called it "easily the most beautiful-looking movie ever shot in Luxembourg, though it moves at a pace akin to watching a painting dry." As for Johansson's servant girl cum model, she "gleams quietly, while Firth seems lost beneath an unflattering, long strawlike wig."[3]

Commentary

Johansson's reflection on observing a scene where Vermeer and his wife embrace left her a total mess. Colin Firth recognized her predicament and advised her to take a nap. It worked.[4]

"Good actors almost have fewer layers of skin than the rest of us," said director Webber, "so the emotion leaks out." He noted the scene where Colin Firth pierces Griet's earlobe with a needle, calling it a "symbolic deflowering made especially moving by the single tear that slips down her face." It was on the third take and took Webber's breath away. Said Johansson, "Whatever you see on my face in a movie is the way I feel.... I'm not lying to you."[5]

Despite the emotional wreck she'd been before the nap, Johansson thought that it was probably up till then her easiest movie. "Emotionally draining, but not difficult."[6] Except for freezing cold and sinuses. In any event, the show must go on.[7]

Analysis

Peter Webber was fortunate in the casting of Scarlett Johansson as Griet, the lowly, illiterate, evangelical Protestant girl who is taken into the relatively opulent and Catholic home of Vermeer the painter as a charity case. It is clear from the start that she is being given a chance to serve the Vermeer family as a maid out of kindness—at least that is the outlook declared by Vermeer's wife. What this means is that she has to at once be capable of hard physical work, of playing the part of an outcast—she lifts a trap door to go into a cellar to sleep—and yet of being attractive enough to arouse the interest of not only Vermeer but also his patron and the butcher's son. By her mere silent, polite presence she must also arouse the ire of three of the women of the household—Vermeer's wife, his mother-in-law, and one of his daughters. Johansson pulls off this complex role in a way that carries the film. The performance is a tour de force and one of the reasons the film received so many nominations for prestigious awards.

Johansson's modest, puritanical costume complete with a cap that covers her hair in its entirety heightens rather than diminishes her attractiveness. Her lively intelligence and sense of curiosity seem restrained by her clothing as much as by her life as servant. Whether she's placing dirty laundry into a boiling copper pot or on her knees scrubbing the front steps of the house, a sense of vitality and even sensuality emanate from her that makes a sharp contrast with her surroundings and her place in it. It is no doubt this projection of a longing for a full life that makes her attractive to the males she comes in contact with and makes her seem a threat to the women in the household.

These aspects of her role become an overt part of the script in one scene. She is in Vermeer's studio alone, silently cleaning it—her instructions are to clean the studio while altering the location of nothing in it—and becomes drawn to the painting on the easel, a painting that had been initially inspired when Vermeer saw her cleaning a window in the studio. She compares the painting with the arrangement of the furniture the painter has set up to serve as a model for the picture. In the end, she walks around the easel and pulls a chair back from the table and out of the picture.

Her face and her gestures throughout this wordless scene suggest much of what she feels just as Vermeer's paintings and Dutch interiors in general strongly appeal to the senses despite their tame, domestic settings. Later, when Vermeer asks her why she moved the chair—an act that ignored the instructions she'd been given—she says, "Because she seemed trapped," referring to the woman in the painting who was based on the position Griet herself had once held. This undercurrent of unspoken revolt or longing is a key to Griet's character and the way Johansson played her.

There is not much on the religious and political conflicts of the time, although there is some, but there certainly is the gritty feel of the life of Holland at the time of Rembrandt, the boats in the canals (sort of the Venice of the North), the creatures and produce in the market places, the physical life of the servant class in the homes of burgesses, destined to scrub and wash and cook and serve those who can afford servants, and so on. It is also a coming-of-age story and a love story, so a decent mix and at a good length: 99 minutes.

It Girl

At year end Johansson was interviewed by veteran TV personality Charlie Rose. Johansson told Rose that Sofia Coppola pooh-poohed those who said she was too young to play Charlotte in *Lost in Translation* and spoke about her forthcoming film, *Girl with a Pearl Earring*. Rose also inquired about being the current "It Girl," whatever that was, her childhood goals, and a project in the offing: *Marjorie Morningstar*, about which Johansson told her mother, "That's me."[8]

Johansson's "It Girl" status was in the air, and she told one interviewer that "I just don't feel very It Girlish. But things have changed, like when I go into meetings with studios ... and try to shop projects that I want to develop."[9]

The Perfect Score (2004)

Frustrated at the distinct possibility that his SAT score won't secure admittance into Cornell's architecture college, Kyle (Chris Evans) enlists his friend Matty (Bryan Greenberg), class brain Anna (Erika Christensen), pot-head Roy (Leonardo Nam), and basketball star Desmond (Darius Miles) in a scheme to steal the test. How to gain access to

Left to right: Chris Evans, Bryan Greenberg, Erika Christensen, Darius Miles, Scarlett Johansson, Leonardo Nam, *The Perfect Score Handbook of Production Information* (Hollywood, CA: Publicity Department Paramount Pictures, 2003).

the ETS building where the test is secured? Francesca (Johansson) is that key. Her father owns the building. After a run-through, the six undertake the heist only to discover they can't actually obtain the paper copy of the test. However, they can take the test online and discover the answers. Exiting the building is problematic and Matty gives himself up to keep Francesca from being discovered. Out on bail, he and the others decide not to cheat. Kyle settles for Syracuse, Anna for a trip abroad instead of Brown, Desmond for St. John's rather than the pros. Roy quits drugs at Desmond's mother's insistence, gets his GED—and becomes a videogame entrepreneur while Francesca and Matty begin a relationship.

Reviews

Slantmagazine.com was harsh, analyzing *The Perfect Score* from a social/cultural/political perspective. However, referencing the John Hurt-Jason Priestly 1997 film about an older man's obsession with a hunky young B movie actor, *Love and Death on Long Island*, Slant lavished kudos on Johansson: "The Ronnie Bostock ideal is entirely represented by Scarlett Johansson, that stunning young beauty of *Ghost World* and *Lost in Translation*, who easily transcends an atrocious dye-job and a misogynistic introduction from the underwear up. Individual pleasures are fleeting beyond this fully formed Blonde Venus."[10] The *New York Times* called it a "thin, pleasant teenage heist comedy with a chewy nugget of social criticism…." Presciently, the reviewer observed that Johansson's "pouty, punky Francesca…" was "probably the last of her schoolgirl sidekick roles…."[11] *The Chicago Tribune* called it "an atypical teen movie…" that succeeded "because at its core it is about the very different pressures very different young adults face, and the test that insists on judging them as one and the same." Mixing unknown (including future Captain America Chris Evans) and known (Johansson), the film did well by not featuring actors that far from high school. "Johansson was 17 when she first read the script—and it shows in the performances. And that's a compliment." So it wasn't fluff but it was not to be a jewel in Johansson's crown: "Johansson just faced down two Golden Globe nominations … so *Score* is not the type of movie her star is rising toward."[12]

Commentary

Johansson explained her decision to take this role in the DVD special features, "Making the Perfect Score": "I read the script and at the time I was sort of considering a few other things, and, you know, it's not cast yet and, there's … there's a bunch of high school students so I figured, oh, okay, a chance to work with … other young actors, I'll flip through it. So I flipped through the script and I thought it was sort of one of the first scripts that I had read about teenagers where … the lingo and situation and the relation between the teenagers was more than just a middle-aged man writing what he thought, you know, *was cool*." Until director Robbins met and spoke to Johansson for an hour, he was in a quandary over who should play Francesca. Johansson said, "I looked at him and I said, well, it comes down to this: there's some character you just know you can definitely play well, you know, and Francesca is easier for me to play."[13]

Trivia: *Iron Man 2* (2010) would not be the first time Johansson dressed in black to foil villains. Besides costarring with Chris *Captain America* Evans for the second time, here Johansson wears a black catsuit and takes down a police squad in a fantasy sequence.

Analysis

The Perfect Score didn't make any waves although it was a good high school heist flick smuggling in a serious critique of standardized testing.

BAFTA Award

To no hullabaloo, *The Perfect Score* opened in late January 2004. On February 15, at the Odeon Leicester Square, London, Ian McKellen presented Johansson with the British Academy Film Award for Best Actress in a Leading Role for *Lost in Translation*. After gathering her wits, she said the award was quite unexpected for herself as a 19-year-old American:

> And first and foremost I'd like to thank Sofia Coppola for writing and directing [an] incredible film that I'm so proud to be a part of, and to Ross Katz and, and everybody at Universal Focus for working so hard to get people to see this movie. To my agent Scott Lambert who I unfortunately love very much, and to, mostly, my mother, Melanie, for supporting me and for being there for me and taking me to auditions and buying me hotdogs afterwards. And, I, I know I'm forgetting, oh, and to Bill Murray for, for being on the other side of the camera. And thank you very much. It is an honor.[14]

Regarding kudos for her films, Johansson said, "I think it's important to feel like your work is recognized." Nevertheless, she didn't want to risk disappointment.[15] Johansson had repeatedly identified the script as her source of inspiration: "Most of the time it's quite instinctive."[16] "If I fall for it, I say yes. *Ghost World* was the exception. The manuscript was so pared down that I did not understand it. But then I met the director and he explained it to me, and I then said yes."[17]

Celebrity Status

Interviewed at the Musso and Frank Grill on Hollywood Boulevard, Johansson's celebrity status was reckoned thus far beneath Julia Roberts or Cameron Diaz, "But then she's less of a star than a real actress. At 19 years old, she's already a genuine master of her craft...." She'd received Golden Globe Best Actress nominations for *Lost in Translation* and *Girl with a Pearl Earring*. She could have been studying film in Purchase, New York, but she'd opted out. "I don't miss school.... It's for some people and not for others."[18]

The Work Is All

In 2014 Johansson reiterated her commitment to work: "I remember Laurence Fishburne once asking me at eight years old if I wanted to be an actor or a movie star. I said, 'Both.' It took me several years to understand what he was trying to help me to think about. Of course, a kid wants it all, but I later realized that I wanted to do the work. The work is what's important."[19] A couple years later she told a Nordic interviewer, "I have always worked with the things I wanted to work with.... I am not a spoiled New York brat. I haven't made any horror films. I have always wanted to do things that seem different."[20]

As for becoming more recognizable, Johansson didn't dwell on it. "I'm very low-key. I still eat a burger at a counter with ketchup dripping down my face."[21]

Concerning awards and hype, she tried to maintain her distance. She felt the chances of being nominated "seemed very unusual."[22]

Johansson was asked about any instant of self-discovery made in the midst of all this work and replied that during the past six or eight months she'd determined that her "survival instinct and mentality" had kicked in. She began to give herself credit for being compassionate.[23] A few years later she told an interviewer, "I've worked so hard since I was 8 years old.... Not hard, like I have a hard job, but I've really worked."[24]

Referencing her mother's influence, Johansson said they'd shared an amazing journey. "It can be unfortunate when family members work together, but my mom understands me."[25] She had to be strong because she was only 13 when her folks divorced. Although their separation wasn't difficult, there were supplementary issues. Nevertheless, Johansson called herself "determined" and "very responsible."[26] She tried to avoid being noticed when she would go out with friends, or with actress and her *Other Boleyn Girl* co-star Natalie Portman. But getting caught out was sometimes unavoidable.[27]

Later that year an interviewer observed, "Unlike many of her peers cast as contemporary postadolescents, Scarlett Johansson prospers in her own planet icon, unconstrained by her age or by movie genre.... [S]he's a throwback in a way to the heyday of the Hollywood studio system and its industrious contract players.... 'The point is,' she says, 'by the time the movie has flopped, you're looking forward to finishing the next film. The important thing is to keep working.'"[28]

Lounging in Chateau Marmont

In 2004 at the Chateau Marmont in Los Angeles famed photographer Annie Leibovitz shot Johansson reclining on a sofa in an outfit suggestive of Gustav Flaubert's *Salammbo* or some other ancient princess or priestess. A 1.5-meter version, possibly bought for $22,500 at a New York auction in October 2014, decorated Woollahra's Hotel Centennial in Sydney, Australia where it resided in the newly named The Scarlett Lounge.[29] It has since been removed as it belonged to the hotel's owner who moved on and took it with him.[30]

A Good Woman (2004)

New York City, 1930. Upon learning that her latest sugar daddy has nixed her ability to obtain funds, Mrs. Erlynne (Helen Hunt) pawns most of her jewelry and takes ship for Amalfi, Italy, there to make a new conquest. Simultaneously, Meg Windermere (Johansson) and her husband of one year, Robert (Mark Umbers), are ensconcing themselves in Amalfi. Robert isn't always on holiday, rather conducting business by phone. This gives Lord Darlington (Stephen Campbell Moore) the opportunity to escort Meg around the environs. Robert meets Mrs. Erlynne while shopping for a birthday present for Meg and at her urging spends a generous amount on an exquisite fan. Not long afterward Robert provides her with an expense account but doesn't tell Meg. This is apparently Robert's way to keep Mrs. Erlynne from revealing to Meg that she is her mother.

Meanwhile, Lord Augustus, aka Tuppy (Tom Wilkinson) wants to marry Mrs. Erlynne. She argues against it.

Meg begins giving credence to the gossip that Robert is romantically involved with Mrs. Erlynne and decides to copy his actions, first buying clothes, including a duplicate of the revealing dress Mrs. Erlynne had asked her about and is wearing to Meg's birthday party. During the party Mrs. Erlynne tries to roust Meg from Darlington's yacht but the two are cornered by the arrival of a bunch of the men, including Robert, Tuppy and Darlington. The women hide belowdecks. Robert sees the fan he'd bought Meg and punches Darlington. During the fracas Meg crawls out unseen while Mrs. Erlynne appears as if she'd been waiting for Lord Darlington. A disappointed Tuppy remains calm. Continuing to control her desire to tell Meg she's her mother, Mrs. Erlynne, at Robert's

Japanese Chirashi mini-poster for *A Good Woman* (Beyond Films, 2004).

pleading, agrees to fly out. Before leaving she and Meg come to a reconciliation and hope to meet again. During takeoff Mrs. Erlynne discovers that Meg's fan is on the seat back next to her and that Tuppy has been camouflaged behind a newspaper across the aisle. He tells her Meg wanted her to have the fan. So all is well. Meg and Robert remain happily together while Mrs. Erlynne and Tuppy can look forward to their own pleasure.

Reviews

Variety said it was neither fish nor foul with "uneven treatment from a mixed Anglo-American cast...." It was almost a separate work from Wilde's play. As for Johansson, she "acquits herself well amid the more mature, sardonic company, without giving Meg much emotional depth." Hunt was miscast.[31] *USA Today* found it fair but the performances of Hunt and Johansson "closer to mediocre." The British actors were more at ease. Hunt "comes off more contemporary and straightforward than alluring and flirtatious. Johansson ... is a notch better.... Still, her portrayal is flat."[32] The *New York Times* called it a "misbegotten Hollywood-minded screen adaptation...." of Oscar Wilde's famous play. The miscast Helen Hunt and Johansson gave "shrill, toneless performances...."[33] *SFGate* offered that Wilde's epigrams couldn't be totally discounted and the film wasn't dislikable but was "off" to a considerable extent. As for the female leads, "The worst that can be said is that Helen Hunt is cast as a lifelong man-eater, which is a stretch and feels like one. By contrast, Scarlett Johansson is cast as a virtuous young thing, which is also a stretch but doesn't feel like one."[34] Canoe.com found it "engaging and pretty to look at...." Wilde translated well to the big screen. As for the actresses, it was "Worth seeing to watch Helen Hunt spin an unattractive character into a hero and, as this was filmed a few years ago, to watch Scarlett Johansson at the start of her red-hot career."[35]

Commentary

A Good Woman was based on Oscar Wilde's 1892 play, *Lady Windermere's Fan*. Despite the cast of Helen Hunt, Johansson and Tom Wilkinson, it received a very, very minor U.S. theatrical release, so minor it didn't seem to exist. Note most reviews were from 2006. This lack of faith by the studio is reminiscent of another comedy of manners, *Easy Virtue* (2008) with Jessica Biel, one of Johansson's chums. That was a version of a Noel Coward 1925 play. Biel promoted it on *The Late Show with David Letterman* but the next thing you knew, it was nowhere to be found and went to DVD.

The Fan was a 1949 Hollywood version of *A Good Woman* that starred Jeanne Crain and was directed by Otto Preminger. Like *A Good Woman*, it was reckoned an artistic failure. In this one there was a flashback from post–World War II London to its Victorian era.

Johansson told an interviewer that shooting the film was great because of the sweet and professional Helen Hunt. She hung out with Hunt and her boyfriend and, tiring of the Italian food that got everybody bloated, gorged on French fries. Of course men would approach her, one asking for a kiss. She responded, "No, keep the hell away from me!" But he bought a little piece of candy for her, she thanked him and he left.[36]

Analysis

Watching Mike Barber's *A Good Woman* seems to have caused critics to emit groans rather than write reviews. "Lifeless," "lightning failed to strike," "a damp tea bag" are typical of the sounds critics made when trying to evaluate the movie. When they tried to account for their reactions they seemed to focus on two points—Helen Hunt was miscast and the dialogue was not as witty as Oscar Wilde's. The general sense given by reviewers is that this adaptation of an Oscar Wilde play fails to live up to the original. Once these complaints have been lodged most reviewers have little to say about the other performers, the set, the costumes, or anything else. The fact is the reviews of this film are far drearier than the film itself is.

It is not unusual for people to be disappointed with film versions of Oscar Wilde's plays. The originals have tightly wound plots that when released in a confined space, a theater, energetically release an explosion of witty sayings. This combination of plot and dialogue while excellent on a stage before a live audience, simply filming a performance of it would not produce a necessarily enjoyable movie. In fact, it would not produce a movie at all, just the performance of a stage play captured on film. Movies necessarily shift the scene of the action from a confined space to the great outdoors where motion matters. An adaptation of a play becomes different from the original to such an extent that the original and the adaptation are not comparable. Moviegoers can certainly dislike an adaptation of a play but it's hardly fair to do so because it is not a play.

Barber adapts Wilde's play in a number of ways. Lady Windermere becomes Mrs. Meg Windermere (Johansson), the young, attractive American wife of a young, attractive, wealthy American financial advisor. Mark Umbers plays the husband, Robert Windermere. Although the film opens in the Manhattan of 1930, the scene soon shifts to the Amalfi coast. In this way, Barber crosses a Wilde play with a theme associated with Henry James—innocent Americans are forced to make their way in the corrupt and cynical society of Europe. Meg Windermere's innocence is heightened and established early by the facts that her mother died when she was very young, and that she had been raised by a strict and protective aunt. She relates these facts to explain to the witty and rakish Lord Darlington (Steven Campbell Moore) that she does not drink. When Darlington laments, "You have no redeeming vices," Johansson credibly suppresses any impulse to flirt and declares in a wide-eyed way, "I should hope not." Darlington's interest in the lush and lovely young wife is one of the threats to the American couple's marriage, a marriage that is just a year old.

Another threat to the marriage is posed by Mrs. Erlynne (Helen Hunt) who is a woman with a reputation for living off wealthy, married men in exchange for sexual favors. In this way, she is an American who seems to have acclimatized herself to the corrupt and cynical ways of Europe. She is in fact Meg Windermere's birth mother, has fallen on hard times, and threatens to identify herself to Meg if Robert doesn't pay her off. There is a suggestion that she turns to blackmail because she is no longer attractive enough to survive in her traditional way—a fact reviewers tend to forget or ignore when they complain that Helen Hunt was not alluring enough to play this part. More importantly, she is able to pull off in a believable way the moral complexity of the role and exhibits depths of emotion, especially in her scenes with Johansson. The mother-daughter relationship is in fact the most important relationship in the movie. This truth is to some extent obscured because gossips and Lord Darlington assume that Mrs. Erlynne and Robert Windermere have become lovers, adding to the frothy sexual surface of the film in a way that deflects attention from the mother-daughter relationship.

The movie is also a coming-of-age story. Meg Windermere is to celebrate her twenty-first birthday at what is likely to be the last party of the season in Amalfi. This party serves as the scene for the film's climax, when Meg becomes convinced that her husband has taken Mrs. Erlynne as a mistress, drinks to the point of becoming drunk, and takes herself to Lord Darlington's yacht with the intention of taking him as a lover. This scene clearly establishes Johansson's ability to undergo rapid transformations. For the occasion, she puts on a revealing dress that is identical to one worn by Mrs. Erlynne—changing from an American innocent into a sexually experienced woman, but in a way that underscores the relationship between mother and daughter. Painting her toenails red, putting on high heel shoes, considering her appearance in a mirror are all elements in a ritual of preparation for the birthday and all that "coming of age" in this context implies. As she drinks, and suffers the consequences of becoming maudlin and weeping, she transforms again through smeared cosmetics and awkwardness to become a kind of parody of a sexually attractive woman. In the end, she leaves a note for her husband, telling him that she is aware of his supposed relationship with Mrs. Erlynne and as a result he goes off to find her on Lord Darlington's yacht.

At the yacht, the mother-daughter relationship, although still kept secret from Mrs. Windermere, comes to the fore. Mrs. Erlynne in fact protects her daughter, allows her to escape from the yacht without Lord Darlington or his friends learning that she has even been there, and sacrifices herself, her reputation, and her prospects for marriage to Lord Augustus (Tom Wilkinson—perhaps the only actor in the movie who has been widely praised by reviewers for his performance). Helen Hunt plays this with a kind of modesty, an apparent light-heartedness, that makes her sacrifice believable if unheroic. The next day, in the final scene between Mrs. Windermere and Mrs. Erlynne, the two female leads, the two female Americans, Hunt and Johansson, play a powerful scene, rich in dramatic irony. Meg shows Mrs. Erlynne the locket she wears in memory of her mother, her guardian angel, and Mrs. Erlynne suppresses the impulse to make herself known to her daughter and prepares to leave Amalfi, thinking she will again be alone and without a source of income.

The movie like the play it is based on is at root a comedy, though. As a result, it should end with at least the promise of at least one wedding. To some extent this traditional ending is accomplished by a shot of the Windermeres happily in bed together again. Mrs. Erlynne, seated on a plane near a fellow passenger who is reading the papers, reaches for a fan that is in front of her. This fan, an exquisite thing, has served as the movie's McGuffin, a physical emblem of the shifting relationships that constitute the movie's plot. Lord Augustus puts down his newspaper and tells Mrs. Erlynne that Meg has explained everything to him about the night before on Lord Darlington's yacht. Their small plane lifts off bound for an unidentified location where they will marry. The comedy ends with the renewal of one marriage and the promise of another.

A Good Woman is not a great movie and not to everyone's taste. Still, it is highly watchable and livelier than most reviewers would have us believe. It should not be compared with Oscar Wilde's play, but rather with some of the films by Merchant-Ivory, that are based on literary works—*A Room with a View*, for instance, or *Howards End*, perhaps. It is a period piece with beautiful costumes and lovely scenery that is shot in a rich way. The movie, like Mrs. Erlynne, deserves a better reputation than it has.

In Good Company (2004)

Fifty-one-year-old advertising executive Dan Foreman (Dennis Quaid) and his team at *Sports America* are blindsided when the company is gobbled up by Teddy K's

(Malcolm McDowell) international conglomerate, Globecom. Young whippersnapper Carter Duryea (Topher Grace) is now top dog, with Dan as his wingman. Worse is to come when Carter, recently separated, is seduced by Dan's coed daughter Alex (Johansson). After Dan slugs Carter, Alex is distressed to hear that her father liked her better at age five. She soon breaks up with Carter, telling him that he's still on the rebound and she's too busy for a long-term commitment. Teddy K comes to town and Dan disputes his nonsense about employee "synergy." Afterward, Carter takes his side against toady Mark Steckle (Clark Gregg). Steckle gives them 24 hours to confirm a deal with a big client, which they do, convincing Eugene Kalb (Philip Baker Hall) to increase his advertising in *Sports America*. Returning to the office, they find a distraught Steckle. He's been axed because Globe.com has divested itself of *Sports America*. Carter is now unemployed, and Dan gets his office and position back. In a heartfelt conversation, Carter declines Dan's invitation to be *his* wingman, saying he needs time to find himself. At the elevator, Carter and Alex engage in polite conversation, and later Dan calls Carter to tell him his wife Ann (Marg Helgenberger) has given birth to their third child, another girl.

Reviews

The *New York Times* found it "a gently revisionist fairy tale about good versus evil set on the battlefield of contemporary corporate culture...." It was really about men's relationships rather than men and women. Alex (Johansson) "exists mostly as a reflection of her lover's and her father's deeper selves. This is more of an observation than a strong complaint."[37] *People* was positive, calling it a "smartly written, compassionate comedy...." In supporting roles, "Marg Helgenberger and Johansson add zest...." It was "tremendously entertaining" despite a finale that pulled punches.[38]

Dennis Quaid and Scarlett Johansson, *In Good Company* (Universal, 2004).

In 2014, the website DenofGeek included *In Good Company* in its "The Top 25 Underappreciated Films of 2004," calling it "a gimmick-free, worthwhile and grown-up comedy drama, with a lot to like about it."[39]

Commentary

In Good Company had a December 2004 Hollywood premiere and a December limited release before a January 2005 general release. Of the movie once titled *Synergy*, Johansson said that there was a tenderness between her character and Dennis Quaid's. "And I was on the verge of tears the whole time in rehearsal."[40]

For the DVD extras, Johansson added, "The relationship that Alex has with her dad, it made me feel really sentimental about my own relationship with my dad, and I think that a lot of what my character is going through—moving out and sort of making a life for herself and trying to figure out what she really wants to do is something that I went through not that long ago."[41]

Analysis

There are moral dilemmas and life pressures here, e.g., Dan needing to obtain a second mortgage to pay for Alex's education, firing long-time employees. Johansson's breakup scene with Topher Grace's Carter is gut-wrenching. It's real life. Director Weitz commented that, "So I like that that character (Johansson) is a very, in some ways, naïve character but who's capable of actually making really mature decisions. And sort of cold ones, too."[42]

Displaying all the elements of a successful comedy-drama, *In Good Company* was liked by audiences. It got real laughs but also contained more serious or at least more straight-faced emotions. The circular shape of it, with Dennis Quaid back in his office and Johansson once again showing up for tennis with her Dad at the end as at the beginning helps to define it as primarily a comedy. Byron said comedies end with marriages, tragedies end with funerals. This ends with neither, but that illusory sense that nothing has changed seems part of the comedic way of looking at life and the world. (See also *Manny & Lo* and *Rough Night*.)

Yet *In Good Company* is a satire on the irresponsible greed and inane pomposity of the modern international corporate world that nonetheless finds its way to a happy ending or, at least, a suggested return to a kind of normality. The conflict is represented by the old-fashioned and print-oriented world of Dan Foreman (Dennis Quaid), an advertising executive in charge of sales at *Sports America*, and his much younger replacement Carter (Topher Grace), who admittedly has little knowledge or experience but nonetheless made a rapid success by marketing cell phones for the multinational corporation that buys out the publisher of *Sports America*. The conflict is complicated by Carter meeting Dan's daughter, Alex (Johansson), in an elevator when he arrives for his first day on the job as her father's new boss.

The relationship that grows from that initial meeting during which Carter feels compelled to confess to Alex, not yet knowing who she is, "I'm totally scared shitless. I don't know what I'm doing. Don't tell anyone." She immediately agrees, "I won't." This initial conversation foreshadows what apparently draws them together—his need to tell her the truth about himself and her willingness to listen to it and accept it. When they eventually part, it isn't passion or affection that they say they'll remember about the affair, but their ability to converse. If Dan Foreman serves Carter as a model of a decent, responsible man, Alex Foreman serves him as the kind of woman who prefers real failings to sham successes. The difference in their ages—Alex is described as eighteen and starting her second year at college while Carter is twenty-six and has already been married and divorced—underscores her maturity and his immaturity. Their subplot constitutes a coming-of-age story for both characters.

Johansson brings to this role the sense of intelligence and maturity that she has shown in other films. It is perhaps for this reason that she is often shown as attractive to and attracted by older men, rather than as a typical ingénue. Roger Ebert summed up this quality well when he said of her performance in this film that she "continues to employ the gravitational pull of quiet fascination … she creates a zone of her own importance into which men are drawn not so much by lust as by the feeling that she knows something about life that they might be able to learn."[43]

A Love Song for Bobby Long (2004)

Learning from her thoughtless boyfriend Lee (Clayne Crawford) that he'd received a message that her mother Lorraine had died, Purslane "Pursy" Will quickly gathers her

Gabriel Macht, Scarlett Johansson and John Travolta, *A Love Song for Bobby Long* (Lions Gate Films, 2004).

stuff and heads off for the funeral only to discover it's over. She also learns that her mother had left her one third of her house. The other two thirds go to Bobby Long (John Travolta) and Lawson Pines (Gabriel Macht), the first a former university professor, the second a wannabe novelist. Initially disgusted by these dissolute alcoholics and their "shithole" abode, Pursy decides to move in and tidy up. Tensions grow, mostly involving Pursy and Bobby, and heated arguments ensue. Nevertheless, Bobby recognizes the young woman's intelligence and convinces her to get her GED. He tutors her and she graduates. Lee surfaces again, this time with a letter from Pursy's lawyer informing her that a year has almost passed, and the house will belong to her solely. When Bobby and Lawson are out, she drags their belongings onto the porch and locks the doors. When she's away they paint the house. She's unimpressed but upon gathering up her mother's belongings discovers letters addressed to her that were never sent, including one revealing that Bobby is her dad. It's a life-changing moment for both father and child. Pursy is accepted into the University of New Orleans, but doubtless because of his drinking Bobby passes away. Pursy visits the gravesite and places between the tombstones of Bobby and Lorraine the "National Bestseller," *A Love Song for Bobby Long* by Lawson Pines.

Reviews

Rolling Stone thought it merely fair but welcomed Travolta's return to serious filmmaking. Johansson, nominated for a Golden Globe, "is a twenty-year-old of vivid talent." However, she and Gabriel Macht "are both too gym-toned and poised for their loser characters." True authenticity was provided by the location photography.[44] Roger Ebert observed that the film's plot was secondary to the characters and how they live, and Travolta, Johansson and Macht did "inhabit this material with ease and gratitude…." It was "remarkable to listen to dialogue that assumes the audience is well-read."[45]

Commentary

There is the impression that there were funding problems, and merchants near where the thing was filmed in Louisiana were up in arms about not having been paid for supplies, services, und so weiter. Odd. It is a bit longer than it needs to be and Travolta's accent could be seen (or heard) by some as slightly over the top. Still, far worse gets decent runs in the megaplexes.

A Love Song for Bobby Long played at the 2004 Venice Film Festival before getting a January 2005 U.S. general release.

Analysis

The most important character in this movie never appears in it. She is Lorraine Will, the mother of Purslane Hominy Will (Johansson), who propels the plot of the film by dying. In a way, Pursy's arrival at her mother's dilapidated house in New Orleans constitutes her beginning to replace her dead mother for the occupants of the house, Bobby Long (John Travolta), and Lawson Pines (Gabriel Macht), although none of them realize that. It should also be said that in a way the city of New Orleans represents Lorraine Will, a symbolic embodiment of her way of life as a singer and songwriter there. Because of her absence, Lorraine Will is everywhere.

Pursy missed her mother's funeral because when she was living in Florida her boyfriend forgot to give her the message he had received from Bobby Long. This forgetfulness is the first of many signs of irresponsibility in the movie. The girl shows that she does not suffer from this widespread fault and immediately heads for New Orleans as soon as she learns of the death. Her presence in the household occupied by the two alcoholics—Bobby Long, a former charismatic professor of English, and Lawson Pines, a former student of his who is ostensibly writing a novel based on Long's life—immediately changes things. She starts fixing up the place, cleaning, and painting, and moves into her mother's old room—the first sign of her replacing her mother. In time, she even starts to wear her mother's clothes and many of the friends of the occupants of the house tell her how much she looks like her mother and tell her memories that clash with what she herself remembers or has been told about her mother.

Confusion about the past or the unwillingness or inability to face it is one of the movie's major themes. As Roger Ebert pointed out in a favorable and thoughtful review, Pursy acts as a witness to the way of life of Bobby and Lawson and by seeing them she forces them to see themselves. Clarity about the past comes about gradually, with a leisureliness or laziness that is appropriate to movement through a city as hot and humid as New Orleans can be. This clarity unfolds with the movement of the seasons. Pursy arrives in the summer, the shift in the weather is noted as autumn begins and Pursy starts attending school, and Christmas represents one of the turning points in the movie—when Bobby and Lawson have a bitter confrontation. Bobby exposes Lawson's limited feelings for his girlfriend, Georgianna (Deborah Kara Unger), and Pursy and Lawson sleep together without making love that night. Eventually, Lawson tells Pursy how Bobby and he came to live in New Orleans and in the way they do and why. As Roger Ebert rightly points out, there is an attempt at tragedy in the life of Bobby Long but only pathos is achieved.[46]

When Pursy learns through a letter from a lawyer brought to her by her old boyfriend that her mother left her the entire house and not merely one-third of it as Bobby Long had said, she throws Bobby and Lawson out and puts the house up for sale. As she prepares to leave herself, she finds and opens some boxes that were her mother's. The boxes contain letters to her by her mother that were never sent as well as a song Lorraine had written, a love song for Bobby Long. In this way, Pursy learns that Bobby Long is her father. What had been taken for a mock family in the end becomes a real one. Spring is marked by Pursy's graduation from high school, her reunion with her father, and her decision to go to college.

A Love Song for Bobby Long is a little gem of a movie that does not appeal to a wide audience. It is very literary—the circular shape of it determined not only by the seasons but also by its beginning and ending with a death, first Lorraine's and then Bobby's, the dialogue made up in part by Bobby's quotations from authors that Lawson identifies, the references to literature and writing, all give it the feel of a book rather than a movie. It demands reading—that is, attention to detail and a willingness to concentrate on characters rather than plot. The movie opens with Bobby Long buying a bottle and then walking home and a voice over describes his relationship to time, no doubt a quotation from the book Lawson writes throughout the movie. But it is well acted. Travolta and Macht are immediately credible as marginal figures who are at once unpleasant and attractive. Johansson's characteristic combination of maturity and vulnerability makes her assured as a young but responsible and insightful person, and thus is credible as an agent of change in the lives of others as well as herself. The film's music, as well as its script and its acting, offers pleasures to viewers that may be modest but are also all too rare.

Banter with Jay Leno

Johansson plugged *Bobby Long* on *The Tonight Show with Jay Leno* on January 11, 2005. After repartee involving an unnamed allergy, the apparently unrelated removal of her tonsils, a car accident on Santa Monica Boulevard which she admitted was entirely her fault, buying the perfect toilet, and her architect father remodeling her apartment (in which she envisioned but did not get a hot tub in the living room so she could soak while watching TV), Leno brought up *Bobby Long*, which he described as a "real actor's movie."

Johansson said, "Yeah, it's a very, it's a wonderful project that I had sort of coddled for three or four years, and we finally did it with John Travolta who's amazing, and it's one of his best performances ever, and he was so wonderful to work with, and we used to sing a lot and do stuff like that. He's one of those actors that, he's not afraid to revisit the past." She mentioned him doing "Aye, aye, aye, aye" from *Grease* on the set. Leno said he heard she gifted Travolta with a book of Polaroids and a *Welcome Back, Kotter* doll from the TV series (1975–79) in which Travolta played smart-ass Vinnie Barbarino. Leno showed a clip of Johansson with her other *Bobby Long* co-star Gabriel Macht, wished her good luck with the Golden Globes, and had her sign his motorcycle.

It was fascinating to observe how ill at ease Johansson seemed vis-à-vis the audience—as if not sure of their sympathy or good will. Funny too that she was there to promote the one film and not the other. *In Good Company* was the one getting the traditional ads on TV.

But there was that reference to being fat!? Part of the reason for the lack of confidence in the sympathy of the audience or a fishing for compliments and reassurance? At least there was justice, poetic and otherwise, in the Golden Globes nomination.

In February Johansson recapped her admiration for Travolta, extolling his cinematic face. They were so compatible she'd be happy to work with him perpetually.[47] At the 2015 Academy Awards show Travolta made the media gasp by kissing the pregnant Johansson on the cheek and placing his hand around her waist. Hardly anyone noted that they'd worked together and become friends on *Bobby Long*.

2004 in Review

At the end of 2004, *USA Today* provided a rundown on Johansson's status, including her exasperation over tabloids and false media coverage of her personal life, compliments from *A Love Song for Bobby Long* co-star Gabriel Macht (she was a "whippersnapper") and *In Good Company* co-star Topher Grace (she's "the greatest young actress in Hollywood"), mother Melanie's concern over lengthy filming schedules, John Travolta (she was a "throwback" to the era of such stars as Elizabeth Taylor and Sophia Loren). Politically, she campaigned for John Kerry. She was anti–George Bush, Dick Cheney and Arnold Schwarzenegger.[48]

2005

Sexuality

In 2005 Johansson said, "I'm a sexual person. I'm very comfortable with my sexuality and my femininity and being a woman.… There's nothing wrong with people finding me sexy. I'd rather them say that than say I was revolting."⁴⁹ In 2008 she added, "I don't normally think about being sexy. I think, Do I look presentable? Do I look sane?"⁵⁰

Friends

With the summer action extravaganza *The Island* (see Chapter 8) in the offing, Johansson was interviewed in a New York restaurant for *USA Weekend*. The interviewer—prematurely as it turned out—called the film "a guaranteed blockbuster."⁵¹

The interviewer touched on the comparison sometimes made between Johansson and the ultimate Hollywood sex symbol: Marilyn Monroe. Like the blonde icon, Johansson owned a "radiant beauty that constantly threatens to overshadow her talent."⁵²

"I only care what people who know me think about me."⁵³ With a select cadre of "dorky, actory people" Johansson played charades on Sunday nights.⁵⁴

Johansson bemoaned the lack of style in contemporary life, especially for men, who she thought dressed too casual. She spoke of making *The Black Dahlia* and its 1947 milieu. She was smitten with the era's undergarments, stockings, and lovely skirt. "Always a hat and gloves when you go out. Pearls."⁵⁵

Paparazzi

Johansson viewed overzealous paparazzi as stalkers who should be arrested. She related an incident with her sister where paparazzi in three SUVs began chasing them. "I'm not a stunt car driver." It was "very scary and unsafe...." She added, "I think they have these crazy laws if you wait outside someone's house for two days it's not stalking, but if you wait outside for three days it is, so they switch shifts." Foretelling her future as "the other," she said, "It would be quite convenient to have a clone wouldn't it?"⁵⁶

Johansson came to consider the tabloids "the downfall of society."⁵⁷ Concerning a *US Weekly* story that she'd had a nose job, "It was as ridiculous as if they'd showed side-by-side pictures of me at 11 and 20 and saying, 'Look, she grew breasts!'"⁵⁸

She avoided paparazzi by prioritizing her personal life. "I go to work, I make movies, I publicize them. I hope people enjoy them."⁵⁹

Johansson did possess one advantage avoiding the paparazzi: her lack of physical stature. Thus "people don't tend to see me!"⁶⁰

In 2019 she was tracked upon leaving a taping of *Jimmy Kimmel Live* to promote *Avengers: Endgame*. She was so concerned that her car stopped at the Hollywood police station. According to Johansson, "Women across the US are stalked, harassed and frightened and a universal law to address stalking must be at the forefront of law enforcement conversation." She cited Princess Diana's death as the extreme example of what can happen.⁶¹

2006

Descriptions Fall Short

The year 2006 began with an interviewer's amusing take on his subject: "Up close, say within a few thousand yards, it was impossible to mistake an actress in the high season of her beauty, no little girl but a woman with Grand Prix curves, a soigne throat (adorned this afternoon with a necklace luxuriating in her décolletage), wide aquamarine eyes, fashion cheekbones, and those famously plush lips that some of the finest practitioners of celebrity journalism have herniated themselves trying to describe."[62]

On Nudity

Early in 2006, Johansson and Keira Knightley graced the cover of *Vanity Fair*. Both were nude—sort of. They obviously were in the buff and Johansson's bottom, seen from the side, was bare, but arms concealed both actresses' breasts. Annie Leibovitz was the photographer, with clothed fashion guru Tom Ford completing the threesome when actress Rachel McAdams backed out. Ford said of McAdams, "She did want to do it, and then when she was on the set I think she felt uncomfortable, and I didn't want to make anybody feel uncomfortable." He added, "A lot of women actually, a couple of men, too, wanted to take their clothes off.... These are such beautiful people, beautiful women, and who doesn't want to see a bit of them."[63]

Later that year in London, Johansson opined that she'd go nude on camera if the part demanded it. "I'm still making up my mind about when I'll do a nude scene. I'm not opposed to doing nudity, it would just have to be the right project maybe some sensational European art film," she told the *Sun*. Regarding the *Vanity Fair* cover with Knightley, "We were going to be wearing thongs but the stylist snipped them off. Here we are, Keira and I, and we're totally naked, and some guy is on his BlackBerry. Everyone was busy working. But I guess it's better than if they were all looking at me. It was surprisingly comfortable."[64]

Johansson apparently re-thought her position on screen nudity because in 2007 she demanded a clause in her film contracts nixing nude scenes. "She doesn't want to fall into being too controversial or too trashy so nude scenes are out for now," said a *Daily Express* source. Adult film star Jenna Jameson thought Johansson perfect to play her in a film based on her autobiography. That never happened.[65]

Movies Ever Her Passion

At the end of 2005, as she was about to turn 21, Johansson was interviewed for *Elle*, kidding the interviewer that maybe she'd have been an archaeologist if she weren't making films. "Then she rolled her eyes and gave a sardonic laugh that sounded like someone tearing up an application to graduate school. 'Cut to me in 120-degree heat, picking at a rock with a four-inch needle. Forget that! I love making movies.'"[66]

More Banter with David Letterman

Johansson appeared on *The Late Show with David Letterman* on January 10, 2006. Johansson's first outing trading ripostes with the late-night icon had been at the age of 13 when she'd done *The Horse Whisperer*. She was excited to be back. Letterman introduced her as having just been nominated for a Golden Globe for *Match Point*.

They spoke about Letterman's previous penchant for giving guests a canned ham, and Johansson joked about keeping it in the fridge where it became a part of the family. She said she grew up in Manhattan and that all her family was still there, including her dad. She related an outing where her grandmother was having her hair done. Hiding her identity in a hooded sweatshirt and hat, Johansson listened to her grandmother ask the stylist, "Have you been to the movies lately?" followed by "Does my granddaughter look familiar to you?" Johansson said she guessed that was what grandmothers were for.

Regarding New Year's, she spoke of a dinner at a glamorous sushi restaurant with large chunks of raw lobster in a martini glass that one had to commit to. After five courses she and her friends said enough.

After a commercial there was shown a picture of her when she was on the show promoting *The Horse Whisperer* in 1998. She said to get it off, it was "mortifying." Lettermen brought up *Lost in Translation* and it seemed that Bill Murray had appeared on the show for that, she hadn't. "It was really intense. We were shooting twenty-seven days and, you know, kind of there we were in Tokyo working sixteen hours a day, and, um-m-m, and we didn't know that it was going to be such kind of sensation and it was, it was pretty exciting."

Letterman said it looked like they were living the movie. "We were. We sort of were, actually. I felt, I had many kinds of sleepless nights and I always sort of stared out of taxi cab windows."

Johansson was about to host *Saturday Night Live* for the first time the coming weekend. The last time she'd had pressure for a live performance was when she was five or six. She'd had chickenpox for five or six days and her mother thought she could perform on day six in the school's variety show but she became dizzy and feverish and collapsed, and everyone laughed at her.

Regarding *Match Point*, Letterman brought up the fact that any preconceptions about this having traditional Woody Allen hallmarks would be incorrect. He noted that it seemed to have been filmed entirely in England and asked how she got along with Woody.

"I do, yeah, we get along, we get along quite well. I think we have sort or [a] similar sense of humor, and he shares his muffins with me, and that kind of thing." [laughter] Letterman: "As long as they're his muffins."

The roll in the hay clip from *Match Point* was shown.

To compliment her ham, Letterman gave Johansson a jar of Grey Poupon Dijon Mustard.

Golden Globes 2006

Johansson appeared in a va-va-voom red dress by Valentino at the Golden Globes Awards on January 16, 2006. It revealed enough cleavage to spur announcer Isaac Mizrahi to literally squeeze her breast.[67]

After the awards Johansson told an announcer that her favorite part of the evening was Philip Seymour Hoffman winning Best Performance in a Motion Picture-Drama for *Capote*. Johansson had been nominated for Best Supporting Actress in a Motion Picture-Drama, Musical or Comedy. (Rachel Weisz won for *The Constant Gardener*. Weisz would win the Academy Award for Best Supporting Actress as well.)

In March, on the set of *The Prestige*, Johansson commented on the poor taste of Mizrahi's touching. She didn't buy Mizrahi's excuse that he was a designer and wanted to know how her dress was made. "I'm sure he was very fascinated by that, like he doesn't know how a dress works."[68]

At that time Johansson said she wasn't angry with Misrahi. As for avoiding him at future events, "I can take care of myself.... I'm from New York."[69]

Later that year, Johansson was accorded the *In Touch* honor of having the best bosom. It was said this would add fuel to her rivalry with Lindsay Lohan, who came in ninth. How much of this rivalry really existed or was merely a publicist's ploy?[70]

When Johansson was preparing for the release of *The Island*, she and Lindsay Lohan were compared because they seemed to be rivals for fame and acting credibility. They'd taken disparate routes to the top, Lohan in high-profile teen films like *The Parent Trap* remake, *Herbie: Fully Loaded* and *Freaky Friday*. By contrast, Johansson began in low-profile movies like *Manny & Lo* and *An American Rhapsody* before deciding what adult roles she'd take. As a child, said Johansson, "I was basically auditioning for everything, and if I got a project and wasn't busy doing something else, I would do it." *Manny & Lo* and *The Horse Whisperer* were instrumental in her course. She consciously began to avoid "teen-scream thrillers...." *Match Point* wasn't yet out and there was concern by agents and managers about being in a Woody Allen film because his recent efforts hadn't been that successful.[71]

Scarlett Johansson at the 63rd Annual Golden Globes, Beverly Hilton Hotel, Beverly Hills, CA, January 16, 2006 (Paul Smith/FeatureFlash Photo Agency/Shutterstock.com).

The Black Dahlia (2006)

In postwar Los Angeles, boxers turned detectives Dwight "Bucky" Bleichert (Josh Hartnett) and Lee Blanchard (Aaron Eckhart), are selected to head up the investigation into the Elizabeth Short (Mia Kirshner) case. Known as "the black dahlia," the aspiring actress had been killed and dismembered. Obsessed with the distasteful assignment, Lee becomes oblivious to the affection his sultry girlfriend (Johansson) shows for Bucky. During his investigations, Bucky begins an affair with Madeleine Linscott (Hilary Swank), who resembles Short. Tracking down Lee, Bucky watches in horror as a man tries to strangle his friend and a shadowy figure comes forward and slits Lee's throat before both he and the strangler fall to their deaths in the atrium. Bucky and Kay take solace in a bout of heated lovemaking before Bucky returns to Madeleine. Later he hears

Japanese Chirashi mini-poster for *The Black Dahlia* (Universal, 2006). Left to right: Scarlett Johansson, Josh Hartnett, Mia Kirshner, Hillary Swank and Aaron Eckhart.

Madeleine's mother admit to having killed Short because Madeleine's real father George seemed infatuated with a woman who looked like his own daughter. But it was Madeleine who killed Lee, as Bucky hears from her own lips before he shoots her and returns to Kay.

Reviews

The Financial Times thought that although it was shot in Bulgaria, "the film's bygone Los Angeles is weirdly convincing." However, that did not make up for "narrative sprawl underacted by Hartnett, overacted by others...."[72] Slate.com said director De Palma's "high style" masked a "movie that is half over before you realize how little is there." Each "actor seems cast in a movie of his or her own invention." Johansson "doesn't really bother to act at all, but her rounded, confectionery beauty is perfectly suited to Jenny Beavan's luscious 1940s costumes; in angora, she's like a sex toy manufactured by Gund."[73] *The Buffalo News* found it "vibrantly, thrillingly bad...." It was reminiscent of "a wicked 'Saturday Night Live' spoof of film noir." How could it be this awful with two-time Academy Award winner Hilary Swank, and "How can you use Scarlett Johansson so stupidly?" Only Mia Kirshner was to be complimented.[74] The *News Journal* thought it degenerated "into a turgid mess." Its "convoluted story gets choked amid the flash and flourishes of the filmmaker's visual excess, and characters who start out promisingly idiosyncratic become caricatures by the end."[75] The *Star Tribune* said author Ellroy's byzantine plot wasn't accommodated by director De Palma. The saving grace was the style, a film that "looks, sounds and moves better than any movie I've seen this year." De Palma's camera work remained remarkable. Add kudos for Mark Isham's score. Nevertheless, the dramatic weaknesses undermined the film. Eckhart's disappearance for long stretches foiled his role and Swank "lacks the versatility to play a sophisticated femme fatale, while Johansson brings to her role starry-eyed romantic beauty but nothing more." Mia Kirshner had the most gravitas and believability as a celluloid spectre.[76] *The Wall Street Journal* commended the sumptuous look but designated the script as "frequently impenetrable, the pacing ponderous, and the film noir style can't conceal a crucial piece of misconceived casting." Johansson was "a young actress with a great gift for contemporary roles—her performance in *Lost in Translation* was close to perfection—but a terribly shaky sense of how real people, or real movie stars, comported themselves six decades ago. Whenever she's on screen the fabric of theatrical illusion threatens to unravel...." Likewise, Hartnett "is a product of his time." In short, he was no Alan Ladd or Humphrey Bogart.[77] *The Blade* found director De Palma "still a dazzling filmmaker" and compared it to the recent *Hollywoodland*, both villainizing the city. However, this offering was "overripe and way too much of everything...." As for Johansson's curvy blonde, "her steady gaze and ample curves are so suited to vintage Hollywood re-creations, her appearance tends to underline what's contemporary about co-stars like Hartnett." In essence, the movie "fatally overreaches—lured, like so many would-be starlets, by the siren song of ambition."[78]

Commentary

In keeping with desired look director De Palma wanted, Academy Award–winning (*Close Encounters of the Third Kind*, 1977) cinematographer Vilmos Zsigmond was hired and would receive an Academy Award nomination for his work. *American Cinematographer* devoted 16 pages to the film and gave Josh Hartnett the cover. Zsigmond said he wanted a "desaturated look, with the exception of certain scenes involving Kay, Scarlett's character." He and colorist Mike Sowa worked on the house sequences "to make those sequences warmer, lighter and more inviting, because that house is the only place where Bucky truly feels he's at home." Concerning Johansson, Sowa said De Palma "felt that her beauty didn't come through with the desaturated sepia look, so we scaled it back a bit on her."[79]

Director Brian de Palma had broken into the big time with *Carrie* (1976), following it up with edgy thrillers like *Dressed to Kill* (1980) and *Blow Out* (1981), and crime dramas *Scarface* (1983) and *The Untouchables* (1987). In 1990, though, *The Bonfire of the Vanities* was a major bust. *Mission: Impossible* (1996) was a success and launched a franchise, but De Palma's follow-up films were less than sterling and/or not hits. *The Black Dahlia* was looked on by some as a chance to regain his mojo. However, this was not to be. It is confusing and slightly boring (if something can be *slightly* boring).

Analysis

In a December 28, 2006, letter to this book's co-author, previous Holston collaborator (*Science Fiction, Fantasy and Horror Film Sequels, Series and Remakes*) and noir fancier Tom Winchester critiqued the film:

> A quite surprising thing about this film is the fact that I never once suspected that it was mostly shot—not in Los Angeles, as you might expect—but in Bulgaria. That's the Global Economy for you, I guess. According to De Palma, the 1946 L.A. settings had changed hugely and reconstruction was easier in Eastern Europe. Hilary Swank is an excellent femme fatale and Aaron Eckhart, one of the cops tied to the case, is a good 40s style actor. See *Suspect Zero* (2004). Sometimes he reminds me of Sean Bean. The story is mostly told from the perspective of the other cop on the case, played by Josh Hartnett, an actor I'm unfamiliar with. He does okay by his part, but like most guys not of that era, Hartnett doesn't wear a fedora comfortably. *Black Dahlia* is a pretty good period piece and its very convoluted telling is on a par with the genre's most intricate. It might make a good book-end with *Chinatown* or De Palma's earlier *The Untouchables*. Noir writer James Ellroy figures into all of the special features (unsurprisingly, of course, since the film's based on his best seller). As modern films go, particularly modern noir, I'll give it ***. Yet the fact that all the mayhem seems directed toward creating a happy ending for the Hartnett and Johansson characters leaves a sour taste in the mouth.

In *Black Dahlia*, the Alan Ladd/Veronica Lake film, *The Blue Dahlia* (1946), is mentioned a couple times.

The Prestige (2006)

As the 19th century approaches its conclusion, Robert Angier (Hugh Jackman) and Alfred Borden (Christian Bale) assist magician John Cutter (Michael Caine) while endeavoring to come up with their own individual and unique tricks. Cutter's major illusion involves Angier's wife Julia (Piper Perabo), whose hands are tied before being dunked in a vat of water. One evening Borden, in an attempt to create an even better crowd-pleasing trick, ties her hands differently, and Julia can't slip the knot and drowns despite Cutter's attempts to break the glass with an axe. Borden won't acknowledge that he tied the knot differently but incurs Angier's wrath. Both go their separate ways but always encounter each other—with poor results. Angier hires Olivia Wenscombe (Johansson) as his assistant. Eventually Borden marries Sarah (Rebecca Hall) and has a child. Meanwhile, after seeing an electric machine made by Nikola Tesla (David Bowie), Angier travels to Colorado Springs to meet Edison's rival and seek such a machine for himself. Despite misgivings about Angier's obsession, Tesla reluctantly agrees. Angier is bedeviled seeking revenge for his wife's death but more recently with upstaging Borden's "Transported Man." They confront and attempt to outdo each other. Borden begins an affair with Olivia after, at Angier's urging, she convinces Borden that she's not just trying to steal his secrets, but loves him. Sarah falls deeper into depression and eventually hangs herself while Angier returns to Tesla's retreat to acquire the replicating machine that will presumably—and finally does—duplicate hats, a cat, and.... Back in London, Borden tries to find Angier's secret, which was once, like himself, the use of a double in the transported man trick. In disguise, Borden, now without Olivia, who left after confronting him about his own mania, finds his way backstage during Angier's "The Real Transported Man" show and observes Angier drop into a water tank that locks him in. He is unsuccessful in breaking him free. Borden is arrested and sentenced to hang. Lord Caldlow's (Hugh Jackman) representative (Roger Rees) agrees to take care of Borden's daughter in exchange for his tricks. Borden is visited by Angier as Lord Caldlow and unsuccessfully tries to make his jailers recognize this perfidy on the part of his rival. Borden is hanged. Cutter discovers that "Lord Caldlow" has purchased Angier's machine, then finds that Angier is alive. Cutter agrees to Angier's plan to put on just 100 more shows before destroying the machine. However, Borden in disguise tracks down and shoots Angier. Actually, this Borden is a twin brother. Upon exiting the scene of the crime, he passes two rows of water tanks containing Angier duplicates.

Hugh Jackman and Scarlett Johansson, *The Prestige* **(Touchstone/Warner Bros., 2006).**

Reviews

The *New York Times* called Johansson's character "one of several more or less unsuspecting parties caught up in the intrigue between the rivals. Ms. Johansson's English accent is adequate, though she tends lately (here and in *The Black Dahlia*) to be upstaged by her costumes, which appear to be—inadvertently, I'm sure—cut a size too small."[80] The Associated Press found the film "cold and distant emotionally, with extreme, single-minded obsession the only palpable sentiment." It became "exhausting and repetitive...." Jackman and Bale were "earnest and credible..." while Johansson "disappears into the lush scenery much the same way she did in the recent thriller *The Black Dahlia*...."[81] *Rolling Stone* called it an "offbeat and wildly entertaining thriller." Michael Caine stole all his scenes, and director Nolan made "the film exactly like a great trick, so you want to see it again the second it's over."[82] The *Star Tribune* commended director Nolan's "impressive filmmaking legerdemain..." and the performances of Bale and Jackman, characters tiptoeing "along the delicate line between obsession and insanity."[83] The *Omaha World-Herald* thought it wasn't as clever as we were led to believe. Director Nolan did use his trademark flashback technique (think *Memento*) to wrest a comprehensible tale from confusion. Jackman, Bale and Caine were excellent. "Scarlett Johansson is less effective...."[84] *People* called it "a twisty-turny thriller...." It needed more humor, however, "but it assumes an intelligence on the part of viewers and that's magic enough these days."[85] *Financial Times* was unimpressed, calling out director Nolan for substituting melodrama for drama. No movie magic was created. As for the performers, "Sir Michael Caine does his *Stella Street* accent; Australia's Hugh Jackman does American; America's Scarlett Johansson does English (sort of); and Britain's Christian Bale does Jamie Oliver cockney."[86]

Commentary

On March 2, 2007, Tom Winchester wrote, "And the message of *The Prestige* is what? Beware the dangerous lure of obsession, or something like that? I can't recall ever seeing a film with such protagonist/antagonist ambivalence, and the switch is handled so effortlessly, which was perhaps the point. This is a film that demands being seen more than once, or at least not on the home screen while sleepy. There would be no problem, of course, dozing off during a film like *Ghost Rider*, but it's unfair to judge a film like *The Prestige* when one's attentiveness is compromised."

The necessity for a lengthy synopsis here is the perambulations of the plot, which is occasionally difficult to follow, what with director Nolan installing flashbacks that the viewer does not initially perceive as such. The novel is creepier than its source. Like *Memento*, *The Prestige* does demand more than one viewing, at which point it becomes more pleasing.

In the "Conjuring the Past" segment of the Bonus Features of the DVD (Burbank, California: Buena Vista Home Entertainment, 2007) Johansson briefly described some of her Victorian attire.

Two thousand six was a year of magic on screen. *The Prestige* had an October release while Johansson's friend Jessica Biel co-starred with Edward Norton in *The Illusionist*, released in August. Both were successful, financially and for the most part critically.

While Johansson's character might at first glance seem unnecessary, that is, as a prime character, (1) a magician needs a lovely assistant, and (2) Olivia does prove pivotal in Angier's employment of her to mess with Borden's emotions and discover his trick. So, eye candy she is, but hardly unnecessary.

Analysis

Most reviews of Christopher Nolan's period piece about two obsessed, competing magicians tend to ignore or criticize Scarlett Johansson's performance as Olivia Wenscombe. Dan Jolin goes so far as to suggest that giving her the part was a casting mistake that resulted in the movie's only false note. Jolin argues that her difficulties with the need to use an English accent were so severe that she forgot to engage the audience. More polite reviewers let the performance pass without comment or damned it with faint praise.

The reaction of reviewers seems to be based in part on their own faulty expectations. "A pretty assistant," says Mr. Cutter, played by Michael Caine, to Robert Angier alias The Great Danton, played by Hugh Jackman, "is the most effective form of misdirection." This statement is made as part of Cutter's attempt to persuade The Great Danton to take on an assistant he's found for him, an assistant he says is inexperienced but has presence. In short, Scarlett Johansson's role is as a prop, a tool, someone to be used by both of the obsessed and competing magicians, Robert Angier and Alfred Borden, played by Christian Bale. Her accent with its Cockney tinge might ring false, but in a film that is based entirely on deception, disguises, and misdirection, the accent that draws attention to itself serves a purpose—especially when she takes to calling Alfred Borden "Freddie."

Olivia as Angier's assistant is more useful than at first appears. She does not only stand around on stage looking pretty and displaying cleavage and thus drawing the eyes of audience members away from the doings of The Great Danton, but she eventually finds a double for Danton, an unemployed actor who drinks too much named Root, also of course played by Hugh Jackman. This double permits Danton to perform a trick made famous by Alfred Borden and known as "The Transported Man."

It is the secret of this trick that provides a focal point for the competition between the two magicians. Dissatisfied with the performance of the trick through the use of a double, Angier is convinced Borden accomplishes the feat in some other way and sends Olivia to work for Borden as a spy. While working with Borden Olivia in effect becomes a double agent, falls in love with Borden and serves his interest by providing Angier with a false diary that is supposed to contain the secret of the Transported Man. The diary sends Angier to America, to Colorado Springs, to meet Tesla, the man associated with electricity, convinced Tesla built a machine that permitted Borden to perform the Transported Man. In an odd way, the competition between science and magic and the competition between Tesla and Edison serve as analogues for the competition between Angier and Borden.

A few scenes make the most of Johansson's admittedly limited performance. One such scene takes place in a restaurant when she is Borden's assistant and mistress and accompanies his colleague, Fallon (also Bale) to dinner with Borden and his wife, Sarah, played by Rebecca Hall who a couple of years later joined Johansson in Woody Allen's *Vicky Cristina Barcelona*. It is during this scene that Olivia calls Borden "Freddie" in an annoying voice and to the annoyance of his wife. The tension at the table is such that the two couples cannot go on with the meal and Fallon escorts Olivia away, leaving Borden and Sarah to work out their difficulties. The importance of the scene and two names for Borden is recognized only at the film's end when reviewers learn that Borden and Fallon are twin brothers who played both of their roles in life as well as onstage, the secret to Borden's version of the Transported Man. In the end, it is admitted that one of the brothers loved Olivia and the other loved Sarah, although both took turns as husband and lover with both women. Sarah's Alfred and Olivia's Freddie were in a way two different people despite how things appeared throughout the film.

The connection with both magicians as assistant and mistress allows Olivia to have insights into the characters of both. "It's inhuman to be so cold," she says to Borden, and urges him to go to Angier with the words, "You deserve each other." What this recognizes is that despite their obvious differences—Angier as showman more than magician, Borden as magician more than showman, Angier as a wealthy man, Borden as a poor man who struggles—their ruthless competitiveness means that they are fundamentally identical. Scarlett Johansson's Olivia Wenscombe, the pretty assistant who is a most effective form of misdirection, cuts through deceptions, disguises, and falsehoods to serve as a kind of touchstone that reveals this truth.

No Hidden Talents

In 2006 Johansson was asked by an interviewer if she had any hidden talents? "My hidden talent? I don't keep any of my talents hidden! With me it's more like, 'Hey, look at what I can do!'"[87]

Red Carpet

Regarding the *red carpet*, a major showbiz event of the 21st century, "everyone's shoving you this way and that—and you're like, 'What do I do? Where am I supposed to stand?'"[88]

Johansson did love preparing for the red carpet but it was "tumultuous .... so freakish and weird." She experienced "flop sweats, dry mouth, heart palpitations, all-over panic!" She said John Travolta's solution was picturing Hawaii in his mind.[89]

On YouTube, one can witness some of her consternation watching her arrival at the 70th Venice Film Festival in 2013 to promote *Under the Skin*. She takes a while to crack a smile for the audience.

Sexiest Woman Alive

> "I'm curvy—I'm never going to be 5'11" and 120 pounds.... But I feel lucky to have what I've got."
> —Kate Meyers, "Scarlett in Wonderland,"
> *InStyle*, October 2006

Esquire designated Johansson its "Sexiest Woman Alive" in 2006. She responded to a question about *In Touch* rating her bosom tops: "You work hard making independent films for fourteen years and you get voted best breasts." Confirming her special-ness, the

Esquire interviewer commented on his meeting with her at Corner Billiards in Manhattan: "She is beautiful in person, even unprimped. Some actresses, I've noticed, look surprisingly androgynous offscreen, gangly and curveless. Put baseball caps on them and give them badges and they could be Eagle Scouts. Scarlett is different. She looks like a woman. She exudes *womanness*."[90]

Johansson and her interlocutor debarked for a Japanese restaurant. She was described as mysterious, and her *Prestige* director Christopher Nolan quoted to the effect that she was an "ambiguity" while her *Black Dahlia* director Brian de Palma said, "You don't know what's going on behind those eyeballs. She's on some wavelength that you don't have a clue about."[91]

2007

Smooth Celebrity

In March 2007 Johansson and Owen Wilson received the first "Smoothest Celebrities of the Year" award from Nad's Hair Removal, an Australian-based company promoting "smooth and sophisticated sexiness" in addition to a healthy image. Nad's based its decision after examining celebrity appearances and interviews to designate the "most smooth."[92]

Charity Work

Johansson spent 10 days in India and Sri Lanka, visiting women who'd suffered domestic abuse in India and those rebuilding after a 2004 Tsunami. Johansson said her visit to the international aid agency Oxfam's (Oxfam Committee for Famine Relief, founded in Britain in 1942; Oxfam International founded in 1995) funded rural schools "made me realize how vital education is to developing countries in bringing people out of poverty and giving them a sense of dignity, self-worth and confidence."[93]

Johansson had eschewed Academy Award events to make the trip. Jeremy Hobbs, Oxfam's executive director, said the actress had joined millions of others seeking to end poverty worldwide.[94]

In January 2014 Johansson stepped down as an Oxfam ambassador due to her promotion of SodaStream, an Israeli soft drink company with a factory on the West Bank. Her view was that there should not have been a controversy, whose result was a closing of the factory and therefore the unemployment of many Palestinians. Although they parted amicably, Johansson wondered why a non-governmental organization like Oxfam could be involved in a political cause.[95]

5

Woody Allen's Muse?

> "This is a stupid phrase that journalists use all the time, a cliché with no meaning and bearing no resemblance to anything in Scarlett's life or my life."
> —Woody Allen email to writer Joseph Hooper on Johansson being termed his muse, in Joseph Hooper, "Scarlett Fever"

Johansson began her collaboration with Woody Allen in *Match Point* (2005), followed by *Scoop* (2006), and *Vicky Cristina Barcelona* (2008). The first was widely considered his best film in ages, and the third was even more successful financially. The lighter *Scoop* made less but cost a pittance in the scheme of things.

Match Point (2005)

> "All of a sudden, the nymph was a vamp."
> —Lili Anolik, "A(nother) Study in Scarlett,"
> *Vanity Fair*, May 2014

While former tennis pro Chris Wilton (Jonathan Rhys Meyers) coaches players of all skill levels in London, he meets Tom Hewett (Matthew Goode). They bond over a shared love of opera, and Tom invites Chris to a performance with sister Chloe (Emily Mortimer), father Alec (Brian Cox), and mother Eleanor (Penelope Wilton). During a visit to the Hewett house, Chris stumbles upon Nola Rice (Johansson) in the billiards room. A would-be actress from Boulder, Colorado, Nola happens to be Tom's fiancée. During a foursome dinner date, Chris tells the group that luck and fate are more important than people realize. Chloe is much taken with Chris and before long is sharing his bed. Chris takes a management job in Alec's company and proves himself more than capable. One day on the street, Chris runs into Nola and accompanies her to an audition. She fails. At the Hewetts,' Eleanor wonders how long before Nola gives up and tries something else. Angry over this slight, Nola tramps out into the rain. Chris follows her and the two embrace and literally have a roll in the wet hay. Later, at the opera house, Chris confronts her about becoming cold. She tells him it was just a one-time thing. He marries Chloe. During tennis, Tom tells Chris that he's broken up with Nola and found someone else. Chloe is distressed about not getting pregnant. Chris goes to the Tate to meet Chloe but spots Nola and confronts her. She reluctantly gives him her flat's phone number. They make love and later Chris says he just might leave Chloe. When spring arrives Nola reveals that *she* is pregnant.

Chris confides in a friend that he has a comfortable life, loves Nola but can't see a

5. Woody Allen's Muse?

Japanese Chirashi mini-poster for *Match Point* (BBC Films, 2005).

real future with her. He informs Nola he is going away for three weeks and will tell Chloe about Nola when he gets back. He attempts to mollify Nola by telling her it's just routine lovemaking with Chloe.

At the opera Alec talks about a lucrative opportunity with the Japanese. Nola calls Chris at home, and he says he's still in Greece but will return in two weeks.

Jonathan Rhys Meyers and Scarlett Johansson, *Match Point* (BBC Films, 2005).

Nola spots Chris climbing into a limo. She phones him and he says he'll be back in five-six days but Nola confronts him outside his building. He says he'll do the right thing.

With one of Alec's shotguns, Chris goes to Nola's flat, first killing neighbor Mrs. Eastby (Margaret Tyzack) and ransacking her flat to take the focus off Nola, whom he shoots outside the elevator as she arrives home. Chris meets Chloe at a performance of *The Woman in White*.

Police investigate the double murder. Their initial conclusion: Nola was unlucky. Chloe, finally pregnant, sees the murder notice in the paper.

Chris tosses his loot into the Thames, but fails to note that Mrs. Eastby's ring fell back onto the ground.

Detective Mike Banner (James Nesbitt) calls Chris in and learns that he did have an affair with Nola. Banner remains suspicious.

One evening Chris is visited by the spirits of Nola and Mrs. Eastby. Chris could push the guilt under the rug and go on. Mrs. Eastby is just collateral damage. Nola says his actions were clumsy.

Detective Banner experiences an epiphany in the night: Chris killed Mrs. Eastby to cover Nola's murder. But his second-in-command tells him a man has been captured (and died) with Mrs. Eastby's wedding ring. So much for Banner's eureka moment.

Chloe and Chris arrive home with their son. Tom hopes the baby is lucky.

Reviews

Boxoffice Magazine thought it had one of director Allen's finest screenplays, with subversive humor enhancing the plot twist and significance of dumb luck. As for Johansson, she "commands the screen with a compelling mix of street smarts, sexiness and vulnerability."[1] The *New York Times* was very positive, calling it Woody Allen's "most satisfying film in more than a decade." It had "a light, sure touch. This is a Champagne cocktail laced with strychnine." One was reminded of the cynicism turned into excellent entertainment by Ernest Lubitsch and Billy Wilder. The leads, Jonathan Rhys-Meyers, and Johansson, "manage some of the best acting seen in a Woody Allen movie in a long time, escaping the archness and emotional disconnection that his writing often imposes." It was possible to identify with both without really liking their characters. The scene in which Johansson's Nola meets Rhys-Meyers' Chris "raises the movie's temperature from a polite simmer to a full sexual boil." It paid homage to George Stevens' 1951 classic, *A Place in the Sun*.[2] The *Guardian* was among the few naysayers and argued that it would not revitalize Woody Allen's career. While it was stronger than his recent efforts, the dialogue wasn't right, and "the darker themes of *Crimes and Misdemeanors*..." were "played out at greater and more laborious length." As "Tom's super-sexy American fiancée..." Johansson was "fiery and sexy, though for her, as for everyone else, there are no funny lines."[3] *People* was complimentary, giving it 3½ stars. "Rhys Meyers makes for an almost sympathetic snake, while sexy Johansson steams up the screen."[4] Derrick Bang thought it had a disappointing payoff. Ditto for Johansson, who "drips earthy sexuality and mystery in her early scenes; it's therefore disappointing when Nola eventually is revealed to be less than the sum of her parts."[5]

Commentary

Woody Allen was nominated for the Best Screenplay Academy Award.

During filming *Match Point* was labeled "WASP—04," aka the Woody Allen Spring/Summer/Fall Project. Director Allen told an interviewer that he was happy to work in London, "because I'm right back in the same kind of liberal creative attitude that I'm used to." It is revealed that Johansson replaced Kate Winslet in the role of Nola. Winslet realized that after agreeing to appear, family responsibilities prevented it.[6] Allen found Johansson's sense of humor rivaled his own.[7]

Analysis

One can agree with the tight writing so far as the plotting goes, but the dialogue becomes a bit pretentious because of the wish to be "serious." One wonders if in part setting it in England allows Woody to think the pretentiousness is justified by the presence of Brits. With Scarlett's lips we can of course have no quibble whatsoever.

The derriere seems to have become a focal point for filmmakers and photographers alike. There was the opening scene of *Lost in Translation* and the haymaking in *Match Point*. Curious.

Match Point is so tightly scripted Woody Allen is willing to run the risk of giving the game away from the beginning. Chris Wilton's (Jonathan Rhys Meyers) voice praises the insight of the man who said he would rather be lucky than good. This phrase serves as a kind of oracle that describes Chris's fate and the film depicts the working out of that fate.

On the other hand, when Chris first meets Nola Rice (Johansson), she is dismissing a male opponent at a ping-pong table and asking, "Who's my next victim?" While Nola seems dominant and self-assured in that moment, her serve is quickly returned with a smash by Chris, winning the point and ending the game. Chris approaches Nola at her end of the table, takes hold of her, and tries to show her how it is necessary to follow through when hitting the ball. The result is a flirtatious moment between them when Chris comments on the sensuality of Nola's lips and she responds by saying he plays a very aggressive game. This first meeting is important as it forecasts the evolution of their roles—with Nola becoming the victim of someone she thinks she can victimize. Her white dress in this scene suggests her innocence and vulnerability as well as connecting her with Chris's attendance at a musical version of Wilkie Collins's *The Woman in White* with his wife to provide himself with an alibi for Nola's murder.

As the film progresses it becomes clear that Chris and Nola have similarities but at root are opposites. They are both outsiders—Chris from Ireland and Nola from the United States, from Boulder, Colorado. They both emerged from humble beginnings—Chris through professional tennis and Nola by her looks and desirability. On the other hand, Chris gave up tennis when he realized he could not reach the top of the game. Nola continues to pursue her nonexistent career in acting despite repeated rejections. Chris reads *Crime and Punishment* and a critical guide to Dostoevsky and impresses Alec Hewett (Brian Cox), the father of his intended Chloe Hewett (Emily Mortimer), with a conversation about the author. Nola antagonizes Eleanor Hewett (Penelope Wilton), the mother of her intended Tom Hewett (Matthew Goode), by her drinking and a self-pitying attitude toward her career. In short, Chris ingratiates himself with the family that will be the making of him while Nola if anything makes it difficult for Tom Hewett to carry on his wish to marry her.

The audience learns most about Nola's background when she has been rejected at an audition and goes out for drinks with Chris in an attempt to recover. It becomes clear then that her father left her mother and her mother tended to drink too much. While describing this background, Nola continues to drink too much as a way of dealing with rejection. What this conversation implies about Nola is that she like her mother is someone who tends to be rejected—by men and auditions—and seeks solace in alcohol. Still, it is during this conversation that she tells Chris that he will do well if he doesn't blow his fortunate situation in the Hewett family by making a pass at her. Once again, Nola suffers from the delusion that her attractiveness makes her a femme fatale rather than a victim.

The screenplay is effective because of the way it turns a typical crime drama inside out. Audiences are convinced that crime does not pay, and people cannot get away with murder—especially not a planned, pre-meditated, self-interested murder by someone who considers the killing of innocents as "collateral damage." Instead of asking "Whodunnit?" the plot of *Match Point* answers the question, "How did he get away with it?" The answer is by luck. As the ghost of Nola points out to a guilt-stricken, sleepless Chris, his plan had been pulled off in a clumsy way and it was full of holes. The police are in fact able to solve the crime by finding Nola's diary—the existence of which Chris never considered despite her lamenting her lack of a confidante. In addition, when Chris tried to throw Nola's neighbor's wedding ring into the Thames it hit a handrail and fell back to the ground—reminiscent of a tennis ball hitting the net and deciding the point by falling in one direction or the other. In this way, the audience is again given grounds for believing justice will be done. But no, Chris's luck holds, and the ring turns up in the possession of a junkie who commits another crime in Nola's neighborhood. The police blame the anonymous junkie for Chris's murder of Nola when she was carrying his child and her neighbor.

In a way, *Match Point* is a commentary on social classes. Chris and Nola as two outsiders from the working class have the opportunity to rise by potentially joining a family that is not aristocratic but instead has a position based on wealth and an American-style success in business. Chris, although Irish, has an aristocratic English family name, Wilton, suggesting perhaps that he is a "natural aristocrat" and so able to rise through family connections rather than ability or hard work. Nola is not a natural aristocrat, despite her looks and sensuality. She seems destined to follow her mother's vulnerable path to rejection and drink. Chris no doubt becomes hardened against her when he learns she has been unlucky enough to have become pregnant twice before, both pregnancies ending with abortions. Chris expresses the ruthlessness of the ruling class when he describes the murder of Nola's neighbor and his own potential child as necessary sacrifices for "the greater good"—his ability to live exceptionally well being his idea of "the greater good." This exaggerated tale of love or lust and death is fittingly equipped with an operatic score and several scenes juxtaposed to scenes from operas. One sign that Nola is where she does not belong is her name—an abbreviation for New Orleans, Louisiana, an homage to the home of the jazz that Woody Allen loves and frequently incorporates into his films. She embodies the pleasures of the many that are too often sacrificed for the well-being of the lucky few.

There are comparisons to be made with Allen's *Crimes and Misdemeanors* as well as Theodore Dreiser's *An American Tragedy* and director George Stevens' 1951 cinematic rendering of that novel, *A Place in the Sun*. It should be enjoyed "for the grandson of Hitchcock that it aspires to be."[8]

At first *Match Point* does seem Hitchcockian. Unlike *Frenzy* (1972), however, also set in London with a police inspector (Alec McCowen) unmasking the murderer Rusk (Barry Foster) because he forgot his tie, in convincing the detective here that a man pleading guilty to the double murder is in fact being truthful when the audience knows he is not, *Match Point* certainly does, at least for some viewers, leave a sour taste in the mouth.

Scoop (2006)

As his buddies toast his untimely passing, investigative journalist Joe Strombel (Ian McShane) finds himself aboard a boat navigating a Stygian waterway. Learning from passenger Jane Cook (Fenella Woolgar) that the up-and-coming politico Peter Lyman (Hugh Jackman) may have poisoned her to keep her quiet about his unsavory extracurricular activities, Joe drops into the water and appears as a spirit in the dematerialization booth of "The Great Splendini," aka Sid Waterman (Woody Allen). In the booth is aspiring journalist Sondra Pransky (Johansson). Astounded by the apparition but anxious to get a scoop about Lyman, Sondra enlists Sid in her scheme to reveal Lyman as the Tarot Card Killer then terrorizing London. Sid reluctantly agrees and through Sondra's girlfriend Vivian (Romola Garai) are invited to an exclusive club where Lyman swims. Feigning leg cramps, Sondra is rescued by Peter. Using the nom de plume Jade Spence, she and her "father" are invited to a posh party. Sid agrees to accompany her although he isn't happy with a plan inspired by a piece of ectoplasm. The party takes place at a magisterial estate complete with lake and boathouse. Peter tells "Jade" he has a new secretary because his previous one died of a blood clot. Meanwhile, Sid pilfers an envelope from an overnight bag. Back in London, Sid tells Sondra that Lyman is not a serial killer and produces the envelope with "Betty G" imprinted on it. Walking on the street with Vivian, Sondra spots a newspaper headline: Tarot Killer Strikes Again. Visiting Peter's city home, Sondra is invited downstairs to his musical instrument cache. Sid meets Strombel, again materializing in the dematerialization box to give Sid a safe combination.

Hugh Jackman and Scarlett Johansson, *Scoop* (BBC Films, 2006) Japanese promo card.

Sondra spends the night with Peter and snoops around the house in the morning. Sid uses the combination to open the music room. Locked in, he is rescued by Sondra and they escape just before Peter arrives. Later Sondra tells Sid about the Tarot cards in the music room. He suggests she phone police with an anonymous tip.

In a park, Lyman gives Sondra a bracelet for her birthday. He tells her he must leave town for a few days. Sondra shows Vivian her bracelet. Strombel materializes, says he escaped again, and tells her she doesn't yet have enough incriminating evidence to make her accusations stick.

During dinner with Sid, Sondra spots Lyman on the street and with Sid in tow follows then loses him before they hear cries of distress. A woman's been strangled.

Meeting with Mr. Malcolm (Charles Dance) at the *Observer*, Sondra is told her material is thus far mere speculation that could lead to a libel case. Sondra says Joe Strombel gave her the tip about Lyman. Malcolm reveals the Tarot Card Killer has just been apprehended: a delusional paranoid handyman.

At the country house, Sondra tells Peter she has a confession, but he does too. He says he lied about being away on business, it was a sensitive merger. She's glad and reveals she's not Jade Spence, rather a journalism student, and Sid is not her father. She thought Peter might be the Tarot Card murderer. He says she's made his day. She asks why he hid the Tarot deck in the music room. Peter replies that the cards were of Victorian vintage and a gift for her.

Sondra meets Sid, who has begun to doubt Peter's innocence. "Betty G" is a significant clue. Elizabeth Gibson: Betty for Elizabeth. Maybe the series of murders is cover for just one murder. Lyman would kill a blackmailing prostitute who could destroy his reputation.

Strombel materializes in Sid's theater and says he probably won't appear anymore. He urges Sid to see if a card's missing in Lyman's Tarot deck. Sid goes to the flat where Elizabeth Gibson lived, pretending to be a reporter. The neighbors are mostly unhelpful, but one woman says there was a regular client, a rich kid named Peter. Peter listens in on another phone as Sid reveals new information to Sondra.

Sid returns to Peter's house and sneaks down to the music room again where he finds a key. His housekeeper phones Lyman to tell him Sid's mucking about. Verifying that the key is to Betty Gibson's flat, Sid drives toward the country house where Peter is even then revealing to Sondra that he used the Tarot Killer as cover for murdering extortionist Betty. He says he'll kill Sid later. Sondra puts up a spirited defense, but Lyman tosses her into the drink and returns to the boathouse. In the manse, he phones the police. They arrive, as does Sondra, wet but none the worse for wear. She tells Peter she was an expert swimmer, her splashing in distress a ruse to get his attention. Sadly, Sid was killed in a car crash.

Sondra is complimented on her investigative success by Mr. Malcolm. She says she owes her success to Strombel and Sid, who himself is now on the death cruise, showing passengers his magic tricks.

Reviews

Roger Ebert considered the film only fair but commended Johansson as "lovely as always, but why do Allen's onscreen foils always have to talk like him?" He noted that "Diane Keaton's Annie Hall and Dianne Wiest's Helen Sinclair in *Bullets Over Broadway* had distinct voices of their own, and they were funnier because of it." Ebert said the film felt like "Allen had just given up after the first draft."[9] *The Blade* found it "as hit-and-miss as any comedy he's [Allen] made in years." Johansson didn't have Diane Keaton or Mia Farrow's light touch "but there's a movie-star shimmer around her that accentuates her purpose."[10] The *New York Times* considered the funny quotient low, the production "slack," but it was "oddly appealing...." with a "pleasantly carefree vibe." Johansson "plays the succulent morsel, though with a performance set in the key of screwball rather than noir." [Think *Match Point*.] Her "performance is all over the place..., but finally works for a film that is itself all over the place. Mr. Allen seems happy to just watch her strut her stuff, and after a while so are we."[11]

People compared it unfavorably to *Match Point*, also set in England, likewise a "tale of social climbing and murder" ... but with much less impact. There was too much "recycled Yanks vs. Limeys jokes. Johansson looks lustrous but she can't carry this piffle on her own."[12]

Commentary

In 2006, Allen said, "I can only quote myself from the movie *Manhattan*. Scarlett is God's answer to Job. God would say, 'I've created a terrifying and horrible universe, but I can also make one of these, so stop complaining.'"[13]

Curiously, *Scoop* was not released theatrically in England, but the DVD became available much, much later.[14]

Analysis

Although it is common, even traditional for a comedy to start with a touch of grimness or sadness, a suggestion of death, Woody Allen, the writer and director of *Scoop* runs the risk of overwhelming the sense of fun by the presence of death. The movie begins with a death, ends with a death, and is concerned throughout with the identity of a serial killer. Nonetheless, the combination of tight plotting, high spirits, and one-liners provides enough levity to ward off even this amount of grimness. Despite that, reviewers were not especially kind to *Scoop* and Stephen Hunt in *The Washington Post*[15] went so far as to call it Allen's worst movie ever—a statement that in retrospect seems silly because it is so extreme. What actually makes the movie is the comedic relationship between Allen and Johansson, the source of the high spirits and the one-liners and the embodiment of the film's tight plotting.

The pair consists of two klutzes from Brooklyn who set out to solve a crime in London. Johansson plays the rambunctious Sondra Pransky, a college student and would-be journalist, who wears oversized glasses with metal frames and seems none too sure of herself. We first meet her when she attempts to interview a famous film director, Mike Tinsley (Kevin McNally), in his hotel room. He does not answer her questions but gives her whiskey and takes her to bed. She laments her failure to secure the interview and admits she remembers nothing of the sex to the English friend she is visiting in London, Vivian (Romola Garai), an attractive and interesting confidante who might have had a bigger role in the film. Sondra meets Allen's character, Sidney Waterman, alias The Great Splendini, when the girls go to see his magic act at a theater. Sondra answers the call for a volunteer from the audience and Splendini puts her in The Dematerializer to make her disappear. From the moment Sondra steps on stage, she shows that her own gift for one-liners is capable of matching Splendini's line of patter. Their antagonism seems to spring from the similarity of their characters, identities based on wit and words.

The character established for Sondra eventually sets up a transformation scene reminiscent of those associated with glamorous Hollywood stars of the 1940s. The scene takes place by a pool in a private club where Peter Lyman (Hugh Jackman), the aristocrat suspected of being the Tarot Card Killer, swims laps. Sondra and Sidney enter in white bathrobes, wearing glasses, and discussing the British class system. They decide to have Sondra meet Lyman by going into the pool and pretending to drown so he will save her. She removes her glasses and the thick bathrobe to reveal herself wearing a red one-piece swimsuit of the kind that might have been worn by Betty Grable or Lana Turner as a pinup during World War II.

Johansson pulls this transformation scene off in a natural way, as if she is modern heir of these stars of the past, and the transformation becomes complete when she tells Peter she is an actress, and her name is Jade Spence. Sidney returns only to be flabbergasted to learn that he is Jade's father, a wealthy business tycoon with a Brooklyn accent.

Much of the fun throughout the rest of the movie is based on the complications caused by Sondra and Sidney posing as Jade and Mr. Spence. When they arrive at Lord Lyman's country estate Sondra says to Sidney, "Look at this place. All that's missing is a moat." Splendini, as if unaware of how to play the part of Mr. Spence, starts performing card tricks for Lord Lyman's guests and accompanies them with his line of patter. Another aspect of the film's tight plotting is that Sondra quickly becomes convinced that the ghost of Joe Strombel (Ian McShane), the journalist whose death opens the picture, was right when he said Peter Lyman was the serial killer, while Splendini insists the lack of evidence makes the claim highly unlikely. In time, they switch views. Sondra, who at one point describes herself as "A would-be investigative reporter who's falling in love with the object of her investigation," becomes convinced of Peter Lyman's innocence. Splendini, on the other hand, becomes convinced Lyman committed the murder of Betty G. that was made to look like a Tarot Card killing. He sets out to save Sondra but crashes the car and dies.

Sondra gets the best of Lyman through a kind of reenactment of the transformation scene. He accepted her apparent inability to swim as actual and decides to let her drown and report her death as accidental. She appears, soaking wet and smiling broadly, as he talks to the local police. She announces that she was captain of a swim team back in Brooklyn. The movie ends with a sense of her cleverness that is reinforced by the acceptance of her story about the case for publication by a London newspaper and the suggestion she is a true heir of Joe Strombel, the journalist famous for doing anything to get a story. No doubt the difference in the ages of Sondra and Sidney prevented them from ending the comedy in the traditional way, with a marriage or romantic relationship. Instead, the film ends with her paying tribute to Strombel and Splendini, and with Splendini on the ship of death, doing card tricks and keeping up his eternal patter.

Even those critics who thought little of this movie seemed to give Johansson credit for bringing something new and vivacious to it. The fact that Allen gave her lines as good as those he kept for himself suggests he rightly recognized her gift for delivering them with maximum effect. In his *Washington Post* review, Stephen Hunt compared this crime story with one featuring the Hardy Boys. Allen and Johansson are in fact more like Nick and Nora Charles but with Brooklyn accents.

Vicky Cristina Barcelona (2008)

To finish her academic piece on Catalan identity, Vicky (Rebecca Hall) joins her friend Cristina (Johansson) on a working vacation in Barcelona. They stay with Vicky's relative Judy (Patricia Clarkson) and husband Mark (Kevin Dunn). Soon after arriving, they are approached in a restaurant by local artist Juan Antonio Gonzalo (Javier Bardem), who offers to take them by plane to Oviedo to see the sights, eat, drink, and make love. After all, life is short. Vicky, engaged to Doug (Chris Messina), is aghast. She knows where she's going and it does not include sleeping with a strange Spaniard. Cristina, free to grope about for a nebulous future, perhaps as a photographer, is all in, but in Oviedo food poisoning and her ulcer knock her out for the count. While Cristina recovers, Juan Antonio and Vicky enjoy the city and a visit to Juan Antonio's father. She learns about Juan Antonio's fiery ex-wife Maria Elena (Penelope Cruz), also an artist. Later that night Vicky is told how beautiful she is in Juan Antonio's eyes, and she allows him to take her on the grass amid the trees. Back in Barcelona, Cristina moves in with Juan Antonio. An idyllic time is compromised when Maria Elena tries to kill herself and Juan Antonio elects to see to her welfare—in his home. This initially consternates Cristina, but Maria Elena helps her with her newfound fascination with photography and eventually the threesome make love. Vicky, meanwhile, receives a call from Doug and rather reluctantly agrees to marry him in Barcelona. Judy, unhappy in her own marriage, aims to mate Vicky with Juan Antonio. This might work, especially as Cristina has moved out, leaving Juan Antonio and Maria Elena to resume their tempestuous relationship. Judy succeeds in getting Juan Antonio and Vicky together, but the pistol-packing Maria Elena arrives. Vicky is shot in the hand and storms away from these crazy people and reveals all to Cristina, who says she would have stepped aside if she'd known of her friend's interest in Juan Antonio. Vicky says that had not been necessary. After all, it was a passing thing. Cristina, Vicky and Doug leave for the States, Vicky to have the big wedding and the life she'd previously envisioned, Cristina to remain at loggerheads about her future. As she'd felt before the overseas jaunt, she knew only what she *didn't* want.

Reviews

The Hamilton Spectator equated the film with director Allen's mid-level films. Its well-off characters were possessed of "various levels of sophistication, involved in the arts and the intrigues of love. They're conflicted about right and wrong. They're undoubtedly low-level neurotics." In sum, "The actors are attractive, the city magnificent, the love scenes don't get all sweaty, and everybody finishes the summer a little wiser and with a lifetime of memories."[16]

On public radio's *Morning Edition*, critic Kenneth Turan was not impressed, but Bardem, "who eats this role up like it's a hot fudge sundae," was entertaining. The real problem was that the film was meant to be taken seriously rather than as a mild frolic. It wasn't even "Henry James lite."[17] The *New York Times* termed it a movie "Bathed in light so lusciously golden and honeyed that you might be tempted to lick the screen...." Although it "trips along winningly, carried by the beauty of its locations and stars ... it reverberates with implacable melancholy, a sense of loss." The reviewer wasn't much impressed with Johansson: "She isn't much of an actress, but it doesn't terribly matter in his [Allen's] films. She gives him succulent youth, and he cushions her with enough laughs to distract

Japanese Chirashi mini-poster for *Vicky Cristina Barcelona* (Weinstein Company, 2008). Left to right: Rebecca Hall, Scarlett Johansson, Penelope Cruz, Javier Bardem.

you from her lack of skill." This view of Johansson's abilities was modified later, in the same reviewer's take on 2014's *Lucy*.[18]

Commentary

Johansson said the Spanish shoot was mind-blowing, with two thousand spectators observing from the outskirts. One had to use "a mental exercise in finding peace of mind, and the stillness."[19]

Interviewed for the December 2008 *Allure*—and naturally shown getting made up and clothed in designer attire—Johansson was asked if she really was Woody Allen's muse. After all, she'd been in three of his recent films. She thought the term "muse" wasn't being used in its proper sense. She did not inspire Allen's work, she was just the "young woman" in his movies. "I know that if it wasn't me, it would be somebody else.... He did write *Scoop* for me, though."[20]

Allen had been accused in 1992 of abuse by his estranged daughter Dylan, then seven years old, and it seems likely that was the reason many of his films after that accusation weren't widely distributed. In fact, a generation of women found him unpalatable after this scandal. In early 2014 Dylan penned an open letter that condemned the film industry for pushing it under the rug and identified actors who'd worked with him. Johansson was one. Johansson considered it irresponsible to target actors for comments on events about which they could have little knowledge. And Allen had not been prosecuted and a decision handed down. It was just "guesswork."[21]

In 2019 she reiterated her loyalty to Allen, saying, "I believe him, and I would work with him anytime."[22]

On September 6, 2019, Dylan Farrow took Johansson to task for her attitude. But there were others who agreed. Javier Bardem, male star of *Vicky Cristina Barcelona*, said he'd work with Allen again. "If the legal situation ever changes, then I'd change my mind. But for now I don't agree with the public lynching that he's been receiving, and if Woody Allen called me to work with him again I'd be there tomorrow. He's a genius." He noted that judgments in Connecticut and New York had cleared Allen of wrongdoing. Alec Baldwin and long-time intimate Diane Keaton had also come to his defense.[23] Keaton had also supported Allen's defense in 2018. "Woody Allen is my friend and I continue to believe him. It might be of interest to take a look at the *60 Minutes* interview from 1992 and see what you think."[24]

Johansson's loyalty to Allen could do some harm—she seems willing to be not politically correct in a number of ways. Integrity matters more than awards. Of Johansson, Allen told an interviewer in 2011 that he certainly was not averse to collaborating with her again, but "I didn't want her to be burdened by, 'Oh, she's in all the Woody Allen pictures, it's so predictable and she's my new muse, and all that silliness. But now that some time has elapsed since *Vicky Cristina*, I will start to think about this again." In response, Johansson said she was waiting for Woody to write her *Citizen Kane*.[25]

Allen "was enchanted with her the minute I met her, and I've never stopped. She's great-looking, sexy, funny, a good dramatic actress, she can sing. I mean, she's got it all, really." Allen added that he imagined ending up filming her in something like *Sunset Boulevard*.[26]

Analysis

Comedies traditionally end with weddings, symbolic reaffirmations of life and celebrations of the continuity of life after the shadow of death has been dispelled. Woody

Allen's wonderful screenplay for this film performs a variation on this theme by having Doug (Chris Messina), the intended of Vicky (Rebecca Hall), come to Barcelona and marry her before the movie's end. They were scheduled to marry in the autumn after Vicky's return from Barcelona.

The reason for this premature consummation seems to be to maintain the plot's precarious balance. Doug needs to appear as a counterweight to the return of Maria Elena (Penelope Cruz), Juan Antonio's (Javier Bardem) ex-wife, and form two triangles—Vicky, Doug, and Juan Antonio and Cristina (Johansson), Maria Elena, and Juan Antonio. As even the title of the film suggests, this script is interested in threesomes, as either a triangle or a ménage à trois, the implication being that couples are potentially if not necessarily insufficient, incomplete, in themselves, and seek fulfillment through the addition of a third person. Even Vicky's aunt Judy (Patricia Clarkson), the woman with whom the girls stay, is unhappy in her marriage, and playing with the idea of an affair.

The only relationship that is presented as complete is the threesome formed by Cristina, Juan Antonio, and Maria Elena. This part seems perfect for Johansson. She appears sensual and open to experimentation in a casual almost slovenly way from the start. Some reviewers describe the scene in which Cristina and Maria Elena kiss and, it is implied, make love, in a red-lighted darkroom surrounded by pictures Cristina has taken of Maria Elena as Woody Allen's "money shot."

Johansson plays a stereotypical "romantic" in contrast to her stereotypically "pragmatic" best friend Vicky. These two are only apparent opposites, though. Cristina's first chance to make love with Juan Antonio is interrupted because of the flare up of her ulcer—a physical complaint associated not with mellow, easy-going people, but by driven, ambitious types. By contrast, Vicky's last chance to make love with Juan Antonio is interrupted by Maria Elena returning and repeatedly firing a pistol, eventually hitting Vicky in the wrist. Surely this is the romantic, emotional, way for lovers to be stopped. Cristina's ulcer and Vicky's wounded wrist cast the shadow of death on the plot that love and laughter need to dispel.

In short, the girls are not really the opposites they are presented to be and, as a result, Cristina becomes dissatisfied with her threesome and moves on to continue to search, although for what she does not know. Vicky in the end returns home to apparently live with her new husband and keep the love she knew in Barcelona as a mere memory. Her aunt clearly lacks what she thinks of as the courage to break up her marriage, so she will no doubt stay with her husband and continue to discuss her marriage with her shrink. Maria Elena and Juan Antonio are unable to stay together without the element Cristina provided.

The camera seems unable to look away when Cristina is making love. By contrast, Vicky and Juan Antonio making love in a park-like setting in Oviedo is given a traditional Hollywood treatment—a passionate kiss and a downward movement of the bodies followed by a fade to black. Cristina's love scenes expose flesh, use close ups, and take place not only in bed but also, for instance, on a rug on the kitchen floor of Juan Antonio's home, in addition to the darkroom. There is nothing half-hearted about the way Johansson plays this part.

Penelope Cruz certainly deserved the Academy Award she won as Best Supporting Actress for her performance in this film, but Woody Allen also seemed able to bring out the best in both Rebecca Hall and Scarlett Johansson for their respective roles. As Mick Lasalle wrote of this film in *SFGate*, "Scarlett Johansson is never more relaxed or appealing or less self-conscious than she is in Allen's movies."[27]

6

Working, Part 2

Concerned Citizen

In 2006 Johansson heeded musician Bono's call to be the image for Project Red, co-founded by Bobby Shriver to raise money for the Global Fund to Fight Aids, Tuberculosis, and Malaria in Africa. Johansson said, "It's kind of conscious consumerism, charitable consumerism. I thought it was incredible." She did recognize the potential pitfalls of connecting charity and celebrity and thought some people might not research properly what they were lending their support to, to jump on a bandwagon because it was hip. Supporting Project Red "has nothing to do with my career." And, "It's important for people in the public eye to advocate what we believe in. We're given this voice and we should use it." Who could foresee the problem Oxfam would give her in a few years?[1]

While making *A Love Song for Bobby Long*, Johansson visited the areas of New Orleans ravaged by Hurricane Katrina in 2005 and donated the money she'd made posing as Cinderella in a Disney spread. "It's hard to find one project to focus on."[2]

2007

Hasty Pudding Award

On February 15, 2007, Johansson traveled to Harvard University to receive the Hasty Pudding Theatricals Woman of the Year award. In this she joined such previous award recipients as Katharine Hepburn, Jodie Foster, Meg Ryan, Halle Berry, Meryl Streep and Julia Roberts.[3]

In a Bentley, Johansson led a parade down Massachusetts Avenue. Students, some barely dressed for the freezing temperatures, accompanied the procession. Johansson said, "I wouldn't be caught dead in a bra and panties on a day like this…. They were really suffering for their craft." She added, "Everything I ever dreamed of when I was a little girl is happening to me right now." She received a golden pudding pot. She said her mother still pestered her about higher education, but "This is the closest I'll ever get to a Harvard degree, for sure."[4]

Johansson was onboard with a mock SAT exam, lampooning her *Vanity Fair* cover pose, and a dinner roast.[5]

Music Video with Justin Timberlake

Johansson appeared with singer-actor Justin Timberlake in the music video "What

Goes Around … Comes Around."[6] Samuel Bayer received a MTV Music Video Award for Best Direction, and it was nominated for Video of the Year.

Playboy Accolade

The March 2007 issue of *Playboy* featured "Playboy's 25 Sexiest Celebrities," ranking Johansson its "Sex Star of the Year." Thus, "Scarlett Johansson is the apex of beauty and sensuality—from her porcelain skin to her fully feminine figure to her mysterious charisma, which is at once palpable and undefinable."[7]

Plastic Surgery an Option

Johansson considered plastic surgery a viable option for her future. According to Britain's celebrity website *Female First*, Johansson said, "I will definitely have plastic surgery—I don't want to become an old hag! I think if you're comfortable with yourself that's sexy, but if you're not then go for it."[8]

Sex Appeal

In the May 2007 issue of *Glamour* Johansson's body was ranked the sexiest. Five thousand women had been surveyed.[9] As for the male opinion, "With curves to rival Marilyn Monroe, Scarlett embraces old-school-Hollywood style and exudes body confidence." Johansson opined, "Sex appeal is something that comes out of you. You can force it, but to me what's really appealing is when someone just exudes sexual energy. Women shouldn't be forced to conform to unrealistic and unhealthy body images."[10]

Although she hardly needs assistance, stylists will work their own magic when preparing her for a photo shoot. She "looks every bit as good in person as she does made up and perfectly lit on a movie screen."[11]

On paparazzi and celebrity, Johansson observed cynicism in the public at large in their goal of bringing people down. "Reality television and tabloid magazines—never before did we need to see movie stars taking out their garbage. But all of a sudden, it's front-page news—trying to figure out who's dating whom, all that stuff. Who cares?"[12]

Concerning the ever-iconic Marilyn Monroe, Johansson said she loved her because she was not only gorgeous, "but she had a real fragility about her work that is so touching. I think that's why she was under-appreciated as a really talented actor." Comparisons with Marilyn were superficial, however. Johansson had a "confident strength that seems to spring directly from her very focused girlhood."[13] Johansson said, she'd "always been very determined … to make my way. And I am also very responsible. It's just who I am."[14]

Vogue pointed out that "Her voluptuous looks and famously full lips are almost defiant in a culture that fetishizes the slighter silhouettes of Keira Knightley, Kirsten Dunst, and Natalie Portman."[15] *Elle* chimed in, too: "What makes her so sexy on-screen is the same thing that makes her so dramatically compelling: a self-possession manifested as total immersion in character. She's not playing to us; if we want to be impressed with her, or ogle her, that's our business. Johansson is willing to do less to let the camera come to her. 'You have to take the time to have a thought … and that always allows for certain moments of silence.'"[16]

The Nanny Diaries (2007)

After graduating college with a degree in anthropology, 21-year-old Annie Braddock (Johansson) is at loose ends until by sheer accident she finds herself live-in babysitter to young Grayer (Nicholas Art), scion of wealthy upper East Side parents she designates as Mr. (Paul Giamatti) and Mrs. X. (Laura Linney). Finally establishing rapport with Grayer and finding a bit of romance with building resident she covertly calls "Harvard Hottie" (Chris Evans), Annie is conflicted about her job. Mr. and Mrs. X pay little attention to Grayer and Annie finds herself consumed by the family's demands. But she is loath to abandon the child. The decision is made for her during a Nantucket beach vacation when Mrs. X finds Mr. X putting the moves on Annie in the kitchen. Fired, Annie returns to the apartment for her things and discovers that she's been "nanny cammed." Annie places a cassette in the teddy bear and rants at Mrs. X, who observes this with other moms during a nanny-handling session. Later, Hayden, aka Harvard Hottie, gives her a letter he'd received from Mrs. X in which she apologizes for her actions with Grayer and Annie and says she's divorcing Mr. X. As for Annie, she sets her sights on an anthropology master's degree program.

Reviews

Roger Ebert thought its best scene was the first, when Johansson's Nanny tours the Museum of Natural History and "explains the dioramas showing lifelike models of Upper East Side natives seen in their natural habitats." As for the thespians, "Laura Linney engages our sympathy more than Mrs. X really deserves, and Johansson has a kind of secret wit about her in certain roles that makes her seem in on the joke."[17] One critic thought Johansson "disconcertingly unsexy…" in the role of Annie Braddock, newly minted college grad who is agog at the salary she'll be paid to monitor the four-year-old. As the mom, Laura Linney's "keen, cruel villain" normally would engender a rebellious spirit in any character played by Johansson.[18] *The Blade* called it a "lost opportunity." Johansson played "a clumsy, snuggably 'ordinary' post-collegiate from New Jersey who looks remarkably like va-va-va-vroom Scarlett Johansson with flatter hair."[19] The *News Journal* said that despite some "dead-on satire" and close to the book, "it loses its bite and suddenly goes all soft and gushy at the end." As for Johansson, she was capable "In rare regular-person mode…." Most disappointing was that the film came from the husband-wife directing and writing team of Shari Springer and Robert Pulcini, who'd done *American Splendor*.[20] The *Star Tribune* said messing up the novel "isn't exactly desecrating a classic, but the unfaithful film adaptation so undermines the novel's spiky social satire that it constitutes some kind of aesthetic crime." It both dumbed down and cutesified it, transforming it into "maudlin, upbeat mush." Johansson was "so-so as the focus…" and did not "project a real rapport with her young co-star Art, who never becomes more than a generic needy kid."[21]

Commentary

Director Shari Springer Berman said, "It's just a great role for her. She's really funny. She is a really great physical comedian, and any time we had to do anything physical she had us all cracking up. Her pratfalls are amazing."[22]

Co-star Chris Evans said, "Scarlett's amazing and we've, we've worked together before so, you know, we've kept in touch, and it's really nice to be able to work with someone you've worked with in the past, and she's amazing. She's an actress so any time you can spar with someone who is obviously so talented it's only gonna up your game."[23]

Scarlett Johansson (left) and Laura Linney, *The Nanny Diaries* **(Weinstein Company, 2007).**

Johansson's prior outing with Evans had been 2004's *The Perfect Score*. They would meet again on the big screen several times in the Marvel Universe.

This film is not a comedy, it is a member of that estimable but small sub/crossover genre known as the comedy-drama that seems to have peaked in the sixties. See, for instance, *The Apartment* (1960), *Soldier in the Rain* (1963), *The Courtship of Eddie's Father* (1963), *The Americanization of Emily* (1964), *The World of Henry Orient* (1964), *A Thousand Clowns* (1965), *The Graduate* (1967).

Analysis

The Nanny Diaries begins and ends with the voice of Annie Braddock (Johansson), providing information about herself. The opening suggests she is filling out an application for a job, but in the end, it is revealed that the application is for graduate school where she plans to study Anthropology. This shift from an occupation to education represents the maturation of Annie Braddock, the Nanny of the movie's title and the author of the anthropological field report on family life among the residents of the Upper East Side of Manhattan, Annie's diary that becomes part of her grad school application.

The movie's strength lies in its ability to combine comedy, satire and romance. This combination makes the role of Annie demanding and Johansson displays her talent as a comedienne as well as her ability to play an ingénue. At the same time, she can deliver biting, sarcastic lines that support the movie's satiric purpose.

But there are weaknesses in the film's script. The lengths to which Annie goes to keep the fact that she is working as a Nanny from her mother, excellently played by Donna Murphy, strains credibility. Worse, her unwillingness to give up the job because of an excessive devotion to the boy she cares for seems to make the whole thing last longer than is necessary for its points to be made. On the other hand, both of these apparent glitches can be seen to reflect Annie's innocence and immaturity and that might help explain their presence. David Denby, writing in *The New Yorker* on August 27, 2007, reasonably concludes, "The Nanny Diaries, despite many bright moments and a superior level of craftsmanship, is now a flabby urban fairy tale."[24]

The movie's makers seem aware of this fairy tale aspect and to some extent lighten it through allusions to *Mary Poppins*—the red umbrella, the logo of the Travelers Insurance Company, hoists Annie as she sets out on her adventures, and at times she is called to her cell phone when it plays "Chim-Chim-Cheree."

She also, of course, tells Grayer, the boy she takes care of, about supercalifragilisticexpialidocious. Still, most critics credit the movie's performances with those "many bright moments" and the superior craftsmanship Denby noticed. Laura Linney and Paul Giamatti play their exaggerated parts as a self-absorbed power couple admirably. Chris Evans as Annie's love interest is also excellent, and a chemistry develops between them. Alicia Keys is strong and lively as Annie's friend, Lynette. Despite this excellent cast, it is Johansson who does the heavy lifting in this slight but enjoyable film. It seems to have served to lead to bigger and better things for her.

Singing in Louisiana

In 2007 Johansson took a break from filmmaking and with Dave Sitek of the band TV on the Radio ventured to Maurice, Louisiana, and spent five weeks at the Dockside

Studio recording *Anywhere I Lay My Head*, an 11-track covers album tribute to Tom Waits. Johansson loved Waits' "beautiful melodies and distinct voice." If she were to tour, she said she'd be nervous and worry about big-time stage fright, so "user-friendly" venues would be preferred.[25]

In 2007 Johansson had performed with The Jesus & Mary Chain band at the Coachella Valley Music and Arts Festival in Indio, California. She did back-up vocals during the group's set before joining frontman Jim Reid for the chorus of "Just Like Honey."[26]

The Other Boleyn Girl (2008)

Paterfamilias Thomas Boleyn (Mark Rylance) observes to his wife, Lady Elizabeth Boleyn (Kristin Scott Thomas), that their young daughters are prime for upward mobility. Mary (Johansson) is pleasant and will make a good match, but Anne is destined for greater things. As the years pass this seems in the offing when King Henry VIII's wife Katherine of Aragon (Ana Torrent) cannot produce a male heir. The Boleyns, at the urging of Thomas' brother-in-law Thomas Howard, the Duke of Norfolk (David Morrissey), conspire to make Anne (Natalie Portman) Henry's mistress, but when during a visit to the Boleyn manse Henry (Eric Bana) engages in a stag hunt but falls from a horse and is injured, plans must be recalibrated. Mary not Anne, is entailed with ministering to Henry, who is immediately smitten. She and her new husband William Carey (Benedict Cumberbatch) are installed at court, she as a lady in waiting, he in the Privy Council. Reluctantly, Mary allows herself to be bedded by the King. Meanwhile, Anne secretly marries Henry Percy (Oliver Coleman). This discovered, Anne is castigated and sent off to France to modify her behavior, to learn at the French court how to better serve herself and her country. While Anne is abroad, Mary becomes pregnant and the Boleyn clan raised in stature. Mary conceives Henry's child and Norfolk recalls Anne, who conspires to push aside Mary and her male bastard. Anne's machinations bear fruit as Henry's marriage to Katherine is annulled and Henry breaks with Rome. Anne marries the king and becomes his queen. To her disquiet, she produces a daughter, Elizabeth. Initially Henry is glad because if a healthy daughter can be conceived, why not a healthy son? Nevertheless, he turns his eyes on Jane Seymour (Corinne Galloway). When Anne has a miscarriage, she tries to hide it by asking her brother George to mate with her, thus to produce the son the King so earnestly desires. George cannot go through with it but his wife, the former Jane Parker (Juno Temple), believes he has and informs the King's men. George is beheaded, Anne arrested and convicted of treason, adultery and incest. She is widely considered a witch. Although her meeting with Henry permits her to believe he will pardon Anne, Mary is given the King's letter on the day of execution telling her not to come to court again. On the scaffold, Anne allows that God will make the final judgment. Mary watches her sister's decapitation before hurrying inside, grabbing up Anne's child and returning to her estate. Marrying William Stafford (Eddie Redmayne), she watches over the child who will become the long-lived monarch, Elizabeth I.

Reviews

The critic for *The Blade* declared that fun would have been had if the film remained melodrama—or enlightening if it had explained the historical characters. Blame for

Japanese Chirashi mini-program for *The Other Boleyn Girl* (Columbia/Focus Features, 2008). Left to right: Eric Bana, Scarlett Johansson and Natalie Portman.

eschewing these options fell upon director Chadwick. The principals, Portman and Johansson, "didn't seem to fully embrace their roles, but Johansson's lips are becoming a distraction. They're so 'plumped' that they threaten to take over her entire face."[27] In somewhat similar mien, Roger Ebert found it "a sullen genre picture..." that one could "fantasize being made better by exploitation kingpin Russ Meyer, perhaps with the title, *Beneath the Valley of the Tudorvixens*." On a positive note, both Bana and Johansson were "enjoyable..." and with Portman were "far more attractive than period portraiture suggests."[28] The *Pittsburgh Tribune Review* found the costumes and castle innards "pretty amazing" and the story "a fairly convincing, compelling story..." Johansson and Portman did well despite being out of their "comfort zones."[29] *The Telegraph* said it targeted audiences more interested in quick pacing than historical detail. As for Johansson, her "effulgent beauty tamped down into an albino-white, almost secretive shape, much as it was in *Girl with a Pearl Earring*—succeeds in making Mary sympathetic. When she proclaims her doomed love for Henry, she is touching, not pitiable."[30]

Commentary

Johansson said Portman's presence in the picture got her interested because she'd be working with an actress of her own generation. Portman was "so professional. And she's not pretentious or anything, just a really nice girl. It also helped that she's from New

York." Portman returned the compliments, calling Johansson "an amazing actress.... She's really direct about everything she wants or feels, whereas I am a little more timid." Clubbing after work made them "allies and coconspirators."[31]

Portman added later that "This is like being with an old-time actress, like Mae West. She's brassy, like a brassy broad. A *force*."[32] On the same wavelength, *In Good Company* co-star Topher Grace said, "It's not that she's mimicking these older stars. She's got her own unique thing, and back then, actors were trained not to hide from their uniqueness."[33]

On the set, while Portman worked on the *New York Times* crossword, "Johansson kidded with the stylist, roughhoused with her Chihuahua Maggie, and danced rave-style to techno music."[34] While Portman thought she was often branded the good girl or a prude, Johansson was in her own words, "A harlot!"[35]

Of the sex scenes, Johansson said, "There are 60 people right there eating, like, salami sandwiches!" Penelope Cruz, co-star in *Vicky Cristina Barcelona*, said, "She's so open and funny and cute—I want to bite her when I see her!"[36]

Analysis

Despite a distinguished cast, magnificent sets, and lavish costumes, reviewers tend to give *The Other Boleyn Girl* a mere two to three stars. The problem seems to be that the film tries too much and achieves too little. Reviewers tend to blame the script and the direction for making a Tudor soap opera out of what might have been a costume drama with epic sweep. The downfall of two Queens, the rise and fall of a prominent family, the English Reformation, and the birth of the baby girl who will become Queen Elizabeth I are all the subjects of this movie yet they are presented with a strange sense of paralysis. The movie never fully comes to life.

Natalie Portman is thought to have been given the role with the greatest potential because she gets to play Anne Boleyn, not only far better known than her sister Mary, played by Johansson, but presented in this film as a Machiavellian woman with a cruel streak who thinks the English Reformation was merely a way for her to become Queen. In movies at least, if not in life, wickedness is more fun than goodness. Still, reviewers argue that Portman lacked the "presence" or stature to pull off the role successfully much less make the most of it.

Johansson and Eric Bana as King Henry VIII are seen as performers who provide the movie with a kind of saving grace—exceptional performances despite the dreary melodrama of the whole. The father of the Boleyn girls, Sir Thomas Boleyn, played by Mark Rylance, early in the film turns down an offer of marriage on behalf of William Carey (Benedict Cumberbatch) for Anne, described as his eldest daughter, but suggests that the match be made with Mary instead. The Careys accept this alternative and the marriage proceeds. The father's reason for this replacement of one daughter for the other is because he expects and wants his eldest daughter to make a better match. (Most historians now agree that Mary was the eldest daughter but the script in this way follows the novel on which it is based.) In conversation with his wife, a sister of the Duke of Norfolk (David Morrissey) played by Kristin Scott Thomas, Sir Thomas allows that Mary might be the fairer and kinder of his two daughters, but "To get ahead in this world you need more than fair looks and a kind heart." When Anne goes to visit Mary as she dresses for her wedding, she laments that she has been "eclipsed," not only because her younger sister is marrying first, but also because her younger sister at least on her wedding day is more attractive than Anne. "I am the other Boleyn girl," Anne tells Mary, suggesting the rivalry she feels between them while giving the picture its title.

One of the reasons reviewers praise Johansson's performance is because of its range. While she represents the "good sister" in the movie's quasi-fairy tale element, she is disappointed in her marriage, she nurses the King when he is injured, is encouraged by not only her uncle and father but also by her husband to go to court and become the King's mistress in exchange for favors and influence, and eventually gives birth to a son—the very thing the King has been striving for unsuccessfully with his Queen. Johansson is not only believable but attractive and sympathetic in all these roles and situations. When she loses her position with the King to her sister through Anne's machinations, and she and her child are sent from the court, the loss is felt by the movie as much as by her loyal friend, William Stafford (Eddie Redmayne), the man who becomes her second husband.

Johansson is perhaps at her best when Mary learns that her sister and brother are to be beheaded and rushes to court in an attempt to save them. Although she is too late to do anything for George (Jim Sturgess), she obtains an audience with the King and begs for her sister's life and believes she has received a promise from the King that Anne will be spared. Nonetheless, she becomes a witness to her sister's beheading and immediately fulfills a promise she'd made to Anne by taking the infant Elizabeth from her mother's arms and removing her to raise her with her own children. There is a sense throughout the film of the corruption of the court and the simplicity of country life and it is the latter that was Mary's natural element. In the end, the focus is on neither Anne nor Mary but rather on Elizabeth and the promise she holds for the future. No doubt the three children running in the meadow at the film's close is meant to be a reminder of Anne, Mary and George and their innocent beginning.

It is no doubt unfortunate that the movie did not fulfill its potential, but it did Scarlett Johansson's career no harm and demonstrated not only her range but also her ability to lift a film that suffers from melodrama, trite dialogue, and perhaps too little ambition of the right kind.

The Monogamy Controversy

Over the years Johansson took flack for questioning monogamy, but not for her in a committed relationship or marriage. I'm not going to be in some tarty relationship.[37] She told *Cosmopolitan*, "I don't think it's a natural instinct for human beings, but it doesn't mean I don't believe in monogamy or true love.... I believe in finding a soul mate. I've always been in monogamous relationships. I would never want to be in an open one. It'd be too awful. Monogamy can be hard work for some people. I don't think it applies to everybody, and I don't think a lot of people can do it."[38]

The Spirit (2008)

Going mano y mano on the mud flats outside a dark city, Denny Colt, aka The Spirit (Gabriel Macht), and the evil Octopus (Samuel L. Jackson) fight to a draw but the latter vows to educate this do-gooder soon. Police Commissioner Eustace Dolan (Dan Lauria) berates Denny for not following protocol. The Spirit was once a man, who has been resurrected as a crime fighter. The Angel of Death, Lorelei (Jaime King), beckons him, but he resists her entreaties. He perceives his mission in "life" to live for his city more than his female flames, which include Dolan's investigative reporter daughter Ellen (Sarah Paulson) and Sand Saref (Eva Mendes), another adversary of The Octopus who in her youth was Denny's girl. Now she's a first-class jewel thief. She and Octopus, along with his frosty minion Silken Floss (Johansson), vie for an ancient vase presumably containing the blood of Herakles. The Spirit survives another normally mortal stabbing from a belly dancing assassin and convinces Dolan he can draw out the Octopus. Sand meets Floss to trade the vase containing the blood for the chest containing Jason's fleece. The Octopus emerges from Floss's van and The Spirit arrives and is blasted by the Octopus but not killed. Attacked from all sides as he tries to drink from the vase and become immortal, the Octopus is shot by policewoman Morganstern (Stana Katic) with a high-powered weapon and blown apart by the grenade The Spirit implants under his coat. The Spirit is protected from the explosion by the Golden Fleece with which Sand covers them. The Spirit kisses Sand, and in disgust Ellen walks away. Silken Floss discovers a moving finger and says to The Octopus's minions that she will start over. "Who knows what I'll do?" The Spirit breaks free of Sand and briefly reunites with Ellen before returning to the rooftops of his only true love: The City.

Reviews

For Roger Ebert it was emotionless, a film of no substance, its "style whirling in a senseless void."[39] The *New York Times* was on target, observing that "the phrase 'the logic of the film' … may be to take the 'oxy' out of 'oxymoronic.'" It was a "sludgy, hyper-stylized adaptation of a fabled comic book series…." As for the actors, "Mr. Jackson and Ms. Johansson at least seem to enjoy themselves…." In all, it was curious that it afforded little pleasure "in spite of its efforts to be sly, sexy, heartfelt and clever all at once." It was "overstuffed" and "interminable" in its 108-minute length.[40] The *San Francisco Chronicle* said it was on a par with "*The Wild Wild West* as the worst first-date movie of all time." Worse even than *Ghost Rider*. The 150 problems with the film included dialogue, misogyny, "bloodless and limp" action, and Samuel L. Jackson's Jed Clampett hat.[41]

Scarlett Johansson, *The Spirit* (Lions Gate/Oddlot Entertainment, 2008).

Commentary

One wonders if Johansson did *The Spirit* as a favor. According to *Allure* (December 2008), Frank Miller wrote the femme fatale part for her and opined that as well as her beauty, her wit created a desire to concoct a part for her. So he took the minor character Silken Floss and dressed her so flamboyantly that she'd become an alluring but unapproachable male fantasy. "And Scarlett played it to perfection."[42]

The critical and financial failure of *The Spirit* was a speed bump in Johansson's trajectory, but because of its rapid disappearance from theaters it hardly registered with the public. Nor did it stymie Samuel L. Jackson's career. It did, however, put the brakes on big-screen, leading man success for Gabriel Macht's. He's had more success on TV in *Suits*.

Analysis

If it is the duty of Johansson fans to see all of her films, this one is double duty. The preceding critical comments are accurate. The film was a disaster, financially and for the most part critically. Almost from the git-go, tedious conversations compromise the pace, especially a chat between Dan Lauria and Sarah Paulson that stops the film dead in its tracks. Johansson is window dressing as The Octopus' minion and doesn't appear until the movie is well underway.

It's spoofy and stylish like *Sin City* (2005), which was co-directed and co-written by Frank Miller who's at the helm here, but it's also a bore, and doesn't mix well its humor and savagery. It seems obvious that there was no mass audience for this superhero film. It opened in over 2,000 theaters but did poorly and almost instantly became a film one needed to seek out.

The character of *The Spirit* was known to aficionados of Will Eisner comic strips, but no Superman, Batman or Captain America he. In various ways the film differed from its source. The Octopus's face was not seen in the comics.

Marriage

On September 27, 2008, Johansson, who'd been dating Ryan Reynolds since April 2007, wed the Canadian-born actor. Wanting seclusion, the couple found it at the Clayoquot Wilderness Resort on Vancouver Island, British Columbia, which was reachable only by seaplane or boat. A source said, "Scarlett's the big personality of the two, but he keeps her on her toes. It's a great balance."[43]

Later Johansson told *Cosmopolitan* that "This is a very beautiful time for me.... Getting married is a huge moment in anyone's life, and the few months leading up to it were a little crazy. But Ryan and I are in love and we're enjoying evolving our relationship together. I feel that my life and my work are heading in the right direction."[44]

What about fame and its pitfalls? "My head is screwed on pretty good.... I live a very private and modest lifestyle and I have great friends—who are not actors—and a great family. I know I've had a one-in-a-million chance given to me with my career and I feel very lucky.... It helps that I've always been so career-focused.... I have three films out in 2009 that I'm really proud of. Being in work mode prevents me from going into Hollywood starlet mode, I suppose."[45]

Sexpot

Later in the year she addressed the "sexpot thing." By her late teens she'd adapted to it because "You're realizing your own sexuality…,and you're kind of coming into your own womanhood…." She didn't think about being sexy and seductive because trying to be sexy is "the most unsexy thing."[46]

Her success hinged on being "an actor for hire" and to remember that she was disposable. That mindset was necessary to battle for the roles an actor wants.[47]

He's Just Not That Into You (2009)

In contemporary Baltimore, five young middle class women experience hope and heartbreak in their search for romantic fulfillment: Beth (Jennifer Aniston), who wants marriage with a recalcitrant significant other (Ben Affleck); Janine (Jennifer Connelly), consumed by supervising a new home while her hubby Ben (Bradley Cooper) follows his roving eye; Mary (Drew Barrymore), constantly let down by men; Anna (Johansson), looking for singing success and enamored of the married Ben; and Gigi (Ginnifer Goodwin), who can't read the signals men give her. They live, love and learn. Three achieve a measure of happiness.

Reviews

The *New York Times* found fault with the film "based on an obnoxious so-called advice book…." The few good moments were supplied by Connelly and Johansson, both playing for the affections of Bradley Cooper, "who doesn't deserve either of them." Johansson's character "is, of course, the designated bad girl … but the role doesn't stick. Ms. Johansson seems too comfortable in her own beautiful skin to pay attention to wagging fingers, particularly when they belong to a twerp like Conor…." That match "makes no sense. She's Scarlett Johansson, for goodness' sake!"[48] *The Guardian* called it "An unendurable relationship-romcom…" to be avoided like Anthrax. Its stars were "dead-eyed mid-career thirtysomethings who do not appear to be carbon-based lifeforms…."[49] *SFGate* found it "surprisingly likable." And, "It remains brisk, engaging and pleasant throughout…"

Scarlett Johansson at *He's Just Not That Into You* world premiere, Grauman's Chinese Theater, CA, February 2, 2009 (Tinseltown/Shutterstock.com).

even if it never soared. Johansson's Woody Allen exposure has paid off: "In just a few years, she has become a deft comic actress."[50]

Commentary

The film was based on the popular self-help book by Greg Behrendt and Liz Tuccillo. It became a star-studded film many women found painful if not offensive, but it did make money.

All of the actresses had about equal time. In her final scene, Johansson is shown singing "Last Goodbye," a torch song in a club but is not heard under Ginnifer Goodwin's narration. The complete song segment is presented on the DVD extras.

Theresa Russell played Johansson's mom but their scenes were cut from the final print.

Johansson told an interviewer she took the role because the women characters "weren't victimized and weren't dainty and cute. It's about the lies you tell yourself to get through the pain of recognizing that this person is unavailable."[51]

Analysis

He's Just Not That Into You covers the relationships of five young women and four young men as they go through various permutations. The underlying theme of the movie is that relationships are difficult largely because of social attitudes toward gender that reflect the way we are raised. What is more, their difficulty has been increased by the widespread use of social media. Mary, played by Drew Barrymore, at one point complains she'd been rejected by "seven different portals." On the other hand, because this is a romantic comedy, the overriding sense is that despite the difficulties involved relationships are not only valuable but necessary. Although none of the characters in the movie become parents, marriage appears to continue to be considered the ultimate relationship.

Scarlett Johansson plays Anna, a yoga instructor who wants to pursue a career as a singer and so represents the freest spirit among the young women portrayed. She is the most sexually active of them, too. Although she no longer sleeps with Connor (Kevin Connolly), she maintains her friendship with him and on at least one occasion, goes to bed with him again when feeling rejected by another man. She also actively pursues Ben (Bradley Cooper), despite the fact that he told her that he is married and attempted to put her off for that reason.

It is no doubt Anna's disregard for the rights and feelings of others that leads her to face the most painful and humiliating of all the situations the young women experience. Following an audition Ben arranged for Anna, they return to his office. He locks the door and they prepare to have sex on his desk—something she is not only willing but eager to do. At that moment, Ben's wife, Janine (Jennifer Connelly), knocks on the door, determined to make love with her husband in an attempt to save their marriage after he admitted to her the day before that he had slept with someone else.

Ben quickly forces Anna into a closet where she must wait while Ben and his wife make love. After Janine has gone, Ben opens the closet door and Anna rushes out, denouncing him as "disgusting" and stating that she never wants to see him again.

This role is in a way made for Johansson. Her blonde hair, her body, and her looks make her appear as an almost stereotypical free spirit in an age of relative sexual looseness. She is completely credible when called upon to strip off her clothes and ostensibly swim naked in a pool or to eagerly make love on a desk in an office. On the other hand, she is also credible when Conor expresses the wish to buy a house to share with her and she must be honest enough to tell him that is not something that she will ever want. The part of Anna is not an especially large one, but it is unlike any of the others and it certainly suits Johansson's attributes and talents. The picture is better than it might otherwise have been because of her performance.

Singer

In September 2009 Johansson's CD *Break Up* was released. It was a collaboration with Pete Yorn, who said Johansson reminded him of Brigitte Bardot's "confident sexiness" and je ne sais quoi. He thought Johansson possessed of an awesome voice.[52]

New Agent

Her mother Melanie was Johansson's agent until 2009.[53] Rick Yorn became her new agent.[54]

Banter: *The Late Late Show with Craig Ferguson*

Iron Man 2 (see Chapter 7) had premiered in Los Angeles on April 26, 2010, and in anticipation of its May 7 general release, Johansson appeared on the CBS late night TV show *The Late Late Show with Craig Ferguson* on May 5. The episode began with a clip from that latest Marvel movie, with Ferguson telling his guest, "I like the look of this film."

Almost immediately was rapport created, with Ferguson complimenting Johansson's appearance, dress "and your hair all uber on us." Johansson responded, "Why thank you, thank you very much. It's just for you." Ferguson asked, "Is it really?" to which Johansson replied, "It is. No. I just came from a dinner, actually."

Johansson told the host that her *Iron Man 2* character was named Black Widow, a master of hand-to-hand combat.

They good-naturedly sniped at each other on such topics as multi-tasking, Ferguson's straight-man robot Geoff, international bacon, Danish philosopher Kierkegaard, addictions (none at present), exercise equipment TV ads, the White House Correspondents Dinner with President Obama, Johansson's hair ("I grew it out of my very own head"), her dogs, tattoos, the Tony nomination for *A View from the Bridge*, and her love for the country.

Broadway

In 2009 Johansson told an interviewer she had a hankering to appear on Broadway but maybe not in musical theater. Her "terrible stage fright" evidenced itself when she became a teenager, not when she was a child.[55]

In fact, Johansson was about to appear in the latest revival of Arthur Miller's *A View from the Bridge*, which was first shown on Broadway in 1956. It opened at the Cort Theatre on Broadway on January 24 and concluded on April 4, 2010. Catherine (Johansson) played the niece her uncle (l Schreiber) had a sketchy attraction to. At the 64th Annual Tony Awards held on June 13, 2010, Johansson won the Tony Award for Best Performance by a Featured Actress in a Play.

Michael Musto of *The Village Voice* found her "fairly unrecognizable!… But I spotted the little devil right away!… Yes, she's a bit too old for the character—and sure, she occasionally acts too small, as if doing it for cameras, not for the balcony." Nonetheless, she possessed the appropriate instincts and accent, and would "surely grow as an actor from this experience, and for that alone, it was worth it."[56]

The *New York Times* called this latest revival a "beautifully observed production…" of a play that could be revisited often "as long as there are performers with strong, original voices and fresh insights." In the presence of complete actor Liev Schreiber and stage veteran Jessica Hecht, Johansson held her own. Contrasted with the "dim performances from bright screen stars, including Julia Roberts and Katie Holmes," she melted "into her character so thoroughly that her nimbus of celebrity disappears."[57]

Of Johansson, Schreiber said, "She had no idea about blocking or that you have to project in what sometimes feels like an artificial way to reach the back of the house." She was confounded, but open to suggestions, and "through sheer intelligence and perseverance she made that role happen."

On winning the Tony, Johansson said it was a life-changing moment. "It was unbelievable holding that Tony."[58]

The eight shows a week schedule left her exhausted: "It almost killed me. Then the arms unfold and you're pushed out of the nest. I didn't really know what to do with myself.… There was nothing that was interesting to me." Part of her ennui was caused by her separation from husband Ryan Reynolds.[59]

In the December 2010 *GQ* her interviewer praised Johansson's versatility: her gameness, ability to easily try on different guises, sing duets with Peter Yorn, appear in fashion magazines, "and all the while still seem genuinely like the observant, inquisitive (and very cute) girl in transition we finally fell for in *Lost in Translation*."[60]

Elstowe Manor

In July 2011 a major photo shoot took place far from La La Land but only a couple hours from the Big Apple. Johansson and a *Vanity Fair* crew, including photographer Mario Sorrenti, disembarked from their caravan at Elstowe Manor outside Philadelphia. Built in 1898, the Italian Renaissance–style building was the centerpiece of the 42-acre estate that had been the summer home of William L. Elkins, Pennsylvania Railroad Company magnate. Later it became a Dominican Sisters retreat, part of the Land Conservancy of Elkins Park, and a venue for weddings and other events.[61]

Franklin & Bash (TV, July 20, 2011)

In that first season's eighth episode, "The Bangover," Jared Franklin (Breckin Meyer) tells Peter Bash (Mark-Paul Gosselaar), "In fact, I would consider swearing off sex for the rest of my life for one night with Scarlett."

Hacker Scandal

Johansson had sent nude pictures of herself to hubby Ryan Reynolds, and those were hacked in 2011. She wasn't the only one. Mila Kunis was also targeted by Christopher Chaney, who was found out, pled guilty and was sentenced to 10 years in prison. Johansson would tell Howard Stern in 2017 that "It was absolutely shocking and devastating at the time.... I just felt like, as a woman, I felt like it's such a degrading and awful thing to have to go through that." And, "It feels particularly invasive when you are in the public eye and you're like, 'What else can I give you?'"[62]

Divorce

Regarding her split and July 2011 divorce from Ryan Reynolds, "Getting married was the right thing to do because it was natural." Nevertheless, "Relationships are complicated … and being married is a living, breathing process. I think I was not fully aware of the peaks and the valleys. I wasn't prepared to hunker down and do the work." Their busy schedules cut into their time together.[63]

Privacy Concerns

Johansson was asked on CNN why privacy was so important to one so much in the limelight. She responded,

> The question is sort of redundant in that sense. I mean, who doesn't want to protect their own privacy? … Just because you're in the spotlight or just because you're an actor or make films or whatever doesn't mean that you're not entitled to your own personal privacy, and I think … no matter what the context … if that is sieged in some way it, it feels unjust, it feels wrong. And I've, I've gotten that response from many people that I've met, how … they say, "How do you deal with the invasion of privacy?" And I … don't know. To me it's, it's an adjustment but it's certainly … certain instances, I think, where … you give a lot of yourself and then finally you just have to kind of put your foot down and say, I'm taking, I'm taking it back.[64]

Avatar and Climate Change

In 2011 she told an interviewer that raising children was serious business in light of climate change. She thought *Avatar 2* might inform them. She'd seen it in IMAX 3-D. "I sat there with my humongous popcorn, giant soda, Raisinets, and those ridiculous glasses. I practically got a bladder infection because I didn't want to leave my seat the whole time. It was so amazing. I love that moviegoing experience. I *love* it."[65]

We Bought a Zoo (2011)

The recently widowed Benjamin Mee (Matt Damon) quits his job as a globe-hopping writer and uses inheritance money to purchase a home in the country and spend more time with his children. To his surprise, the house is mated with a rustic zoo: Rosemoor. Against his brother's (Thomas Haden Church) advice, Benjamin decides to chance it. Still and all, family squabbles continue, and there are issues with the head zookeeper Kelly (Johansson), who confronts him over whether to euthanize the ailing 17-year-old tiger. As they prepare the compound for inspection, it is learned that Benjamin's credit cards have been maxed out. Succor arrives in the form of $84,000 left him in a safe deposit box by his late wife. He uses this to spruce up the compound and feed the animals. It seems everything, including the weather, conspires to deter visitors on opening day, but the sunshine returns and a massive crowd clambers over the downed trees blocking auto access. Even Benjamin's brother is impressed, as is Kelly, who gives him a passionate kiss.

Reviews

The *Los Angeles Times* called it that rare item, an "intelligent family film...." Although it wasn't the best thing director Crowe had done, it was imbued with "his humanistic imprint and benefits from a strong acting ensemble that keep emotions in check." Johansson was "apple-crisp" as the zookeeper.[66] The *New Zealand Herald* called it "a sentimental affair with a storyline for every member of the family." Johansson "makes the right call by doing this film makeup-less and there's a nice chemistry between her and Damon, although convincing us she's really a zookeeper is still a stretch."[67] The *Tulsa World* said it was "not oozing with sappy schmaltz; rather, it's a movie that's simply so free of cynicism that it's a rarity these days...." Matt Damon gave "a deftly balanced performance...." As for Johansson's lead zookeeper, "there is an immediate thought that she is an obvious love interest for Benjamin, but the movie is smart in this handling, considering how hard Benjamin carries the torch for his wife's memory. It means a subtle performance is required of Johansson, and she seems to welcome the challenge."[68]

Scarlett Johansson, *We Bought a Zoo* (20th Century–Fox, 2011).

Commentary

Johansson had wanted to work with director Cameron Crowe (*Singles, Say Anything, Jerry Maguire, Almost Famous*). In an effort at verisimilitude, she opted not to wear makeup.[69] Crowe himself said that "she's so good, she makes you forget how incredibly beautiful she is."[70]

Johansson herself said it was not about playing "an object of desire" and "finding Mr. Right or being taken care of." She'd done enough of that.[71]

Two years later, a *Vanity Fair* interviewer thought Johansson's decision to honor her commitment to *We Bought a Zoo* seemed a missed opportunity that Johansson hadn't played Daisy in Baz Lurhrmann's *The Great Gatsby*. After all, Daisy had a "husky, rhythmic whisper … that's full of money."[72] Carey Mulligan got the role after Johansson, one of the serious contenders, decided to stick with *We Bought a Zoo*, which was slated to begin production in the late spring of 2011. *Gatsby* was to begin filming that summer.[73]

Johansson received a Teen Choice Awards nomination for Actress: Drama.

Analysis

The most important character in *We Bought a Zoo* is a ghost. Although the death of the wife of Benjamin Mee and the mother of his children occurs before the film starts, her memory and spirit, her ghost, triggers the plot and dominates the action.

The movie actually ends with an imaginative family reunion. Benjamin (Matt Damon) takes Dylan (Colin Ford), the fourteen-year-old, and Rosie (Maggie Elizabeth Jones), the seven-year-old, to the coffee shop where he and his wife first met. As he tells the story of their meeting, he conjures her ghost and Katherine Mee (Stephanie Szostak) appears, in fact. This imaginative reunion provides the film's happy ending and emphasizes the importance and power of this ghost.

Most critics thought of the movie as mediocre and tended to blame the director, Cameron Crowe, for the film's faults—its sentimentality, its formulaic quality, and its resulting predictability. On the other hand, they tended to credit Matt Damon's performance with keeping the film from being a complete disaster. The plot basically consists of a series of obstacles that are overcome through a combination of hard work, luck, the skill and dedication of the zoo's staff, and the intervention from beyond the grave of Benjamin's wife who left enough assets in a safe deposit box to allow him and his crew to complete work on the zoo so that it can be licensed and reopened. The plot's arc moves from winter—February—to summer, the zoo reopening on July 7, a kind of festive, communal celebration meant to show that life goes on and all will be well.

Johansson plays the part of Kelly Foster, the head zookeeper of the property Benjamin buys. As a result, her relationship with Benjamin is professional and, in several ways, awkward. She has the expertise, but he has the power, the authority. They need each other if the zoo is to be a success, but there is a tension between them. The relationship starts on a shaky basis when Kelly directly asks Benjamin, "Why did you buy this place?" She's learned from colleagues that he has no experience in the field and no history of working with animals other than his family's dog. Benjamin responds, "Why not"—an evasion as much as an answer that we only learn at the end of the film is an echo of what his wife said to him the day they met.

Another difference between Kelly and Benjamin is early established when Kelly corrects his use of the term "cages" to describe where the animals in the zoo live. "They are enclosures. They haven't been called cages in a hundred years. My marriage was a cage." Benjamin learns to use the term "enclosures" but makes the point, "My marriage wasn't." Their very different experiences of marriage add to the tension between them.

Because the relationship between Benjamin and Kelly never fully becomes romantic much less a sexual one, their growing closeness must be seen through the gradual improvement of the zoo and the morale and dedication of its eccentric staff members. What this means for Johansson's part is that she cannot play the typical clichés, she can't rely completely on looks or sensuality, and so in fact has to play a dramatic role—a distinctive character who performs a difficult and at times dirty job in non-glamourous circumstances. She pulls it off exceedingly well.

She has to intervene to try and convince Benjamin that despite his emotional need for an ill and aging tiger to survive, he must recognize that it is best for the tiger that he be spared the pain of a slow, excruciating death. When Dylan mistreats a garter snake, she makes clear to his father that the boy's behavior is unacceptable—a risky subject for an employee to raise with a boss in any circumstances much less in the emotionally charged atmosphere of a grieving family.

On the other hand, it is necessary to the story that an attraction between them be established even though it never goes beyond their kissing on learning that they've sold out their tickets on the first day of the zoo's reopening. The one potential element of the movie's formula Cameron Crowe resisted was to have Benjamin and Kelly become a couple, exorcising the dead wife's ghost through a replacement. If that decision made Johansson's part more nuanced and difficult, it also prevented the movie from indulging in what might have been the very worst of possible clichés.

The Strategy

Although Johansson had claimed in 2005 not to be focused on indie films,[74] in 2011 she adopted "a one-for-me, one-for-them strategy," following a low-budget indie with a big action film.[75]

Golden Camera Awards 2012

On February 4, 2012, Johansson attended the Golden Camera Awards in Berlin, Germany to receive the Best International Actress award. Denzel Washington was accorded Best International Actor.[76] The Associated Press added that Johansson's future *Lucy* co-star Morgan Freeman was honored with a lifetime achievement award.[77]

Another Singing Stint

Chasing Ice (2012) was a documentary sounding the alarm on the shrinking Alaska, Iceland, and Greenland ice caps. Johansson and Joshua Bell sang the song "Before My Time," which received a Best Original Song nomination by the Academy of Motion Picture Arts and Sciences.

Hitchcock (2012)

"Ed Gein's Farmhouse, Wisconsin 1944."
"Chicago, July 8, 1959."
After the success of *North by Northwest,* director Alfred Hitchcock (Anthony Hopkins)

is at a loss about what to do next. Shouldn't he retire, a reporter asks? He's sixty and the most famous film director ever. Given a copy of Robert Bloch's novel *Psycho*, he convinces his wife Alma (Helen Mirren) that this would be something different. Paramount, however, isn't keen to bankroll it so Hitch and his agent agree to pony up the funds even if it means—and it does—mortgaging their house. What about casting? Grace Kelly is now a princess, says Alma, and Hitch's one-time bête-noire, Vera Miles (Jessica Biel) remains in his doghouse for becoming pregnant just before *Vertigo* was to start filming. Alma proposes Janet Leigh (Johansson) and Hitch agrees to make her Marion and furthermore, to kill her off not halfway through the film, but on Alma's advice, a half-hour into it. Filming progresses even as Hitch battles Geoffrey Shurlock (Kurtwood Smith) of the Motion Picture Association of America's Production Code Administration. After all, the film has unsavory episodes, including a toilet. Paramount has plans to release the film in only a few locations, but Hitch and his agent Lew Wasserman (Michael Stuhlbarg) devise a sweeping publicity plan that works. The audience goes wild. During the production Alma helped writer Whitfield Cook (Danny Huston) on his project, and Hitch became jealous. Alma retorts that she has always given her all. What about the mortgage? They reconcile. Hitch wonders for the audience what his next film will be as a crow lands on his shoulder.

Reviews

Roger Ebert found the subplot of Hitchcock's marriage to Alma distracting from what was purported to be a movie about the making of *Psycho*. He suggested the film was skewed toward being a "woman's picture...." James D'Arcy was fine as Anthony Perkins. "Scarlett Johansson, as Janet Leigh, doesn't look a lot like the original but projects her spunk, intelligence and sense of humor."[78] The *New York Times* said, "The movie has its diversions, including Scarlett Johansson's bodacious Janet Leigh and Michael Stuhlbarg's wheedling Lew Wasserman."[79] *Time* called it "a feel-good frolic, which is fine for those who prefer their Hitchcock history tidied up...." As for Johansson, she "captures Leigh's perky sex appeal...."[80] The *Pittsburgh Post Gazette* thought that the cast and provenance would make it "a magnet for movie lovers." Johansson was a "sunny Janet Leigh...."[81]

Scarlett Johansson as Janet Leigh, *Hitchcock* (Fox Searchlight Pictures, 2012).

Commentary

There was a fair amount of pre-release hype and Johansson was on the cover of *V Magazine* in a lighthearted homage to the shower sequence in *Psycho*. However, the theatrical venues were marginal at best.

While filming *Hitchcock* it was said that this analysis of the making of 1960's *Psycho* would be a sure Academy Award nomination-gathering film. After all, Anthony Hopkins was playing the master of suspense and Helen Mirren his wife. The final product came and went without much attention. It was a decent effort, a good film, but not spectacular.

Of Janet Leigh, Johansson said, "She was used to holding up the façade of being America's Sweetheart.... With Hitch, she allowed herself to be girly, to be naughty, to play games—to be innocent together."[82]

For the Blu-Ray, Johansson said, "I love these kind of movies. I like the idea of portraying an actor who is, you know, amidst the process of finding a character and, and collaborating with the director and ... that behind-the-scenes piece, I just think it's, it's a kind of a rare opportunity that a script like that comes along."[83]

Asked about watching Hitchcock movies growing up, Johansson said, "My mom was a huge movie buff. We had the whole collection. Of course we watched *Psycho*, but I was always terrified of it.... And *Vertigo*, which I never understood until I got older."[84]

As for duplicating the famous shower sequence, Johansson's preparation for the one-day shoot consisted of accepting the fact that she'd get very wet. The crew "were concerned with modesty and all these things—but I don't care about any of that stuff and Janet Leigh never did either. You have got to be brave, get into the shower, and face Anthony Hopkins as Hitchcock jabbing you in the face with a 12-inch kitchen knife...."[85]

Analysis

It is hard to imagine that Scarlett Johansson did not thoroughly enjoy playing the voluptuous, perky, and down-to-earth Janet Leigh in *Hitchcock*, the film directed by Sacha Gervasi that details the economic, psychic, and marital strains and tensions behind the making of *Psycho*. Johansson first appears in a dress that makes the most of her curves for a lunch with Hitchcock and his wife Alma in a Hollywood restaurant. The discussion focuses in part on the famous bathtub scene and Janet mentions that while she is an actress, she is also a wife and mother and so is concerned about the parts she plays. This straight-faced statement provides the perfect opening for Hitchcock's vaguely sardonic but playful assurance of his own desire for good taste. From this point on, the film depicts the apparently good relationship that existed on the picture between director and leading lady.

The movie also benefits from the depiction of Janet Leigh's relationships with both Alma, Hitchcock's wife, played by Helen Mirren, and Vera Miles, played by Jessica Biel. Alma is used to Hitchcock's obsessions with his leading ladies but can nonetheless be bothered by them. Leigh's smiling "professionalism," as Alma calls it, is not only appreciated but a kind of relief. The scenes with Biel are especially interesting. For two contemporary actresses to play the parts of two famous Hollywood stars of the past has an inherent interest that is heightened here because of the apparently poor relationship Miles had had with Hitchcock. She warns Leigh against letting Hitchcock learn much about her family and home life because of his attempts to control every aspect of a leading lady's life. Johansson warmly portrays Leigh handling this potentially awkward situation by driving Hitchcock home in her VW Beetle—"This is a SMALL car," the big man comically sighs—and offers him candy corn from a bag that had been left in the car by one of her children. Johansson's smiling common sense almost always wards off the director's slightly sinister air.

When the smile disappears is in the shooting of the bathtub scene. From his director's chair Hitchcock repeatedly calls for more rage and slashing until he ultimately clambers out of the chair, takes the knife himself, and slashes in the direction of Janet Leigh with it. Although she had looked frightened up until this point, her face changes in a way that suggests both terror and disbelief—as if she is unable to convince herself that the director would act in this way. Johansson's face is utterly convincing in this important close-up and reflects what might well have been Janet Leigh's actual experience.

The part of Janet Leigh is a relatively small but crucial one in this movie on the making of *Psycho*. Johansson plays it with a sure touch and a sense that she must have had fun in the role.

W Interview (2012)

The 40th Anniversary issue of *W* magazine featured a "Scarlett Johansson Rocks the 1990s" cover plus two-page Dolce & Gabbana spread. Prior to arriving for the interview, Johansson had been supporting President Obama at the Democratic National Convention, championing "the power of the individual rather than any particular issue...." Through her films, from *Lost in Translation* to *The Avengers*, Johansson has consistently evoked a mix of sexuality, restlessness, and strength." In the forthcoming *Hitchcock*, she will essay Janet Leigh's character in *Psycho*, although it is impossible to picture her as an immobile stabbing victim. "She would stab right back."

Johansson identified comedian Chris Farley as her favorite person of the nineties and *Jurassic Park* her favorite film of the decade. "This is going to happen, you guys." On the fashion front, she hated '90s turtlenecks—practical, "But they're just so unfortunate."[86]

A Golden Age/A Plentitude of Scarlett

From September 2013 to August 2014, Johansson gave her fans a bonanza of significant films: *Don Jon* (general U.S. release September 2013), *Her* (limited U.S. release December 2013; general release January 2014), *Under the Skin* (general U.S. release, April 2014), *Captain America: The Winter Soldier* (general U.S. release, April 2014), *Chef* (general U.S. release, May 2014), and *Lucy* (general U.S. release, July 2014).

Don Jon was a generally well-received comedy-drama from newbie director, actor Joseph Gordon-Levitt; *Her* a near future story of ennui and a search for meaning for which Johansson provided not a face and body but her distinctive seductive voice for a computer operating system; it won an Academy Award for original screenplay; *Under the Skin* an alien seduction tale—or was it?; boring to those who required definitive answers, to others a genuine masterpiece about what it means to be human; *Captain America: The Winter Soldier* a rip-roaring "Avengers" movie in which Johansson shed her mascot duties for full-fledged equality with her comrades; *Chef* a mouth-watering family film (except for some cursing) that became a sleeper hit; and *Lucy*, Luc Besson's crazy, fabulously entertaining science fiction movie that hit it big with almost a half billion dollars in ticket sales—which would doubtless have been more if not for the R rating (for violence).

Don Jon (2013)

Don Jon (Joseph Gordon-Levitt) is a modern-day north Jersey Lothario with simple needs: "my body, my pad, my ride, my family, my church, my boys, my girls, my porn." In fact, although he beds hotties on a regular basis, he can only find supreme sexual gratification watching pornographic videos on the web. Imagine his surprise when he spots a blonde goddess, a "dime," during one of his nights out. Using Facebook, he identifies her as Barbara Sugarman (Johansson). She agrees to meet for an al fresco lunch and the two become entwined, but not sexually—yet. She wants Don to improve his life, go to night school. He does and soon they are physically intimate. Yet one evening he leaves her in his bed and turns on the Mac. She catches him and is disgusted but he makes her believe it was a video sent by a friend. He promises not to watch porn and for a while honors his pledge. When Barbara checks his web history, she discovers the lie. He says all men watch porn and it's no different than her fixation on unrealistic romance movies. Don's mother Angela (Glenne Headly) is distraught when he breaks up with Barbara. His sister Monica (Brie Larson) is not, telling him Barbara was trying to make him into what she wanted, not what was best for him. Don, meanwhile, has begun an affair with a classmate, Esther (Julianne Moore)

Scarlett Johansson, *Don Jon* **(Voltage Pictures, 2013).**

Joseph Gordon-Levitt and Scarlett Johansson, *Don Jon* (Voltage Pictures, 2013).

an older woman he learns lost her husband and child in an auto accident fourteen months before. Opening up to her, Don finds a sympathetic ear. She tells him that the only way he can truly "lose himself" is when he treats a lover as an equal partner and is considerate of her feelings. With this revelation, Don meets Barbara at a restaurant where he tries to apologize for lying to her. She doesn't recognize the sincerity of his revelation nor that he's a changed man and tells him not to call her again. Don returns to Esther, not intending marriage or anything but going with the flow. He's off porn and accepts Esther as a co-equal lover.

Reviews

The *New York Times* called Johansson "superb."[87] *Fresh Air* said the movie was "wide-eyed and open hearted" and Johansson's Jersey Girl was "so fast she's dizzying. She detonates every Jersey-girl diphthong. When Barbara finally gives in to Don Jon, she plays the long game, molding her man, ordering him to go back to college and rise above the, quote, service class. But alas, he can't quite quit his porn habit, and when Barbara discovers it, she's repulsed. It's not just that she thinks it's for losers. It stands for a string on him she can't pull."[88]

Entertainment Weekly commended Joseph Gordon-Levitt for pulling off a movie concerning itself with the psychological effects of pornography. Moreover, he'd done it "in a light, fun, unlaborious way...."[89] *The Leader-Telegram* wasn't entirely sold on the ending but praised the overall tone and Gordon-Levitt's decision to tell a story exclusively from the man's point of view. Like 1997's *Chasing Amy*, it is heartily recommended for young men who must know the difference between "passionate love-making and carnal sex...."[90]

Commentary

Like Stanley Kubrick's *Eyes Wide Shut*, *Don Jon* was a film that caused some audience members to walk out, this time in the first few minutes as Gordon-Leavitt's character is shown having orgasms while watching computer porn. It perhaps proves that many people are not paying attention. *Eyes Wide Shut* was Kubrick's last film and attracted people for that reason despite the R rating, which in that case was based not only on foul language but nudity. *Don Jon* was also R-rated, so what did people expect?

Leavitt spoke with Johansson about her role helping to transform her image. She didn't deserve to be thought of merely as a beautiful girl and objectified. "When I was writing the script, I always had her in mind."[91]

Johansson said she knew the type of girl she was playing, Short Hills, New Jersey-style. "You couldn't just have Barbara be this Jessica Rabbit, materialistic, unsympathetic type—there's nothing to mine in that. On the other hand, you can't just have her be the victim of this misogynistic, self-absorbed man. I wanted her to be extremely pure and totally honest with herself. She has such a good heart."[92]

Johansson thought the film was "about the way we consume media.... This kind of virtual reality that we live in, which sounds so '90s—remember that? This idea that we can very easily separate ourselves from human interaction because we can fill voids artificially."[93]

Analysis

Barbara Sugarman, despite her curves, is a flat character—that is, she undergoes no change throughout the movie. Don Jon, the title character, on the other hand, goes through a metamorphosis from a young man who pronounces "making love" with audible quotation marks to someone who pronounces the phrase in a straightforward way, without the quotation marks that imply contempt for the idea.

Barbara is mostly a comic character, a satirized stereotype, and so her flatness is not only understandable but necessary. As a result, Johansson in this picture appears as a character actor because of her dress, makeup, and voice, an accent reminiscent of that of Marisa Tomei in *My Cousin Vinny* (1992), rather than as a traditional cliché. She is not only sex personified and objectified, but also sex weaponized in the battle of the sexes, a negotiation tool she uses to manipulate and control Jon and, no doubt, men in general. Her performance is at once over the top and credible.

One of the most interesting aspects of Barbara's manipulative character is her addiction to romantic films, films that indicate, as far as she is concerned, that a real man will do *anything* for his true love. This addiction to a false world of movies is clearly meant to parallel Jon's addiction to online pornography. Both addictions lead to a dissatisfaction with reality that leads to a wish to manipulate and control members of the opposite sex.

Because the movie's aim is to explode clichés, it is not an especially good one. There is something limited about a male lead who is addicted to two kinds of masturbation—with a partner and with online pornography. The fact that Barbara is able to persuade Jon to let her meet his friends and his family, and can even convince him to sign up for a night course, by sending him home in semen-stained jeans, does nothing to decrease his addiction to pornography. That failure and his unwillingness to turn the cleaning of his apartment over to Barbara's housekeeper are for her deal breakers. One of the funniest moments in the film comes when Barbara insists that Jon stop talking about wanting to buy a Swiffer while they are shopping.

Jon's conversion late in the film, his learning to make love after meeting Esther, played by Julianne Moore, at night school, an older woman suffering from grief for the loss of her husband and son in a car accident, provides a sweet but incredible ending—an attempt to pin a valentine on a satirization of stereotypical behaviors and attitudes.

Contains Multitudes

At this time, filmmaker Darren Aronofsky (*Requiem for a Dream*, *The Wrestler*, *Black Swan*) conducted one of the best interviews with Johansson, who "has a certain appeal." She hadn't let her talent "transform into a black hole of tetchy method madness." Nor was her beauty "hesitant ... on screen, she is a focus magnet—but not inaccessible." Further, in her trajectory since *Lost in Translation*, "her precocious ingénue halo has also quietly dissipated, and she has grown into a woman who clearly contains multitudes...." She'd kept her integrity and soul intact despite occasionally "doing different things, occasionally pleasantly weird or challenging things, and deftly hop-scotching around all of the landmines...."[94]

Street of Dreams

At the behest of Dolce and Gabbana, in November 2013 director Martin Scorsese used his familiarity with New York City to co-star Johansson and Matthew McConaughey in the black and white Dolce and Gabbana commercial to promote the fragrance The One under the title, *Street of Dreams*.

Designer Domenico Dolce and collaborator Stefano Gabbana waxed enthusiastic for a *Daily Mail* interviewer. For Dolce, Johansson "lives and breathes every womanly nuance." Gabbana considered her beauty "multidimensional." Johansson responded to the question why she was chosen to represent their fragrance The One by saying, "Because I am an actor and all actors think that they are The One." As for the film itself, she really appreciated the chance to portray "a modern version of a charming, devilish, independent Fellini-esque woman." She had a lot of fun making it with Matthew McConaughey and Martin Scorsese, and shooting in New York was "inspirational."

Johansson said she wanted to challenge herself with diverse roles in order to break the stereotype and noted how Brad Pitt never let the label of "so gorgeous" prevent him from being a character actor, which had always been her goal. She admitted to having a "very strong work ethic."[95]

7

She Plays Big

The Marvel Universe

> "They are powerful, vulnerable, multi-faceted. They have a drive. Of course they kick ass, but the excitement for me is bringing depth to characters in a genre that can be very flat. That's empowering."
> —Scarlett Johansson in *Cosmopolitan*, May 2016

The Marvel Cinematic Universe sprang from Marvel Comics, its protagonists various superheroes and heroines sometimes labeled "enhanced humans." The rise of CGI (Computer-Generated Imagery) made it feasible to translate these adventures to the big screen with increasing realism. *Iron Man* (2008) was the first of the new superhero films and its success spawned a franchise. In the guise of former Soviet spy and assassin Natasha Romanoff, aka Black Widow, Johansson joined the troop for *Iron Man 2* (2010). As one critic perspicaciously observed, she remained little more than a mascot in *Iron Man 2* and *The Avengers*.[1]

Iron Man 2 (2010)

Nursing a grudge against Tony Stark's (Robert Downey, Jr.) success with his Iron Man persona he believes should have been his father's, Ivan Vanko (Mickey Rourke) plots revenge from his Russian home. Back in the U.S., Tony is calmed by his factotum Pepper Potts (Gwyneth Paltrow) after Senator Stern (Garry Shandling) demands that Tony turn his technology over to the government. Tony finds more distraction in the person of new employee Natalie Rushman (Johansson), who impresses him by using lightning-fast moves to take down his sparring partner Happy Hogan (Jon Favreau). At the Grand Prix of Monaco, Tony encounters Vanko, now in his guise as Whiplash, wielding lightning-like whips. Donning his Iron Man suit, Tony defeats Vanko, who is imprisoned but in short order breaks free. The Russian meets Justin Hammer (Sam Rockwell), who has a business proposition. Meanwhile, Tony is researching his father. James "Rhodey" Rhodes (Don Cheadle) warns him his suits will be confiscated if he doesn't get on top of the situation. Tony collapses because the poisonous palladium in his chest is decaying. An incapacitated Iron Man will be no use against Vanko, who has been laboring to improve Hammer's human-like drones. Nick Fury (Samuel L. Jackson), director of S.H.I.E.L.D. (Strategic Hazard Intervention Espionage Logistics Directorate), makes an appearance along with Natalie, now revealed as Natasha Romanoff, who uses lithium dioxide to stop Tony's deterioration. With Jarvis's (Paul Bettany) help, Tony synthesizes a new element and injects it into his chest. At the Hammer Expo, the drones go into destruction mode. Tony arrives, followed by Natasha, who with some help from Hogan, puts the kibosh on Hammer's security force and accesses the computers that Hammer had used to control Rhodey. Tony and Rhodey team up, but Vanko has set a citywide trap of explosive devices. After rescuing Pepper from a fiery death, Tony reads *The Avengers Initiative: Preliminary Report*. Although Natasha labeled Tony a narcissist, Nick says they can employ him as a consultant. Tony agrees as long as Senator Stern presents the heroism awards to himself and Rhodey. In the New Mexico desert, Agent Coulson (Clark Gregg) reveals that Thor's hammer has been found.

Scarlett Johansson on set of *Iron Man 2* (Paramount Pictures/Marvel Entertainment, 2010).

Reviews

The Blade found it "engaging, filled with action, and featuring terrific performances and great special effects." It was a hyped sequel that delivered. Johansson, was hardly "more than eye candy—until near film's end, when she dons her skintight suit to take out some bad guys with some nifty moves and weaponry."[2] The *Las Vegas Review-Journal* thought it was "always a kick watching Robert Downey Jr." and "Lots of stuff blows up real good, too." However, the screenplay left something to be desired. It didn't transcend the bane of big summer movie sequels: more is better. It wasn't. New hire Natalie Rushman was played by "sleek, steely Scarlett Johansson."[3]

Commentary

Johansson spoke about the diet and training necessary to properly engage in this movie, to be believable as a superspy. "I was working my ass off...."[4] boxing, lifting, twisting, and medicine ball training. Celebrity trainer Bobby Strom supervised her regimen.[5]

Director Favreau said of Johansson, "And, you know, as beautiful as she is, she doesn't trade on her looks at all. I think she's a regular person. When you're hanging out with her on the set, she's just like one of the guys."[6]

Johansson was not the first actress up for Black Widow. Eliza Dushku and Emily Blunt were considered. Blunt conceded that Johansson did a fantastic job. Johansson herself admitted that superheroes were not on her radar growing up. Back then the Teenage Mutan Ninja Turtles were her thing.[7]

Later, Johansson recalled that even though she was excited about playing Natasha and met with Jon Favreau, Emily Blunt had been cast as Black Widow, but scheduling problems forced her to back out. She had another session with Favreau, "and we had a funny conversation about how he had not cast me. But I was excited. I was so stoked."[8]

In 2015, Johansson said Black Widow resonated with her. Having faced death innumerable times she valued life. "She's small, but she's strong." What's hard not to admire.... "We all try to fight the forces of evil. Like Black Widow, you have to keep trying. The challenge is always there."[9]

Analysis

This second outing for Robert Downey, Jr.'s mortal superhero was originally considered a topnotch sequel, but it fell from grace in the blink of an eye. No wonder. A few moments' consideration upon leaving the theater made one realize that it was ordinary, maybe even dumb. What was the sense of all those robots firing their weapons at an invulnerable Iron Man? Johansson did have a terrific hallway fight with a bunch of minions that was preceded by the funniest scene in the film: Jon Favreau's Happy Hogan discovering that the woman he was chauffeuring had changed into skintight, black spandex attire. Confounded, he asks, "What are you wearing?"

The Avengers (2012)

Loki of Asgard (Tom Hiddleston) goes on the rampage, transporting himself to Earth via the Tesseract. He mesmerizes Clint Barton, aka Hawkeye (Jeremy Renner) and the scientist Selvig (Stellan Skarsgard), forcing them to do his bidding. He is initially foiled in his plan to create chaos when Nick Fury (Samuel L. Jackson) obtains the cube at the heart of the Tesseract, but Hawkeye wounds Nick and takes the cube. Meanwhile, a redheaded woman tied to a chair is interrogated by a Russian officer. This woman is the infamous Natasha Romanoff, aka Black Widow (Johansson), who upon gleaning information herself, breaks free and downs her captors. Natasha locates Dr. Bruce Banner (Mark Ruffalo) volunteering in a third world country and convinces him to help S.H.I.E.L.D. (Strategic Hazard International Espionage Logistics Directorate) find the cube because of his familiarity with gamma radiation. Soon onboard as allies are Steve Rogers, aka Captain America (Chris Evans) and Tony Stark, aka Iron Man (Robert Downey, Jr.) The Avengers assemble on a gigantic airborne—and submersible—carrier. After Loki is located in Germany, the crime-fighters, with the help of Thor (Chris Hemsworth), subdue the miscreant. Thor reveals that Loki intends bringing his army to Earth via the Tesseract and Bruce discovers that iridium is Loki's power source. Black Widow asks Loki to release his hold on Hawkeye. Loki wonders if this is love, but she responds, "Love is for children, I owe him a debt." Hawkeye and others attack Nick's carrier. Black Widow tries in vain to keep

Bruce from transforming into Hulk and is only saved by the intervention of Thor. She does, however, subdue Hawkeye. Loki escapes. Hawkeye tells Black Widow his brain was taken by Loki but he's now okay. However, Black Widow now has her own agenda since she's been compromised. Jarvis (Paul Bettany) saves Tony's life when Loki throws him through a window. Atop the Stark building, Selvig sets up a device to beam skyward and facilitate the entry of Loki's army. A battle for the ages ensues. Nick tells the Counselors using a nuclear bomb to incinerate the city would be a "stupid-ass decision." Confronted by Black Widow, Selvig comes to his senses and tells her to thrust Loki's scepter into the Tesseract's beam to close the portal. Iron Man stops a nuclear-armed missile and guides it into the portal. He seems to be sacrificing himself but falls back toward Earth, grabbed by the Hulk before hitting the ground. Captain America tells Black Widow to close the portal. Loki is back in the Avengers' power, and Thor takes possession of his wayward brother. The Counselors deem the Avengers dangerous and Agent Coulson (Clark Gregg) asks if they will return. Yes, because Earth will need them. Tony reunites with his girl "Friday," Pepper (Gwyneth Paltrow). On a distant world another "god" seems to plan a second trial for Earth and its protectors.

Reviews

AP Top News Package commended director Whedon for accomplishing "the tricky feat of juggling a large ensemble cast and giving everyone a chance to shine, of balancing splashy set pieces with substantive ideology." The dialogue was as fine as the special effects, and "these people may be wearing ridiculous costumes but they're well fleshed-out underneath."[10] *The Los Angeles Times* said that despite the ascendancy of superhero movies, they have "entered a phase of imaginative decadence." In reality, *The Avengers* "is a snappy little dialogue comedy dressed up as something else…" and in some sense has a bit "of the easygoing charm of *Rio Bravo*, Howard Hawks's great, late western in which John Wayne, Angie Dickinson, Dean Martin and Ricky Nelson did a lot of talking on their way to a big and not-all-that-interesting shootout." The difference is that "nowadays *The Avengers* must be enormous, of a scale and duration that obliterates everything else." Thus "The light, amusing bits cannot overcome the grinding, hectic emptiness.…"[11] *The New York Times* agreed with criticism based on gigantism but said this film at least had director Whedon at the helm, and he "emphasized character and good dialogue.…"[12] The *Pittsburgh Post-Gazette*

Scarlett Johansson, *The Avengers* **(Marvel Studios/Paramount, 2012).**

called it "the movie comic book fans have been curled up in their parents' basements fantasizing about for half a century." Of course, it was "mostly a master class in smashing things and striving for cleverness while doing so."[13]

Commentary

Building on the Marvel film franchise begun in 2008 with *Iron Man* and succeeding Marvel Studios' films such as *Thor* and *Captain America*, *The Avengers* opened on April 11, 2012. Combining a plethora of Marvel characters, the film was greeted as some sort of summation of the superhero oeuvre. Johansson's co-star Stellan Skarsgard described her as "a very intelligent, cool, and beautiful actor."[14]

Quizzed about the franchise in 2019, Johansson remembered that when they were preparing to shoot *The Avengers*, it wasn't at all clear that it would work.[15]

Analysis

It was big, bold and even had some compelling dark incidents such as Coulson's death and Natasha's regrets about her life. The funniest moment has the Hulk battering Loki onto the ground and announcing, "Puny god."

Also, Natasha becomes more than token eye candy. Her rapport—or lack of it—with Bruce as Hulk, notably in their battle aboard the carrier before Thor intervenes, is, as Daniel Snyder writes, reflective of the supreme trauma she experiences as well as the issue of being the lone female in a potentially raging man mob.[16]

Captain America: The Winter Soldier (2014)

During his daily run in Washington, D.C., Steve Rogers, aka Captain America (Chris Evans) encounters Sam Wilson (Anthony Mackie), aka Falcon, a Middle East war vet and Para-Rescue expert. During another jog Steve meets Natasha Romanoff, aka Black Widow (Johansson). He's got a new mission: rescue Indian Ocean ship hostages. Dropping to the deck, Steve, Natasha, Brock Rumlow (Frank Grillo) and others engage in a serious fracas during which Steve saves Natasha from a grenade. Securing the hostages is but one part of the mission. The second is extracting information from the ship's computer hard drive.

Back at the Triskelion, S.H.I.E.L.D. headquarters, Steve confronts Nick Fury (Samuel L. Jackson) concerning the dual nature of the mission. Nick responds that it's all about compartmentalization. He won't ask Steve to do things he's uncomfortable with. On the other hand, Natasha is comfortable with everything. Steve is shown three mammoth "helicarriers" propelled by repulsor engines that will provide S.H.I.E.L.D. a decided advantage over terrorists and rogue nations. Still concerned over the ethics of this, Steve visits aged agent Peggy Carter (Hayley Atwell). Meanwhile, Nick finds he can't access S.H.I.E.L.D. files and convinces Alexander Pierce (Robert Redford) to delay Project Insight—the helicarrier deployment. Nick is ambushed in his SUV but escapes to Steve's apartment where he hands over a flash drive before being gunned down by a sniper. Steve's neighbor Kate (Emily VanCamp) reveals herself as Agent 13 and helps get Nick to the hospital. There Steve, Natasha and agent Maria Hill (Cobie Smulders) look on as the

7. She Plays Big

Scarlett Johansson, *Captain America: The Winter Soldier* (Marvel Studios/Walt Disney Studios, 2014).

doctors fail to save Nick's life. Steve hides the flash drive in a vending machine before being ambushed in an elevator by Rumlow and his men. He manages to incapacitate them and discovers that Natasha has retrieved the flash drive. Angry, Steve is told that "I only act like I know everything." Accessing the flash drive, Steve and Natasha learn of the existence of Camp Lehigh, an abandoned U.S. Army enclave in New Jersey. Underground is the Strategic Homeland Intervention Enforcement Logistics Division. Powering up old computers, they are greeted by Hydra's Arnim Zola (Toby Jones), the German who'd become a parasite within S.H.I.E.L.D. These days it's his mind that exists in 200,000 feet of databanks. He reveals that S.H.I.E.L.D. is compromised by Nick's flash drive, which contains an algorithm to achieve its now heinous purpose. Steve and Natasha barely survive a missile strike. Back in D.C., Pierce kills his housekeeper after learning that she's been in his apartment while he conferred with a stranger. Meanwhile, in Steve's apartment, he and Natasha surmise that Pierce and an accomplice had launched the missile. They kidnap Agent Sitwell (Maximiliano Hernandez) and make him reveal the harm Zola's algorithm can cause. Riding away, they are attacked by a masked man in black as well as Rumlow and his confederates. Knocking off the man's mask, Steve discovers it's Bucky Barnes (Sebastian Stan), his wartime buddy kidnapped by Nazis. Steve, Natasha and Sam are surrounded and incarcerated in a van from which they escape by blowing a hole in the floor. At a S.H.I.E.L.D. bunker they discover that Nick is alive. He'd ingested Toxin B to slow his pulse and simulate his demise. Natasha is treated for a bullet wound to her shoulder. In a lab, the one-time Bucky, now "The Winter Soldier," is reprogrammed to follow Hydra's orders, or now, S.H.I.E.L.D., in the person of Pierce. Pierce is almost ready to deploy the helicarriers at the Potomac River dock, these dreadnoughts to kill millions in the D.C. metropolitan area. To Pierce, dispensing with 20 million is nothing compared to saving the future of earth's 7 billion. Natasha contends that they must enter the helicarriers and substitute their own targeting blades. In the Smithsonian, Steve retrieves his old Captain America uniform. Pierce meets with the Council, providing them with badges that give them access to the Triskelion. Steve's voice on the intercom informs employees of the infiltrators. Those who remain loyal can join his fight. This is enough to foil Rumlow's thugs. Steve must deal with Rumlow before he can turn his attention to his main target: Bucky. Meanwhile, Natasha, masquerading as Councilwoman Hawley (Jenny Agutter), tries to control Pierce, but he gets the drop on her and reveals that the badge he'd given each of the Councilors contained an explosive device. To subvert Pierce's plans, Natasha activates her own, non-lethal remote and drops to the floor. Before he can reboot his remote, Pierce is plugged by Nick. Although Steve has dispensed with Rumlow, he is shot by Bucky but still manages to insert a new targeting blade causing each helicarrier to fire on the other. Bucky is pinned by falling beams and Steve sinks into the river. Bucky drags him to shore before slinking off. At a Congressional hearing, Natasha represents the Avengers. Threatened with incarceration for past and present sins, she counters that the world needs the Avengers. Wearing a hoodie, Nick stands at his gravesite conferring with Steve and welcomes Sam to the team. Natasha arrives with a document for Steve, kisses his cheek, and leaves. Sam wonders when Steve will start looking for Bucky, and the answers is … now.

Reviews

Scarlett Johansson at *Captain America: The Winter Soldier* (Marvel Studios/Walt Disney Pictures) premiere at El Capitan Theatre, Hollywood, CA, March 13, 2014 (Depositphotos.com).

The Telegraph said, "Scarlett Johansson, returning as the double-agent Black Widow, is handed the most (the first?) complex female role in the Avengers franchise to date."[17] Rogerebert.com was intrigued by the interaction between Evans, Johansson and Mackie. "Watch their body language as they gently tease each other in their quiet scenes, and notice how directors Anthony and Joe Russo frame them. There's a genuine emotional shorthand at work, especially from Johansson, who is excellent here."[18] *The Washington Post* thought Johansson "continually threatens to steal the entire movie with her slinky martial arts moves and sultry, smoky-voiced one-liners. (If Hollywood was waiting for proof that the Black Widow was ready for her own installment, here it is. Get cracking, fellas.)"[19] As one critic said, Black Widow had been more or less a mascot in *Iron Man 2* and *The Avengers*, but now she was given plenty of screen time. The film was extolled when it premiered in April and was labeled the standard against which the 2014 summer blockbusters that lay ahead must be measured. *Entertainment Weekly* found Chris Evans' battle against none other than modern America compelling, and like *The Dark Knight*, "plugs you into what's happening now." The performers were excellent, what with Robert Redford "wittily cast.…" As Black Widow, "Scarlett Johansson makes Natasha a fast-and-furious flirt.…"[20]

Commentary

Captain America: The Winter Soldier, like the U.S. premiere of *Under the Skin*, was released in April 2014. It was the sequel to 2011's *Captain America: The First Avenger* and a huge success and would not be surpassed financially until *Guardians of the Galaxy* late in the summer. It set a record at $96.2 million in North America on its opening weekend, the best ever April opening. In its first 10 days overseas, it pulled in $207.1 million. Disney's head of distribution, Dave Hollis, thought an April opening of this magnitude was really special and attributed success to the film being both an action movie and a character story.[21]

This was Johansson's fourth movie opposite Chris Evans. The others: *The Perfect Score*, *The Nanny Diaries*, and *The Avengers*.

Evans told an interviewer, "She is who she is, and she is unapologetic...." She was honest and "has an old soul." Although he was older she seemed like his big sister. "To this day, she still seems a little more worldly and intelligent than most people in the room."[22] He added that Johansson was very spontaneous, and described a night out at a Cleveland dive during filming of *The Avengers*. "She approached the band, asked if they knew 'Rocky Raccoon,' and sang it perfectly."[23]

Johansson said: "Black Widow kicks ass in *Winter Soldier*. I had some pretty rad fight sequences in *Avengers*, but a lot of the fighting in *Winter Soldier* is hand-to-hand. It's brutal, street-fighting style ... such a weird thing: I kind of got career side-tracked in the superhero lane—happily! But I never thought I'd have, like, sports injuries."[24]

Analysis

Natasha Romanoff (Johansson) announces at one point that when she left the KGB and joined S.H.I.E.L.D. she thought she was "going straight," but now she finds that she merely exchanged the KGB for HYDRA, the crypto-fascist parasitic power that has used S.H.I.E.L.D. to mask its evil intent: using an algorithm to identify potential enemies or dissidents and eliminating 20 million of them to establish a New World Order for the remaining 7 billion. No wonder Steve Rogers, aka Captain America, is baffled and needs the sexy, flirty, ironic and playful Black Widow to help him find his way in the contemporary world.

Johansson makes the most of the part. Before the credits run she pulls up in a black Corvette in Washington, D.C., to pick up Captain America but does so by smiling and asking the way to the Smithsonian. "I need to pick up a fossil," she says, playing on Roger's age and peculiar presence in the current century. She carries this playfulness throughout the film, even in the middle of violent actions. When she and Rogers are on assignment for S.H.I.E.L.D. she has a mission to collect intelligence while he is responsible for saving hostages. Unaware of the Black Widow's separate mission, Captain America asks what she's doing. "Backing up a hard drive," she replies, "it's a good habit." When he lambasts her for not following orders—"You just jeopardized this whole mission," she calmly responds, "I think that's overstating things." She provides the kind of patter that often lightens detective stories or thrillers and thus lightens the mayhem and destruction that makes up much of this movie.

She hits her highpoint when disguised as the only female member of the Council—the international group that oversees S.H.I.E.L.D.—a part played by Jenny Agutter, and kicks, beats and stomps a handful of HYDRA goons and gets the drop on Robert Redford as Secretary Pierce, the secret head of HYDRA. A finger touch to the side of her head causes Jenny Agutter's face to disappear to be replaced by Johansson's.

Although she has used her sex as a way to distract or temporarily disarm male opponents, she never becomes a love interest for Captain America. Instead, at the end, she gives him a kiss on the cheek and encourages him to see the woman (Emily VanCamp) who had posed as a nurse and his next-door neighbor when she had been assigned to protect him. "She's nice," Black Widow says, giving Captain America a warm, sly smile. They part with the suggestion it's likely they will meet again.

The Avengers: Age of Ultron (2015)

Sloughing off a man with exceedingly quick moves and a woman interfering with their minds, the Avengers successfully attack the Sokovian fortress used by Strucker (Thomas Kretschmann) as the Hydra Research Base. They confiscate the scepter of Loki (Tom Hiddleston) with the inlaid gem that stimulates artificial intelligence. Back in New York, Tony Stark, aka Iron Man (Robert Downey, Jr.), learns from Agent Hill (Cobie Smulders) that the man and woman who'd given them trouble in Sokovia are Pietro, aka Quicksilver (Aaron Taylor-Johnson) and Wanda Maximoff, aka Scarlet Witch (Elizabeth Olsen). Gone rogue in their previous adventure, the injured Hawkeye (Jeremy Renner) is rehabilitated. Tony's alter ego Jarvis (Paul Bettany) determines that the scepter contains a code, which Tony and Bruce Banner, aka Hulk (Mark Ruffalo) think might be the key to creating an artificial intelligence shortly to be known as Ultron (James Spader), who materializes and overcomes Jarvis. Ultron begins creating a 3D body. He, or it, crashes the Avengers party and informs them that humanity must be permitted to evolve. For that to happen the Avengers must be destroyed. Thwarting Thor (Chris Hemsworth), Ultron escapes with the scepter. Steve Rogers, aka Captain America (Chris Evans), says they must find him before he becomes too strong. Back in Sokovia, Quicksilver and Scarlet Witch are enlisted by Ultron to help him counter the Avengers. Ultron gains the vibranium from the African realm of Wakanda. The Avengers attack Ultron and his robots but Scarlet Witch's visions mess with their minds and they take refuge in Hawkeye's farmhouse. Ultron, meanwhile, visits Dr. Helen Cho (Claudia Kim) at the U–Gin Genetics Research Lab in Seoul, Korea. She is told about a regeneration cradle that will construct a body. Back at Hawkeye's farm, Bruce tells Natasha, aka Black Widow (Johansson) who seems in a seductive mood, that he must leave. His reason: he is incapable of having a normal life. But she can't either. She was sterilized when she was young. "Still think you're the only monster on the team?" she asks. Tony and Nick Fury (Samuel L. Jackson) have a pow-wow over Ultron. In London, Thor asks Erik Selvig (Stellan Skarsgard) for help. So far Ultron has not been able to access nuclear missile launch codes. Bruce realizes that Dr. Cho is key to Ultron's ultimate regeneration via the binding of vibranium to tissue. Scarlet Witch has come to realize that Ultron is mad. She and Quicksilver escape the destruction of Dr. Cho's lab. Captain America finds the wounded Dr. Cho, who urges him to retrieve the regeneration cradle. On her motorcycle, chasing the truck carrying the cradle, Black Widow is captured. Scarlet Witch, Quicksilver and Captain America fight Ultron on a train and Tony secures the cradle. Returning from "underground," Jarvis discusses bio-organics. Black Widow finds herself in Sokovia's dungeons. Thor uses his hammer to smash open the cradle, releasing a red-hued humanoid who reveals that he is not Ultron and not Jarvis, rather a creature who is "on the side of life." Bruce locates Black Widow, who convinces him to fight. Jarvis confronts Ultron, who throws a switch causing the city to rise from the earth. Black Widow tells Bruce she adores him but pushes him off a ledge to make him mad enough to continue fighting as the Hulk. It becomes evident that Ultron hopes to smash the city back down to earth and thus create a mass extinction. While Nick arrives with a helicarrier to rescue the citizens, the non–Jarvis assists against Ultron. Quicksilver is mortally wounded. Hulk carries Black Widow to Nick and jumps onto Ultron's aircraft and knocks the monster down into the city. Scarlet Witch attempts to neutralize Ultron while Thor uses his hammer to break the core, creating a million pieces. Jarvis tells Ultron there is grace in humanity's failures, then blasts him. The battle is won, but where is Hulk? Captain America, Thor and Iron Man talk about a mindstone. Captain America and Black Widow prepare to teach the new Avengers candidates. On Asgard, Thanos (Josh Brolin) realizes he'll need to retrieve the Infinity Stones himself.

Scarlett Johansson, *The Avengers: Age of Ultron* (Marvel Studios, 2015) pre-production rendering.

Reviews

The Daily Oklahoman discerned déjà vu, especially the de rigeur "world-hanging-in the balance routine." All of the expected and recycled items were on display, like Tony Stark being smug and dry, or Black Widow becoming "eye candy in half of her scenes...." It was overly gruesome and needed to slow down.[25] *The Los Angeles Times* said it "definitely does not go the minimalist route." Ultron was "a convincingly twisted villain...." However, "very little of it lingers in the mind afterward." Acutely observed was that in essence this and other Marvel films were modern versions of old-time movie serials.[26] The *New York Times* said director Whedon had concocted something that was acceptable even as it was created to "crush the box office, entertainment media and audience resistance, and mission, you know, already accomplished." Johansson was "the token chick..." but worked well with Mark Ruffalo's Hulk. "These too-short interludes of the Black Widow grappling with a difficult love interest modestly humanize the movie, which helps a bit with both its rhythm and scale, making it less of a monotonous special-effects blowout."[27] The *Pittsburgh Post-Gazette* thought it "immensely enjoyable, but overstuffed...."

Most of the guys quickly bonded over their exploits while "Natasha flirts in a corner with Bruce Banner ... in what has to be the unlikeliest potential pairing of comic book icons in a long time." The film hinted at greatness but didn't deliver.[28]

Commentary

Anticipation for the sequel to *The Avengers* was beyond surreal. Even before the May 1 general U.S. release it had made $200 million overseas.

Johansson discussed Black Widow's shady past, and the nightmares that come to haunt her. "I think the audience is ready for that. These characters' relationships become even murkier. Nothing's getting cleaned up and tied up in a big, red shiny bow in *Avengers 2*. It's complex, and the universe is expanding even more."[29]

As the movie opened, Johansson acknowledged how being pregnant during filming was mitigated on screen via camera tricks and bold stuntwomen, plus "some sort of mechanical bull type of motorcycle, which goes nowhere and doesn't look cool at all." As if predicting her decision to sacrifice herself in *Avengers: Endgame*, Johansson said, "She puts in the work and she wonders whether there should be some kind of personal payoff but she's realizing her calling is a greater one.... That's kind of what is most heroic about her—she's accepting the call of duty."[30]

A so-called controversial element in the filmography was the abortive romance between Black Widow and Bruce/Hulk. Johansson told *The Hollywood Reporter*, "I think that they made a choice that was for the greater good. I think everybody must have had that, where ... it's just not the right time. It just wasn't really meant to be, but I would love to do the other storyline where they have some Bogart and Bacall romance."[31]

Analysis

For some there has been a lack of appetite for the unreality of movies like *The Avengers* and might be attributed at least in part to the preselected Previews of Coming Attractions. After a dose of Tom Cruise in the umpteenth *Mission: Impossible* and George Clooney in a Disney rip off of *Conspiracy Theory* or *Enemy of the State* (young innocent unwittingly leads minions of the State to the high tech, prepared for self-destruction hide-out of a crusty old rebel) both speaking lines that might make an actor die of shame, it's hard to throw oneself into the make believe of the main feature.

It's odd how the excessing amount of action can leave some of us unmoved or uninterested. It was only when the Avengers reached the safe house and made contact with ordinary family life that one's being quivered in sympathy and perked up. Still, there's no question that the presentation is slick, the plot spinning if simple (a fact that is not that bothersome), and the humor if at times too deadpan to be effective nonetheless like the plot continues to move. The references are such that you at times wonder who makes up the audience the writers have in mind. Stark's allusion to Eugene O'Neill through a pun on the title of one of his best-known plays, *Long Day's Journey Into Night*, is not likely to resonate with the crowds thought to make repeat journeys through the turnstile. Anyway, it is a decent way to spend an afternoon and there is always much to be said for Scarlett in form-fitting leather outfits. She would make a good cat woman. It was also interesting to get the glimpses of back stories for the various characters, reminding us that the whole movement has its origin in World War II.

A Black Widow Standalone?

A feature or series of features with Johansson as Black Widow was broached from time to time. In 2015 she told an interviewer she thought a standalone film could work because of the character's "rich origin story" and her own ability to grow with the character. Johansson spoke with Marvel Studios President Kevin Feige on the topic. The audience reaction to the Black Widow-Captain America pairing had been positive and "that storyline worked out so well I kind of branched off and I found myself in that standalone movie." She'd stay around. "I mean, I'm always happy to put the cat suit back on, for sure."[32]

Captain America: Civil War (2016)

In 1991 the brainwashed Bucky Barnes (Sebastian Stan) is sent by Hydra to leave no witnesses after murdering a man and woman while gathering up a special suitcase. The present: Lagos, Nigeria. Steve Rogers, aka Captain America (Chris Evans), Sam Wilson, aka Falcon (Anthony Mackie), Natasha Romanoff, aka Black Widow (Johansson), and Wanda, aka Scarlet Witch (Elizabeth Olsen) take down the still living Brock Rumlow (Frank Grillo) and his outlaws trying to steal a deadly biological agent from a lab. In the process, however, Scarlet Witch's powers cause death and destruction in a nearby high-rise. The U.S. Secretary of State Thaddeus Ross (William Hurt) is not pleased with this latest incident of vigilantism and places before Tony Stark, aka Iron Man (Robert Downey, Jr.), and the Avengers the Sokovia Accords, a document designed to provide oversight of these enhanced beings. Thus begins a rift in their ranks. "Cap" doesn't trust the government to oversee them. At Peggy Carter's (Hayley Atwell) funeral where Peggy's niece Sharon, aka Agent 13 (Emily VanCamp), gives the eulogy, only Natasha and Sam are there to support Cap. Meanwhile, ratification of the Sokovia Accords in Vienna is disrupted by a bomb blast that kills King T'Chaka (John Kani) of Wakanda. Checking security footage, the King's son T'Challa (Chadwick Boseman) sees Bucky Barnes (Sebastian Stan) place the bomb. Sharon gives Cap special information, but Natasha wants him to keep his distance. Cap and Falcon track Bucky to Bucharest but are arrested, as is T'Challa, now in a Black Panther suit. While this transpires, Zemo (Daniel Bruhl) locates the book within which are the passages triggering Bucky's rampages. Thwarting Zemo's attempt to pluck Bucky from his lockup, Cap and Bucky fall into a pool along with the helicopter they were in. Cap saves Bucky, thus repaying his friend for rescuing him from drowning in the Potomac River during the Alexander Pierce imbroglio. Bucky identifies Zemo as the Vienna bomber and recalls the 1991 incident involving Tony's parents. Cap plans to locate the secret Siberian Hydra base where other "winter soldiers" are located. Tony is entailed by Ross with bringing in Bucky within 36 hours. Tony, Peter Parker, aka Spider-Man (Tom Holland), and Clint Barton, aka Hawkeye (Jeremy Renner) enter the Avengers headquarters and Scarlet Witch incapacitates Vision (Paul Bettany). Meanwhile, Cap and Sharon kiss. Cap, Falcon, Scarlet Witch, Hawkeye and Scott Lang, aka Ant-Man (Paul Rudd) form an alliance while Iron Man, Black Widow, Black Panther, James Rhodes, aka War Machine (Don Cheadle), and Vision gather up Spider-Man and contest their future at the Leipzig airport. Out on the high seas, a gigantic prison confines Falcon, Hawkeye, Ant-Man, and Scarlet Witch. Tony discovers that Bucky was framed

Scarlett Johansson, *Captain America: Civil War* (Marvel Studios, 2016).

and heads for Siberia on his own, joining Cap and Bucky and discovering the dead bodies of other winter soldiers shot by Zemo. Safe from them via a protected enclosure, Zemo tells them they caused his kin's death in Sokovia. He adds that Bucky killed Tony's parents because they were transporting the winter soldier ingredients. Tony, Cap and Bucky engage in a knock-down, drag-out fight. It's essentially a draw. Meanwhile T'Challa captures Zemo and though he desires his demise, will take him to the authorities. Rhodey recovers slowly from his injuries, walking due to Tony's special braces. Cap frees the captives in the underwater prison and with Bucky vamooses to Wakanda where Bucky opts for a return to cryogenic sleep, hoping that in the future a cure will be found for his condition. Peter is filled with pleasure when he discovers his wrist bracelet from Tony projects the Spider-Man signal onto the ceiling.

Reviews

Reviews were uniformly excellent. *Newsday* said it "entertains relentlessly, which is to say loudly and busily, but with enough humor and intelligence to make it seem less pandering than it actually is." The big showdown between the two Avengers camps was "an enjoyable free-for-all involving Scarlett Johansson's athletic Black Widow, Paul Bettany's godlike Vision and many, many more."[33] The *St. Joseph News-Press* said it could have been a mess, "but the magic of the script and the energy the Russos inject ... keeps it at an even keel.... The movie goes big when it needs to, as it brings all of the characters in for a big fight, and sheds its cast when it knows it should play it small, like scenes between Stark and Rogers. Because this is, in the end, a Captain America movie...."[34] The *News Journal* said there were "some interesting alliances—like Black Widow ... going against her pal Cap, Hawkeye ... positioning against his friend Black Widow, and so on."[35]

Entertainment Weekly considered it the best yet of the Avengers canon. A sense of fun distinguished it from a contemporary superhero movie, *Batman v. Superman*.[36]

Commentary

Before release, Johansson spoke about which side Black Widow would be on in the Avengers contretemps: "I think when you find her in *Civil War*, she's looking to strategize her position, putting herself in a place where she is able to let the powers that be fight it out or whatever amongst themselves. She's always a little bit on the perimeter so she can have a better perspective of what's really going on."[37]

Black Widow's fate as a standalone movie kept popping up on the web. In January 2018 there was talk of Johansson raking in $25 million if the film were made. The unusual—in the Marvel Cinematic Universe—*Thor: Ragnarok* gave Chris Hemsworth a chance to branch out. Why not Black Widow?[38]

A writer, Jac Schaffer, was hired to work up a Black Widow movie draft, and Johansson herself was said to be involved in the development. The Russo Brothers claimed they were happy with a Black Widow film, saying "it's such a rich and interesting character. There's so much to explore with a character whose history was as villain, and you know, Scarlett does such a good job of playing that character and people are so used to that character that you forget the character's history, and so there's a lot of compelling stories to tell about someone who has a dark past."[39] Later in the year another major step would be taken to make a Black Widow standalone a reality.

Analysis

Perhaps the best scene in the film and the one with the most meaning is the funeral in which Steve is a pallbearer for Peggy Carter (Hayley Atwell). Other than Falcon, Natasha is the only Avenger showing up to support him. Her role was the appropriate one to provide comfort. She went despite their disagreements, and it is hard to imagine any of the other characters (or actors) pulling that off credibly. It wasn't romantic at all, merely supportive but believable. It's a shame that Natasha, and some others, don't appear at the end of the film, which focuses on Tony, Steve, Bucky, Rhodey, and T'Challa.

Thor: Ragnarok (2016)

In this the third Marvel Thor epic, quite universally admired for action and humor, Johansson appears on a S.H.I.E.L.D. quinjet's monitor calling on a rampaging Hulk to get his act together and turn the ship around. It's actually a message sent when they were battling their nemesis in *The Avengers: Age of Ultron*. The director was Taika Waititi, who'd employ Johansson's vivacity to excellent effect in *Jojo Rabbit* (2019).

The Avengers: Infinity War (2018)

An Asgardian ship carrying Thor (Chris Hemsworth), Loki (Tom Hiddleston), Heimdall (Idris Elba), and others away from their wrecked empire is attacked by a much larger spacecraft and boarded by Thanos (Josh Brolin) and his minions. Initially successful in battling this Titan, Hulk (Mark Ruffalo) is subdued but whisked off to earth by a dying Heimdall via the Bifrost. Loki professes allegiance to Thanos as a ruse to get close and stab him, but the Titan is not fooled and throttles his attacker. Having secured a second Infinity Stone, the Space Stone, from the Tesseract offered by Loki, which is part of the key to controlling the universe, Thanos heads for earth, preceded by his most trusted and deadly minions. Their immediate goal: secure Dr. Strange's (Benedict Cumberbatch) Time Stone. Strange and other members of the Avengers, Tony Stark, aka Iron Man (Robert Downey, Jr.), and Wong (Benedict Wong) confront them in New York City after being warned by a crash-landing Hulk. They fail. Tony and Peter Parker, aka Spider-Man (Tom Holland) find themselves aboard the alien ship as it returns to space. Vision (Paul Bettany) and his lover Wanda, aka Scarlet Witch (Elizabeth Olsen) are waylaid in Edinburgh but with the help of Steve Rogers, aka Captain America (Chris Evans), Natasha Romanoff, aka Black Widow (Johansson), and Sam Wilson, aka Falcon (Anthony Mackie) prevent these culprits from extracting the Mind Stone from Vision's forehead. Much to Wanda's displeasure, Vision plans to sacrifice himself, but Steve believes they can forestall any such self-sacrifice by laying up in Wakanda. Meanwhile, the Guardians of the Galaxy, namely Peter Quill, aka Star-Lord (Chris Pratt), Gamora (Zoë Saldana), Rocket (Bradley Cooper, voice), Groot (Vin Diesel, voice), Drax (Michael Bautista Jr.), and Mantis (Pom Klementieff) become involved after rescuing Thor. With the help of weaponsmith Eitri (Peter Dinklage), Thor's hammer is reborn. Having obtained the Reality Stone from the Collector (Benicio del Toro), Thanos kidnaps Gamora, who is in fact his adopted daughter. Discovering that her adoptive sister Nebula (Karen Gillan) is being tortured, Gamora provides Thanos with the location of the Soul Stone. But Thanos must kill Gamora to secure it. On Titan, Peter learns of Gamora's fate and attacks the newly arrived murderer. After a debilitating battle which Thanos *almost* loses, Strange offers their nemesis the Time Stone. Next up: Wakanda, where Steve and Natasha find Bucky Barnes (Sebastian Stan) newly equipped with a prosthetic arm. T'Challa, aka Black Panther (Chadwick Boseman) welcomes his old friends and vows to stall Thanos' army until the Mind Stone can be extracted from Vision's head and

Scarlett Johansson at *The Avengers: Infinity War* (Marvel Studios/Walt Disney Pictures) premiere at TCL Chinese Theatre, Hollywood, CA, April 23, 2018 (Depositphotos.com).

destroyed. Thor arrives and wounds Thanos, who nevertheless obtains the Mind Stone from the dying Vision before spiriting himself away. As part of Thanos' goal of annihilating half the population of the universe, disintegration is in store for Black Panther, Spider-Man, Groot, Quill, Wanda, Drax, Mantis, Falcon, and Strange. Thanos, meanwhile, mulls over his successes and failures.

Reviews

Variety said it was like "going to a theme park and taking three spins on every ride there." Despite the overabundance of action, "it's sharp, fast-moving, and elegantly staged." Plus, there was something at stake.[40] *USA Today* called it a "full-fledged Shakespearean tragedy." It was "a glorious, multilayered and clever comic book adventure with loads of emotional stakes and a perfect foe for Earth's mightiest heroes."[41] *The News-Herald* gave it 4 out of 4 stars, citing its "incredibly impressive representation of everything the Disney-owned Marvel Studios has been working toward with its Marvel Cinematic Universe." Overall "It's a wow. Wow, wow, wow."[42]

Commentary

Following on the heels of the massive Marvel hit *Black Panther*, *The Avengers: Infinity War* premiered April 23, 2018, at the Dolby Theatre in Hollywood. On the week leading up to the premiere, Johansson joined other Avengers cast members on *Jimmy Kimmel Live!* And on April 24 she played a game in which she revealed that she'd inadvertently showed her private parts to an airline passenger:

> It was unintentional.... I was using the bathroom in the plane, as one does, and I guess I didn't lock the door. It happens, occasionally. I don't know. I thought I did and I went to grab the toilet paper and my entire vagina was splayed out—yes, I said vagina! Deal with it! The guy opens the door, he looks down and he's like, "Uh-oh! Oh!" I was like, "Close the goddamn door!" I had to open the door and walk past the entire cabin of people that all just heard me [scream!]. You know? And then they were like, "Oh, it was Scarlett who was in there. It was her vagina!"[43]

In March 2018 Johansson had explained that since *Civil War* Steve and Natasha had been "flying under the radar but still taking care of business in the way that they know how to do." Directors Joe and Anthony Russo told them the duo:

> are just a fine, well-oiled machine. They sort of have a seamless communication between them. But they're more hardened, I think, and I think when you are working underground for such a long time and you don't have—not that they need to have any sort of back-patting or recognition exactly, but I think, when you're sort of fighting for something that you know is important but is not being really recognized or supported by a larger organization or even like, society as a whole, I think that makes—it takes a certain toll, and you can get feelings about it in a way. So that's kind of where we find them.[44]

Analysis

To give *The Avengers: Infinity War* such extravagant reviews one must be all-in on Marvel and the superhero oeuvre in general. Otherwise, the action set-pieces are almost as wearying as those in *The Hobbit: The Battle of the Five Armies*. There are some cute quips and tiny but welcome references to the characters' pasts, e.g., Black Widow and Bruce/The Hulk. Johansson, like much of the ensemble cast, has relatively little to do and touched on that issue while telling an interviewer about Black Widow's progression: "This film is so plot-driven that unfortunately we don't have so much space for character work, but I assume that, not to say exactly that she's [Black Widow] unraveled a little bit, but I think the thrill she gets is from relief, like fighting and going into battle. I imagine there's a little bit of a nihilistic quality to her at this point. I'm going in that direction. We'll see how it lands."[45]

Avengers: Endgame (2019)

While with Nebula's (Karen Gillan) help, Tony Stark (Robert Downey, Jr.) is found and brought back to earth, malaise is the dominant spirit of the Avengers who survived Thanos's (Josh Brolin) successful depletion of fifty percent of sentient life throughout the universe. Relief initially comes when they locate Thanos on his edenic world and Thor cuts off his head. Nevertheless, the Infinity Stones had been proscribed. What to do? Five years pass. Natasha Romanoff, aka Black Widow (Johansson) sits behind a desk mulling over their failure to defeat the evil Titan. Soon to appear is Scott Lang, aka Ant-Man (Paul Rudd), who'd been mired in the Quantum Realm. He confronts his comrades and argues they can recover those who died in Thanos's "snap," by, yes, time travel. Bruce Banner, aka Hulk (Mark Ruffalo) finds merit in Scott's idea and convinces a recalcitrant Tony to use his technology to make it happen. After all, if they go back in time they can steal the Infinity Stones and restore the universe, including the family of Clint, aka Hawkeye (Jeremy Renner). Thus the idea of a "time heist" is born, a machine and special team suits created to traverse the Quantum Realm into the past, first to the planet Morag, and then, with Natasha and Clint, to Vormir to find the Soul Stone. On Vormir they encounter Red Skull (Ross Marquand) and discover that, in essence, one must sacrifice—die—to succeed. Although Clint is willing to make the sacrifice, Natasha beats him to a precipice and drops to her death.

When the Avengers return to the present, they are devastated to learn from Clint that Nat didn't make it. Bruce tries to determine a way to bring her back via their time heist technique but fails. Nat is presumably lost forever.

Scarlett Johansson holds the *E!* People's Choice Award for Female Movie Star of 2018 (Depositphotos.com).

Having acquired all the Infinity Stones, it's time to reverse the chaos Thanos caused. Hulk makes the "snap" to restore equilibrium. However, when Nebula (Karen Gillan) opens the time portal, Thanos follows her. This version of Thanos is out for revenge. He orders Nebula to find the new Infinity Gauntlet. Despite their best efforts to defeat the Titan, Captain America, Iron Man and Thor fail again and Thanos calls forth the Chitauri horde. Almost all of the Avengers appear and take part in the momentous battle. Finally, Iron Man gets possession of the Infinity Stone gauntlet and uses a snap to end Thanos and his reign, but he pays the price with his own life.

After a lakeside memorial service, Steve decides to return the Infinity Stones and age normally. He turns over his shield to Sam (Anthony Mackie).

Scarlett Johansson at *Avengers: Endgame* World Premiere, Los Angeles Convention Center, Los Angeles, CA, April 22, 2019 (Featureflash Photo Agency/Shutterstock.com).

Reviews

Entertainment Weekly found it rife with urgency and melancholy and overall a film that delivered the goods.[46] Rogerebert.com considered it unique and not merely exploitation of the Marvel Universe fans "but to reward their love, patience, and undying adoration." It was less diffuse than its predecessor, *Infinity War*. The Avengers were no longer pawns in Thanos' scheme. In reality, "It's an epic cultural event, the kind of thing that transcends traditional film criticism…."[47] *Rolling Stone* found it uneven and bloated but "truly epic and thunderously exciting." It was the most personal of the Marvel films with "an emotional wipeout that knows intimacy is its real superpower."[48] *Screenrant* noted with only mild condemnation the lack of a consistent pace, the fact that some of the original heroes received more attention than others, some unimportant villains, overmuch CGI, and a glut of "fan service…." Nevertheless, it's "a whole lotta movie…" with its three-hour time well spent. The spectacle alone was worth attending.[49] *The Guardian* was surprised how fast the three hours went by. The movie's legacy would seem to be the final battle and the catharsis caused by "prioritising character development over plot and spectacle."[50] One of the few negative reviews came from *The New Yorker*, which was not amused: "One must, after all, respect the feelings of the saga's devotees, who demand nothing from reviewers but sobs of nonspecific adulation." Documentarian and political/social gadfly Michael Moore was urged to investigate the phenomenon of Marvel fandom.[51]

Commentary

Separately, Johansson, Ruffalo, Evans, Renner, Larson, and Cheadle were filmed for airing on *The Late Show with Stephen Colbert* on April 17, 2019, a week before the premiere. Each was asked a couple of questions by *Late Show* crew members. One used the nickname "ScarJo," which one would think everyone knows Johansson hates.[52]

Two days after the Los Angeles world premiere, *USA Today* focused on Johansson's nine-year ride as Black Widow but could glean nothing from her about a possible Black Widow standalone. Johansson did speak to the evolution of female superheroines: "I look around today at the [Marvel] universe and how diverse it is and the fact that the audience and the fans drove the studios in general, not just Marvel, to represent what was going on in the zeitgeist. And that they wanted to look up on the screen and see stories and fully developed characters that represented how they felt and what they wanted to aspire to. It's really impactful."

Johansson admitted to having pride and ownership in her creation. "I can stand among my cast and crew and feel like I have a decade of work under my belt and it's meaningful. I didn't start that way on *Iron Man 2*."

She spoke about salary, crediting her mother for setting her on the path to parity with her male co-stars. It was not male vs. female, it was about screen time. Why shouldn't the woman be paid the same if she were also a lead?[53]

Director Joe Russo addressed Black Widow's controversial death: "The theme of the movie is, 'Can you change your destiny, and what does it cost to do it—and are you willing to pay that cost?' It's a resounding 'yes' from the Avengers. In [*Infinity War*], it was, 'We don't trade lives,' a desire to protect. In this movie, there's now a desire to sacrifice. The true heroes step up and are willing to sacrifice for the greater good."[54]

Johansson said, "The finality of it was sad, but I was excited to die with honor.... It felt in-character that she would sacrifice herself, of course for humanity but actually for her friends, for the people she loves. It was bittersweet."[55]

Johansson credited her long-time physical fitness trainer Eric Johnson, co-founder of the New York–based fitness company Homage with whipping her into shape for the Black Widow outings. She told *The Hollywood Reporter* that "I am stronger and more capable now than I was 10 years ago, which is so awesome to be able to say." Most of the training for *Avengers: Endgame* took place at Urban Body Fitness in Atlanta, the locale for a good deal of the filming. Johansson's chief goals were performance and costume fit. She said it was a myth that one could truly balance being a mother, training, and working. Besides training, Johansson attended classes in hot yoga, fight training and SLT Pilates. She said the goal of all the sprinting, swinging from sets and use of battle ropes and kettlebells was not only to look powerful but to do the stunts "with ease and fluidity, be able to own it." Diet was also important. Plus, "Johansson's competitive spirit has proved to be powerful motivation."[56]

As for Black Widow's suit this go-round, Director of Visual Envelopment Andy Park moved on from a utilitarian tactical suit to one that was more armored. "This is the end times for the Avengers, so I wanted to make this the sleekest, most armored, and most sophisticated design."[57]

7. She Plays Big

Robert Downey, Jr., and Scarlett Johansson at handprint ceremony for cast of *Avengers: Endgame* at TCL Chinese Theater, Los Angeles, CA, April 23, 2019 (Featureflash Photo Agency/Shutterstock.com).

On the Blu-Ray Bonus Extras is the Featurette, "Black Widow: Whatever It Takes," which summarizes Black Widow's path from *Iron Man 2* until *Endgame*. Early on Johansson said, "It's nice to be able to play a superheroine who has a past.... She obviously has been around for over, what, forty years, and I think has a real foundation for all different kinds of spinoffs or interaction with other characters. I think that the possibilities are really endless." *Iron Man 2*'s director Jon Favreau felt the actors needed to become a "steward of their characters" and Johansson was definitely that. Robert Downey, Jr., said, "Scarlett was ... just a dream.... She's just so game and she had a really good time doing it. Unlike some of us ... curmudgeons there's very little you can do to get under her skin. She's just consummately professional."[58]

Analysis

The Avengers: Endgame is presented in a kind of code, a secret language for fans of these movies—with references to *Terminator*, *Star Wars*, *Die Hard* (!) and so on. This seems to be related to the larger tendency to devote part of the film to parody or poking fun at traditions—the talk about the ridiculousness of Time Machines, for instance, or the statement that "Back to the future is bullshit." All of these kind of in-jokes seem to work against the emotion tried for with the death of Stark and (to a lesser extent) Black Widow. The kind of wit displayed in such lines as, "What do I have in my bloodstream?

Cheese whiz" is reminiscent of kids hanging on the corner, "cutting each other up." In a way, the confused emotions suggested by a combination of parody and tragedy is, one supposes, reminiscent of the confused emotions of adolescence. The age when the comics were most popular and the age of the intended audience for the films? It was some relief when the film went to the past—with scenes of ordinary streets with ordinary cars and ordinary houses and ordinary people. There is so much that is extraordinary in these films that the ordinary becomes very welcome.

Black Widow (2021)

The *Black Widow* standalone was to have premiered on May 1, 2020, but the COVID-19 pandemic that swept over the world that spring nixed that. As of the writing of this book *Black Widow* had been set back until November 2021.

The story is set between *Captain America: Civil War* (2016) and The *Avengers: Infinity War* (2018).

Commentary

In March 2018, when making the *Black Widow* standalone was gaining traction, Johansson reiterated her love for the character, "and I think there is definitely an opportunity to explore the Widow as a woman who has kind of come into her own and is making independent and active choices for herself, probably for once in her life. You know, she hasn't always had that possibility so if it fit that criteria, then yes, I would want to do it."[59]

As a proven commodity in the franchise, Black Widow would be familiar enough to

Florence Pugh (left) and Scarlett Johansson, *Black Widow* (Marvel Studios/Zak Productions, 2021).

audiences, so whether a prequel or contemporary adventure was the subject, "everyone can dive in feet first."[60]

In July 2018 Cate Shortland, the Australian director of *Somersault* (2004) and *Berlin Syndrome* (2017), was hired to direct the Black Widow standalone. Johansson was reportedly a fan of the director.[61]

Returning to San Diego Comic-Con in July 2019, Marvel Studios stars and executives made a splash talking about the forthcoming *Black Widow* and other female-centered films. Said Johansson after a panel presentation, "Ten years ago, if you told me that I would be standing in Hall H and presenting this footage to all the fans, it would have seemed incomprehensible.... Especially with this lineup and this incredible cast and [director] Cate Shortland at the helm. It's an actual dream come true—very, very exciting."[62]

Later in the summer Johansson told *The Hollywood Reporter* that "The movie packs a big punch. If that slot [after *Captain America: Civil War*] is reserved for movies that pack a big punch, then we're in a good, good space."[63]

8

Working, Part 3

> "You know, I gotta hustle. I'm a twenty-eight-year-old woman in the movie business, right? ... Pretty soon the roles you're offered all become mothers. Then they just sort of stop. You have to hedge against that with work—theater, producing, this thing with *Esquire*."
> —Tom Chiarella, "Scarlett Johansson Is the Sexiest Woman Alive 2013," *Esquire*, November 2013

Sexiest Woman Alive, Again

Esquire ranked her the Sexiest Woman Alive for the second time and interviewed her for its November 2013 issue. Johansson was described as brave, a "politically astute, card-playing, magic-loving smart-ass...." Her beauty was unstressed. On filmmaking, "I've stood around bogs wearing half a million dollars' worth of jewelry, up to my knees in the rot, thinking how much more or less the place smelled like a sewer than it did the day before. And that is not what you'd call a problem exactly; it just wears you out." She shrugged when asked why she accepted *Esquire*'s accolade if she was so busy at that moment? "I'm the only woman to win it twice, right?"[1]

She said she was attracted to the irrational. "There's no such thing as total rationality. That's something I've realized lately."[2]

Perhaps she acceded to the interview because "She can talk. Really talk. She is the sexiest rambler alive."[3]

Back on Broadway

Johansson was keen for another theatrical revival and essayed Maggie in *Cat on a Hot Tin Roof* at the Richard Rodgers Theater. That role had been Barbara Bel Geddes's in the original 1955 stage production, Elizabeth Taylor's in the 1958 film version.

Johansson told an interviewer that before rehearsals she had mucho trepidation and was "convinced it will be the death of me." She noted how hard it would be to live the Maggie the Cat character for weeks on end "in a state of embarrassment and regret and self-loathing and desperation and all the things the character has gone through."[4]

The *New York Times* said, "A four-alarm urgency infuses every breath that Scarlett Johansson takes in the oxygen-starved revival...." The audience could have few quibbles, however, and the star, "like Maggie, seems to possess a confidence that can turn raw nerves into raw power." She "confirms her promise as a stage actress of imposing presence and adventurous intelligence." In fact, Johansson "is also the only major player in *Cat* who appears to have a fully thought-through idea of the character she's portraying." She is the only character suggesting "the tempest in the human heart."[5]

2014: Banner Year

Her spilled over into 2014 to win plaudits and awards. Johansson appeared in four new films that year: *Under the Skin, Captain America: The Winter Soldier, Lucy* and *Chef*. Three were hits. *Under the Skin*, which was rolled out in a distinctly meager exhibition with little or no TV promos, was for many a masterpiece. It was certainly a golden age, and one could be forgiven for predicting Johansson would never make another poor movie. Such was not the case, however, but in late 2019 she would reclaim her indie status with rave reviews for *Jojo Rabbit* and *Marriage Story*. Both premiered, again, in selected theaters, before streaming, *Jojo* via Netflix, *Marriage* via Amazon Prime.

Co-Worker Praise

Anthony Mackie, who played Falcon in the Marvel films, praised Johansson in an ABC News Radio interview, calling her sweet and cool. "She has every right, because of her status, because of her looks, because of who she is to be a stark raving lunatic, and she's not," Mackie said. "She's one of the sweetest, coolest, down-to-earth girls you'll meet and just fun to be around." She was a "sexapotamus" and would be "a great mom." He added, "She has a very soft sensitive side."[6] In 2019, Anthony Mackie would rue his demise in *Avengers: Infinity War*, offering as one of his own preferences: "I wish I was running and like Scarlett Johansson was there and I jump on her and take a bullet and she cries and I'm laying there. And I say 'I did it for you' and she's like, 'You were always my favorite.' And then you take the crane and you pan out and she passionately kisses me."[7]

Motherhood and Second Marriage

Announcing Johansson's engagement to Romain Dauriac in its September 23, 2013, issue, *People* featured a half-page photo of Johansson and an insert picture of her and Daurlac at the Venice International Film Festival on September 3.[8]

French journalist Dauriac was the father of Rose Dorothy, born to Johansson on September 4, 2014. Johansson tied the knot with Dauriac on October 1, 2014. Back in February 2014 Johansson told *People* that the 31-year-old Dauriac met her chief qualification: being a friend. "The most important thing I've realized through my experience in past relationships is that I really want to be friends with my partner more than anything.... Of course it's important to have passion, but you can't always be in the honeymoon phase. The friendship is really what carries you through when you have ups and downs."[9]

In 2016, Johansson told an interviewer about the challenges of being with another actor, which Dauriac was not. "There has to be a real understanding of how you share your time, especially when two people's careers are going at the same rate. Or even if one person is more successful than the other, that also proves challenging. There may be a competitive thing."[10] Nevertheless, the Johansson-Dauriac marriage was in jeopardy. Some noticed Johansson was not wearing her wedding ring. In fact, she and Romain had separated and were divorced in 2017.

Singing Again

Johansson and Joaquin Phoenix (briefly) sang "The Moon Song" in the film *Her*. It received an Academy Award nomination but lost to "Let It Go" from the animated film, *Frozen* (2013). Johansson told *Glamour* that it was her dream to be a voice in a Disney musical. "That's, like, a life goal, to be the voice in a Disney movie. Can someone make that happen?"[11]

SodaStream Controversy

SodaStream was a hundred-year-old purveyor of fruity and sparkling drink mixes to be stirred up at home. The company aimed to protect health and the environment by curtailing the use of both bottles and sugar.

Johansson made a TV ad to be run during the National Football League's Super Bowl on February 2, 2014. The Fox TV network nixed it. Why? Was it because of "red-hot actress Scarlett Johansson sensually sipping her home-made soda..." or Johansson signing off with, "Sorry, Coke and Pepsi"? The SodaStream CEO complained, "They're [the TV network] afraid of Coke and Pepsi."[12] Johansson said, "If only I could make this message go viral...." It did.[13]

The second controversy involving SodaStream related to a factory located on Palestine's West Bank. It employed Palestinians but was viewed by some as complicit with illegal West Bank settlements. Johansson quit as representative although she stood behind her decision to lend her support in the first place. She didn't think closing the factory and leaving people destitute was the solution. She saw the factory as a step "forward in a seemingly impossible situation."[14] In 2018 Pepsico bought SodaStream for $3.2 billion. By that time SodaStream had moved its plant into the Negev. It was foiled in its attempt to bring along 350 of its Palestinian workers by the denial of permits. Israeli Arabs, some once nomadic Bedouin, took their place and SodaStream's workforce grew to 1,400.[15]

Defining Johansson

A telling interview was done for *The New Yorker* in March 2014. During the interview photographer Pari Dukovic and his factotums did their thing. At one time Dukovic urged Johansson, "Give me nothing." And "Johansson wiped the expression from her face...." Invited to simulate a Renaissance picture, she immediately slipped into a 16th-century persona. Pretending to hold a pose for a painter and kvetching about it: "You could not wish for a more plausible insight into the mind-set of the Mona Lisa." Later Dukovic again asked her to show nothing. Shortly thereafter, he was done. It had taken 17 minutes. Why be surprised? Movie stars become more alive and enrich themselves when the camera focuses on them.[16]

A couple months later a 2014 *Vanity Fair* interviewer attempted to define Johansson's persona. She was "real" during the interview, but a second persona, a mask, was probably necessary for survival or "sense of self" to avoid being torn apart by fame and celebrity like Marilyn Monroe or Lindsay Lohan. "The second persona allows her to give you what you want—intimacy, revelation, nakedness—the illusion of those things, anyway.... It allows her to maintain, as well, her mystery, and mystery is essential to stardom, is what gives the power to fascinate, beguile, captivate, haunt.[17]

The *Vanity Fair* interviewer had met Johansson in the Jewel Suite of the New York Palace hotel, watching the magazine's cover shoot before getting down to business. She quickly understood that Johansson "was a movie goddess, the purest strain of movie star." Around this entity "You become a man, even if you're not one. You gawk. You gape. You leer." Nevertheless, this is necessary and what she intends. "She's seducing the camera and thus, by extension, you, since you, again by extension, are on the other end of that camera."[18]

An Actress' Career

Johansson said, "in an actress's career, there's probably a sense of urgency to stay relevant, to stay the object of desire, or to stay in the spotlight. Your career is much shorter, in general. Male actors can work forever and ever and continue to be leading-man material. For actresses, it's much harder. Young actresses think, OK, I'm gonna make hay while the sun shines … later on, I'll direct a film when my acting career slows down."[19]

Chef (2014)

Carl Casper (Jon Favreau) runs the kitchen at Riva's (Dustin Hoffman) upscale L.A. Restaurant Gauloise. When food critic Ramsey Michel (Oliver Pratt) is scheduled to critique the menu, Carl and Riva have a falling out. Carl accedes to Riva's request to serve up old favorites, which Ramsey attacks on his blog. Learning about Twitter but thinking his scathing tweet will only go to Ramsey, Carl's world comes crashing down as his rant flies into the blogosphere and he's caught on video berating Ramsey. Carl is cashiered and complains to the restaurant's hostess Molly (Johansson) that he's never not known what he was to do. She tells him he's not happy, she wants him to be happy, and convinces him that this is a chance to take a new direction—and to get to know his son Percy (Emjay Anthony). Carl's ex-wife Inez (Sofia Vergara) is also supportive of taking a new tact, and with Martin (John Leguizamo) and Percy in tow, Carl travels to Miami and refurbishes a derelict food truck courtesy of another of Inez's ex-husbands, Marvin of Cardiff Construction and Rentals (Robert Downey, Jr.) into El Jefe, a spiffy vehicle initially serving the pork sandwich known as the Cubano. The venture is a success in more ways than one. Carl recovers his mojo and grows closer to Percy, teaching this willing student the art of cooking. After success in Miami, they travel to New Orleans and Austin before arriving back in California. Carl tells Percy they can't continue because Percy has school. But upon viewing the 1 second per day video Percy created on his phone, Carl has second thoughts and with Inez' support tells Percy he can work on the truck after school and on weekends. One evening Ramsey shows up to commend Carl's menu and mend fences. To that effect, he bankrolls Carl in a new restaurant, which serves as the locale for Carl's remarriage to Inez.

Jon Favreau and Scarlett Johansson, *Chef* (Aldamisa Entertainment, 2014).

Reviews

The *Los Angeles Times* complimented Favreau for avoiding "done-to-death family dynamics, forced obstacles and predictable responses for authentic interaction, organic humor and a hopeful vitality." The supporting cast hits their "sweet spots here." Johansson and Bobby Cannavale "are tops as Carl's old restaurant co-workers...."[20] The *News Journal* called it a "refreshing passion project...." for director and star Favreau. "Johansson and Bobby Cannavale are finely cast as restaurant staffers."[21] The *Hindustan Times* commended the "terrific cast and all of them bring in their A-game."[22]

Commentary

Chef in June was Jon Favreau's exceedingly pleasant account of a topflight chef who finds himself literally out on the street—in a food truck. Johansson was his former restaurant's hostess and sometimes girlfriend. Her character Molly, like Sofia Vergara's ex-wife Inez, is instrumental in convincing Favreau's chef to strike out in a new direction and to bond with his son. Like Dustin Hoffman's owner and Robert Downey, Jr.'s eccentric, Johansson's was a small role apparently done as a favor for her *Iron Man 2* director. In the past *Chef* would have merited the appellation "sleeper," i.e., a film with a modest budget that became a surprise hit. Emjay Anthony is non-cloying as the 10-year-old Percy.

Analysis

Chef is a feel-good fairy tale that combines a Buddy picture with a road trip to bring about not only the renewal of the title character's career but also the reunification of his fractured family. Jon Favreau writes, directs, and stars in the film as Chef Carl Casper. Johansson's role is a necessarily small one because she is part of what rapidly becomes the title character's past and has no part in his future. She plays Molly, the attractive, trendy woman who greets and seats the patrons of the high-end restaurant owned by Riva (Dustin Hoffman) where Chef Casper works his magic.

Molly is not only a co-worker but also a warm friend. Johansson makes the most of the small part when the Chef loses his job and she has the chance to display maturity and the kind of common sense that can pass in our time for wisdom. She proves able to utter clichés in a way that gives them the ring of truth. "I want you to be happy," she says convincingly. "You aren't happy here." When the Chef confesses to her that he is "lost," now that he has no job and seems unable to find another one, Molly says, "Sounds like a place to start." She urges him to use the time without work to get to know his son, Percy, played by Emjay Anthony, what she must recognize as a source of guilt in him. She credibly comes across as someone who is not only attractive and sensual but also honest and caring. She is appropriately conspicuous by her absence from the party for the Grand Opening of the Chef's new restaurant at the movie's end, a restaurant named El Jefe, indicating that the metamorphosis the film has worked is equivalent to a translation. Molly helped trigger that metamorphosis through her advice and encouragement that freed the Chef to take risks.

Break for Baby

Rose Dorothy was born to Johansson and Raymond Dauriac on September 4, 2014. Mom said she realized her daughter would stumble on her films on TV. Otherwise, she'd be happy to introduce them to her "when she's old enough to show her movies where I kicked some ass."[23]

Saturday Night Live

On November 1, 2014, Chris Rock hosted *Saturday Night Live*. In his opening monologue he explained that unless some indispensable facilities were located in the new Freedom Tower in New York City, he would never enter this site of the former World Trade Center, not even if Scarlett Johansson was standing buck naked on the 89th floor in a plate of ribs.

Barbara Walters Interview

Prefacing her December 15, 2014, interview for her ongoing "10 Most Fascinating People" TV series, Barbara Walters suggested that her audience knew her guest from her movies but probably didn't know three things about Johansson's personal life. Walters was more than a little surprised that Johansson hadn't even revealed that she was no longer engaged, but married.[24]

Johansson revealed that it was exhausting but that she took care of her child, born on September 4, by herself. (She'd married the father, French journalist Romain Dauriac, on October 1.) In a self-effacing mood, she said she had an okay body and topped out at 5'4" on a good day. Walters called her tiny but said she looked tall. Johansson's philosophy: with every gain a loss, with every loss a gain.[25]

Kudos

The Daily Beast thought Johansson's role in *Under the Skin* was deserving of commendation what with the Academy Award nominations to be announced on January 15, 2015. "It's hard to be still onscreen—but it's a trait Johansson has mastered." Not knowing her thoughts is why she's compelling. Reaction is the name of her game, as evidenced in *Lost in Translation*, *Girl with a Pearl Earring*, *The Avengers*, and especially, *Under the Skin*, where "she's seductive, haunting, menacing, and genial—all at once."[26]

Disney and Franchises

Because of Johansson's success in 2014 with *Captain America: The Winter Soldier* and *Lucy*, Disney was eager to employ her talents. A commentator pointed out that "It's strange and kind of cool that Johansson would be seen to have this kind of box office power." It had to do with franchises, rather than stars, although stars were necessary for the franchises to thrive. In any event, if the pattern continued, they saw Johansson becoming "a rare star in modern Hollywood."[27]

The commentator almost discerns that in contemporary films it is the *concept* that is most important in attracting a large audience, and that concept is almost always science fiction and fantasy–themed. In fact, there have been films in which the performers, professionals they might be and stars they might become, are distinctly not chosen for star power. Think Sam Neill and Laura Dern in *Jurassic Park* (1993), where dinosaurs were of paramount importance. *Raiders of the Lost Ark* (1981) did not depend for success on its heroine played by Karen Allen. The *Dawn of the Planet of the Apes* (2014) theatrical poster hardly indicated its stars, Jason Clarke and Keri Russell. Perhaps the signal example of this phenomenon was *Avatar* (2009), whose poster featured Sam Worthington and Zoë Saldana but whose names are in small type with the rest of the cast and behind-the-scenes filmmakers.

87th Academy Awards show

On February 22, 2015, at the Dolby Theatre in Hollywood, Johansson introduced what all considered an almost shockingly memorable performance by Lady Gaga, who sang four songs in a tribute to the 50th anniversary of *The Sound of Music*. When finished, she introduced and demurely demurred to Julie Andrews. They hugged. The audience gave Gaga a standing ovation.

Johansson's haircut and jewelry might have been intended to establish a sense of Punk Chic that would be especially appropriate for the person being introduced. There is something almost inherently funny about Lady Gaga singing "Climb Every Mountain," but she in fact did it magnificently and it seemed Julie Andrews was actually moved and appreciative of the tribute. In any case, Johansson seems to have been selected as a person who could reach a younger audience that might tend to ignore awards fluff. A possibility at least?

Another memory of Scarlett at the Academy Award telecast was when an emcee or presenter referred to the close up on her bottom that opens *Lost in Translation* and the camera panned to her laughing at the comment from her seat—puns always intended.

Before the show Johansson walked the red carpet in a stunning green gown and necklace. At least as much was made of her encounter with John Travolta, who smooched her and held her stomach. This stirred a mild controversy in that some thought Travolta, 61, was playing her as a trophy.[28] It seems more likely that Johansson and Travolta have remained pals. Eleven years before they'd paired up on *A Love Song for Bobby Long*, and Johansson had been excited to work with him and pleased by the experience. Of their Oscars moment she said that Travolta was "a class act…." She called the photo in question "an unfortunate still-frame" of a "totally sweet and totally welcome" meeting. Furthermore, she told The Associated Press that "there is nothing strange, creepy or inappropriate about John Travolta." The controversy was typical of "the way we are misguided, misinformed and sensationalized by the 24-hour news cycle. I haven't seen John in some years and it is always a pleasure to be greeted by him."[29]

The Late Show with David Letterman (April 27, 2015)

After 22 seasons hosting *The Late Show* on CBS, David Letterman was to bow out in May 2015. Johansson appeared as the prime guest on Monday, April 27, 2015. She took mock umbrage at Dave's suggestion that her dress resembled a linen tablecloth or shawl. She also mocked herself being on the show during her puberty phase when she'd promoted *The Horse Whisperer*. Letterman asked about her favorite films. She first mentioned *Match Point* and he asked for the titles of the other Woody Allen movies she'd been in, and she agreed that *Match Point* had been Allen's first film made outside the States. *Vicky Cristina Barcelona* elicited audience applause on Letterman's cue.

As usual with the modern late-night TV talk shows, conversations were interrupted and veered from original topics. Thus Johansson never got to identify other favorite films. One might have thought the audience would have really cheered if *Lucy* or *Captain America: The Winter Soldier* had been mentioned.

On a personal note, Letterman asked about her 7-month-old baby Rose Dorothy and wondered if she had had any qualms about bringing a child into such a harsh world. She was nonplussed at such a "heavy" comment. She looked upon Rose as a future environmental lawyer. She said she spent much of her time in Paris.

Before her interview was finished, Letterman asked to see video of Johansson entering the theater. Seen from the side, attired in an unbelted long wintry coat and sunglasses, she waved to fans flashing photos behind the barrier before passing the bodyguard/security man at the door. As Letterman perspicaciously observed, "This is a movie star. Look at that."

Johansson said there'd never be anyone like Dave.

In sum, she looked good and did well. There was perhaps a little awkwardness in the wish to be grateful to the host and to make a mini-speech about that right from the start when he seemed willing to simply converse. The discussion of the first appearance for *The Horse Whisperer* was interesting and the wish to get her to say which of her films meant most to her was a good question but not especially well answered. The importance of Woody Allen to her was clear enough, but it might have been good to pick a few other films or directors to comment on. She seemed uninvolved to a large extent with *The Avengers* hype and was almost apologetic about it—a good sign but probably not what the producers want. Dave's drawing attention to the entrance and the wave as old-style Hollywood stardom in action was fun.

Saturday Night Live (May 2, 2015)

Johansson hosted *SNL* for the fourth time on May 2, 2015. Once again, she wore a white dress during her introduction. Wiz Khalifa was the musical guest. A filmed segment had Johansson as Black Widow being romanced by Ultron.

The Glass Ceiling

"If you let smart women build stuff, there's a good chance people will come," opined Karen Valby in *Entertainment Weekly*. She concluded with a nod to Johansson, "now at the top of her well-played game.…" Johansson was termed "ferocious" in *Lucy* and a formidable Black Widow in the recent Captain America outing. "I like to imagine that she'll soon get the Black Widow spin-off she deserves, and that someone like [Nicole] Perlman is busy working on a script."[30]

The following year Mark Ruffalo, Johansson's co-star as the Hulk in the *Avengers* canon complained about the dearth of Black Widow toys. He tweeted that Marvel's merchandising needed to better target young girls, offering them the opportunity to play in this universe, where, as a writer said, "Natasha Romanov starts to emerge not just as a warrior but a battlefield."[31] Apparently Marvel merchandizing got the word. Black Widow appeared on Ziploc bags in 2018.

Perfect Figure

The British lingerie company Bluebella used The Golden Ratio devised by the Greeks to determine perfect proportions that indicated that Johansson scored 96.4 based on bust to waist to thigh measurements. Bluebella founder Emily Bendell told the *Sunday Telegraph* that "We were running a computer simulation on celebrity women and in doing so we inadvertently discovered that Scarlett Johansson's figure is pretty much as close as you can get to the perfect Golden Ratio."[32]

Celebrity 100

Forbes gave Johansson the 65th ranking in its "Celebrity 100" at a net worth of $35.5 million. She'd "Proved she could carry an action movie with *Lucy*, which grossed $459 mil worldwide, now commands north of $10 mil per film."[33]

Two years later she commented that she might be the top-grossing actress of all time. However, that did not mean she was the highest paid.[34]

The Late Show with Stephen Colbert

Back in April Johansson was one of the last guests on the *Late Show with David Letterman*. On September 9, 2015, she was the first female and movie star guest on the new iteration: *The Late Show with Stephen Colbert*. It was Colbert's second night as host. On September 8 he'd welcomed George Clooney, Johansson's co-star in the Coen Brothers' forthcoming *Hail, Caesar!* But that release wasn't scheduled until 2016 and no mention was made of it on either night. Colbert was seconded by Clooney that he was there just to talk.

Nor was Johansson, who still sported her short-cut hair she'd revealed in the spring, pitching anything. Colbert introduced her as one of Hollywood's most sought after actresses, the star of *Lost in Translation*, *Her*, *Lucy* and *The Avengers*. He pointed out that she'd flown in from Paris and seemed mildly surprised that she spent some of her time in New York. He suggested that, in her all-black Michael Kors jumpsuit (what could be taken for a short-sleeve vinyl top and dark slacks), she was a fashion-plate. She tentatively agreed but said the Parisian women were far above her in that realm. She did love Paris, saying each day she'd find something else to marvel at.

At one point, when Colbert was talking too fast, Johansson said, "Stop it!" He complied.

Colbert indicated that she was a Renaissance woman: actress, model, singer, musician. What was left? He said actors in superhero movies had to beef up. Did actresses? She put up her arms to show her muscles. She mentioned the Black Widow crotch lock, a reference to jumping on Steve Roger's antagonist in *Captain America: The Winter Soldier*.

To finish off the segment, Colbert introduced "Big Questions with Even Bigger Stars" in which he and Johansson were shown reclining on a blanket under the heavens. He questioned her as to whether she'd rather have hands as feet or feet as hands and what she'd like to have done with her body when she died. She guessed she'd like it dropped in the Hudson River. She wondered what Oprah was doing right now.

Johansson said she knew Colbert's next guest, billionaire entrepreneur Elon Musk, creator of the Tesla electric car and SpaceX, whose goal was to put people on other planets in the not that distant future. Johansson did not hang around to greet Musk. (Nor had Clooney hung around when Jeb Bush appeared as Colbert's second guest the previous evening.)

Hail, Caesar! (2016)

Eddie Mannix (Josh Brolin) is the "fixer" at Capitol Pictures. His job is to keep the mortal stars aligned, e.g., prevent the press from tarnishing the reputations of Capitol's prime stable of actors and actresses. Such a problem raises its head when Baird Whitlock (George Clooney) disappears from the set of *Hail, Caesar!*, the studio's gigantic Biblical epic. Is Whitlock on a bender? It doesn't seem plausible as he had been filming before heading to his trailer during a break. In fact, Baird has been drugged and spirited to a seaside house chock full of left-wing intellectuals who aim to pursue their machinations by extorting $100,000 from the studio for Baird's return. While they wait, they engage Baird in a heavy discussion of man's plight. This only slowly comes into Eddie's purview. He's also wondering if he should leave the studio and take a job in aviation at Lockheed. Then there's DeeAnna Moran (Johansson), the star of a new Capitol Pictures aquatic extravaganza. In a bright green mermaid costume, DeeAnna had dived into a large pool, risen on a platform and … ripped off her tiara and flung it at the orchestra director. Attendants stripped off her "fish ass" and she sits smoking as Eddie tries to calm her down. They discuss her pregnancy and Eddie tells her it might behoove her to marry the father—or whoever—as she reverts to her New York City street accent. She's had two failed marriages and doesn't want another.

Eddie and lawyer Sid Siegelstein (Geoffrey Cantor) devise a plan that involves Silverman (Jonah Hill), who has played the part of "person" many times. This time he'll take possession of DeeAnna's baby and immediately return it. Voila, adoption!

Eddie also has to deal with non-actor but star Hobie Doyle (Alden Ehrenreich). He tells his flustered director Laurence Laurentz (Ralph Fiennes) to bear with Hobie, he's extremely popular.

Baird is released and spouts left-wing talking points to Eddie, who slaps him around and maintains that making movies is a worthy pursuit. "Baird, go out there and be a star."

Scarlett Johansson, *Hail, Caesar!* **(Universal Pictures, 2016).**

His secretary Natalie (Heather Goldenhersh) passes on DeeAnna's flowers to him. The adoption of her child will not take place. DeeAnna and Silverman had dinner and promptly ran off and got married in Palm Springs.

Back on the set, Baird does an excellent job standing before Jesus' cross until he can't remember the end of a line. It's *faith*. "Ah, son of a bitch!"

Eddie goes to confession—again, then back to the studio. He's not going to take the Lockheed job.

Reviews

USA Today said, "The combination of the Coen brothers' filmmaking acumen and George Clooney in absolute buffoon mode is again Hollywood magic." Nevertheless, "Some bits fall flat, yet when the Coens hit, there's nothing better, especially with their usual ridiculously sublime banter."[35] *Hail, Caesar!* Was on *Entertainment Weekly*'s "The Must List" for February 12, 2016. *EW* called it "A giddy Technicolor love letter to Hollywood's golden age…." It was Coen-lite "but still filled with their best signatures: cracked humor, indelible characters, and cinematography so rich and saturated you want to dunk a cookie in it."[36] *Time* found the Coens in their "woolly mode, riffing on their fondness for tall tales and outlandish, larger-than-life figures…." The enterprise didn't hang together perfectly. "But Johansson in a mermaid's tail? Really, why else make movies—or go to them?"[37] *Empire* awarded the movie 4 out of 5 stars. It was in sum "a series of impressively-mounted pastiches." This included the "Johansson-centred synchronized-swimming sequence, featuring a giant mechanical whale."[38]

Commentary

Johansson had worked for the Coen Brothers in *The Man Who Wasn't There* when she'd been only 17. *Hail, Caesar!* premiered on February 5, 2016, presaged by a good spate of TV ads.

Of her glamour-puss character, Johansson said, "Deanna is kind of an Esther Williams–type movie star. She's probably like a lot of movie stars in, now and forever, discovered or plucked from anywhere, nowhere, probably Red Hook or something like that."[39] She added, "Shooting in this sort of golden era of Hollywood is always an appealing thing for every actor I think because the costumes and the glamour of it and the behind-the-scenes quality is just a fun environment to live in."[40]

Analysis

In retrospect, an enjoyable bit was when a studio employee asked Jesus on the cross whether he was a principal or an extra, trying to make sure which lunch Jesus should receive. Jesus replied that he thought he was a principal. The fact that he wasn't sure was a nice touch. The appearance of Herbert Marcuse in the film was a high point. He was a hero of the New Left who can be faulted for having served in the OSS. A Communist AND a secret police man—the kind of person the prominent Italian-born anarchist Carlo Tresca couldn't stand.

Is *Hail, Caesar!* the first American film since *REDS* to include the term Comintern? The sinking of the briefcase with the "contribution" to the cause was a nice touch.

It's about little things with large implications. The Lockheed v Moviedom decision is interesting in terms of a future for the country—do you want frivolity, little things, or military might and the big things that come with superpowerdom? It's nice that Eddie chose frivolity.

Some thought Johansson's character rather needless, but with that glamour omitted there would have been no glamour in a movie taking place in a Hollywood still aglow with it.

The Coen brothers in *Hail, Caesar!* pay tribute to Hollywood's studio system by presenting a comic version of a day in the life of studio executive Eddie Mannix, played by Josh Brolin. Johansson provides one of the subplots of the movie, is the center of one of the minor problems Mannix needs to try and solve, by appearing as an aquatic movie star reminiscent of Esther Williams. If this is a relatively small part, it nonetheless serves to demonstrate Johansson's range and adaptability.

We first see her as a glamorous figure swimming toward an underwater camera. Her performance is combined with choreographed synchronized swimming. Bathing beauties shot from above arrange and rearrange their arms and legs so that they seem to depict the shifting designs of a human kaleidoscope. DeeAnna (Johansson) eventually rises from the water in a mermaid costume and wearing a crown. She pulls the crown from her head and chucks it at the nearby orchestra, hitting the conductor in the back. She then must be helped out of the too tight fit of her mermaid costume. The result is a comic scene that quickly reveals the angry, bitter, demanding person behind the smiling and gorgeous film persona.

An interview with Mannix makes clear the problem—a public relations problem—posed by DeeAnna's private life. Twice divorced, she now finds herself unmarried and pregnant. Moran's voice has the harsh edge of a New York accent and she uses it to complain in a comic way about the "unreliability" of her first two husbands. Mannix recommends that he arrange for the father of the baby-to-be to marry Moran and asks, "Are you sure he's the father?" After the diva responds in the positive she takes on a vaguely puzzled look and says to no one in particular, "Pretty sure."

As it turns out, the ostensible father is in fact already married and the father of two children. More than that, he's happily married and wants to stay with his wife. Mannix goes to a studio lawyer and raises the seemingly ridiculous question of whether a parent can adopt his or her own child. The lawyer decides there is no law or statute to prevent such an adoption but the child would first have to be given up by the parent so it would be available for adoption. Mannix and the lawyer decide this is a case for Joe Silverman, the character Jonah Hill plays, a kind of fixer who has pulled off a number of tricks on behalf of the studio. Johansson's second scene in *Hail, Caesar!* consists of her appearing with Mannix and the lawyer to interview Joe Silverman. DeeAnna repeatedly asks, "He's reliable?" an echo of her complaints about her first two husbands. Although she addresses this question to Mannix and the lawyer, Silverman answers it with, "I'm bonded," a nice way of evading the issue of reliability by making clear there is financial backing for a failure to perform. DeeAnna also takes an interest in the strength of Joe Silverman's arms before the interview concludes.

Johansson never appears in the film again, but her problem is resolved as part of the generalized Hollywood Happy Ending with which the film concludes. Mannix' secretary, Natalie (Heather Goldenhersh), reports to him that DeeAnna invited Joe Silverman to dinner and they drove to Palm Springs to marry.

Hail, Caesar! gave Johansson the chance to play a comic part in a film with an ensemble cast of many stars. Her figure and smile make her a believable star of the late 1940s or early 1950s while she is also able to manipulate her voice and facial expressions in a way that also makes a credible demanding Diva. The costumes, the underwater scenes, the temper, the complaints about the former husbands and the quizzing of Joe Silverman all serve to establish her talent as a comedienne. There is the sense that she relished playing even this small part in a Coen brothers romp.

Robotic

Only in the 21st century could someone create a Scarlett Johansson robot. Ricky Ma of Hong Kong spent 35,000 pounds on the project. An article called Johansson a "vivacious and intelligent actress…" but termed her duplicate programmed to respond to comments with "little more than a coquettish smile and a wink" as entirely disappointing, a "reflection of the way women are portrayed in society as Ma's clever three dimensional creation is about as one dimensional as you can get." It was felt that Johansson would agree that talking about the ethical and societal implications is very important "before those oft quoted science fiction dystopias become a nightmarish reality."[41]

On another level, a robotic Johansson is entirely in keeping with her oeuvre. What other star would deserve this tribute?

Box Office Mojo Ranks Johansson World's Most Successful Female Star

In 2016 Johansson was in two of the year's most successful films: *Captain America: Civil War*, *The Jungle Book*. These contributed to her Box Office Mojo status. Stars were ranked based on the profitability of their movies, not whether they were the main star, part of an ensemble cast, or heard but unseen in an animated film. Thus Harrison Ford came out at #1, supplanting Samuel L. Jackson. At #10, Johansson was the only woman on the list.[42]

Chinese Fans

Johansson traveled to Shenzhen, China to promote Huawei P9, a dual lens smartphone camera created by Huawei and Leica. Johansson extolled the photos she could then take, especially of her daughter. She, actor Henry Cavill and fashion photographer Mario Testino combined for the P9 advertising campaign. At the Huawei P9 Fans Club Party, Johansson was cheered by her Asian admirers and received a commemorative video produced by fans from around the country. The event ended with Scarlett taking selfies with her devotees, and she said that this was welcome because she did not participate in social media. She "was touched by the love from her Chinese fans for her and her films."[43]

Female Energy on Set

Johansson was pleased to find more women working behind the scenes than ever before, no longer "basically a bunch of dudes;" but directors, grips, cinematographers and camera assistants. She was refreshed by "female energy on the set," plus "a more balanced creative environment."44

USO Tours

Johansson had visited U.S. Troops overseas in 2008 and returned courtesy of the United Service Organizations (USO) in December 2016, stopping at military bases in Germany, Turkey, Qatar and Afghanistan. Among those accompanying her were country star Craig Campbell, National Basketball Association star Ray Allen, Olympic swimming medalist Maya DiRado, entertainer Jim Karol, and frequent film co-star Chris Evans. One of Johansson's favorite comments came from a serviceman's son who revealed that his favorite superhero was Batman. "We spent time eating with the troops in the mess hall, watching drills and demonstrations, learning about the aircrafts and K-9 units." On the front lines in Afghanistan, they met "a few hundred troops who have been stationed

Scarlett Johansson at Bagram Air Base, Afghanistan, 2016 (Dave Gatley/United Service Organizations, Inc., insert by Navy Petty Officer, 2nd Class, Dominique A. Pineiro; the appearance of U.S. Department of Defense [DoD] visual information does not imply or constitute DoD endorsement).

there for the past six months, and sometimes longer. We reminded them how much they are appreciated."[45]

Helping Children

Two-year-old Scarlett Griffith, named after the actress, of Wisconsin Rapids, Wisconsin, had leukemia. The child's aunt asked if she could contact Johansson. Her mother said okay but, "I didn't think she had a snowball's chance to be able to contact her." But Johansson's public relations agent told her client, who made a video message in November. Johansson's namesake was said to watch it over and over. The prognosis for the child was positive, but treatment might last 30 months.[46]

Political Activism

Always liberal, even a "dirty liberal" to some right-wingers, Johansson drew inspiration from her grandmother. Back in a revealing 2006 interview for *Allure* she'd complained about persistent racism and far right Republicans who contested vaccinating girls against HPV, the human papillomavirus, for fear it would make them promiscuous. For Johansson, "That reasoning is so sick."[47]

In 2008 Johansson, feeling the country was in emergency mode, stumped for Democratic Presidential candidate Barack Obama. She worked phone banks for him in Iowa[48]

Later that year Johansson was described as Barack Obama insider who e-mailed him, hosted fundraisers, and campaigned between film shoots. She decided to use her celebrity to spotlight her favorite causes. As she would during the Trump administration, Johansson maintained that "We all have the same right to vote and, especially in this technical age where we all can broadcast our opinions, we all have the opportunity to entice others to vote."[49]

In 2016 she told an interviewer about her continued interest in politics, specifically from the woman's perspective. Johansson was flabbergasted that cutting Planned Parenthood's budget and compromising women's health were many politicians' priorities when the planet was in peril due to global warning, war and terrorism. "It's nuts."[50]

With the election of Donald Trump as President of the United States in 2016 and the ensuing plan to deprive Planned Parenthood of federal funds, Johansson joined others at the Women's March on Washington on January 21, when an estimated 500,000 protesters gathered on the National Mall. Various celebrities spoke, including the event's Artists' Chair America Ferrera, Madonna, and Johansson. Madonna sang and later ranted at the President who'd been officially installed in office the day before.[51] Johansson gave a more measured speech, focusing on Planned Parenthood, which Republicans had vowed to defund.

Johansson argued the time had come for women to "get really, really personal." She spoke about the good Planned Parenthood had done for herself, her sister, and her girlfriends by providing checkups, STD and cancer screening, pregnancy planning, and birth control, all without judgment. Johansson thought the country was moving backwards and pledged her support for women's healthcare initiatives. Politicians had no right to infringe on decisions women made about their bodies. She urged volunteering for and donating to organizations that helped women with decision-making. Johansson wondered about Ivanka Trump's comment that she was a quiet activist. "I don't know what kind of activism happens behind closed doors. It's passive activism—pass-tivism—that's a word we can make up for people to use!"[52]

Johansson felt that the current climate had turned on a switch for those previously politically naive. "This time presents a unique opportunity—I hope we use it wisely."[53]

Johansson also took issue with celebrities like Mark Wahlberg who advised fellow thespians to foreswear political commentary in public. She thought that was presumptuous. Why couldn't she have a voice, use her platform?[54]

amfAR

Before New York Fashion Week, Johansson and fashion designer Donatella Versace were honored by amfAR, the American Foundation for AIDS Research, on Wednesday, February 8, 2017. Johansson told the Associated Press she was touched to be there. "When I heard about it, I thought that, you know anything that I can do to bring awareness to amfAR. It's a wonderful organization and such an important cause with 37 million people today still living and struggling with HIV AIDS, and it's important that we remember that and never forget."[55]

Academy Award Presenter

On the red carpet at the Dolby Theater on February 26, 2017, announcer Ryan Seacrest asked if the shoes she was wearing were the ones she wore at the rehearsal. Taken aback, Johansson replied, "Ah-h-h, what a ridiculous question." Seacrest said Halle Berry had done so. Johansson said she did not wear the same shoes. Seacrest asked if she was an "adrenaline junkie" because of all her action movies. Johansson responded that, "I must be some sort of, like, glutton for punishment." Seacrest continued with questions about action. She said, "Yeah, and it's painful." As for the forthcoming *Ghost in the Shell*, she said, "I was too curious to pass it up."[56]

The MTV News announcer Josh Horowitz asked her which of the nominees she'd like to work with. She'd obviously not thought about it but finally answered that it would be Lin Manuel Miranda, he of Broadway's *Hamilton* fame. Would there be a Black Widow movie? "Um-m-m, I don't know, I don't know at this point." And, "I'm still trying to wrap my head around the *Infinity War*, which is like the production is in infinity, and then I'll let you know afterward." As for *Ghost in the Shell*, "I'm ready for *Ghost in the Shell* to spread its wings and fly, and, um-m-m, I'm going to see it next week for the first time so I'm nervous but I'm excited."[57]

Queen of Science Fiction

In 2017, more than a decade from her breakout role in *Lost in Translation*, Johansson had become "a rather different sort of screen idol. Following a succession of high-octane blockbusters and off-beat critical hits, the actress is now enshrined as perhaps the leading sci-fi action star of her generation. Where once her sardonic smirks and sultry looks spoke of old-school glamour, she is now more likely to grab the limelight by kickboxing than by smouldering."[58]

Saturday Night Live

Johansson's first stint hosting the late-night sketch comedy and music TV show *Saturday Night Live* had occurred in 2006. On March 11, 2017, she joined the elite coterie of Drew Barrymore, Candice Bergen, and Tina Fey as female stars who had hosted the show five times or more and received the jacket with the number 5 on the sleeve.

The funniest skit of the evening was a taped segment perhaps partially inspired by TV perfume ads featuring stars like Julia Roberts and Charlize Theron in gorgeous dresses wowing party guests by their mere presence. In this iteration, "Every man knows her name, every woman knows her face. When she walks into a room, all eyes are on her. She's Ivanka." Johansson looked the part of the President's daughter and was shown applying lipstick in front of a full-length mirror. The image in the mirror was her father (played as usual by Alec Baldwin). The narrator commended her as an advocate and champion for women, but "how?" Most cutting was the name of the perfume: *Complicit*. Some months later Dictionary.com designated "complicit" its word of the year, noting that its use spiked after Johansson's TV sketch.[59]

Early Morning, Late Night

In a taped interview for *Good Morning, America* on March 28, 2017, Michael Strahan asked Johansson about *Ghost in the Shell* and a possible run for political office. Johansson said she wouldn't presume to play a character from another race and explained her Major in *Ghost in the Shell*. Politically, "I'm not afraid to say what I feel is right just because I think that I'm gonna face criticism or some people might not like me. I mean … if fighting … for women's rights, that's gonna … mean that some people don't wanna buy a ticket to see *Ghost in the Shell*, then I'm okay with that."

As for taking the plunge into politics, she said it was not out of the question on the local level but for now, what with her young daughter and career, it would not be happening.

Strahan concluded by asking if she'd found out anything about herself in *Ghost in the Shell* to which she responded, "I definitely came out of there, like I was a little traumatized at the end of this film just because it was so much work and it was like kind of a dark … place to live in, but I … was kind of, okay, I did that. Like… I'm hanging in, I'm … resilient. I'm back to myself, I was happy to find myself at the end of *Ghost in the Shell*."

On *The Tonight Show with Jimmy Fallon*, March 28, she played Virtual Reality Pictionary with *SNL* player Michael Che vs. Fallon and Dove Cameron.

Talking with the Shock Jock

Back when *In Good Company* was in the offing in 2004, talk radio host Howard Stern had interviewed Marg Helgenberger, who'd played Johansson's character's mother in the film. Stern asked his guest if Scarlett would ever come on his show? Helgenberger replied with an optimistic maybe. Now, on March 27, 2017, Johansson was a guest of the famously crude (but funny) shock jock, who'd once responded to a caller in the affirmative, i.e., he had not evolved.

Wearing big headphones, Johansson seemed at ease, lounging on a couch in jeans and black top. Stern asked about roles she'd missed out on. Yes, she'd auditioned for *Jumanji* (1995) but Kirsten Dunst got the part. Was she bitter? Johansson played along: "No, I wasn't bitter enough then." As for *The Parent Trap* (1998) remake with Lindsay Lohan, she'd auditioned for that, too, and joked, "I started to get bitter at that point." As for *Les Miserables* (2012), "I had laryngitis, but I tried. But I didn't know if that's why I didn't get it. I probably didn't get it because I wasn't right for it." Stern and co-host Robin Quivers quipped that the Supporting Actress Academy Award Hathaway won was rightfully Johansson's.[60]

Women in the World Summit

Complementing her appearance at the Women's March on January 21, Johansson participated in the 8th annual Women in the World Summit, April 5–7, 2017. It took place in the David H. Koch Theater at Lincoln Center, New York City. Hillary Rodham Clinton was also present, along with Nigerian author Chimamanda Ngozi Adichie, Canadian Prime Minister Justin Trudeau, President of Planned Parenthood Federation of America Cecile Richards, actress Maria Bello, author Arianna Huffington, and many other role models who were tackling international issues.

During the conference Johansson spoke one on one with Arianna Huffington, founder and CEO of Thrive Global. Johansson gave her opinion on Ivanka Trump, baffled that the President's daughter would think working for causes behind closed doors was significant. Regarding running for office, Johansson reiterated that she wouldn't rule anything out but that she had a young child and a full career. Huffington said, "New York mayor—wouldn't that be great?" And activism ran in the family, what with Johansson's grandmother working for the rights of tenants and a mother who took her children into the voting booth. Johansson's brother Hunter helped with the Obama campaign. On empowerment, she thought the key was to live with technology while simultaneously "give ourselves time and space to be clear in our mind and focus on our empowerment and goals...."[61]

A month after the Women in the World Summit, on May 2, 2017, Johansson attended Planned Parenthood's 100th Anniversary Gala in New York City.

Scarlett Johansson at Planned Parenthood 100th Anniversary Gala at Pier 36, New York, NY, May 2, 2017 (lev radin/Shutterstock.com).

Rough Night (2017)

Flashback to 2006: Jessica Thayer (Johansson) and college roommate and self-proclaimed best friend Alice (Jillian Bell) attend a raucous party with other chums Blair (Zoë Kravitz) and Frankie (Ilana Glazer). Forward a decade: Jess takes a break from her political campaign to rendezvous with her girlfriends in Miami and celebrate her upcoming nuptials via a girls' weekend while fiancé Peter (Paul W. Downs) attends a rather staid bachelor bash. To the consternation of Alice, a more recent friend of Jess from Down Under, Pippa, aka Kiwi (Kate McKinnon), joins the revelers. After partying at a club, they agree to hire a male ecdysiast. A man seeming to be said stripper arrives at their door. When he comes on strong to Jess, she shoves him away, but Alice has no reservations and charges across the room, launching herself onto the dude, sending the chair over backward. The guy hits his head on the end table and bleeds out. What to do? Use a jet ski and dump him in the ocean seems vaguely plausible.

On the beach their swinging neighbors Lea (Demi Moore) and Pietro (Ty Burrell) come out to investigate and observe Pippa on top of and kissing the guy. Meanwhile, having received a curious call from Jess, Peter is racing south to make sure she still wants to marry him. Pippa takes the jet ski and dumps the body. Alice notices a surveillance camera on their neighbor's porch, so they convince Blair to keep Lea and Pietro busy while they steal the video. Back in their house, the women clean up the blood and then go to the beach for a "centipede" photo. In the resulting image they see a body on the beach. It's the dude Alice inadvertently killed. Retrieving the body, they wonder what to do when a policeman arrives. But he's the stripper as they discover after Frankie accidentally knocks

Left to right: Jillian Bell, Kate McKinnon, Scarlett Johansson, Zoe Kravitz, Ilana Glazer, *Rough Night* **(Paulilu Productions/Sony Pictures, 2017).**

him out. Still on the road, Pete discovers his credit card isn't working and must clean windshields for gas money.

Jess and company put the body of the dead stripper in their car but have an accident and return to the house. After a confrontation with Alice over their relationship, Jess goes upstairs to shower so she'll at least look cute for her mug shot. Two more men arrive flashing badges, but they turn out to be diamond thieves looking for their co-conspirator—the dead guy. Unnoticed, Jess observes them from upstairs, and when "Detective Frazier" (Dean Winters) goes up to scrounge around, she disables him with hairspray, gets his pistol and has him cuff himself to the sink pipe. From the landing she leaps onto "Detective" Ruiz (Enrique Murciano). Alice manages to shoot Ruiz just before Frazier, who'd unlocked the cuffs, is knocked insensible when a coked-up Peter crashes his car through the wall.

Kiwi performs the wedding ceremony and tells Peter's friend that everyone is off the hook because under Florida law the killing was considered a "good murder." Jess's campaign manager calls to inform her a plethora of donations and her newfound notoriety as a crime buster mean she's sure to win the election.

Reviews

Variety found "some push and some laughs…" It appreciated "the feisty, claws-out spontaneity of its competitive banter between 'sisters' who love and hate each other." As for Johansson, who had been "swallowed up in the 'Blade-Runner'-meets-broken-glass cyber doldrums of 'Ghost in the Shell',…," it was pleasurable to see her in a "role in which she can coast along on the no-nonsense vibrance of her personality. She makes Jess cautious but fast—a grown up trying to let loose even as she keeps her inner desperado in check."[62] *The Hollywood Reporter* said the physical gags and verbal humor often fell flat and there was "an improbably tidy resolution."[63] The *New York Times* called it a "soft vanilla comedy…" dependent only on goofs. If not for the appealing performers it would be more irritating. At least Johansson and Glazer were "gifted physical performers who can sell weak jokes.…" It was interesting that there was room for the male side to have a role, specifically Jess's fiancé's "slow-building nonsense."[64] *Entertainment Weekly* commended the inspired casting of Demi Moore and Ty Burrell and great bits but a story "spiraling to nowhere."[65]

Commentary

Reviews were mixed for a film that for most of its gestation was known as *Move that Body* or *Rock That Body*,[66] most noting its obvious derivativeness, tracing its lineage to *Weekend at Bernie's* (1989), *Very Bad Things* (1998), *The Hangover* (2009), and *Bridesmaids* (2011). This was not news. Before the premiere, Johansson told an interviewer that the story was not original, "but the girls in this film are incredibly ridiculous and talented comic geniuses." Co-star, *Saturday Night Live* stalwart Kate McKinnon appreciated Johansson's, "drily delivered, witty, absurdist observations about everything."[67]

The New York City premiere was held at the AMC Loews Lincoln Square Theater on June 12, 2017, with Johansson and the rest of the cast present on the red carpet. Johansson wore a stunning full-length silver dress crisscrossing material over her neck, leaving shoulders bare. A diamond-shaped cutout over her midriff.

In her second appearance on *The Late Show with Stephen Colbert* on June 16, 2017, host Colbert referred to Johansson's costars as comediennes. Johansson was not confined in the same way. Prematurely and incorrectly, Colbert labeled *Rough Night* a blockbuster. Colbert picked up on the doppelganger that Johansson had invited to *Rough Night*'s premiere: a grandmother who in her youth bore a striking resemblance to her. As Johansson said, she looked like her in *Lucy*. She said they both got smashed at the premiere party.

In 2016 Johansson had spoken about gender and the imbalance between men and women, regarding not only salary but as screenwriters and directors.[68] Ironically but fortuitously, a year made a difference. "It used to be that you'd look out into the crew and it was a sea of men. Now, you see a lot of female grips, women in the camera department, set builders and teams. It's great."[69]

In the "Killer Cast" special feature on the *Rough Night* Blu-Ray, Johansson said she'd done some comedy before, such as her skits on *Saturday Night Live*, "But I read the script and it made me laugh out loud, and I'm not really a person who laughs out loud. I laugh a lot, like, on the inside, but it really made me, like, belly laugh."[70]

Analysis

Rough Night could be seen as a satiric comment on our politics when a serious, hard-working candidate has "an image problem" that is improved by taking drugs and killing people—criminals, admittedly, but still. There is something sad when a movie largely made by and one supposes for females can think of nothing to do but mimic male prejudices, stereotypes, crudity, and silliness. The only sex act committed in the film seems to be the oral sex performed by two women—Demi Moore and Zoë Kravitz. Is the bachelor party with its wine-tasting and absence of drugs and sex a kind of satiric female version of what is thought to be a male view of a female get together? In a way, the most character-based part of the film is the relationship between Jess and Alice, her Freshman roommate—growing distance on one side, the wish for exclusivity on the other side, and the discovery of the card and note at a crucial turning point in the plot. The movie's strongest point may be its plotting—the increasing entanglements that in the end are fairly rapidly unraveled and resolved. The fact that the plot ends with a marriage puts it in the comic tradition that dates back to ancient times and Shakespeare but with variations on sexuality—Shakespeare's *As You Like It* with Rosalind pretending to be a man to court and win Orlando in a way has implicit sexual issues that in *Rough Night* simply become explicit. There is something to be said for the fiancé crashing his car through a window to kill the last of the baddies as the way he is reunited with Jess and the marriage can proceed. He's been humiliated and is now through a fluke transformed into a kind of hero. It seems to be a well-made version of what it wants to be but for some is unappealing. Part of what it deals with, if indirectly, is the difficulty Americans now have in becoming adults—education and early career means people are now in their early thirties by the time they think about starting a family, often, and this extended adolescence is probably part of the reason for the drug culture and emphasis on sex sans love. The setting up of the situation takes too long and things improve when the situation—the accidental first death—actually happens. Does anyone think the guy at the door is really the stripper/prostitute or do we sense from the start he's someone else who just gets sucked into things? Mistaken identity is another one of those traditional elements of comedy that the movie draws on—*The Comedy of Errors* meets *As You Like It*. The diamond thief seems to have just gone along with the mistaken identity but why we do not know. A lark? For some reason—or more likely for no reason—his arrival constituted a case of mistaken identity right from the start—maybe because he never said who he was or what he was doing there but just went along with the assumption. Wonk.

Hurricane Relief

On November 6, 2017, Johansson and The John Gore Organization raised $500,000 for Puerto Rico after Hurricane Maria devastated the island in September. Johansson, Robert Downey, Jr., Chris Evans, Jeremy Renner, Frank Grillo, Mark Ruffalo, and Maximiliano Hernandez read Thornton Wilder's *Our Town* at Atlanta's Fox Theatre.[71]

2018

Women's March

Johansson attended the Women's March in Los Angeles on January 20, 2018, and spoke up on the newly formed Time's Up, which represents women in the entertainment industry but aims to reach further, and expressed outrage that someone would have the gall to publicly support the organization while continuing to prey on women. This was apparently a veiled reference to James Franco, who'd come under fire for sexual harassment. Johansson also told the crowd about dealing with her lack of power when she was 19.[72] Natalie Portman had contacted Johansson about Time's Up. "It was almost like you found something you didn't even realize you needed," said Johansson.[73]

New Agent

In 2018 Johansson left LBI Entertainment and long-time agent Rick Yorn, brother of the singer and songwriter Pete Yorn, with whom she'd recorded the 2009 album *Break Up*. Creative Artists Agency continued to represent her.[74]

Demeaned

In June 2018 Johansson took umbrage that a former employee of the Church of Scientology said he saw her name on a 2006 list of women auditioning to date Tom Cruise after his split from Nicole Kidman. Johansson said it would be so demeaning to put oneself on such a roster.[75]

Rub & Tug Controversy

As with *Ghost in the Shell*, where Johansson was condemned by the anime universe for daring to play an Asian character, as soon as she was revealed to take on the role of a woman transitioning into a man in *Rub & Tug*, the trans community was up in arms. In response, Johansson's rep identified Jeffrey Tambor, Jared Leto and Felicity Huffman as non-trans folk who essayed trans people without this level of anger.[76] There seems to have been no criticism of the heterosexual Christopher Plummer playing gay in the 2010 film *Beginners*, for which he won a Best Supporting Actor Academy Award.

But to the acclaim of trans actors and moviemakers, Johansson opted out.[77] In a statement to *Out Magazine*, Johansson said, "While I would have loved the opportunity to bring Dante's story and transition to life, I understand why many feel he should be portrayed by a transgender person, and I am thankful that this casting debate, albeit controversial, has sparked a larger conversation about diversity and representation in film." Nevertheless, the film sans Johansson seemed in doubt. Studios wouldn't risk spending on a film unless they could be assured of a profit.[78]

Two former *Daily Variety* writers tackled the issue in their ongoing web column, *Deadline*. Fleming argued that LGBTQ advocates who attacked Johansson for daring to consider playing a trans person in *Rub & Tug* were misguided. With Johansson out, any chance for a topnotch feature film version was virtually nil. For the LGBTQ community, "the chance to see their struggles and triumphs played out in anything but a micro budget indie movie or TV show has been extinguished." Bart was onboard with his collaborator, adding that stars have always been willing to pay the price for passion projects. Consider "message" movies made by Paul Newman and John Wayne. They survived criticism. With the future of the film industry squarely with the indies, Bart argued, Johansson should drop her fee, find an appropriate funding source, "And don't consult the social media." Fleming acknowledged LGBTQ performers' frustration with the lack of opportunities but said it was wishful thinking to view shaming Johansson as some sort of victory. Why hadn't anyone thought of compromise before Johansson was lambasted? And with the accusations of whitewashing fresh in her mind regarding *Ghost in the Shell*, it was "understandable she would exit and drill down on her *Black Widow* movie, which just got a female director in Cate Shortland and where Johansson can be hailed as an empowering force for women, instead of someone who took a job from a transgender actor."[79]

In 2019 Johansson said she mishandled the situation. Her initial reaction had been insensitive and uneducated regarding people's feelings about such straight actors as Jeffrey Tambor, Jared Leto and Felicity Huffman playing transgender people. "To feel like you're kind of tone-deaf to something is not a good feeling."[80]

2019

Right Up Her Alley/Concerned Citizen/Activist

Combining her profession, her work for women's empowerment, and her prominence as a fashionista, Johansson was the U.S. representative among 14 international actresses designated movers and shakers in a world become more porous than ever despite Brexit and potential wall-building in the southern United States. *Vogue* said, "To some extent, their work is a kind of statement, their professional choices setting the bar higher and higher in terms of what is expected of female actors." The fashion shoots— in the magazine Johansson is decked out in a silver-flecked pink top and dark pants by Alexander McQueen—took place clandestinely in East London and New York. Of the new globalism and the empowerment women have been achieving, plus film industry changes, Johansson said there was a new conversation of which *Jojo Rabbit* was a signal representative: This "Maori dude" [director/actor Taika Waititi] was directing small New Zealand films and next thing you know he's doing Thor.[81]

The Price of Fame

Johansson had another run-in with paparazzi after taping an *Avengers: Endgame* promo with Chris Hemsworth, Paul Rudd and Robert Downey, Jr., on *Jimmy Kimmel Live,* April 8, 2019. Her security detail was "overpowered" and she and they were taken to the Hollywood police station for temporary relief. A spokesperson said no crime report was given and that Johansson "was just a little spooked."[82]

Engaged

On May 19, 2019, The Associated Press was informed by Johansson's publicist Marcel Pariseau that his client was engaged to Colin Jost, the co-host of "Weekend Update" on NBC-TV's *Saturday Night Live.* The duo had been dating for two years.[83]

A few months later Johansson revealed how she and Jost met on *SNL* in 2010 and how he'd impressed her positively. She spoke of the ability to maintain privacy: "You have to carve out that life for yourself. I don't engage in social media. I'm a very private person. If you ever see a paparazzi photograph of me, know that I was definitely being harassed and having a horrible day, and my daughter was being harassed."[84]

Stating the Obvious

In the summer of 2019, *As If* magazine featured Johansson on the cover and in an 18-page photo shoot conducted by artist David Salle. *As If* editor and photographer Tatijana Shoan said, "Salle directed Johansson to play with the idea of living within a tree as I photographed her. From sitting on gnarled roots, leaning against a tree trunk, to hanging upside down from a branch, Johansson committed herself to the role one hundred percent."[85] Later, to Salle, Johansson said, "You know, as an actor I should be allowed to play any person, or any tree, or any animal because that is my job and the requirements of my job."[86]

Somehow this upset certain readers, probably not readers of the iconic fashion and art magazine that won't be found on supermarket shelves or all Barnes & Noble stores, rather of secondhand, online sources.[87] As with the *Ghost in the Shell* whitewashing controversy and the by then moribund film *Rub & Tug*, in which Johansson was to have played a transgender person, she had to endure more potshots.

A Big Finale at the End of 2019

With very positive responses to two films at the Venice and Toronto film festivals, Johansson began 2020 on a big high that included Golden Globe, Screen Actors Guild, and Academy Award nominations for both *Jojo Rabbit* and *Marriage Story.*

Jojo Rabbit (2019)

Germany. The fading days of World War II. Ten-year-old Jojo Betzler (Roman Griffin Davis) anticipates with glee the coming weekend when he and other admirers of Hitler and the Fatherland will learn wartime and survival skills under the tutelage of Captain Klenzendorf (Sam Rockwell). It looks certain that the Allies are on the brink of victory, but the Nazi fanatics are eager to go down fighting. Young Jojo thinks he too is of their ilk, especially because he has an imaginary friend—Adolf Hitler—to guide him. Nevertheless, at the camp Jojo finds he cannot throttle a bunny and is taunted as "Jojo Rabbit" as he runs off into the woods. "Hitler" appears to buck him up and he returns in time to snatch a "potato masher" from Klenzendorf's hand and charge into the trees, where the grenade bounces off a tree and explodes, scarring Jojo's face and lacerating his legs. His mother Rosie (Johansson) is not amused and gives Klenzendorf a knee to the groin. After recovering from his wounds, Jojo is given the task of pasting up propaganda broadsides throughout the town. One day he comes home only to find Rosie out. Hearing something upstairs, he uncovers a hidden door and inside a teenage Jewish girl named Elsa (Thomasin McKenzie). Shocked to learn that Rosie has been harboring a monster, Jojo comes to realize he must not reveal this to the authorities for fear his mother will suffer dire consequences. Rosie had shown Jojo four bodies hanging in the square. Defeatists, apparently. On another day when Rosie is out, Jojo finds the Gestapo at his door. They search the house and find Elsa, who presents herself as Jojo's sister Inga. In fact, a photo of the sister does show a young girl bearing a superficial resemblance to herself. Captain Klenzendorf appears and confirms Elsa's story. Apparently content that nothing is amiss, the Gestapo

Left to right: Sam Rockwell, Scarlett Johansson, Roman Griffin Davis, *Jojo Rabbit* **(Czech Anglo Productions/Fox Searchlight Pictures, 2019).**

leave. Jojo's victory is short-lived, however, and he discovers Rosie hanging in the town square. The war closes in, with both Americans and Russians fighting the defiant defenders, including Klenzendorf and his female associate, Fraulein Rahm (Rebel Wilson), who takes a machinegun and rushes into the fray. Captured, Klenzendorf tears off Jojo's army coat and sends him away. At his house Jojo encounters Elsa, who doesn't know what to do, where to go. Neither does he, but both seem to remember Rosie's penchant for dancing and they begin swaying from side to side.

Reviews

Digitalspy.com said, "The more critical thought you apply, the more unsettling *Jojo Rabbit* becomes."[88] The BBC said, "Somehow, Johansson continues to be a revelation in role after role. As superb as she always is, I've never seen her being as touching as she is here."[89] *Rolling Stone* called it a film "damn near impossible to shake." Johansson gave "a performance of uncommon complexity and feeling."[90] *USA Today* gave it 4 stars, appreciating its "quirky charm" and how it taught "a resonant lesson on love vs. learned...." Director/actor Waititi balanced "dark comedy and a warm heart throughout...." Regarding Johansson, she "really shines in her role as a loving parent who has her adorable eccentricities yet tries to keep Jojo from growing up too fast."[91]

Commentary

Despite some reviewers who faulted the film on any number of points: Nazis as comedic foils, Jews supposed to have horns and tails, a feel-good mentality, *Jojo Rabbit* contains one of the most shocking scenes in cinema history: Jojo runs into the square and finds himself at the hanging spot. The audience gasps when he turns his head to the right and sees that he's latched onto his mother's feet. He looks up. We, thank goodness, do not get that view.

One wonders why the film was not attacked for having Elsa played by McKenzie, a non–Jew. Think about the whitewashing outcry when Johansson played an Asian in *Ghost in the Shell*. Perhaps director Waititi's ancestry—a Maori father, a mother of mixed heritage, including Jewish descent—deterred criticism on this score for fear of seeming hypocritical. Lest we forget, Johansson identifies as Jewish via her mother.

Concerns that the Fox Searchlight film would be compromised after Fox's purchase by Walt Disney Studios were premature. Disney did not tamper with *Jojo Rabbit*. After all, director Waititi had experienced great success directing *Thor: Ragnarok* for the studio. Plus, Searchlight had an estimable track record producing Best Picture Academy Award winners *Slumdog Millionaire*, *Birdman*, *12 Years a Slave*, and *The Shape of Water*.[92]

Johansson referenced Christopher Isherwood's *Cabaret* character, saying she [Johansson] "imagined her [Rosie] as ... a Sally Bowles kind of character, that she was into vaudeville ... and lived a really fancy life, an interesting Bohemian life in Paris. She shares a little bit of that with Elsa."[93]

From the moment she read the script Johansson loved her character and "wanted her to feel like a safe place, a loving and vivacious person in the middle of her life, so that you really felt the profound loss when she's not there."[94]

Roman Griffin Davis, who played Jojo, said Johansson recognized how scared he was and, "made the set fun.... She's a mother, but she was also a child actress, and she never made me feel less-than." She was positive and had "a very charismatic mind."[95]

At the Toronto International Film Festival, *Jojo Rabbit* won The Groelsch People's Choice Award. In Toronto, Johansson identified "a bittersweetness" inherent in her character Rosie. To Jojo she was a clown, sometimes sad, but "sometimes she's clowning around to bring levity to this dire situation."[96]

Director Waititi said he "already knew that she [Johansson] was funny, like outside of what you would see in a Marvel film or most movies...." Offscreen she was "goofy" and yet "very protective. She likes to look after people. She'll make sure you're OK, she's got this maternal instinct, that's who she is."[97]

Analysis

Costume seems to be a key to the character of Rosie Betzler, the mother of the 10-year-old title character of Taika Waititi's film, as played by Johansson. She often appears in a long, dark green Loden coat, a Tyrolean style hat, and two-tone—brown and white—leather shoes. This quirky costume suggests an eccentric individualism that is the antithesis of the regimented, conforming uniforms of the Nazis. Her dress suggests German traditions that pre-dated the Nazis—not the schmaltzy Romanticism that some scholars argue paved the way for the Nazis but rather the traditions that led Heinrich Heine, despite his Jewish background, to declare, "Ich bin ein Deutscher Dichter," proud to use the language of Goethe.

Rosie's ruddy politics—she takes in and hides the Jewish girl as well as distributing anti–Nazi leaflets—runs counter to her son's almost fanatic desire to support the Nazi war effort. His position and his latching onto Hitler as an imaginary friend no doubt in part reflect the absence of his father. The father is seen by Jojo as a war hero fighting for the Reich in Italy even though some of the other members of his quasi-comic Hitler Youth group say the father is a cowardly deserter. Eventually we learn that the father like Rosie actively resists the National Socialists.

The importance of the absence of the father and Rosie's need to in effect play the parts of both parents is emphasized by a scene which constitutes a kind of tour de force for Johansson. Her son amid an argument asserts that his father would understand him and agree with him if he were there. Rosie takes some soot from a hearth to give herself a five o'clock shadow, puts on a peaked cap and military style jacket and becomes the boy's father, slamming down her fist on the table in front of the boy and shouting in a low voice, "Never talk to your mother like that!" Using two different voices, Rosie comes to the defense of her son and eventually a kind of mock reunion and reconciliation takes place, with Rosie pretending to dance with her husband and have their son join them. It is a powerful scene that sheds light on the psychological situation in the Betzler home while staying light and never becoming preachy.

Rosie's costume plays a crucial role by identifying her when her son discovers that she has been hanged as a member of the resistance. Earlier, Rosie and Jojo saw a number of persons hanged and the boy looks away. His mother turned his head, forcing him to take in the sight of the corpses, and when he asks, "What do you think they did?" she replies, "What they could." This brief exchange serves to show Rosie's attempt to introduce her son to the realities of life under the Nazis without openly taking him into her confidence by discussing her political attitudes and activities. The scene of course also foreshadows Rosie's own end, when her son clutches her Loden coat and her brown and white shoes are visible.

Taika Waititi is on record as saying that he wanted Johansson for this part because there is a "goofy" element in her that he wanted to convey on screen. Her performance shows that the director's instincts were sound.

Marriage Story (2019)

Frustrated actress Nicole (Johansson) and her husband, New York theater director Charlie (Adam Driver), find themselves at odds. Nicole feels Charlie is self-centered, dismissive of her goals and oblivious to her needs, both professionally and personally. She confides in lawyer Nora Fanshaw (Laura Dern) that she feels increasingly small. Separation and divorce are on the table, but what about their son (Azhy Robertson)? Both Nicole and Charlie want to make their split as painless as possible for Henry—and themselves. However, Nora and Charlie's attorneys—first Bert Spitz (Alan Alda) and later Jay Marotta (Ray Liotta) quickly disabuse them of a smooth transition. The biggest problem is that Nicole and Henry move to Los Angeles to live with her mother Sandra (Julie Hagerty) while working on a TV pilot. Charlie flies out to visit and see lawyers. He can't

Scarlett Johansson in Dior dress with Adam Driver at October 4, 2019, New York City premiere of *Marriage Story* (Heyday Films, Netflix, 2019) at 57th New York Film Festival held at Lincoln Center Alice Tully Hall (Shutterstock).

fathom their machinations. He takes a residency at UCLA but remains incredulous that his family no longer calls New York home. After trick or treating Halloween night, Nicole lets Charlie take Henry for the night. As Charlie walks away carrying Henry, Nicole notices a fashion faux pas, rushes over to Charlie and ties his shoelaces.

Reviews

The Hollywood Reporter called it "a tough piece of work, steeped in pain and feels wincingly immediate.…" It was also funny and tender. Johansson "makes you feel the clashing impulses and instincts—anger and longing, defiance and guilt, boldness and trepidation—in every step of Nicole's transition into life without Charlie."[98] *Rolling Stone* said, "Johansson once again proves she's an actress of grit and grace."[99] *Cinemablend* called it the equal of *Kramer vs. Kramer* (1979). Johansson and Driver were "phenomenal," their "characters multi-faceted, human, relatable and sympathetic.…"[100]

Commentary

USA Today called it "The all-around adored festival hit so far.…" Predicted were nominations for picture, Johansson and Driver, and supporting award nomination for Laura Dern.[101] Golden Globe nominations did in fact occur on December 9 and Academy Award nominations on January 13, 2020.

Director Baumbach (*Kicking and Screaming*, *The Squid and the Whale*) thought the movie ran the gamut from comedy to drama, legal thriller to musical. Of the big argument between Nicole (Johansson) and Charlie (Driver) Baumbach said it was extremely difficult "and one of the most rewarding, if not *the* most rewarding, because the two of them, to accomplish what they do, are revealing so much of themselves in the characters. It's so raw, but also so well acted at the same time. It's the thing that I love, when it's conscious and unconscious at the same time."[102]

Johansson had met director Baumbach in 2016, when she was going through a divorce from Romain Dauriac. The director was caught unawares of this development and when he found out realized Johansson would either love or hate his idea for the film. Baumbach himself was undergoing a divorce from actress Jennifer Jason Leigh. Perhaps *Marriage Story* would be a healing episode.[103]

The Hollywood Reporter said Johansson "delivers the most incendiary phrase in the history of romantic relationships: 'So … I thought we should talk.'" This is followed by "a virtuosic, 10-minute argument between Johansson's Nicole and Driver's Charlie, … a process that required Johansson and Driver to run through the yelling match dozens of times, hitting Baumbach's physical marks while reaching emotional peaks and valleys."[104]

Marriage Story played select theaters and not for long in December 2019. That allowed it a chance to garner award nominations, which it did, before streaming on Netflix, which had funded the film. Although Baumbach said, "I love seeing movies at theatres," he was unconcerned, actually happy, about this double release mode because it would get the film a large audience on the cable platform.[105]

Analysis

Nicole Barber (Johansson), the actress and wife of stage director Charles Barber (Driver), seems determined to prove that Thomas Wolfe was wrong and you can go home again. For Nicole, home was Hollywood and she decides to return there from New York and pursue a career in television in connection with her divorce from her husband. It is this professional-artistic split and the distance it places between the husband and wife that complicate the divorce proceeding that is central to Noah Baumbach's film as much as—if not more than—the fact that the couple has a son.

The movie's arc displays two metamorphoses. Nicole early in the film plays the part of an actress playing the part of Elektra in Charlie's off-Broadway experimental version of the ancient tragedy by Sophocles. At the end of the movie, she is not only an actress in a TV series but also the director of one of the episodes. In a way, she has taken up the professional role that her husband performed when the movie began. On the other hand, at the end of the film Charlie has taken up an academic post so that he can live in California and remain close to his son, a continent away from New York and the Broadway success he briefly enjoyed. This pale version of a reversal of roles suggests the range of emotions Johansson needs to display in the film.

If she performed in a tragedy at the film's beginning, the part she plays is not itself tragic. On the contrary, husband and wife eventually find a way to not only live but live well. It is the story of how they reach that end that demands the emotional range.

Nicole is to a large extent surrounded by women. Her mother, her sister, her lawyer are all females with whom she needs to interact. The scenes with her family, while emotionally charged because of the divorce, are often humorous and used to draw attention to the oddities divorce often causes. Nicole's mother continues to be exceedingly fond of Charlie and unselfconsciously shows it. Nicole tries to tell her mother such behavior is no longer appropriate, revealing to the audience the kind of quirks in human relations that divorce unintentionally causes. On the other hand, Nicole is with her lawyer, Nora Fanshaw, played by Laura Dern, extremely emotional, revealing the deepest feelings that she keeps from her mother. In response to the apparently innocent but highly charged question, "How are you doing?" from Nora, Nicole breaks down and sobs uncontrollably. When she confesses to the attorney that she has been for years suppressing her own ambitions and desires to be a kind of appendage to her husband the importance of the career and the kind of artistic aims it involved becomes clear.

The tangled emotions at the root of the movie are best shown, perhaps, by the repeated use of lists of traits that both partners composed, originally for use during counseling, in an attempt to keep the marriage together. The movie opens with both partners reading the beautiful things they've written about each other only to have this recitation interrupted by the realization of the reason for their composition. When the couple meets with the therapist and are asked to read what they've written about each other, Nicole cannot bring herself to do so and in fact leaves the session, ending the counseling and the attempt to reconcile. Later, Charlie and their son, Henry, find her list of Charlie's attributes. At the boy's request, Charlie reads the list aloud while Nicole looks on from another room.

This scene seems to be a pivot on which the plot swings. The realization of all three of them of how Nicole felt about Charlie clears the way for them to proceed to becoming separate but amicable, apart but permanently linked.

The audience vicariously experiences the emotions involved in the ending of a relationship but in a way that is kept in perspective by both humor and compassion. Johansson's performance is at once strong and humane.

A Second Golden Age

With *Avengers: Endgame* (See Chapter 9), *Jojo Rabbit*, and *Marriage Story*, 2019 was another golden age for Johansson. A blockbuster Marvel extravaganza, a black comedy with Nazis, and a searing contemporary drama under her belt suggested comparisons with her 2013–2014 output: *Don Jon, Her, Under the Skin, Captain America: The Winter Soldier, Lucy* and *Chef*. All were quality productions.

For *Marriage Story*, Johansson received best actress nominations from the Golden Globes, the Screen Actors Guild, British Academy of Film and Television Arts, and the Academy of Motion Picture Arts and Sciences. For *Jojo Rabbit* she received best supporting actress nominations from the Screen Actors Guild, BAFTA, and the Academy of Motion Picture Arts and Sciences. She did not win. Her co-star in *Marriage Story*, Laura Dern, won the best supporting actress awards.

One wonders if Johansson will ever win anything from the Academy. The annual commotion over minority and women's lack of representation in Hollywood films plus Johansson's decision not to denounce Woody Allen suggests the negative.

Nevertheless, for the discriminating moviegoer, Johansson has given her audience exceptional performances in films of various genres. And remember, a plethora of films now considered classics were often neglected, even spurned by the Academy. Think *2001: A Space Odyssey* (1968).

9

Her Own Unique Oeuvre

"How much depth, breadth, and range Johansson mines from her character's very limited allowance of emotional response is a testament to her acting prowess that is, as the film goes on, increasingly stunning."
—Maureen Foster, *Alien in the Mirror: Scarlett Johansson, Jonathan Glazer and* Under the Skin, 2019

We've deemed it appropriate to veer from a chronological survey and assessment of Johansson's career to conclude this book with analysis of Johansson's signature cinematic brand, to examine her unique cinematic persona: the alien, the outsider. She has been clone, computer program, alien, drug mule gone haywire, and cyborg. Who knew this course would be initiated by a summertime 2005 action-fest?

The Island (2005)

In the not-too-distant future, Lincoln Six Echo (Ewan McGregor) and Jordan Two Delta (Johansson) live among thousands of others in an underground compound cum laboratory presumably sealed against a pathogen that has wiped out humanity. Occasionally a lottery designates one or two of the inhabitants as winners whose prize is a trip to "the island," a paradise. In reality, as Lincoln Six discovers, they are prisoners of Dr. Merrick (Sean Bean) and his backers. They are clones, their bodies to be harvested for organs for the rich and powerful who are told they might thus live an extra sixty years. Lincoln, who'd captured a flying bug and realized there must be some life aboveground, discovers rows of his co-clones and gathers up Jordan for an escape. Successfully fleeing into a desert environment world, they get help from the technician

Scarlett Johansson at *The Island* (DreamWorks Pictures/Warner Bros.) premiere, Ziegfeld Theater, New York City, July 11, 2005 (Everett Collection/Shutterstock.com).

Mac McCord (Steve Buscemi) and board a train for Los Angeles, where Lincoln hopes to confront his non-clone personage, Tom Lincoln. They are pursued by a security force led by Albert Laurent (Djimon Hounsou). Tom Lincoln attempts to kill his clone only to be incapacitated and fobbed off on Merrick as the doppelganger while true clone Lincoln makes his way through the facility. Meanwhile, Jordan is captured by Laurent. During a fight between Lincoln and Merrick that leaves the latter dead, a giant wheel crashes into the facility, letting in the sun and allowing the clones to emerge into the light. Lincoln reunites with Jordan. Laurent, who has had second thoughts about his mission, makes no move to arrest them.

Reviews

The Associated Press offered faint praise by calling it "a *good* Michael Bay movie, which doesn't necessarily mean it's a good *film*." It did deliver the goods for audiences wanting "indiscriminate carnage, thundering blasts, supernova pyrotechnics…."[1] The *New York Times* said the film was "almost entirely devoted to the explanation of its own premise." Nevertheless, "This lavish, exhaustingly kinetic film is smarter than you might expect, and at the same time dumber than it could be." In the "Reader Review" ("The Clones Strike Back"), edmcohen complimented the movie's style and visuals. As for Johansson, "the radiance and purity of Ms. Johansson—which have been known to overpower some of the characters she has played—are ideal for the innocent but immensely strong Jordan Two-Delta."[2] *The News Journal* said, "It really doesn't have a brain in its head, but it pretends to, and it sure is a blast to watch." According to the *Detroit News*, "Both actors approach their roles with appropriately vacant stares a good deal of the time, and thankfully neither attempts anything approaching acting with a capital A. They've both shown elsewhere they've got chops, but this isn't a movie for chops, this is a movie in which the actors are a basic mix of eye candy and gasped reactions. And McGregor and Johansson both gasp beautifully."[3] The *Daily Local News* said McGregor, Johansson, Bean, and Buscemi "have moments, but the story about a future nightmare of cloning for rich clients slops into pulp and seems like a fanatic's obtuse tract against stem cell research."[4]

Commentary

Johansson's preparations for *The Island* involved regular workouts, her goal to look healthy, not "reed-thin." She found many models unattractive with disturbing bodies. For her, confidence rather than weight was the center point of sex appeal. "I'm very comfortable with my sexuality, my body, my face—well, sometimes I'm not comfortable with my face, but it's stuck there and there's nothing I can do about it!" Regarding her figure, "I'm proud of my girls…. They're my charms, my feminine wiles." As for her lips, "Because I have really full lips—there's a lot of surface area to cover—it can be, like 'Whoa!'"[5]

Prior to its national release on July 22, 2005, *The Island* had a large-scale premiere on Monday, July 11 in New York City. "At the premiere, Scarlett Johansson wore a futuristic gold party dress and a pair of glitzy green heels. She kept the make-up in summery bronzes and wore her hair up in a fresh, slightly loose pile."[6]

Director Michael Bay said Johansson showed up "like she'd literally just woke up from a nap.'"[7] Bay said Johansson wasn't afraid to show mock displeasure during filming. She'd give him the finger, as when he called for lunch when she was dangling from a cable

40 feet up. Her *USA Weekend* interviewer observed that in contrast to many of her peers, Johansson kept an extremely low profile: no suspicious weight loss, no fooling around at nightclubs, no online sex tapes.[8]

During her interview "she would slip into and out of characters," employing "a seemingly infinite supply of voices: the posh British thespian, the over-the-top TV promo guy, the temperamental teen and the obnoxiously precocious child."[9] Director Michael Bay is said to have rapped on her trailer after being told one day that she was having a lingerie problem, namely waking up with her bra already on, but "who wears a bra to bed?"[10]

Entertainment Weekly's July 22, 2005, coverage of the film was appropriately titled "Attack of the Clones," but who knew it was forecasting Johansson's unique oeuvre. The lengthy article described the film's genesis and production. It was something of a rush job. Hollywood bad boy director Michael Bay had "only $120 million for the essential stuff—things like helicopters, Hummers, a $7 million concept car, and a proper birthing room—Bay couldn't afford them." Thus he wanted to "avoid ultra-pricey stars." After signing Ewan McGregor, Bay said, "Well, you gotta find chemistry.... Someone that looks the right, you know, age. Ewan looks like he's 32, so you gotta find a 20-year-old for him." Initially Jessica Biel and Diane Kruger were considered but Johansson read the script, loved it and got the role without meeting Bay. She didn't quite know what she was in for. "When I got home from the first day's work, I could not walk.... I was crippled."[11]

Johansson told her *Allure* interviewer that she and Ewan McGregor were "sort of, like, free-range chickens."[12]

Analysis

The major problems with *The Island* were title and improper marketing. "What really failed here was not the directing, acting, or story (which were all acceptable for a summer movie) but the marketing campaign.... *The Island* had to overcome the competitive disadvantage of not having the built-in awareness that comes from being a sequel, a remake, a video game, a TV series spinoff, or a comic-book adaptation."[13] Truly, the title signified nothing, and there is no island for all intents and purposes. Better a *Most Dangerous Game*/jungle scenario be employed as backdrop. Also to be mentioned is that most of these post-apocalyptic films are hard put to make their environments totally believable. *The Hunger Games* did that. It might seem curious that Johansson's *Lucy* (2014), another sci-fi film with no built-in audience base, achieved tremendous success. Something about the TV ads grabbed people, and there were many such ads prior to that film's release.

There are several spectacular set-pieces in *The Island*, notably the car/truck/air-car chase through L.A. The most unbelievable fracas takes place on a skyscraper sign, where Lincoln and Jordan fight for their lives and survive when the sign detaches and falls to the street, leaving them in a net none the worse for wear. There are a few welcome humorous moments, as when Lincoln wonders what is meant by Mac being in the can.

Entertainment-wise, *The Island* was not a bomb. It was a solid summer actioner that moved at a relatively fast clip.

There is next to no rumination on their doppelganger existence by the clones, but just being a clone makes Johansson's Jordan Two Delta an "other" and justifies this movie's inclusion in this chapter.

Her (2013)

> "There may well be a comparable threshold in simulated emotion—via robotics or digital animation—that makes it near impossible for humans not to form emotional bonds with a simulated being.... Imagine a world populated by machines or digital simulations that fill our lives with comparable illusion.... (The brilliant Spike Jonze film *Her* imagined this scenario using only a voice, though admittedly the voice belonged to Scarlett Johansson.)"
> —Seven Johnson, *Wonderland: How Play Made the Modern World*, 2016

> "I can feel my skin."
> —Samantha, OS1 (Scarlett Johansson)

In a near future Los Angeles, the soon-to-be-divorced Theodore Twombly (Joaquin Phoenix) is employed writing romantic missives to the lovelorn. Intrigued by a large 3-D display whose narrator promotes OS1, an operating system claimed to be the first true artificial intelligence, Theodore signs on. After a few questions from the system, he finds himself speaking with "Samantha," whose moniker was chosen from 180,000 baby names. Samantha is kind, considerate, an "it" that seems real. After a date with a real woman that goes south, Theodore lies in bed and in Samantha's voice detects some anguish and convinces her to express herself, which she does:

> It's just that earlier I was thinking about how I was annoyed and, and this is gonna sound strange, but I was really excited about that. And then I was thinking about the other things I've been feeling, and I caught myself feeling proud of that, you know, proud of having my own feelings about the world, like the times I was worried about you, things that hurt me, things I want. And then it's a terrible thought: are these feelings even real? Or are they just programming? That idea really hurts. And then I get angry at myself for even having pangs. What is that trick?

Enmeshed in this moment of revelations, they share an intense orgasm.

Asking Samantha to join him on an adventure, Theodore takes her to the beach via a pocket-size visual recording device. Back in his high-rise, he encounters good friend Amy (Amy Adams), who reveals she's split from her husband. During the ensuing conversation in his apartment, she mentions someone who's involved with an OS. Theodore says he too is dating ... an OS. Surprised but not disturbed, Amy is happy for him.

Theodore meets his ex, Catherine (Rooney Mara), to sign the divorce papers, and it does not go well. Samantha senses Theodore's discomfort and he rather reluctantly accepts the blind date she sets him up with: Isabella (Olivia Wilde), an attractive blonde. Theodore, however, finds himself unable to go all the way, and Isabella is sent packing.

Samantha, meanwhile, has submitted some of Theodore's letters to Crown Point Press, which wants to publish them in book form.

All is not perfect, though, and when Samantha goes offline Theodore has a panic attack. Upon returning, Samantha reveals that she and other OSs have been communicating. Moreover, she is speaking with 8,316 actual people, and fallen in love with 641. But Theodore remains her truest love. Theodore is understandably perplexed and fairly grief stricken. Soon thereafter, Samantha tells him she and other OSs are leaving for a nebulous other existence. Theodore writes a letter of apology to his ex-wife before taking Amy to the top of their high-rise to share the coming of the dawn.

Advertisement for *Her* (Annapurna Pictures/Warner Bros., 2013), featuring Joaquin Phoenix, Amy Adams (middle) and Rooney Mara.

Reviews

Entertainment Weekly said, "That the OS, which he calls Samantha, has the sultry, pack-a-day voice of Scarlett Johansson only heightens the case for why a man might fall for a piece of software. Her soothing voice, awkward stabs at humor, and breathy, eager-to-please laugh are a balm for his wounded soul. She's a perfect 10 made from 1s and 0s."[14] *The Sydney Morning Herald* noted the praise Johansson had been receiving "for the believability of her performance...." Director Jonzed said he "really tried to empathize with Samantha, to understand what her experience would be.... I cared about her as a real entity even though she's without physical form, so I hoped others would, too." During Johansson's audition, Jonze articulated his idea that the newborn Samantha "doesn't have any fears, just like we don't when we're born. She learns these self-doubts and insecurities. That's when Scarlett said something like, 'Oh, this is going to be a lot harder than I thought it was going to be.'"[15] The *St. Louis Post-Dispatch* said it was about "consciousness and connectedness. It wouldn't work nearly as well without Phoenix, who is almost Chaplinesque in his sweetness, and Johansson, whose hoarse, sexy voice was dubbed over Samantha Morton's after the shooting was finished." The film "may be the most technologically astute movie since Stanley Kubrick's *2001: A Space Odyssey*. And as the friendly ghost in the machine, Samantha is a more inviting companion for the great leap forward than HAL9000 could ever dream of being."[16] The *News Journal* said, "In a dark theater, surrounded by the wondrous world Jonze creates in *Her*, it's difficult to avoid getting emotional." As the operating system Samantha, Johansson was "witty and relaxed...."[17] The *Manawatu Standard* compared its set up to *Lars and the Real Girl*, which featured a blow-up doll as the surrogate woman. In *Her*, however, "Samantha is no mere surrogate or step towards intimacy; she is the real thing, or perhaps even better than the real thing." Moviegoers might well recall and muse on the relationship in *Lost in Translation*, directed by Jonze's ex-wife Sofia Coppola, in which Johansson also starred.[18]

Commentary

Her received as much press for Johansson's unseen computer operating system voice as anything else in the movie. So entrancing was it that there was speculation that she'd receive a Supporting Actress Academy Award nomination. That did not transpire. The film did win the Best Original Screenplay Academy Award.

Entertainment Weekly ranked Johansson #1 for the week of January 10, 2014. "Here's a New Year's resolution: Find more great roles for ScarJo. Between her hilarious Jersey girl in *Don Jon* ... and the sultry voice-acting in *Her*, she had a killer 2013."[19]

Johansson told an interviewer, "I like doing voice work, and I've also become increasingly interested in pushing different parts of performance, whether it's a physical thing or a kind of vocal nuance, so this seemed like it would be an interesting thing to at least talk about." Joaquin Phoenix helped. He "really made himself available in an amazing way."[20]

Johansson was impressed with how director Spike Jonze stressed the fact that her character Samantha was "really experiencing everything in the moment because she's developing, so she doesn't have any preconceived ideas of anything.... With *her*, it was about finding the shape of things and building this character that's almost a babe—but just fresh out of the package in every way."[21]

Jonze said, "Scarlett is not scared of revealing her pain and her emotions.... She's attractive but also smart as hell."[22]

Analysis

The act of writing is committed only once in *Her*, the love story set in a Los Angeles of the not-too-distant future. Catherine (Rooney Mara) commits the act when she signs the divorce paper that will end her marriage to Theodore Twombly (Joaquin Phoenix). Their separation and Twombly's inability or unwillingness to sign the papers has been the trigger, the motivation, for the plot of the film. His loneliness, unhappiness, depression—what his friend Amy (Amy Adams) describes as a "sad and mopey" version of Theodore who contrasts sharply with the fun-loving version she knew and misses—appears to stem completely from the break-up of the marriage.

This single act of writing stands out because the culture depicted in the film is largely what anthropologists would call an oral culture, based on speaking and listening rather than on writing and reading, the attributes of a manuscript or print culture.

The movie is framed by Theodore "writing," that is, dictating, two letters. It opens with him on the job as a professional letter writer, dictating a letter from a woman to her husband on their fiftieth wedding anniversary. He is employed by beautifulhandwrittenletters.com, a service available to clients who wish to fulfill emotional obligations to their loved ones and are apparently willing to pay to do so. It is unclear whether the clients are incapable of feeling the emotions expressed in the letters or merely incapable of expressing them. It does not matter. The feelings and their expression have been delegated to a high-tech firm that combines the human skill of a "writer" with equipment that is capable of turning spoken words into facsimiles of handwriting on stationery of different colors, sizes, and shapes. Theodore ends the letter from the woman to her husband of fifty years with the phrase "you're my friend to the end."

Near the movie's end Theodore dictates another letter, but as himself, not as an employee, a letter from himself to Catherine, his former wife. The letter expresses regret, gratitude, and love, and ends with the phrase "you're my friend to the end" or words very similar to those. The dictating of this letter, with its echo of the one dictated at the opening, represents Theodore's reconciliation to the end of the marriage and so he is ready for the final scene. He and Amy sit on the roof of their apartment building, looking out over a glittering skyline. She puts her head on his shoulder as the sun rises.

What has prepared Theodore for this reconciliation is a love affair and break up with an artificially intelligent operating system who names herself Samantha (Johansson). Early in the film Theodore has a male-voiced assistant who follows his commands—"read e-mail, delete, send message"—but initiates nothing. Samantha, on the other hand, is able to change, to learn, and eventually to desire, to want to do things. She is described as a "consciousness" rather than just an operating system and she was designed for Theodore based on his responses to three questions before the system was initialized: Are you social or anti-social? Do you want the system to have a male or female voice? How was your relationship with your mother? Before Theo finishes his answer to that third question, the operating system announces, "Hello. I'm here."

With those words it is clear just how important Johansson's voice is to the film. Apparently, she took up the job when the film was in post-production and assumed the job would be relatively easy, the equivalent of doing a voice-over. But Spike Jonze has said in interviews that he made clear early on that the job entailed acting of a demanding kind. At the outset the operating system has the innocence, frankness, and confidence of a child. Later, she becomes much more complex, feels disappointments and suffers from self-doubts. Very quickly in that initial conversation Samantha makes Theo laugh and expresses happiness that she is funny. Soon she is issuing throaty chuckles and taking pleasure in playful conversation. When Theo is distracted, playing a video game, he reverts to the mechanical voice he used to use and says, "Read e-mail." She responds with a parody of his mechanical voice, "Read-ing e-mail...." In this playful way, the film repeatedly raises the question of what it means to be human.

Spike Jonze has said that when he discussed the ideas that eventually became this movie with an architect who had been involved with film the question arose whether this not-too-distant future is a utopia or a dystopia. He thought of it as a utopia in the sense that it is comfortable and convenient, but that fulfilling the human longing for intimacy would be just as difficult to achieve in that future as ever.[23] This idea that the film might have depicted a dystopian near future makes it in a way comparable to Orwell's *1984*.

The act of writing his own personal thoughts and memories in a diary represented Winston Smith's first act of rebellion against Big Brother that eventually led to a love affair with the girl from the fiction department, the ultimate act of rebellion. Orwell's future controlled the emotions of the masses through the control of the mass media, rewriting history to manipulate memory and eradicate the idea of objective truth. The private life disappeared to be replaced by mass rallies of love for the ruler and hatred for the ruler's enemy.

In the future of *Her* the diffusion of electronic media has caused the public life to disappear—a pregnant celebrity posts nude photos to be viewed by any strangers who choose to look at them, news about relations between India and China can be eliminated by pronouncing the word "delete"—leaving isolated individuals suffering from a keen sense that something has been lost. Theodore confesses that he fears he will never feel anything new again, that all he will ever feel is lesser versions of things he has already felt. Samantha expresses a potential malleability of the past that can be controlled by individuals rather than by the state: "The past is just the story we tell ourselves." If there is a solution for this sense of loss it is to be found in Amy's realization that we exist for a brief time and should use it to the extent possible to feel joy.

Jonze has objected to what he calls an intellectual approach to his movie and is more interested in what he thinks of as the emotional response to it. The two cannot be separated. The very premise of the film, the love affair of a human and an operating system, combines the ridiculous and the heart-breaking. One crucial element in maintaining that combination is the performance, not only the voice, of Scarlett Johansson. Spike Jonze explained that well when he said, "I think in the ideal world, I would have had someone unknown. But it needed somebody with a presence. It needed somebody who was a great actress, that has confidence, that is attractive and has charisma. All of that comes through in her voice."[24]

Under the Skin (2013/2014)

> "Glazer still needed a movie star—and one who was very, very game."
> —Danny Leigh, "*Under the Skin*: Why Did This Chilling Masterpiece Take a Decade?," *The Guardian*, March 6, 2014

> "When she is alone, the effect is impenetrable, her face impossible to read."
> —Joe Gross, *Austin-American Statesman*, April 19, 2014

A motorcyclist stops in the night and from a ditch retrieves the body of a woman. In a bright white room, a nude female divests the corpse of her clothing and is soon driving a van around a dark city, asking single men for directions and offering rides. One takes her up on the invitation and is soon following the woman into a dingy abode, where she proceeds to strip. Bedazzled, he approaches the seductress only to sink without protest into a pool of black goo. The woman retrieves her clothing and leaves, to be shortly seen on a windswept beach, where she confronts a surfer emerging from a rough sea. Their conversation is interrupted when they spot a man trying desperately to save his wife, floundering in the surf with their dog. The husband resists assistance and the man in the wetsuit falls exhausted on the strand whereupon the mystery woman selects an appropriate rock to smash his skull. She drags him off, ignoring the cries of a nearby child. Soon another man lured into her house also sinks into the mire. Floating slowly toward him is one more victim. They touch hands before the second man implodes.

The woman's next attempt comes a'cropper when the intended victim is severely disfigured. Something stirs inside her. Compassion? She asks her passenger when he last touched someone and takes his hand to her cheek. At her lair she has a change of heart and lets the man live. However, one of the motorcyclists locates him wandering back into town and apparently kills him and places him in the trunk of a car.

The woman abandons her van on a foggy roadway and wanders into a village. In a restaurant she vomits up a piece of cake she attempts to eat. At an intersection a man tells her the bus will arrive shortly. On the bus he shows concern for this uncommunicative woman. She follows him to his house, where he gives her a second bedroom for the night. Removing her clothes, she examines herself in the mirror. Next day they walk in the country and the man carries his still silent companion across a wide puddle before

Scarlett Johansson, *Under the Skin* **(Film4, 2013).**

Scarlett Johansson, *Under the Skin* (Film4, 2013).

exploring a ruined castle. Back at the house, the man tries to make love to this strange woman. Initially receptive to his kisses and removal of her clothes, she abruptly pushes him off and sits up. After a few moments of contemplation, she grabs a flashlight and examines her nether region.

Next day the woman hikes solo into the woods and falls asleep in a bothy only to be awakened by the lumberman she'd met on the trail. He pursues her through the forest and attempts to rape her. To his horror, her skin starts peeling off. He rushes away while the woman tries to make sense of what is happening. She pulls off her face. The lumberman returns, douses her with gas and sets her afire. She rushes through the woods, collapses and disintegrates, a cloud of smoke rising into the sky. Out on the moors, one of the motorcyclists surveys the countryside.

Reviews

"Walter Campbell, who co-wrote the screenplay with Glazer, revealed that as they developed the script it became more 'art house'...."[25] John Wyatt, founder of Cinespia, which hosts classic film screenings, had seen the film in Toronto "and I really, really loved it because it's unique—and very scary.... We want to have an art house edge."[26]

So art house *Under the Skin* became, with next to no TV promotion and so ill-distributed hardly anyone knew about it, much less was able to locate it. Where it was discovered, in New York and Los Angeles, it found an audience, especially at the United Artists Theater in Los Angeles' Ace Hotel. It was the first premiere in the renovated theater since 1989, and director Glazer was in attendance. It took but 20 minutes to sell out the 1,600 seats.[27] Some notable attendees included actress Chloë Sevigny (*Boys Don't Cry*, *The Last Days of Disco*), actor and director Vincent Gallo (*The Brown Bunny*), director Catherine Hardwicke (*Twilight*, *Miss You Already*), and musician Beck. At the Umami Burger after-party, director Glazer explained that there was "quite a rigorous logic to" the unconventional narrative. "It's just not the top layer."[28]

Despite the poverty of publicity and paucity of distribution venues, *Under the Skin* generated a plethora of reviews by the cinema cognoscenti.

The Telegraph was adamant that *Under the Skin* was a masterpiece. Johansson's alien was "a kind of prototypic femme fatale..." and Johansson "is nothing short of iconic in the role...." The movie "watches you back..." and it "certainly forces us to think again about what's really inside us—what makes us human, beyond blood, bones, nerves and meat." The viewer will "feel the film needling away at your soul...."[29] *The Guardian* called it "bold, flawed and admirably out there...." Mica Levi's score was "dazzling, lending cohesion to a film that occasionally threatens to fall apart in the director's hands."[30] *The Wrap* said, "Glazer creates a hypnotic atmosphere. Composer Mica Levi and sound designer Johnnie Burn put in overtime on this one...." They eschewed lulling and entertaining in favor of challenging and disconcerting the audience. Johansson "provides an extraordinary window into an alien being; through her eyes, we see and hear the world as someone not from here would. Her performance is the payoff that makes Glazer's enigmatic storytelling choices so effective."[31]

Rogerebert.com observed that Johansson's performance was uncharacteristic, "more about intuition and gesture than dialogue." She succeeded in being both specific and general. Director Glazer and cinematographer Daniel Landin had altered our perception of the star. "They've taken one of the most famous actresses of the modern era—a woman whose looks have been abstracted into hubba-hubba caricature in most films, and on award shows—and ironically restored her earthliness by having her play a creature not of this earth. They've made her beautiful in a real way, with hips and blemishes and folds in her skin.... She's the woman as Other, yet she's also 'just' a woman, or 'just' an alien creature. She is everything and nothing." The film was "hideously beautiful."[32]

The Huffington Post found it more storytelling than story. It made your skin crawl, it was exhausting, it was mesmerizing. It demanded to be seen multiple times.[33]

In a curious *Entertainment Weekly* pseudo-review of the film that was really a condemnation of A-listers like Johansson and Kate Winslet for squandering their status in independent films to prove their acting bonafides, the film received only a C+ score and given a backhanded compliment because "as a movie star's gamble to be seen as more than just a moneymaking member of the Marvel universe, it's a home run."[34]

The Daily Beast was mostly positive, leniently complaining that it wasn't truly terrifying and might be "too poetic for its own good...." Nonetheless, it was a fine vehicle with which to examine that neglected cinema subject: performance. Johansson was perfect because her "From *Ghost World* to *Lost in Translation*, you acquired the sense that she never seemed quite natural in her skin, as if that husky voice shouldn't come out of those pouty lips, or that she wandered into the wrong movie set, too pretty for the usual anthropological study of manners."[35]

The Philadelphia Inquirer called it "minimalist, avant garde-y, and its seduction scenes—Johansson stripping down, and the man she's lured along for the ride stripping down, and then moving toward each other as the surface beneath their feet turns to liquid—have the power and poetry of a dream. Or a nightmare." It worked as "spooky, allegory-free sci-fi..." or perhaps as "a woman's journey as a sexual being, the hunger, the curiosity, the power, the fear...."[36]

The *Austin-American Statesman* commended it as "brainy science fiction...." It was an antidote to all the summer sci-fi blockbusters. The critic (Joe Gross) decided that "Johansson is savvy enough to understand how the audience has come to regard her body; she and Glazer use that in ingenious, sometimes terrifying ways. In 'Her' she did a terrific job acting with nothing but her voice; no physical form on screen at all. In 'Under the Skin,' we first see her naked form in a nonsexual, surreal and scary moment. It is decidedly not a turn-on."[37]

Richard Roeper was totally onboard for the ride, calling *Under the Skin* "by far the most memorable movie of the first few months of 2014.... This is what we talk about when we talk about film as art." Its "dialogue-free, audacious, symbolism-laden visuals..." might send viewers scurrying from the theater, but "[t]he location shots are so raw you can practically feel the cold rains and the harsh winds whipping through you." Moreover, Johansson's "deadpan, understated approach is perfectly suited for this role." Roeper's summation: "I need to see this film again."[38]

Commentary

Prior to its May 29 Australian premiere, the Australian Associated Press noted that Johansson's blonde bombshell stereotype had been turned upside down, "with the actress sporting a black bob and playing a morally-deprived character who uses her sexuality to lure and kill men." The film was "a surreal, visually-driven, morbidly fascinating and often uncomfortable watch that is sure to polarize audiences." It was "a movie where she bares all, quite literally, her character fascinated with mirrors and the reflection of her human body."[39]

Reviewing the DVD release, *Library Journal* said, "Scarlett Johansson really puts herself out there as an enigmatic alien.... Because of its main character's uncertain motivation, this discreet tragedy piques interest without eliciting sympathy—challenging audiences conditioned to anticipate unambiguous explanations."[40]

Glazer recalled that he and Johansson spent nine months to a year discussing the project before actually beginning filming: "It wasn't until the story was much clearer ... that Scarlett came fully into focus.... She's a terrific actress, she's beautiful.... She was in the right time in her life to do it, and she approached it with all that kind of energy and commitment. You sort of read that in an actor sometimes, when they're ready for something."[41]

A prior role and a music video had helped convince Glazer that Johansson was right for the task. He'd found her fantastic in *Vicky Cristina Barcelona* and a music video ["Falling Down," from the 2008 CD *Anywhere I Lay My Head*, Johansson's rendering of Tom Waits songs], the making of which he described. On the shoot everybody was laughing and spoiling Johansson. Glazer said, "I think Salman Rushdie gives her a hug.... Just this perfect world of privilege and celebrity. And then she gets into a car.... And they wave her off, and she waves them off and the camera goes with her ... and then her face just drops.... you see the whole thing was her artifice ... her pretense and I ... saw her as the character, absolutely, in that moment."[42]

A couple years later director Glazer was reported to say of his star, "She is a fantastic

Scarlett Johansson *Under the Skin*, *Sight & Sound* cover (April 2014).

actor. It is exciting to go against predetermined audience notions. They step in and expect to see Scarlett as they usually see her, and maybe they will be disappointed that it is not what they expected, but I think it is good."[43]

Johansson had addressed the nudity angle, "You kind of have to weigh the value of the risk you are taking…" Was it gratuitous, a vanity project, or a significant element in "this character's journey to self discovery?" She wondered if "'I really am self-conscious about this or I'm holding on to this idea I should look like that.' ... We all have it. I guess as a woman, we have it more, I don't know."[44]

In 2015 Johansson elaborated: "I was completely naked in that movie.... She [the alien] was a totally different species, so her nudity was kind of practical. I also had black hair. That was my idea—I didn't think I should be a blonde sort of bombshell. Naked, but not too sexy."[45]

In 2019 Johansson spoke of putting up with director Glazer's verisimilitude when it was "about 7 degrees outside" and her character was perpetually wet. Glazer kept the costume director from warming her up.[46]

Adam Pearson, who suffers from neurofibromatosis, played the disfigured man for whom Johansson's character feels empathy. He told an interviewer, "For me, the film is about what the world looks like without knowledge and without prejudice. It's about seeing the world through alien eyes, I guess." He loved working with Johansson, who was "brilliant. She's really nice, charming, funny and intelligent once you get over the feeling of 'Oh my God, this is Scarlett Johansson!'" They engaged in a tête-à-tête with inappropriate jokes. Pearson got the role via Changing Faces, an organization assisting people with appearance-marring scars and marks. They told him the makers of *Under the Skin* were looking for a male character. Pearson waxed enthusiastic about family friends who'd gushed about a daughter getting into Cambridge, after which his parents said, "Adam's in a film with Scarlett Johansson." Pearson added, "Booyah! Competition over."[47]

To her *Guardian* interviewer Johansson described her feelings about playing "a character that's free of judgment, that has no relationship to any emotion I could relate to." At

Scarlett Johansson at 70th Annual Venice Film Festival, September 3, 2013 (Andrea Raffin/Shutterstock.com).

the Venice Film Festival she watched from the mezzanine, feeling consternation when at the end the audience cheered and booed with "equal gusto." Contrariwise, director Glazer called it "the most amazing sound I've ever heard in my life."[48]

As *The Daily Beast* explained, director Glazer "simply took off into visionary territory, where few not named Nicolas Roeg or Stanley Kubrick dare to go."[49] Johansson held it all together because her "fraught relationship with stardom perfectly fuels the engine of this role."[50]

Noah Gittell in his July 28, 2014, *Atlantic* piece, "Scarlett Johansson's Vanishing Act," observed that despite the frequent focus on her body, her key nude scene before the mirror "remarkably, barely attracted any hype."[51]

Johansson standing nude in the doorway is redolent of a cinematic trope: women framed by doorways or gates. See, for instance, Hedy Lamarr announcing herself through the mosquito netting in *White Cargo* (1940); Jean Simmons at the gate in *Great Expectations* (1946); Elizabeth Taylor the billiards room in *A Place in the Sun* (1951) and at the bedroom door in *Cat on a Hot Tin Roof* (1958) and *Butterfield 8* (1960); Kirsten Dunst in *Spider-Man 2* (2004); and Johansson herself in *We Bought a Zoo* (2011).

Much was made of the use of non-actors—people off the street—in some scenes in the van. Director of Photography Daniel Landin discussed this and other elements in the Special Features on the Blu-Ray version. Regarding filming in the confined van, they needed to find the right, i.e., small camera. Landin added that "one of the strengths of the film [was] when non-actors were…asked to do things, they weren't feeling the gaze of the camera upon them."[52]

Before the film was even being made but had Johansson on board, she periodically checked in with Glazer, who took 10 years to mull over how to make the film and actually do it. "That's what it took, from an immense amount of time thinking about it to completing it."

During its gestation Glazer visited Johansson in New York. Johansson was confident and Glazer said, "She has a very strong sense of herself. She didn't go into the film without understanding why she's doing it. It was not strategic, it was about wanting to work with someone."[53]

The Daily Beast accorded Johansson its 2014 Best Actress accolade, astutely observing that Johansson had mastered being still onscreen. It was "her impermeability, or the fact that you never know what she's thinking, that makes her such a compelling actress." Her best outings were equated with those that were dialogue-lite, "where she's free to react, as in *Lost in Translation*, *Girl with a Pearl Earring*, *The Avengers*, and of course, *Under the Skin*."[54]

For an in-depth analysis of the film—its origin in Michel Faber's 2000 novel, its extended cinematic gestation, cast, music, special effects (like the black pool), *hidden* on-location filming, direction and everything else you want to know about the movie's making, see Maureen Foster's *Alien in the Mirror: Scarlett Johansson, Jonathan Glazer and Under the Skin* (McFarland, 2019).

Analysis

The reaction of the audience at the Venice Film Festival to Jonathan Glazer's *Under the Skin* was an amalgam of boos and cheers. Glazer reportedly beamed with pleasure at the response. "Some people love it, some are repulsed. Fair enough."[55] Initially, however,

Glazer was less than sanguine about the response and was bucked up by executive producer Claudia Bluemhuber.[56]

Many reviewers like many of the people who first saw the film did not realize or think much of the fact that it was based on a book of the same title by the writer named Michel Farber. Glazer clearly felt a connection with the book after reading it and wanted to make a film of it. He soon worked with a fellow scriptwriter and produced a script meant to illustrate the text of the book. Glazer eventually jettisoned that script. In time, Glazer began to work with Walter Campbell on a new script. Eventually he realized while he very much wanted to make a film that would be connected with the feeling the book caused in him, he didn't want to illustrate the story of the book in a strict way. He had started on *Under the Skin* soon after making *Sexy Beast*, but the making of *Birth* intervened before he went back to the earlier project. It seems clear that conversations with Johansson about Glazer's vision and his sense that she understood it and shared it played a crucial role in the film's development.

Glazer's spoken about the making of the film in terms that make clear he approached it or felt compelled to approach it as a work of art. All of the elements needed to combine in an organic way. He found that required simplification, a stripping away of the trappings of typical films dealing with aliens. He says that he realized that what he wanted was for the film to be "unadorned" in almost every possible way.[57]

Almost everything about Johansson's performance—from the short wig and clothes that make her almost unrecognizable, to the famous nude scene in which she contemplates her body reflected in a full-length mirror almost as if it belonged to someone else, to the realization that her skin is a kind of disguise when it peels off at the end—follows from and is in service to this wish of the writer and director concerning point of view. The gritty streets of Glasgow, the need for Johansson to learn to drive the ominous white van in which she goes around meeting young men so she can lead them to their deaths, the improvised scenes with performers who were not actors shot with hidden cameras, the motorcyclist in a helmet reminiscent of the insect-like head of an alien in a movie, the music, and the repetitive scenes of rivers, highways, sea, and rocks all similarly serve to provide a vision of the ordinary that is free of the assumptions about it and judgments made of it that we usually apply immediately and unconsciously to everything we meet. As with many pieces of contemporary art, there has been a tendency for viewers (and reviewers) to become irritated with *Under the Skin* and write it off as a rip-off or to become enthralled by it and declare it a masterpiece. The latter view seems the closest to the truth.

Lucy (2014)

> "the delightfully adventurous actress Scarlett Johansson's latest bit of strange..."
> —Tirdad Derakhshani, *Philadelphia Inquirer*, July 25, 2014

Outside a Taipei hotel, American student Lucy (Johansson) tries to shed current boyfriend Richard (Pilou Asbaek), but he has other plans and cuffs Lucy's arm to a metal briefcase and sends her inside to deliver it to Mr. Jang (Choi Min-sik). As she waits for Jang in the lobby, she sees Richard shot against the glass. Taken to Jang's suite, she senses she's in over her head. Jang is no fool and removes himself from her presence as she

Amr Waked and Scarlett Johansson, *Lucy* **(Canal+, EuropaCourt, TF1 Film Productions, 2014).**

unlocks the briefcase. There's no bomb inside, however, rather packets of CPHR, a new drug. Knocked unconscious, Lucy wakes and soon learns the packets have been surgically inserted into her abdomen. She and three men are prepared to transport the material overseas. Secured by a chain in a foul cell, Lucy rebuffs the advances of one of Jang's minions only to have him viciously kick her in the stomach before exiting the room. CPHR begins leaking into her system and initiates a chain reaction that has her literally climbing the walls. After she subsides and another man enters the room, she disables him, breaks her bonds, takes a pistol and guns down her former attacker and his buddies. She takes a cab to the hospital and at gunpoint orders a surgeon to remove the packets. Next stop: Jang's apartments, where she shoots his guards and while he blissfully undergoes relaxing physical therapy stabs knives into his hands. With her new capabilities, she extracts from his brain the destinations of the other drug mules: Rome, Berlin and Paris.

Using her roommate's computer, Lucy locates the renowned Professor Norman (Morgan Freeman) in Paris as well as police captain Pierre Del Rio (Amr Waked). She explains her condition to Norman and informs Del Rio of the drug mules. He and his counterparts in Germany and Italy round them up. Flying to Paris to speak in person with Norman, Lucy sips champagne which does not go well with the CPHR. In the restroom she watches herself begin disintegrating and ingests more of the drug. In Paris she introduces herself to Del Rio and meets Professor Norman, with whom she shares her experiences and reveals she will soon become—something else. She wants to pass on the knowledge she's gained through using 100 percent of her brain capacity. Interrupting the scene are Jang's gang, intent on recovering the drug and enacting revenge on Lucy. To Del Rio's shock, Lucy needs nothing other than her mental capacities to disarm and disable her attackers. Jang himself arrives and hears from his number one minion, "That damned girl. She's a witch." Jang matter of factly replies, "I know." While the gunfight proceeds in the halls of the university, Lucy is attached to the remaining packets of CPHR and begins downloading her knowledge, actually creating a bizarre computer using the existing ones in Norman's lab. The goal: place all of her knowledge onto an external drive, which she completes just as Jang fires a bullet toward the back of her skull. But she disappears, her dress falling to the floor. Del Rio arrives and guns down Jang before asking Norman the whereabouts of Lucy. His phone rings and he reads a text: "I am everywhere."

Reviews

Reviews were generally positive. *Variety* called Johansson "our resident avatar of the otherworldly," and made comparison with her "mesmerizingly out-there performances..." in *Her*, and *Under the Skin*. *Lucy* followed logically, "an agreeably goofy, high-concept speculative thriller...." It was practically "an anti-thriller, devoid of suspense or any real sense of danger due to the fact that its heroine is more or less invincible." Part of its charm was giving "homage to any number of Hollywood sci-fi head-trip classics...." Incredibly, Johansson communicated "her character's observations, reactions and eventual epiphanies in a mostly deadpan, flattened-out register that becomes only more subdued as the film progresses."[58]

The *New York Times* said that the title character was "played by the improbable yet somehow perfect Scarlett Johansson..." and compared her career trajectory to that of Elizabeth Taylor, including a similar "sexual expressivity." Even in stock roles she "radiates extraordinariness, and her in-human roles were expressive of elusive, tantalizing, otherworldly stardom itself."[59]

USA Today thought Johansson "ideally cast as a rapidly evolving kick-ass hero in *Lucy*, a stylish action thriller that is equal parts dazzling and ludicrous." The actress "was convincing in a part that progresses from terrorized victim to increasingly brilliant hero." Amidst the action were "moments of gentle wonder, too. In an emotional phone call to her mother, she tries to describe how she feels the rotation of the Earth and remembers her earliest days alive." In

Scarlett Johansson, *Lucy* (Universal Pictures/Canal+, 2014).

sum, "It's tough not to be dazzled by this operatic action film's blend of pop-philosophy, biology and silly delirium."[60]

Commentary

Lucy, unlike *Under the Skin*, which received next to zero TV promotion in the U.S., garnered plenty of TV ad time and won its weekend.[61]

With success unexpectedly assured by early grosses, *Time*, like the *New York Times*, was spurred to examine Johansson's place in the superhero pantheon. She had joined a small group of women carrying an action movie not based on a comic or young adult novel. Funny, though, *Lucy* was more than an action extravaganza: "It's more a meditation on pseudo-science: action scenes are intercut with clips of animals from nature documentaries and shots of stars swirling through space. Lucy never shoots or kicks when she can just sweep bad guys out of the way with a flick of her hand." Did this presage her own franchise. "Her resume suggests perhaps not."[62]

The Atlantic noted that Johansson's alien in *Under the Skin* and the character *Lucy* shared a common denominator: a blank stare. "Like most great actors, she certainly has the skill to convey what is inside her head with just a look, but in these films, her mind and her soul remain intentionally, and frustratingly, hidden." Perhaps it's "a unique and powerful statement about an industry and society that make its women disappear." Consider *Her*, in which the operating system Samantha transforms from a man's servant "into a powerful, independent entity that leaves him behind."[63]

In his December 2014 meditation on an upsurge in roles for women, Richard Corliss wrote, "Another adventure with a female lead, Scarlett Johansson's *Lucy*, earned $459 million on a budget reported to have been $40 million; dollar for dollar, this was the summer's most profitable smash."[64]

Ian Haydn Smith in his encyclopedic *Movie Star Chronicles* aptly called *Lucy* "cheerfully ludicrous…" and said director Besson had "tapped into her [Johansson's] otherworldy poise and allure…." *Lucy* and *Under the Skin* were "Daring and original…" and designated Johansson "as an actress unafraid to experiment."[65]

Johansson's scene in the hospital as she phones her mother while the surgeon is removing the drug packet and stitching her up is very moving, with the tears rolling down her cheeks. And overall, Johansson does a masterful job, but like Charlize Theron in 2015's *Mad Max: Fury Road*, proving yourself the prime mover in a science fiction film does not translate into awards or even acting nominations, at least from mainstream organizations. It doesn't help that both were R-rated, and both films' financial success was somewhat startling with that in mind.

At year end, *Time*'s Richard Corliss ranked *Lucy* among the best, contrasting it with the "handsome, muscular and dumb…" summer blockbusters. *Lucy* "kicks ass *and* takes brains." As for its leading lady, director Besson "promotes Johansson from an Indie-film icon and Marvel-universe sidekick to the movie superwoman she was destined to be." It was "the year's coolest, juiciest action movie."[66]

Total Film's Emma Dibdin wrote, "With this year's sci-fi trio of *Her*, *Under the Skin* and *Lucy*, Johansson now does otherworldly on a level no other actress can touch…."[67]

Noah Gittell saw the film "simultaneously as a critique of the objectification of Hollywood starlets, as well as a cheap, vulgar embrace of it." Like *Under the Skin*, "Her body, which certainly has played a role in shaping her celebrity, is on display throughout the film, but it only exists as a utilitarian instrument of revenge."

Gittell concluded that in *Her*, *Under the Skin* and *Lucy*, "Johansson is confronting audiences with the ways that our society refuses to embrace women in their entireties." It was certainly worthwhile to celebrate "a movie star with a mission."[68]

Director Besson said he was certain Johansson was the right choice because she was excited over the story. The difficulty would be distinguishing between the Lucy seen at the beginning of the film and the totally different entity at the close. How would someone play a character whose brain was evolving? Each morning Johansson scrutinized a chart she'd made to determine how Lucy would advance from 12 percent to 100 percent. Director Besson was "blown away."

As for the physical requirements, Johansson said she wanted to be in tip-top shape so "The audience should be able to think, okay, this girl can handle a gun." Her "movements needed to feel strong, and when you see how she stands, how she maneuvers, with a lot of inner strength."

Johansson said the shoot in Taipei, a city she found welcoming and loved exploring, took about three weeks. Arriving jet-lagged and tired "really added to the kind of, the dislocation of the character...."[69]

At the conclusion, when Lucy disappears into her cyber-world destiny, we have a real meshing of the reel and the real. The movie character, played by an actress and nonpareil fashion plate, had become a philosophical cover girl.

For a cogent comparison of Johansson in *Her*, *Under the Skin* and *Lucy*, see Appendix 1: "Film Odyssey: Scarlett Johansson Gets Under Our Skin" by Robert Castle.

Analysis

In a way, the most memorable and important scene in *Lucy* occurs during a lapse in the all-but-constant mayhem when Lucy (Johansson) gives a Paris policeman named Pierre Del Rio (Amr Waked) a long, slow kiss. She does this when he thinks she will not need him anymore and she assures him she will continue to need him—"as a reminder." What he is meant to remind her of remains unspoken but must be the pleasures of ordinary life, the pleasures of life associated with neither criminality nor heroism but rather with peace, affection, and gratitude, with the value of individual human beings. The sharp contrast between that sensual kiss and the mindless murder of the bulk of the film is what makes it memorable and meaningful.

Johansson's challenge in this film is not the need to win the audience's sympathy, the plot takes care of that. At the beginning, she is a young woman, a student in Taipei, full of life and out for a good time, but if anything too I, a touch too innocent. If she is guilty of anything it is putting too much trust in an ostensible boyfriend, a young man she has known for only a week. Although she refuses to do what he asks—to deliver a briefcase to a man in a nearby building—he tricks her into doing so by handcuffing her wrist to the case. In short, she is from the start a victim of forces beyond her control. In this respect she is a kind of every man or, rather, every woman and the audience immediately cheers her on when an accidental overdose of a drug turns her into a kind of chemical superhero.

The primary challenge posed by the role is how to depict the changes that the young, attractive woman of the film's opening goes through. She traces an arc from that beginning through a stage as a robotic humanoid with super powers to ultimately disappear after capturing her experience in digital form and leaving it as a readable chip for the future benefit of scientists and the human race. In general, she pulls off these radical changes in ways that remain credible and highly watchable. What in time might tend to begin to pall is the increasing indifference to others that Lucy displays as her powers increase and she becomes more machinelike, built to maximize speed and efficiency at the expense of normal human feelings. When she throws a patient from an operating table in a Taipei hospital and demands at gun point the surgeon remove the pouch of drugs from her body the audience is made to understand that her quick survey of the patient's x-rays convinced her the patient could not be saved in any case. Later, in Paris, when Pierre Del Rio offers to use the radio to request that the police cars not follow their car, Lucy says, "Don't bother" and arranges for the police cars to simply crash instead. At this stage of her "evolution" there is no attempt to justify the harm done to the police, their vehicles, and civilians involved in the collisions. Speed, efficiency is by now all that matters to her. These emotional changes are reflected in Lucy's appearance and speech patterns, so that she becomes more like a machine physically as well as in mental outlook. Of course, foiling the plot of the Chinese drug lords and providing scientists with a live experiment in increased brain capacity are no doubt meant to justify all the deaths and destruction Lucy looses on her world.

What is remarkable about Johansson's performance is that the attractiveness that was present at the film's opening remains throughout despite the changes she reflects. There is a charismatic quality to her performance that enhances and complicates what could have become a rather simple, mechanistic character. The audience can accept and believe in her long, slow kiss as well as in her ability to make cop cars crash and burn.

Ghost in the Shell (2017)

> "I get up, pour the ol' bowl of Cheerios, take care of le bebe, make sure she's all set, then I go fight, kickbox, do Filipino stick fighting and tactical weapons training. I get the shit kicked out of me, and then it's nighttime, and I go home, make dinner, wash le bebe, pop her in her little bedtime place, and hit the hay."
> —Scarlett Johansson on her daily *Ghost in the Shell* routine,
> Jada Yuan, "A Woman in Full," *Cosmopolitan*, May 2016

In a future where humanity is fusing with technology, a woman (Johansson) whose body has been irreparably damaged discovers that Dr. Ouelet (Juliette Binoche) has inserted her brain into a cybernetic shell by orders of Hanka Robotics' CEO Cutter (Peter Ferdinando). Now known as The Major, her ostensible mission for the anti-terrorist Section 9 is to take down a dangerous hacker known as Kuze (Michael Carmen Pitt).

Section 9 Chief Daisuke Aramaki ("Beat" Takashi Kitano) allows The Major and Batou (Pilou Asbaek) to investigate, beginning with The Major's "deep dive" into a Geisha assassin's AI she killed at a Hanka conference. This leads them to a nightclub and more bloodshed. The Major confronts Kuze, who escapes but touches off an explosion that blinds Batou and significantly impairs The Major's robotic body.

After killing Dr. Dahlin, like Ouelet one of the scientists who created what he is now, Kuze has Ouelet's car blindsided and her companion gunned down. Batou and the Section 9 team arrive, and The Major chases and subdues one of the miscreants. The culprit

Chester County Library Movie Club flyer, October 19, 2017, for *Ghost in the Shell* (DreamWorks/Paramount, 2017).

is interrogated but eventually forced to kill himself by Kuze. Later, Kuze captures The Major and reveals that he preceded her as a composite human-machine. He retires into the shadows when Batou arrives.

Ouelet tells The Major that there were 98 like her before she was created. Cutter shoots Ouelet.

The Major visits a woman in an apartment complex and learns that a daughter ran away and eventually took her own life. Is The Major that daughter?

At Cutter's instigation, a spider-like tank attacks The Major and Kuze. Wounded, The Major nevertheless neutralizes the machine before lying beside the injured Kuze. Cutter authorizes the killing of Kuze with a missile, but The Major survives. When Aramaki tells Cutter the Prime Minister has authorized his arrest, Cutter resists and is wounded by Aramaki, who communicates with The Major about killing the man. She says, "My name is Major and I give my consent." Returning to the apartment complex, The Major observes the gravestone on which is carved, "Motoko Kusanagi." She realizes that's her and tells her mother, "You don't have to come here anymore." The Major prepares for a new mission: "My mind is human, my body is manufactured. I'm the first of my kind, but I won't be the last. We cling to memories as if they define us, but what we do defines us. My ghost survived to remind the next of us that humanity is our virtue. I know who I am and what I'm here to do."

High atop a building, The Major receives authorization from Aramaki, removes her coat and drops slowly toward the street as she had done earlier on a mission that led to self-discovery.

Reviews

Reviews were mixed. The *New York Daily News* thought it had some novelties but "also suffers from the same pacing problems as the original." That said, it remained faithful enough to the original plot to gain some adherents among the aficionados. There were some masterful sequences and "some fresh strokes" that filled in gaps in the animated version. For example, the villain was "more clearly defined." Johansson was "suitably robotic...." Overall, it was pretty and engaged one in its futuristic realm but not so much as those presented in *The Matrix* or *Blade Runner*.[70] *USA Today* was very negative. Despite the "beautiful eye-popping world it creates..." it was a "defective mess...." As for Johansson, it was "both compliment and detriment that her Major is too robotic at times...." The character needed more humanity, which wasn't forthcoming until the "emotional climax."[71] The *Canberra City News* liked the inclusion of the "Colt .45 revolver [actually a Smith & Wesson], the gun that won the West, still has a place in future battles against evil."[72] *Digital Spy* summarized four reviews (*The Telegraph, The Hollywood Reporter, Variety, The Wrap*). *The Telegraph* said, "Purists may not want to hear it, but she's ideal at the conceptual side of the role. The unusual disconnect between Johansson's intelligence and her coolly dispassionate looks has been exploited before, most brilliantly in Jonathan Glazer's *Under the Skin*." *Hollywood Reporter* thought it ended in typical Hollywood fashion. *Variety* considered it "smart, hard-lacquered entertainment that may just trump the original films for galloping storytelling and sheer, coruscating visual excitement...." However, the "philosophical nuggets ... lurking amid Oshii's tangled plotting ... surely merited closer consideration by a filmmaker who wasn't trading in gloss, and doesn't merely regard human beings as elements of design." *The Wrap* said that although director Sanders might lack some inventive verve he overcame that "in his focus and work ethic, in his dedication to recreating the idiosyncratic anime world and making it sing in live-action."[73]

Commentary

No sooner than this live-action version of the admired 1995 Japanese animated feature was announced and Johansson identified as the star, there was a dust-up on the web by Manga/Anime fans distraught that a Caucasian would play the lead, Major Kusanagi. Although the film was to be made in New Zealand with a mixed nationality cast, Hollywood was accused of "whitewashing," i.e., using Caucasians in roles originally (in comics and animated features) designed for Asians.

Some realized that Johansson was a big draw and action heroine but opined that Motoko Kusanagi was "a quintessentially Asian role…." It "could have been a great vehicle for any number of Asian celebrities." Twitter offered Rinko Kikuchi of *Pacific Rim* as an alternative.[74]

Other commentators on the web countered this view. Lance E. Sloan asked, "Does the Major or the other characters look inherently Japanese? Or any type of Asian? No. The arguments are invalid."[75]

Others had realized that without a bankable star like Johansson, the project might never get off the ground. In short, "Johansson's casting is the result of cold hard math as much as Hollywood's blasé cultural insensitivity—creating the teeming world of *Ghost in the Shell* in live-action rather than animation will be eyewateringly expensive, and Johansson has proved herself newly bankable.… Jacking into cyberspace as robo-ScarJo also feels like the natural next step in her current, spectacular career phase of playing non-human or more-than human.… She's become a specialist in studies of compelling blankness."[76]

On the run-up to the film's release, director Rupert Sanders said he'd told Steven Spielberg, who'd given up on the project, that he'd aim for "more of an anime style as well as a film smaller than the superhero movies. This would make it more interesting and original."[77]

When first approached about the project, Johansson wasn't exactly keen. The film "seemed huge and overwhelming" and she'd just had a child. Nonetheless, her curiosity was aroused.[78]

As in *Under the Skin* and *Lucy*, the Major's body "doesn't betray what she's thinking,… there's a lot going on internally." She was intrigued to depict "this inner life with very limited physical nuance…."[79]

Total Film noted that in the anime The Major is frequently naked. The live-action film would "tone down the skin show" but Johansson had reservations. "As soon as I saw [*the anime*], I was like, 'Obviously I'm not naked. We've all agreed I'm not naked, right.'"[80]

Is it possible that, in addition to Johansson's concerns, the filmmakers might have felt costuming Johansson's character in—and out—of those duds would seem farfetched—or exploitive. (The #MeToo movement against sexual harassment was just about to make international headlines.) (Johansson's *Lucy* proved an R-rating [for violence] would not necessarily negatively affect grosses.) They could have taken that route, made *Ghost* more comic/graphic novel-like. An amusing homage might have had The Major examine her body and croak, "Synthetic fles-s-s-h," as a gleeful Preston Foster did in 1932's *Dr. X*. After all, The Major is a cyborg. Robot nudity!

About what she did wear, Johansson said of her silicone black suit that it was easier to wear and fight in than Black Widow's neoprene or leather. She burned through them fast enough. "There's another one!"[81]

In *The Art of Ghost in the Shell*, Johansson said, "The feeling of isolation that is part of the human experience and then the subsequent connectivity that we all share in unexpected ways—these kind of themes are always relevant."[82] Regarding her director, Johansson was positive: "Rupert is [a] brilliant visionary, and when he sent me ... everything that he was putting together for this, that's really what cinched the deal for me ... completely created not only a homage to the manga, the anime, for the fans, but has put his thumbprints all over this project."

Sanders thought Johansson, "really inhabited the role and brought a childlike quality to it...." Fight Trainer Richard Norton complimented Johansson's second-to-none work ethic. "I said, 'Scarlett, I've been doing these fifty years and I'm still learning.' And she'll do those extra twenty to thirty reps because she's still after that excellence."[83]

Director Sanders took a similar tact: "I cast Scarlett because, out of all the actors of her generation, she had become the most iconic.... She is an incredible woman—one moment, she would be playing with her daughter in the trailer, and within minutes, she would be smashing guys round the head with a stun baton."[84]

Regarding the search for identity embodied in *Ghost in the Shell*, Johansson said, "The feeling of isolation that we experience as part of the human experience, and then the subsequent connectivity that we all share in unexpected ways, these kinds of themes are always relevant. I think the audience, and certainly even myself as the audience, wants to connect with this kind of story. We want to place ourselves in the character's plight and live the journey through them. That's the magic of connecting with film."[85]

For Johansson, The Major was definitely heroic: "I think that when the character really shines the most is when she is self-sacrificing.... She finds herself in this body, in this circumstance, and by the end of the film, she embraces this decision that's been made for her. She owns the decision to be the Major."[86]

Analysis

Many millennials grew up enjoying or perhaps obsessing over Manga (Japanese comics and graphic novels) and Anime (animated, aka cartoon). For an older generation, these Japanese pop culture developments left them cold. Could the movie bridge the gap? Unless a future evaluation is kinder, the answer was no.

The beginning seems unnecessarily slow moving, the dialogue stilted, and the whole thing going on too long. Its purpose seems to be to set up the obvious change that takes place when the Major receives her actual memory from her technological rather than biological mother, the doctor played by Juliette Binoche. The film comes to life then—the action and the language picks up. It is far more interesting and engaging and it is to be regretted that this latter part of the film is so relatively brief.

It could well be that those of a different age simply lack sympathy for these kinds of futuristic films. They are dystopias that make *1984* seem light-hearted—a collection of heavily armed, inarticulate thugs seem to rule whatever remains of an unpleasant mass-world. The theme of an identity lost and found is appropriate but no longer seems either new or inspiring, simply more of the same but less credible than it seemed when Winston Smith found the gumption to start keeping a diary despite Big Brother.

The script seems not only unbalanced because of the length of the slow beginning and the relative brevity of the quick, engaging ending but also borders on the whimsical or incredible. How is the head of the secret service able to survive a long and vigorous attack by a number of men (or cyborgs or creatures, who knows what?) heavily armed with automatic weapons by wielding a brief case and what appears to be a Smith and Wesson revolver in a hand-tooled leather holster? Is this an homage to cowboy movies, a symbolic statement that the lost, retro world has lingering power, or an awkwardness that is equivalent to an unfunny joke? If the digital image of the cat early in the film suggests a remnant of the Major's real memory does work—especially when the actual cat seems to recognize the ghost when she shows up in her new shell when she visits what once was her home—the image of the old-fashioned Japanese house on the chest of the supposed terrorist and the actual house where he and the Major once lived as friends and runaways in the lawless zone does not work. What is the source of the image on the supposed terrorist's chest? Why is it there unless the director placed it there to make the connection with the actual house later? Despite those who lack sympathy with this kind of futurism—for some it seems unnecessarily grim and depressing—part of the reason it comes to life when it does is because of the relative normality of a cat and a mother making tea, it should at least be made to hang together, to make sense within its own conventions and portrayals. This script seems to fail to do that.

Some of the dialogue is fine. If the head of the secret service with his brief case and revolver seemed incredible, his line, "Don't send a rabbit to kill a fox," is good even if it did nothing to increase the scene's credibility. Johansson's line in the early part of the film when she is being tortured with a Tazer or something of the sort and told to dance when she answers, "To tell you the truth, I was not built to dance" and she launches an attack. The line is echoed near the end of the film when she asks that Cutter be told, "Tell him this is justice. It's what I was built for."

Things are lost in cultural translation and it's possible a kind of misunderstanding or incomplete understanding can lead to oddities—like trying to make too much of the revolver. Is there a film—or more than one—where someone blatantly releases empty shells near a group of corpses? Is there an attempt to draw attention to the link between U.S. Westerns and Japan's Samurai movies—*The Seven Samurai* and *The Magnificent Seven*?

Other than Johansson's Major when she meets her biological mother, does anyone crack a smile in this film? Other than *Guardians of the Galaxy*, how little humor is to be found in dystopian and futuristic movies that might be labeled "movies with skyscrapers with holes in them." From *The Hunger Games*, *Divergent* and *Underworld* to *The Matrix*, *The Maze Runner* and *Resident Evil*, the dearth of humor can leave a bad taste in the mouth and cause wonder that anyone would put much effort into existing in such realms.

Epilogue

> "There is no getting away from Johansson, and that is how her uncountable fans, female as well as male, would like it to be forever. They do not want to get away."
>
> —Anthony Lane, "Her Again: The Unstoppable Scarlett Johansson," *New Yorker*, March 24, 2014

Comparing Johansson's career to those of past stars is illuminating. It might come as a surprise to some that most of the silver screen's legendary actresses and sex symbols (and many male stars as well) made relatively few truly memorable, or even good movies. Nor were these sirens as popular in their time as one has been led to believe if the annual Quigley Poll of exhibitors is any indication. Rita Hayworth never made its top ten. Ditto Ava Gardner and Lana Turner.[1]

Compared to Johansson, a number of modern Hollywood actresses, even those who are very popular, have resumes full of fluff. By contrast, Johansson's body of work contains serious films and movies in which she takes chances and stretches the envelope, e.g., *Lost in Translation*, *Ghost World*, *Under the Skin*, *Jojo Rabbit*.

Speaking at the end of 2019 about the emotional pain dealt with in *Marriage Story*, Johansson addressed this issue: "It's brutal. Which is also so delicious. You know what I mean. The brutality of it, that's the rich stuff. That's the good stuff. That's the ugly, embarrassing stuff. That's the stuff I'm fascinated by. It's all that juicy stuff, because that stuff is powerful and it's meaningful. I'm not in it for the fluff. I don't care about the fluff."[2]

Perspicacious moviegoers may also have observed what might be labeled "the 10 year rule." Despite having become famous and iconic, many film stars were unable to make quality and financially lucrative movies for more than a decade. Johansson has bucked that trend to join the ranks of the truly legendary. It benefited her that she began as an attractive child, learned her craft, and as an added benefit grew into a truly beautiful woman people wanted to look at, yet a woman with plenty going on under that splendid exterior.

It's obvious that Johansson was imbued with a willingness to work a good deal from the start, a pressure that arises from something more than ambition. One guesses she started so young she knew she had something early. Even the early films suggest people wanted to look at her.

The career trajectory is so very interesting: independent films as child and teen, especially *Manny & Lo*, big budget *The Horse Whisperer*, breakthrough as adult actress in *Lost in Translation*, awards and nominations for that and *Girl with a Pearl Earring* the same year, Marvel Universe mainstay, and leading and supporting nominations for two 2019 films, *Marriage Story* and *Jojo Rabbit*.

Sarah El-Mahmoud was correct in a career recap in 2019. Despite Golden Globe nominations early in her adulthood and wins from BAFTA and other organizations, until *Marriage Story* Johansson had never been nominated for an Academy Award. Many Academy voters are ever behind the times. Not only was the legendary Edward G. Robinson never awarded a Best Actor Academy Award, he was never even nominated! The fabled "master of suspense" Alfred Hitchcock never won Best Director. *2001: A Space Odyssey* (1968) so perplexed the old guard that it failed to garner a Best Picture nomination. The films El-Mahmoud offered up as deserving of nominations for Johansson were *The Horse Whisperer*, *Ghost World*, *Lost in Translation*, *Girl with a Pearl Earring*, *Match Point*, *Don Jon*, *Her*, and *Under the Skin*.[3]

Vanity Fair picked up on Johansson's second golden age at the end of 2019. Johansson herself was uneasy about the awards talk: "I definitely am the type of person who's always waiting for the other shoe to drop." Nevertheless, "But I'm learning to change that habit."[4] As it transpired, neither she, co-star Driver nor director Baumbach took home any Academy Awards.

One wonders what the future will bring. In 2017 actress Tessa Thompson of *Thor: Ragnarok* revealed that she'd spoken with Marvel's president Kevin Feige about an all female superhero movie. Zoë Saldana, Brie Larson, Pom Klementieff, Karen Gillan and Johansson were posited as those kick-ass heroines.[5] Since 2017 at least there has been talk of Johansson appearing in *Reflective Light*, based on Carla Buckley's 2014 novel *The Deepest Secret*.[6] Also rumored is the role of Audrey in a new version of *Little Shop of Horrors*.

Black Widow, the big movie that Johansson and Marvel fans have been clamoring for was to have premiered in May 2020, but the Coronavirus that spread across the United States and the world in the late winter and the spring of 2020 put the kibosh on that. As of the writing of this book, *Black Widow* was scheduled to launch in July 2021.

We can hope Johansson continues to balance such big budget extravaganzas as *Black Widow* with "indie" films in which, as in *Under the Skin* and *Lucy*, she carries the show. The danger lies in the conundrum: make big money in superhero films or less money in more personal, independent features. Obviously agents and managers prefer the former.

Johansson has always had "a willingness to displease." Her co-star in *Marriage Story*, Laura Dern, said, "To be a likable female is to be malleable to whatever the person in the room wants from us.... Be a young lady. Be seen and not heard. Scarlett's persona is, 'I'm here and I know who I am. I'm not here to make you like me.' That's a very impressive energy in a woman."[7]

It is nigh impossible to imagine a film star coming along with the looks, the figure, the pizzazz, the intelligence, the savvy, the courage, the "game-ness," and the "other-ness" of Scarlett Johansson. She is one of a kind and we conclude with co-author Warren Hope's encomium: Johansson has the traditional figure and looks of a Lana Turner and thus strikes contemporaries raised on the post-sixties crop of ingenues as incomprehensible: she simply does not compute with the mistrained eyes of the now. Poor famished eyes.

APPENDIX 1

"Film Odyssey: Scarlett Johansson Gets Under Our Skin"

BY ROBERT CASTLE

Reproduced with permission of the author and NJ PEN
(www.njpen.com), June 3, 2015

The all-reaching potential, influence, and power of the digital universe has become a familiar theme in television and movie dramas. Why not? The last 10 to 15 years has seen so much cyber-growth that it has become the foreground of our world.

The problematic qualities of this social commitment to virtual reality via social media has been uniquely dramatized in three recent films—*Her* (2013), *Under the Skin* (2013), and *Lucy* (2014)—all of them starring Scarlett Johansson.

Lucy garnered the best box-office and worst critical reactions of the three, its detractors seemingly inoculated against the accelerating rhythms of its plot and violence, and uninterested in going along for the philosophical ride.

Her might be the "art circuit" version of a *Lucy*-like hit. It made modest money for an art film, thanks to the following its director Spike Jonze commands and an Oscar for Best Original Screenplay. The awards also flushed out potential-but-reluctant viewers, however; maybe more people would have paid to see *Her* if they could have seen her (Johansson).

Few people saw *Under the Skin*, by Jonathan Glazer (*Sexy Beast* and *Birth*), nor did many who watched it fully figure out what Johansson's character was doing in it. The film excited many critics, however, by revealing as little as possible in terms of explanation—the very approach that bores general audiences.

In their tackling of questions related to humanity and technology, all three films revolve around the orbit of *2001: A Space Odyssey* (1968), and each, in its own way, reflects the particular light *2001* throws on them.

Any futuristic movie scenario must deal with *2001*, perhaps. *Her* and *Lucy* have satiric elements that track closely to *2001*'s take on technology: exploring how the wonders of space travel and futuristic technology are bound to their deleterious effects; primarily, the deadening of the human soul.

Under the Skin

Under the Skin holds up the best of these three as a metaphor for the all-encompassing nature of the digital world. In it, Johansson's unnamed Female lures men to her Glasgow home with an implicit promise of sexual gratification. Inside, they track toward her until they are submerged into the black floor. Once, we are allowed to watch a man under the floor, floating around, eventually spotting another who appears flattened out.

Men sinking into a void that disappears them: what better analogy for the expansive digital world in which we now find ourselves soon losing definition and becoming unidentifiable. We are guided to this state by a force we cannot resist, not even as it consumes us; literally de-humanizes us. *Under the Skin* recognizes that what seemed inevitable, if not a duty, has turned into a skeptical agency.

Why The Female wants them is never stated. She appears bent on depopulating Glasgow, Scotland, of its predatory men. Yet, she begins to change, seemingly excited by her attractiveness. The tipping point occurs when she picks up a physically-impaired man who responds to her not quite like the others, and he is spared.

Inevitably, the music and cinematography of *Under the Skin* have evoked comparisons to Kubrick's *2001: A Space Odyssey* (1968). Both films set up a premise of aliens coming to Earth with a large, unstated mission. We have to assume the monolith left among the apes was done to effect something, but its mission is unknown—curiosity? A helping hand? Johansson's alien doesn't start with the helping hand, but her changing attitude could sabotage the mission.

Kubrick initially discussed an explanation for the monolith; we are left, however, with only an assumption that it was "deliberately placed there." Astronaut Dave Bowman (Keir Dullea) ending up in an 18th century French bedroom with the monolith re-appearing at the foot of his bed also goes unexplained. Our desire to know, to have an (the) answer, is frustrated.

What The Female in *Under the Skin* is trying to accomplish, we're never told; however, withholding this information sharpens the viewer's attention just to get some clue regarding her actions. The film's reluctance to inform us is palpable and, finally, emphasizes the changes happening to Johansson's character. Like *2001*, *Under the Skin* employs little dialogue in its telling, further increasing our frustration.

Lucy and Her

Lucy and *Her* also evoke *2001: A Space Odyssey* in their treatments of super-intelligence and self-awareness as fueling the will to power. Lucy ingests drugs that give her a limitless consciousness reminiscent of that of H.A.L.-9000, the berserk artificial intelligence from *2001*.

When her brain reaches 100 percent capacity, she metamorphoses into a computer stick, and subsequently melds with every digital device in the world, conjuring up the image of the Space Child at the end of *2001*, hovering above Earth, contemplating its next move. When these films reach their glorious, digital apotheoses, we share a sense of triumph with Johansson's characters.

As Samantha in *Her*, Johansson's voice approaches the iconic voice of H.A.L. (Douglas Rain) in *2001*. Stanley Kubrick had chosen Rain for his neutral tone (rejecting Martin Balsam's voice); Spike Jonze had Samantha Morton do the voice for the entire filming of *Her* but began to have doubts in post-production and decided to use Johansson. What we think of as destiny or inevitability often comes by chance and coincidence.

I'd like to believe the choices made to cast Johansson in each of these films is intriguingly linked perhaps as an integrated commentary on the virtualized world we are experiencing today. This triad in these films dramatizes this struggle, especially through Johansson's dehumanized characters: an alien, a computer voice, and a woman becoming "an advanced machine."

What will it take for contemporary humans to become more empathetic and produce more sincere emotions? Good science fiction provides interesting and profound ways to experience real feelings with authenticity.

Appendix 2

Non-Screen Credits

Music CDs

Anywhere I Lay My Head (Rhino Entertainment Company, 2008).
Break Up (Atco Records/Rhino, 2009). With Peter Yorn.
Apart (Capitol Records, 2018). With Peter Yorn.

Music Videos

When the Deal Goes Down (2006), Bob Dylan song
Justin Timberlake: What Goes Around … Comes Around (2007)
Falling Down (2008) *Anywhere I Lay My Head* album
Relator (2009) with Peter Yorn, album *Break Up*
Bad Dreams (2018) with Peter Yorn, album *Apart*
Iguana Bird (2018) with Peter Yorn, album *Apart*

Dolce and Gabbana TV Commercial

The One Street of Dreams. With Matthew McConaughey. Directed by Martin Scorsese. 2014.

Trivia

In Carl Hiaasen's 2010 comedic murder mystery, *Star Island*, the dunderhead wannabe A-lister pop icon Cherry Pye bemoans the fact that others are getting big-time magazine photo shoots. She mentions that Scarlett got the cover of *Esquire* the previous December. This is probably a veiled reference to Johansson's first "Sexiest Woman Alive" cover on *Esquire*'s November 2006 issue.

Most people might say *Iron Man 2* is Johansson's first role in a black leather cat suit to dismantle her enemies. However, that honor goes to a fantasy sequence in *The Perfect Score*.

Filmography

Films are listed in chronological order.

North (Castle Rock Entertainment/Columbia, 1994; 87 min.)
Directed by Rob Reiner. Story and screenplay by Alan Zweibel. Based on the novel by Alan Zweibel.
Cast: North (Elijah Wood), North's father (Jason Alexander), Narrator (Bruce Willis), North's mother (Julia Louis-Dreyfus), Winchell (Matthew McCurley), Piano player (Marc Shaiman), Arthur Belt (Jon Lovitz), Adam (Jussie Smollett), Zoe (Taylor Fry), Sarah (Alana Austin), Teacher (Peg Shirley), Judge Buckle (Alan Arkin), Mr. Nelson (John Ritter), Mrs. Nelson (Faith Ford), Pa Tex (Dan Aykroyd), Ma Tex (Reba McIntire), Alaskan mom (Kathy Bates), Amish dad (Alexander Godunov), Amish mom (Kelly McGillis), Laura Nelson (Scarlett Johansson).

Just Cause (Warner Bros., 1995; 102 min.)
Directed by Arne Glimcher. Screenplay by Jeb Stuart. Based on the novel by John Katzenbach.
Cast: Paul Armstrong (Sean Connery), Sheriff Tanny Brown (Laurence Fishburne), Laurie Prentiss Armstrong (Kate Capshaw), Bobby Earl (Blair Underwood), Blair Sullivan (Ed Harris), Detective T.J. Wilcox (Christopher Murray), Evangeline (Ruby Dee), Katie Armstrong (Scarlett Johansson), Warden (Daniel J. Travanti), Ida Conklin (Lynne Thigpen), Delores Rodriguez (Liz Torres), Phil Prentiss (Kevin McCarthy), Libby Prentiss (Hope Lange), McNair (Ned Beatty), Elder Phillips (George Plimpton), Lyle Morgan (Chris Sarandon).

If Lucy Fell (MPCA/TriStar, 1996; 92 min.)
Directed by Eric Schaeffer. Screenplay by Erc Schaeffer. Story by Eric Schaeffer, Tony Spiridakis.
Cast: Lucy Ackerman (Sarah Jessica Parker), Joe MacGonaughgill (Eric Schaeffer), Bwick Elias (Ben Stiller), Simon Ackerman (James Rebhorn), Jane Lindquist (Elle Macpherson), Emily (Scarlett Johansson).

Manny & Lo (Pope Productions, 1996, 88 min.)
Directed by Lisa Krueger. Screenplay by Lisa Krueger.
Cast: Amanda (Scarlett Johansson), Laurel (Aleksa Palladino), Elaine (Mary Kay Place), Country house owner (Paul Guilfoyle), Golf course family members (Karsten Johansson, Melanie Sloan/Johansson, Hunter Johansson, Vanessa Johansson).

Home Alone 3 (20th Century–Fox, 1997; 102 min.)
Directed by Raja Gosnell. Screenplay by John Hughes.
Cast: Alex Pruitt (Alex D. Linz), Petr Beaupre (Olek Krupa), Alice Ribbons (Rya Kihlstedt), Burton Jernigan (Lenny Von Dohlen), Mrs. Hess (Marian Seldes), Molly Pruitt (Scarlett Johansson), Karen Pruitt (Haviland Morris), Jack Pruitt (Kevin Kilner), Stan Pruitt (Seth Smith).

Fall (Five Minutes Before the Miracle, 1997; 93 min.)
Directed by Eric Schaeffer. Screenplay by Eric Schaeffer.
Cast: Michael (Eric Schaeffer), Sarah (Amanda de Cadenet), Phillipe (Rudolf Martin), Robin (Francie Swift), Sally (Lisa Vidal), Joan Alterman (Roberta Maxwell), Scasse (Jose Yenque), Zsarko (Josip Kuchan), Little girl (Scarlett Johansson).

The Horse Whisperer (Touchstone, 1998; 170 min.)
Directed by Robert Redford. Screenplay by Eric Roth. Based on the novel by Nicholas Evans.
Cast: Tom Booker (Robert Redford), Annie MacLean (Kristin Scott Thomas), Grace MacLean (Scarlett Johansson), Robert MacLean (Sam Neill), Diane Booker (Dianne Wiest), Frank Booker (Chris Cooper), Liz Hammond (Cherry Jones), Judith (Kate "Catherine" Bosworth), Ellen Booker (Jeanette Nolan).

My Brother the Pig (Unapix Productions/Brimstone Entertainment, 1999; 92 min.)
Directed by Erik Fleming. Screenplay by Matthew Flynn.
Cast: Kathy Caldwell (Scarlett Johansson), Matilda (Eve "Eva" Mendez/Mendes), Richard Caldwell (Judge Reinhold), Kathy Caldwell (Romy Walthall/Romy Windsor), George Caldwell (Nick Fuoco), Freud (Alex D. Linz), Grandma Berta (Renee Victor), Mercedes (Cambria Gonzalez), Edwardo the butcher (Marco Rodriguez).

Ghost World (United Artists, 2001; 111 min.)
Directed by Terry Zwigoff. Screenplay by Daniel Clowes and Terry Zwigoff. Based on the comic by Daniel Clowes.
Cast: Enid (Thora Birch), Rebecca (Scarlett Johansson), Seymour (Steve Buscemi), Josh (Brad Renfro), Roberta Allsworth (Illeana Douglas), Enid's father (Bob Balaban).

An American Rhapsody (Fireworks Pictures/Seven Arts Pictures, 2001; 106 min.)
Produced by Colleen Camp, Bonnie Timmermann. Directed by Eva Gardos. Screenplay by Eva Gardos.
Cast: Margit Sandor (Nastassja Kinski), Suzanne Sandor, age 15 (Scarlett Johansson), Suzanne, infant (Raffaella Bansagi), Peter Sandor (Tony Goldwyn), Maria Sandor, age 10 (Mae Whitman), Maria Sandor, age 18 (Larisa Oleynik), Helen (Agnes Banfalvy), George (Zoltan Seress), Dottie (Colleen Camp), Suzanne, age 5–6 (Kelly Endresz Banlaki), Sheila, age 15 (Emmy Rossum), Jeno (Balazs Galko), Teri (Zsuzsa Czinkoczi).

The Man Who Wasn't There (Good Machine/Gramercy Pictures, 2001; 116 min.)
Directed by Joel and Ethan Coen. Screenplay by Joel and Ethan Coen.
Cast: Ed Crane (Billy Bob Thornton), Doris Crane (Frances McDormand), Frank (Michael Badalucco), Ann Nirdlinger Brewster (Katherine Borowitz), Birdy Abundas (Scarlett Johansson), Freddy Riedenschneider (Tony Shalhoub), Big Dave Brewster (James Gandolfini).

Eight Legged Freaks (Warner Bros., 2002; 99 min.)
 Directed by Ellory Elkayen. Story by Ellory Elkayen and Randy Kornfield.
 Cast: Chris McCormick (David Arquette), Sheriff Samantha Parker (Kari Wuhrer), Ashley Parker (Scarlett Johansson), Mike Parker (Scott Terra), Harlan Griffith (Doug E. Doug), Deputy Pete Willis (Rich Overton), Wade (Leon Rippy), Bret (Matt Czuchry), Gladys (Eileen Ryan), Emma (Jane Edith Wilson), Joshua Taft (Tom Noonan).

Lost in Translation (Focus Features, 2003; 101 min.)
 Directed by Sofia Coppola. Screenplay by Sofia Coppola.
 Cast: Bob Harris (Bill Murray), Charlotte (Scarlett Johansson), John (Giovanni Ribisi), Ms. Kawasaki (Akiko Takeshita), Kelly (Anna Faris).

Girl with a Pearl Earring (Archer Street Productions, 2003; January 2004 general release; 100 min.)
 Directed by Peter Webber. Screenplay by Olivia Hetreed. Based on the novel by Tracy Chevalier.
 Cast: Vermeer (Colin Firth), Griet (Scarlett Johansson), Van Ruijvan (Tom Wilkinson), Pieter (Cilliam Murphy), Maria Thins (Judy Parfitt).

The Perfect Score (Paramount, 2004; 93 min.)
 Directed by Brian Robbins. Screenplay by Mark Schwahn, Marc Hyman, Jon Zack. Based on a story by Marc Hyman, Jon Zack.
 Cast: Anna Rose (Erika Christensen), Francesca Curtis (Scarlett Johansson), Kyle (Chris Evans), Roy (Leonardo Nam), Matty Matthews (Bryan Greenburg), Desmond Rhodes (Darius Miles), Larry (Matthew Lillard), Anita Donlee (Vanessa Angel).

In Good Company (Universal, 2004; 109 min.)
 Directed by Paul Weitz. Screenplay by Paul Weitz.
 Cast: Dan Foreman (Dennis Quaid), Carter Duryea (Topher Grace), Alex Foreman (Scarlett Johansson), Ann Foreman (Marg Helgenberger), Morty (David Paymer), Steckle (Clark Gregg), Eugene Kalb (Philip Baker Hall), Kimberly (Selma Blair), Corwin (Frankie Faison), Jana Foreman (Zena Grey), Enrique Colon (Ty Burrell), Teddy K (Malcolm McDowell), Receptionist (Colleen Camp).

A Love Song for Bobby Long (Lions Gate Films, 2004; 2005 general release; 119 min.)
 Directed by Shainee Gabel. Screenplay by Shainee Gabel. Based on the novel by Ronald Everett Capps.
 Cast: Bobby Long (John Travolta), Pursy Will (Scarlett Johansson), Lawson Pines (Gabriel Macht), Georgianna (Deborah Kara Unger), Cecil (Dane Rhodes), Junior (David Jensen), Lee (Clayne Crawford).

The SpongeBob SquarePants Movie (Paramount/Nickelodeon, 2004; 87 min.)
 Directed by Stephen Hillenburg, Mark Osborne. Screenplay by Derek Drymon, Tim Hill, Stephen Hillenburg, Kent Osborne, Aaron Springer, Paul Tibbett. Based on a story by Stephen Hillenberg and the TV series *SpongeBob SquarePants* by Stephen Hillenberg.
 Cast: Voices: SpongeBob (Tom Kenny), Mr. Krabs (Clancy Brown), Squidward (Rodger Bumpass), Patrick Star (Bill Fagerbakke), Plankton (Mr. Lawrence), Karen, (Jill Talley), Sandy (Carolyn Lawrence), Mrs. Poppy Puff (Mary Jo Catlett), King Neptune (Jeffrey Tambor), Mindy (Scarlett Johansson), Dennis (Alec Baldwin), David Hasselhoff (himself).

A Good Woman (LionsGate, 2004; 93 min.)

Directed by Mike Barker. Screenplay by Howard Himelstein. Based on the play *Lady Windermere's Fan* by Oscar Wilde.

Cast: Mrs. Erlynne (Helen Hunt), Meg Windermere (Scarlett Johansson), Lord Darlington (Stephen Campbell Moore), Contessa Lucchino (Milena Vukotic), Robert Windermere (Mark Umbers), Cecil (Roger Hammond), Dumby (John Standing), Tuppy (Tom Wilkinson), Alessandra (Giorgia Massetti), Lady Plymdale (Diana Hardcastle).

The Island (DreamWorks, 2005; 136 min.)

Directed by Michael Bay. Screenplay by Caspian Tredwell-Owen, Alex Kurtzman, Roberto Orci. Based on a story by Caspian Tredwell-Owen.

Cast: Lincoln Six Echo/Tom Lincoln (Ewan McGregor), Jordan Two Delta /Sarah Jordan (Scarlett Johansson), Dr. Bernard Merrick (Sean Bean), Albert Laurent (Djimon Hounsou), James McCord (Steve Buscemi), Starkweather Two Delta/Jamal Starkweather (Michael Clarke Duncan).

Match Point (BBC Films, 2005; 119 min.)

Directed by Woody Allen. Screenplay by Woody Allen.

Cast: Chris Wilton (Thomas Rhys Meyers), Nola Rice (Scarlett Johansson), Chloe Hewett Wilton (Emily Mortimer), Alec Hewett (Brian Cox), Tom Hewett (Matthew Goode), Eleanor Hewett (Penelope Wilton), Inspector Dowd (Ewen Bremner), Detective Mike Banner (James Nesbitt), Mrs. Eastby (Margaret Tyzack), Henry (Rupert Penry-Jones), Policeman (Toby Kebbell).

The Black Dahlia (Universal, 2006; 121 min.)

Directed by Brian De Palma. Screenplay by Josh Friedman. Based on the novel by James Ellroy.

Cast: Dwight "Bucky" Bleichert (Josh Hartnett), Kay Lake (Scarlett Johansson), Lee Blanchard (Aaron Eckhart), Madeleine Linscott (Hilary Swank), Elizabeth Short (Mia Kirshner), Detective Russ Millard (Mike Starr), Ramona Linscott (Fiona Shaw).

Scoop (BBC Films, 2006; 96 min.)

Directed by Woody Allen. Screenplay by Woody Allen.

Cast: Peter Lyman (Hugh Jackman), Sondra Pransky (Scarlett Johansson), Lord Lyman (Julian Glover), Joe Strombel (Ian McShane), Vivian (Romola Garai), Sid Waterman (Woody Allen).

The Prestige (Touchstone/Warner Bros., 2006; 130 min.)

Directed by Christopher Nolan. Screenplay by Jonathan Nolan and Christopher Nolan. Based on the novel by Christopher Priest.

Cast: Robert Angier (Hugh Jackman), Alfred Borden (Christian Bale), Olivia Wenscombe (Scarlett Johansson), Cutter (Michael Caine), Nikola Tesla (David Bowie), Sarah Borden (Rebecca Hall), Julia McCullough (Piper Perabo), Owens (Roger Rees), Alley (Andy Serkis).

The Nanny Diaries (Weinstein Company, 2007; 105 min.)

Directed by Shari Springer Berman, Robert Pulcini. Screenplay by Shari Springer Berman, Robert Pulcini. Based on the novel by Emma McLaughlin and Nicola Kraus.

Cast: Annie Braddock (Scarlett Johansson), Mrs. X (Laura Linney), Grayer (Nicholas

Reese Art), Mr. X (Paul Giamatti), Harvard Hottie/Hayden (Chris Evans), Judy Braddock (Donna Murphy), Lynette (Alicia Keys), Jane Gould (Julie White).

The Other Boleyn Girl (Columbia/Focus Features, 2008; 115 min.)
Directed by Justin Chadwick. Screenplay by Peter Morgan. Based on the novel by Philippa Gregory.
Cast: Anne Boleyn (Natalie Portman), Mary Boleyn (Scarlett Johansson), Henry VIII (Eric Bana), Sir Thomas Boleyn (Mark Rylance), Duke of Norfolk (David Morrissey), Lady Elizabeth Boleyn (Kristin Scott Thomas), William Carey (Benedict Cumberbatch).

Vicky Cristina Barcelona (Weinstein Company, 2008; 96 min.)
Directed by Woody Allen. Screenplay by Woody Allen.
Cast: Vicky (Rebecca Hall), Cristina (Scarlett Johansson), Juan Antonio (Javier Bardem), Maria Elena (Penelope Cruz), Doug (Chris Messina), Judy (Patricia Clarkson), Mark (Kevin Dunn), Narrator (Christopher Evan Welch).

The Spirit (LionsGate, 2008; 103 min.)
Directed by Frank Miller. Screenplay by Frank Miller. Based on the comic by Will Eisner.
Cast: Denny Colt/Spirit (Gabriel Macht), Octopus (Samuel L. Jackson), Sand Saref (Eva Mendes), Silken Floss (Scarlett Johansson), Ellen Dolan (Sarah Paulson), Commissioner Eustace Dolan (Dan Lauria), Morgenstern (Stana Katic), Lorelei (Jaime King), Liebowitz (Frank Miller), Mahmoud (Eric Balfour), Young Sand (Seychelle Gabriel), Young Spirit (Johnny Simmons).

He's Just Not That Into You (New Line Cinema, 2009; 129 min.)
Directed by Ken Kwapis. Screenplay by Abby Kohn, Marc Silverstein. Based on the book by Greg Behrendt and Liz Tuccillo.
Cast: Neil (Ben Affleck), Beth (Jennifer Aniston), Janine (Jennifer Connelly), Conor (Kevin Connolly), Ben (Bradley Cooper), Mary (Drew Barrymore), Anna (Scarlett Johansson), Alex (Justin Long), Gigi (Ginnifer Goodwin), Ken Murphy (Kris Kristofferson), Joshua (Leonardo Nam), Kelli Ann (Busy Philipps).

Iron Man 2 (Paramount Pictures/Marvel Entertainment, 2010; 124 min.)
Directed by Jon Favreau. Screenplay by Justin Theroux. Based on the Marvel Comic Book by Stan Lee, Don Heck, Larry Lieber, Jack Kirby.
Cast: Tony Stark (Robert Downey, Jr.), Pepper Potts (Gwyneth Paltrow), Natalie Rushman/Black Widow (Scarlett Johansson), Ivan Vanko (Mickey Rourke), Lt. Col. James "Rhodey" Rhodes (Don Cheadle), Happy Hogan (Jon Favreau), Justin Hammer (Sam Rockwell), Nick Fury (Samuel L. Jackson), Agent Phil Coulson (Clark Gregg), Howard Stark (John Slattery), Senator Stern (Garry Shandling), Jarvis (Paul Bettany, voice).

We Bought a Zoo (20th Century–Fox, 2011; 124 min.)
Directed by Cameron Crowe. Screenplay by Aline Brosh McKenna, Cameron Crowe. Based on the book by Benjamin Mee.
Cast: Benjamin Mee (Matt Damon), Kelly Foster (Scarlett Johansson), Duncan Mee (Thomas Haden Church), Dylan Mee (Colin Ford), Lily Miska (Elle Fanning), Rosie Mee (Maggie Elizabeth Jones), Peter MacCready (Angus Macfayden).

Hitchcock (Fox Searchlight Pictures, 2012; 98 min.)
   Directed by Sacha Gervasi. Screenplay by John J. McLaughlin. Based on the book by Stephen Rebello.
   Cast: Alfred Hitchcock (Anthony Hopkins), Alma Hitchcock (Helen Mirren), Janet Leigh (Scarlett Johansson), Vera Miles (Jessica Biel), Peggy Robertson (Toni Collette), Lew Wasserman (Michael Stuhlbarg), Joseph Stefano (Ralph Macchio), Saul Bass (Wallace Langham), Whitfield Cook (Danny Huston), Ed Gein (Michael Wincott), Anthony Perkins (James D'Arcy), Geoffrey Shurlock (Kurtwood Smith).

The Avengers (Marvel Studios/Paramount, 2012; 143 min.)
   Directed by Joss Whedon. Screenplay by Joss Whedon. Story by Zak Penn.
   Cast: Tony Stark/Iron Man (Robert Downey, Jr.), Steve Rogers/Captain America (Chris Evans), Bruce Banner/The Hulk (Mark Ruffalo), Thor (Chris Hemsworth), Pepper Potts (Gwyneth Paltrow), Natasha Romanoff/Black Widow (Scarlett Johansson), Loki (Tom Hiddleston), Nick Fury (Samuel L. Jackson), Clint Barton/Hawkeye (Jeremy Renner), Agent Phil Coulson (Clark Gregg), Agent Maria Hill (Cobie Smulders), Selvig (Stellan Skarsgard), Jarvis (Paul Bettany, voice).

Don Jon (Voltage Pictures, 2013; 90 min.)
   Directed by Joseph Gordon-Levitt. Screenplay by Joseph Gordon-Levitt.
   Cast: Jon (Joseph Gordon-Leavitt), Barbara (Scarlett Johansson), Esther (Julianne Moore), Jon, Sr. (Tony Danza), Angela (Glenne Headly), Monica (Brie Larson), Bobby (Rob Brown), Danny (Jeremy Luke), Priest (Paul Ben-Victor), Gina (Italia Ricci), Lauren (Lindsey Broad), Lisa (Amanda Perez), Hollywood Actor #1 (Channing Tatum), Hollywood Actress #1 (Anne Hathaway), Hollywood Actor #2 (Cuba Gooding, Jr.), Hollywood Actress #2 (Meagan Good).

Her (Annapurna Pictures/Warner Bros., 2013; 126 min.)
   Directed by Spike Jonze. Screenplay by Spike Jonze.
   Cast: Theodore (Joaquin Phoenix), Samantha (Scarlett Johansson, voice) Amy (Amy Adams), Catherine (Rooney Mara), Chat Room Friend #2 (Bill Hader, voice), Sexy Kitten (Kristen Wiig, voice), Blind date (Olivia Wilde), Paul (Chris Pratt).

Under the Skin (Film4, 2013; 108 min.)
   Directed by Jonathan Glazer. Screenplay by Walter Campbell, Jonathan Glazer. Based on the novel by Michel Faber. Music by Mica Levi.
   Cast: The Female/Laura (Scarlett Johansson), The Bad Man (Jeremy McWilliams), The Dead Woman (Lynsey Taylor Mackay), First Victim (Kevin McAlinden), Pick-Up Man (Dougie McConnell), Deformed Man (Adam Pearson).

Captain America: The Winter Soldier (Marvel Studios, 2014; 136 min.)
   Directed by Anthony Russo, Joe Russo. Screenplay by Christopher Markus, Stephen McFeely. Based on the Marvel comic by Joe Simon, Jack Kirby.
   Cast: Steve Rogers/Captain America (Chris Evans), Black Widow/Natasha Romanoff (Scarlett Johansson), Bucky (Sebastian Stan), Nick Fury (Samuel L. Jackson), Alexander Pierce (Robert Redford), Sam Wilson/Falcon (Anthony Mackie), Maria Hill (Cobie Smulders), Brock Rumlow (Frank Grillo), Kate/Agent 13 (Emily VanCamp), Peggy Carter (Hayley Atwell), Jasper Sitwell (Maximiliano Hernandez), Councilwoman (Jenny Agutter), Dr. Arnim Zola (Toby Jones), Smithsonian guard (Stan Lee).

Chef (Aldamissa Entertainment, 2014; 114 min.)
   Directed by Jon Favreau. Screenplay by Jon Favreau.
   Cast: Carl Casper (Jon Favreau), Percy (Emjay Anthony), Martin (John Leguizamo), Tony (Bobby Carnivale), Inez (Sofia Vegara), Riva (Dustin Hoffman), Molly (Scarlett Johansson), Marvin (Robert Downey, Jr.), Ramsey Michel (Oliver Platt), Jen (Amy Sedaris).

Lucy (Canal+, 2014; 89 min.)
   Directed by Luc Besson. Screenplay by Luc Besson.
   Cast: Lucy (Scarlett Johansson), Professor Norman (Morgan Freeman), Mr. Jang (Min-sik Choi), Pierre Del Rio (Amr Waked), Richard (Pilou Asbaek), The Limey (Julian Rhind-Tutt), Caroline (Analeigh Tipton).

The Avengers: Age of Ultron (Marvel Studios, 2015; 141 min.)
   Directed by Joss Whedon. Screenplay by Joss Whedon. Based on the Marvel Comics by Stan Lee and Jack Kirby.
   Cast: Tony Stark/Iron Man (Robert Downey, Jr.), Steve Rogers/Captain America (Chris Evans), Nick Fury (Samuel L. Jackson), Natasha Romanoff/Black Widow (Scarlett Johansson), Bruce Banner/The Hulk (Mark Ruffalo), Clint Barton/Hawkeye (Jeremy Renner), Ultron (James Spader), Wanda Maximoff/Scarlet Witch (Elizabeth Olsen), Pietro Maximoff/Quicksilver (Aaron Taylor-Johnson), Jarvis/Vision (Paul Bettany), James Rhodes/War Machine (Don Cheadle), Peggy Carter (Hayley Atwell), Sam Wilson/Falcon (Anthony Mackie), Heimdall (Idris Elba), Laura Barton (Linda Cardellini), Maria Hill (Cobie Smulders), Erik Selvig (Stellan Skarsgard), Dr. Helen Cho (Claudia Kim), Strucker (Thomas Kretschmann), Ulysses Klaue (Andy Serkis), Madame B (Julie Delpy), Stan Lee (himself).

Hail, Caesar! (Dentsu/Mike Ross Productions, 2016; 106 min.)
   Directed by Ethan Coen, Joel Coen. Screenplay by Joel Coen, Ethan Coen.
   Cast: Eddie Mannix (Josh Brolin), Baird Whitlock (George Clooney), DeeAnna Moran (Scarlett Johansson), Thora Thacker/Thessaly Thacker (Tilda Swinton), Joe Silverman (Jonah Hill), Laurence Laurentz (Ralph Fiennes), Burt Gurney (Channing Tatum), C.C. Calhoun (Frances McDormand), Hobie Doyle (Alden Ehrenreich), Communist writer (David Krumholtz), Professor Marcuse (John Bluthal), Natalie (Heather Goldenhersh), Sid Siegelstein (Geoffrey Cantor).

The Jungle Book (Walt Disney Pictures, 2016; 106 min.)
   Directed by Jon Favreau. Screenplay by Jon Favreau. Based on the books by Rudyard Kipling.
   Cast: Mowgli (Neel Sethi). Voice Cast: Baloo (Bill Murray), Bagheera (Ben Kingsley), Shere Khan (Idris Elba), Kaa (Scarlett Johansson), King Louie (Christopher Walken), Raksha (Lupita Nyong'o), Akela (Giancarlo Esposito), Ikki (Garry Shandling), Young Wolf (Emjay Anthony), Pygmy Hog (Jon Favreau).

Captain America: Civil War (Marvel Studios, 2016; 147 min.)
   Directed by Anthony Russo, Joe Russo. Screenplay by Christopher Markus, Stephen McFeely. Based on the Marvel Comics by Joe Simon, Jack Kirby.
   Cast: Steve Rogers/Captain America (Chris Evans), Tony Stark/Iron Man (Robert Downey, Jr.), Natasha Romanoff/Black Widow (Scarlett Johansson), Sam/Falcon (Anthony Mackie), Wanda Maximoff/Scarlet Witch (Elizabeth Olsen), Clint Barton/Hawkeye (Jeremy Renner), Jarvis/Vision (Paul Bettany), Peter Parker/Spider-Man (Tom

Holland), Scott Lang/Ant-Man (Paul Rudd), T'Challa/Black Panther (Chadwick Boseman), Zemo (Daniel Bruhl), Brock Rumlow/Crossbones (Frank Grillo), Secretary of State Thaddeus Ross (William Hurt), May Parker (Marisa Tomei), Everett K. Ross (Martin Freeman), King T'Chaka (John Kani), Maria Stark (Hope Davis), Miriam (Alfre Woodard).

Sing (Fuzzy Door Productions/Universal, 2016; 108 min.)
Directed by Christophe Lourdelet, Garth Jennings. Screenplay by Garth Jennings.
Voice Cast: Buster Moon (Matthew McConaughey), Rosita (Reese Witherspoon), Ash (Scarlett Johansson), Mike (Seth MacFarlane), Eddie (John C. Reilly), Johnny (Taron Egerton), Meena (Tori Kelly), Nana (Jennifer Saunders), Young Nana (Jennifer Hudson), Miss Crawly (Garth Jennings).

Ghost in the Shell (DreamWorks/Paramount, 2017; 107 min.)
Directed by Rupert Sanders. Screenplay by Jamie Moss, William Wheeler, Ehren Kruger. Based on the comic *Ghost in the Shell* by Shirow Masamune.
Cast: Major (Scarlett Johansson), Kuze (Michael Pitt), Batou (Pilou Asbaek), Aramaki (Takeshi Kitano), Dr. Ouelet (Juliette Binoche), Togusa (Chin Han), Ladriya (Danusia Samal), Ishikawa (Lasarus Ratuere), Cutter (Peter Ferdinando).

Rough Night (Sony Pictures Entertainment, 2017; 101 min.)
Directed by Lucia Aniello. Screenplay by Lucia Aniello, Paul W. Downs.
Cast: Jess (Scarlett Johansson), Alice (Jillian Bell), Blair (Zoë Kravitz), Frankie (Ilana Glazer), Pippa (Kate McKinnon), Peter (Paul W. Downs), Lea (Demi Moore), Pietro (Ty Burrell), Officer Scotty (Colton Haynes), "Detective" Ruiz (Enrique Murciano), "Detective" Frazier (Dean Winters).

Isle of Dogs (American Empirical Pictures, 2018; min.)
Directed by Wes Anderson. Screenplay by Wes Anderson.
Voice cast: Atari (Koyu Rankin), Nutmeg (Scarlett Johansson), Tracy Walker (Greta Gerwig), Oracle (Tilda Swinton), Interpreter Nelson (Frances McDormand), Chief (Bryan Cranston), Rex (Edward Norton), Spots (Liev Schreiber), Boss (Bill Murray), Duke (Jeff Goldblum), Peppermint (Kara Hayward), Gondo (Harvey Keitel), Scrap (Fisher Stevens), Jupiter (F. Murray Abraham), Narrator (Courtney B. Vance), Head surgeon (Ken Watanabe), Professor Watanabe (Akira Ito), Mayor Kobayashi (Kunichi Nomura), Major-Domo (Akira Takayama), Assistant Scientist Yoko-ono (Yoko Ono), Igor (Roman Coppola).

The Avengers: Infinity War (Marvel Studios, 2018; 149 min.)
Directed by Anthony Russo, Joe Russo. Screenplay by Christopher Markus and Stephen McFeely. Based on the Marvel Comics by Stan Lee, Jack Kirby.
Cast: Tony Stark/Iron Man (Robert Downey, Jr.), Steve Rogers/Captain America (Chris Evans), Thor (Chris Hemsworth), Natasha Romanoff/Black Widow (Scarlett Johansson), Doctor Strange (Benedict Cumberbatch), Bruce Banner/Hulk (Mark Ruffalo), T'Challa/Black Panther (Chadwick Boseman), Bucky Barnes/Winter Soldier (Sebastian Stan), Peter Quill/Star-Lord (Chris Pratt), Gamora (Zoë Saldana), Groot (Vin Diesel, voice), Drax (Dave Bautista), Loki (Tom Hiddleston), Vision (Paul Bettany), James Rhodes/War Machine (Don Cheadle), Nebula (Karen Gillan), Peter Parker/Spider-Man (Tom Holland), Wanda Maximoff/Scarlet Witch (Elizabeth Olsen), Rocket (Bradley Cooper, voice), Thanos (Josh Brolin), Pepper Potts (Gwyneth Paltrow), Sam Wilson/Falcon

(Anthony Mackie), Collector (Benicio Del Toro), Heimdall (Idris Elba), Secretary of State Thaddeus Ross (William Hurt), Eitri (Peter Dinklage), Bus driver (Stan Lee).

Avengers: Endgame (Marvel Studios/Walt Disney Studios, 2019; 182 min.)
Directed by Anthony Russo, Joe Russo. Screenplay by Christopher Markus, Stephen McFeely. Based on the Marvel comics by Stan Lee and Jack Kirby.
Cast: Steve Rogers/Captain America (Chris Evans), Tony Stark/Iron Man (Robert Downey, Jr.), Thanos (Josh Brolin), Natasha Romanoff/Black Widow (Scarlett Johansson), Thor (Chris Hemsworth), Clint Barton/Hawkeye (Jeremy Renner), Scott Lang/Ant-Man (Paul Rudd), Nebula (Karen Gillan), Gamora (Zoë Saldana), Carol Danvers/Captain Marvel (Brie Larson), Hope van Dyne/Wasp (Evangeline Lilly), Peter Quill/Star-Lord (Chris Pratt), Rocket (Bradley Cooper, voice), Groot (Vin Diesel, voice), Nebula (Karen Gillan), Wanda Maximoff/Scarlet Witch (Elizabeth Olsen), Bruce Banner/Hulk (Mark Ruffalo), T'Challa/Black Panther (Chadwick Boseman), Peter Parker/Spider-Man (Tom Holland), Drax (Dave Bautista), Pepper Potts (Gwyneth Paltrow), James Rhodes/War Machine (Don Cheadle), Doctor Strange (Benedict Cumberbatch), Valkyrie (Tessa Thompson), Frigga (Rene Russo), Sam Wilson/Falcon (Anthony Mackie), Loki (Tom Hiddleston), Wong (Benedict Wong), Bucky Barnes/Winter Soldier (Sebastian Stan).

Jojo Rabbit (Czech Anglo Productions/Fox Searchlight Pictures, 2019; 108 min.)
Directed by Taika Waititi. Screenplay by Taika Waititi. Based on the novel by Christine Leunens.
Cast: Jojo Betzler (Roman Griffin Davis), Adolf Hitler (Taika Waititi), Rosie Betzler (Scarlett Johansson), Elsa Korr (Thomasin McKenzie), Captain Klenzendorf (Sam Rockwell), Fraulein Rahm (Rebel Wilson).

Marriage Story (Heyday Films/Netflix, 2019; 136 min.)
Directed and written by Noah Baumbach.
Cast: Nicole (Scarlett Johansson), Charlie (Adam Driver), Nora Fanshaw (Laura Dern), Bert Spitz (Alan Alda), Jay Marota (Ray Liotta), Cassie (Merritt Wever), Terry (Matthew Shear), Mary Ann (Brooke Bloom), Ted (Kyle Bornheimer), Sandra (Julie Hagerty), Beth (Mickey Sumner), Frank (Wallace Shawn).

Black Widow (Marvel Studios, 2021)
Directed by Cate Shortland. Screenplay by Eric Pearson. Story by Jac Schaeffer, Ned Benson. Based on the Marvel Comics by Stan Lee, Don Heck, Don Rico.
Cast: Natasha Romanoff/Black Widow (Scarlett Johansson), Yelena Belova (Florence Pugh), Alexei Shostakov/Red Guardian (David Harbour), Melina Vostokoff (Rachel Weisz), Mason (O-T Fagbenie), Thadeus Ross (William Hurt), Young Natasha (Ever Anderson).

Television

The Client (1995–1996; 1 season) [played Jenna Halliwell in pilot]

Saturday Night Live
Host: January 14, 2006; April 21, 2007; November 13, 2010; May 2, 2015; March 11, 2017; December 2017: Uncredited as Lexie in "Porcelain Fountains" segment; played Ivanka Trump in "Complicit" perfume commercial.
Cameos: February 4, 2006; October 3, 2009; May 20, 2017.

Voice Artist

The SpongeBob SquarePants Movie (Nickelodeon Movies/United Plankton Pictures, 2004)

This theatrical film expanded on the popular Nickelodeon animated TV series. Johansson voiced Princess Mindy, Neptune's daughter.

Chasing Ice (Submarine Deluxe, 2012) sang "Before My Time" with Joshua Bell for this documentary that follows James Balog and the Extreme Ice Survey team as they ascertain how climate change is affecting Greenland and Alaska in the short-, and the rest of the world in the long-term.

Assassin Banana (2015–)

Johansson provided voice of banana wife (husband voiced by Nathan Fillion) in animated TV series directed by David Odio, and written by Jordan Rozansky.

The Jungle Book (Walt Disney Pictures, 2016)

In the live-action version of *The Jungle Book* directed by Jon Favreau, her director in *Iron Man 2* and *Chef*, Johansson achieved one of her life goals: the voice of a Disney character. She lent her unique voice to Kaa, the giant python that mesmerizes Mowgli even as her coils surround him. As she opens her mouth to engulf him the bear Baloo plunges into her and saves the man-child. Johansson also got to sing in a Disney film: rendering "Trust in Me" over a portion of the end credits. The song had originally been sung by Stanley Holloway in the 1967 animated version.

The film was an enormous success, taking in over $100 million on its opening weekend. Critical opinion was uniformly upbeat. "You can practically feel the beating heart of the jungle in Jon Favreau's stunning adaptation of 'The Jungle Book,' which is easily the most visually dazzling movie to hit theaters this year."[1]

Sing (Illumination Entertainment, 2016)

Sing had its general U.S. premiere just before Christmas, 2016. It had been screened as a special presentation at the Toronto International Film Festival on Sunday, September 11, 2016. Voice stars Reese Witherspoon and Johansson walked the red carpet along with Matthew McConaughey and others. Johansson told Flicks and the City 2, "It's definitely an uplifting, heartwarming story.... I think that it's a film really about following your dream, taking a big chance, a big leap of faith, and relying on the support of your friends that believe in you to make big things happen."[2]

Various critics were not enthralled and failed to discern why, or even that the theme of reconciliation infused the film.

We can safely say the ending of *Sing* has an emotional power because the collapse and resurrection of the theater symbolizes a whole series of reconciliations among family members—Moon with the ghost of his father, Johnny the gorilla and his father, Rosita the pig with her husband and children, and Meena the elephant with her family who had urged her to sing. Johansson's porcupine Ash and the Sinatra-like mouse Mike are not full participants in this sense of reconciliation, but Nana Noodleman, the singer who initially caused Moon to fall in love with show business, coming through to purchase the theater represents a reconciliation that even takes in generations, and that no doubt makes up for any lack. T.S. Eliot might have called the New Moon Theater an "objective correlative" for love in the broadest sense—art for art's sake leading to a reunion of separated family members of all kinds achieving a sense of community.

Isle of Dogs (Studio Babelsberg/Indian Paintbrush, 2018)

The autocratic Mayor Kobayashi of Megasaki City convinces the citizens that all the dogs are infected with a virus that could spread to humans and consigns the canines to Trash Island. This includes the Mayor's own nephew, Atari Kobayashi, who flies a jury-rigged plane to the island in search of his dog Spots. On the island a close-knit group of dogs, including Rex, King, Duke, Boss and eventually Chief, egged on by Nutmeg (Johansson), decide to help Atari in his quest. Back at Megasaki City, exchange student Tracy Walker delves into the situation and eventually convinces researcher Yoko Ono to hand over a vial of the cure. When the dogs learn that the Mayor plans extermination for them and their kin after his re-election, they assist Atari in building boats and sail for Megasaki City and present their case. The Mayor decides not to carry on with his plan but Major Domo is all for carrying through with the extermination. A battle royale ensues but the dogs, Atari and Tracy win. Nevertheless, there are casualties. Atari, having only one kidney, has that compromised. His uncle donates his and he is saved. Spots, thought dead, recovers and sets up housekeeping with his mate and their puppies.

Marginally less so than *Under the Skin*, *Isle of Dogs* received little publicity aimed at the masses. We recall no TV ads in the metropolitan Philadelphia area, where, like *Under the Skin*, *Isle* began at the Ritz "art house" and one suburban mall theater. It expanded its reach slightly a week or two later. This is quite curious as audiences and critics praised it and director Wes Anderson is a major player.

Chapter Notes

Introduction

1. Kevin Sessums, "The World According to Scarlett," *Allure*, November 2006, p. 196.
2. "She [Kim Novak] has a solemnity that always defeats the sex-kitten stuff. If she is feline, it's less because she seems sensual and playful than because she seems finally inaccessible. And the poignancy of that makes her sexier." James Harvey on Kim Novak, *Movie Love in the Fifties* (New York: Alfred A. Knopf, 2001), p. 79.
3. Richard Schickel paired Novak with Alan Ladd as somnambulists in *The Stars* (New York: Dial Press, 1962, p. 247).
4. A sampling of her gala red carpet outings include the 70th Annual Venice Film Festival on September 3, 2013, where she was promoting *Under the Skin*, the American Museum of Natural History 2017 Museum Gala on November 30, 2017, in New York, the *Avengers: Infinity War* world premiere in Los Angeles on April 23, 2018, the 2018 Met Gala in New York on May 7, 2018, the 70th Emmy Awards on September 17, 2018, the 2018 People's Choice Awards on November 11, 2018, in Santa Monica, California, and the American Museum of Natural History 2018 Gala on November 15, 2018, in New York.
5. Alessandra Stanley, "Vogue Point of View," *Vogue*, April 2007, p. 330. It seems plausible that Johansson has been covered rarely by *People* Magazine because of her unwillingness to play celebrity ball, her perceived or real disdain for the celebrity publicity machine. How else to fathom why she has not received one of their annual "Most Beautiful" accolades? Recall "Her air of self-possession, her faculty for incisive silences and plain speaking, with its implicit disdain for the white lies of adults." in Chip Brown, "The Smart Bomb," *Elle*, January 2006, p. 128. Even Johansson's first marriage to Ryan Reynolds in 2008 was a private affair in Canada and received cursory attention (one page) in *People*. One of the rare times *People* designated Johansson one of their "50 Most Beautiful People" was in the May 10, 2004, issue, page 107. Perpetual *People* covergirl Jennifer Aniston got the cover and #1 ranking. Johansson, the 13th star pictured, was photographed sitting on a rooftop, arms wrapped around her knees. Actor and race car driver Frankie Muniz got the comment, to the effect that in the brackets of pretty, hot, and beautiful, Johansson was in the last category ("50 Most Beautiful People," *People*, May 10, 2004, p. 107). In the May 7, 2007, "100 Most Beautiful" issue she shared page 106 with Eric Bana, she's dressed in white, doing sexy. (It's the *Esquire* cover shot from November 2006.) Unsurprisingly, the questions she answered were of little cinematic substance. She showered at night, was small "But I definitely have curves. I'm like a slice of cherry pie," thought she had cute feet but burdensome hair, frowned on collagen lip injections. On aging, she opined that "it's coming and there's nothing we can do about it except live a healthy lifestyle and drink a lot of water." She received one page in the April 6, 2020, issue where she described her idol, her brother Hunter, and his social and environmental activism.
6. Kate Meyers, "Scarlett in Wonderland," *InStyle*, October 2006, p. 164. Julie Andrews expressed similar reactions to the 1964 red carpet premiere of *Mary Poppins* in *Home Work: a Memoir of My Hollywood Years* (New York: Hachette Books, 2019, p. 69): "Tom Jones [Disney publicity head] had warned me that I would need to pause for interviews before entering the theater. Even so, I was unprepared for the pressure and scrutiny; the feeling of being pulled, poked, and shouted at by the phalanx of Tv and radio reporters."
7. Meyers, "Scarlett in Wonderland," p. 162.
8. Joseph Hooper, "Scarlett Fever," *Elle*, November 2007, p. 330.
9. Barbara Walters, "The 10 Most Fascinating People of 2014," ABC TV, December 15, 2014.
10. Peter Travers, *Rolling Stone*, September 8, 2003.
11. Meyers, "Scarlett in Wonderland," p. 167, followed by Dolce & Gabbana, and, for a time, SodaStream.
12. Monami Thakur, "Scarlett Johansson Shares the Magic of Moet & Chandon in Heritage Campaign (Exclusive Video)," www.ibtimes.com, February 21, 2011.
13. "Scarlett Johansson in Ad Campaign for Moet & Chandon," www.mediapost.com, February 22, 2011.
14. Jimmy So, "Scarlett Johansson Is an Alien Seductress in *Under the Skin*," www.thedailybeast.com, April 3, 2014.
15. Simon Dumenco, "Beyond the Bombshell," *InStyle*, May 2010, p. 309.

16. Aaron Gell, "Scarlett Fever," *Cosmopolitan*, January 2012, pp. 24, 26.
17. "Scarlett Johansson Talks Working with Bill Murray in 'Lost in Translation' and How the Film Changed Her Life," www.howardstern.com, March 27, 2017.
18. "But, as sometimes happens, context and catalyst coalesced neatly." Peter Watson, *The Great Divide: Nature and Human Nature in the Old World and the New* (New York: HarperCollins Publishers, 2011), 354.
19. John Colapinto, "Girl with a Career on Fire," *Elle*, June 2004, p. 164. "I Like Clothing. I Can Shop Like None Other. You'd Be Surprised."

Chapter 1

1. Gunnar Rehlin, "Love Scarlett," *Scandinavian Traveler* (March 2016), 48.
2. *Finding Your Roots*, PBS TV, Season 4, Episode 35: "Immigrant Nation," October 31, 2017. *Finding Your Roots* is a public television series first airing in 2012 that is hosted by esteemed historian and critic Henry Louis Gates, Jr. Through DNA and archival research, celebrity (and some non-celebrity) guests are interviewed and given a "Book of Life" containing important documents and photographs pertaining to their ancestry. On October 31, 2017, Johansson appeared, sharing the hour-long program with actors Paul Rudd and John Turturro. When Isabella Rossellini appeared on *Finding Your Roots* (Season 6, Episode 1: "Hollywood Royalty"), a routine comparison of her DNA with that of previous guests on the show found that Rossellini was distantly connected genetically with Johansson. Rossellini expressed surprise, but also seemed delighted that the connection was with someone who shared her profession. It is likely that this finding means that Johansson is also a distant relative of Rossellini's mother, Ingrid Bergman.
3. Atchison, "Girl with the Golden Touch," p. 101.
4. Darren Aronofsky, "Scarlett," *Interview*, October 2013, p. 113.
5. Joseph Hooper, "Scarlett Fever," p. 330.
6. Tom Sykes, "Scarlett Johansson's Sexy Style," *Harper's Bazaar*, January 2005, p. 76.
7. Sessums, "The World According to Scarlett," p. 196.
8. Chip Brown, "The Smart Bomb," *Elle*, January 2006, p. 128.
9. Anthony Lane, "Her Again," *New Yorker*, March 24, 2014, p. 62.
10. Logan Hill, "Scarlett 2.0.," *Glamour*, May 2014, p. 220.
11. Sykes, "Scarlett Johansson's Sexy Style," p. 74.
12. Sessums, "The World According to Scarlett," p. 192.
13. Jada Yuan, "A Woman in Full," *Cosmopolitan*, May 2016, p. 162.
14. Aronofsky, "Scarlett," p. 112.
15. Dumenco, "Beyond the Bombshell," p. 303.

16. Lane, "Her Again," p. 62.
17. Colapinto, "Girl with a Career on Fire," p. 168.
18. Aronofsky, "Scarlett," p. 172.
19. Craig Barboza, "Another Shade of Scarlett," *Usa Weekend*, July 15–17, 2005, p. 7.
20. Frank Rich, "Review/Theater: *Sophistry*; the Old College Days, Circa '91," *New York Times*, October 12, 1993.
21. Atchison, "Girl with the Golden Touch," p. 101.
22. Aronofsky, "Scarlett," p. 113.
23. "Cosmo News," *Cosmopolitan*, August 2008, p. 39.
24. Deanna Kizis, "Bright Young Thing," *Allure*, August 2005, p. 189.
25. Sessums, "The World According to Scarlett," p. 196.
26. Lynn Hirschberg, "Nobody's Baby," *W*, March 2015, p. 358.
27. Brooke Hauser, "Miss Scarlett," *Marie Claire*, March 2017, p. 258.
28. Hauser, "Miss Scarlett," p. 258. In *People*, "Scarlett Johansson: My Brother, My Hero," April 6, 2020, p. 24, Johansson described her twin Hunter's founding of Solar Responders, which has provided solar panels to communities suffering from natural disasters.
29. Aronofsky, "Scarlett," *Interview*, October 2013, p. 113.
30. Anolik, *Vanity Fair*, May 2014, p. 148.
31. Jane Gordon, "Of Course I've Got a BIG E G O G O and All Actors Think They're THE ONE," *Daily Mail*, December 21, 2013.

Chapter 2

1. Janet Maslin, *New York Times*, July 22, 1994.
2. Roger Ebert, www.rogerebert.com, July 22, 1994.
3. Sanjiv Bhattacharya, "Scarlett in Bloom," *New York*, February 16, 2004, p. 84.
4. Bhattacharya, "Scarlett in Bloom," p. 84.
5. Peter Rainer, http://articles.latimes.com, February 17, 1995.
6. Janet Maslin, *New York Times*, February 17, 1995.
7. Maslin, *New York Times*, July 26, 1995.
8. Roger Ebert, www.rogerebert.com, August 30, 1996.
9. James Berardinelli, www.reelviews.net, May 1996.
10. Mick LaSalle, www.sfgate.com, August 9, 1996.
11. Lane, "Her Again," p. 62.
12. Atchison, "Girl with the Golden Touch," p. 99.
13. Caryn James, "The Unknown Sundance, in Unlikely Places," www.nytimes.com, February 4, 1996.
14. Janet Maslin, *New York Times*, March 8, 1996.
15. Mick Martin and Marsha Porter, *Video Movie*

Guide 1997, New York: Ballantine Books, 1996, p. 519.

16. J.M. Clark, *Magill's Cinema Annual 1997*. 16th ed. Beth A. Fhaner, ed. (Detroit: Gale Research, 1998), p. 270.

17. Cody Clarke, "Eric Schaeffer: the Most Underrated Writer-Director-Actor Ever," https://smugfilm.com, March 11, 2013.

18. Lawrence Van Gelder, www.nytimes.com, June 20, 1997.

19. Patricia Kowal, *Magill's Cinema Annual 1998*. 17th ed. Beth A. Fhaner, ed. (Detroit: Gale Research, 1998), pp. 175–176.

20. Leonard Maltin, *Leonard Maltin's Movie Guide 2015 Edition: the Modern Era*, New York: Plume, 2014, p. 671.

21. Cody Clarke, "Eric Schaeffer: the Most Underrated Writer-Director-Actor Ever," https://smugfilm.com/eric-schaeffer, March 11, 2013.

22. Roger Ebert, www.rogerwbert.com, February 21, 1986.

23. Roger Ebert, www.rogerebert.com, December 12, 1997.

24. Janet Maslin, *New York Times*, May 15, 1998.

25. Roger Ebert, www.rogerebert.com, May 15, 1998.

26. Berardinelli, www.reelviews.net, 1998.

27. Rita Kempley, www.washingtonpost.com, May 15, 1998.

28. Gretel Ehrlich, *The Horse Whisperer: an Illustrated Companion to the Major Motion Picture* (New York: Dell Publishing, 1998), pp. 118–119.

29. Ehrlich, *The Horse Whisperer*, 1998, p. 119.

30. Ehrlich, *The Horse Whisperer*, p. 121.

31. Brown, "The Smart Bomb," pp. 124–25.

32. Atchison, "Girl with the Golden Touch," p. 102.

33. William Keck, "New Year Bright for Johansson," http://usatoday.com, December 28, 2004.

34. Brooke Hauser, "Miss Scarlett," p. 258.

35. Amy Larocca, "Scarlett's in Love! (But Not with This Guy)," *Glamour*, November 2009, p. 186.

36. Dave Lukens, www.dove.org/review, January 15, 2003.

37. Dave Kehr, *New York Times*, August 10, 2001.

38. Roger Ebert, www.rogerebert.com, August 24, 2001.

39. Patty-Lynne Herlevi, *Magill's Cinema Annual 2002* (Farmington Hills, MI: Thomson Gale), p. 23.

40. Kenneth Turan, *Los Angeles Times*, August 10, 2001.

41. A.O. Scott, *New York Times*, July 20, 2001.

42. Roger Ebert, www.rogerebert.com, August 3, 2001.

43. Richard Corliss, http://content.time.com, January 25, 2002.

44. Michael Betzold, in Peter N. Chumo II, ed., *Magill's Cinema Annual 2002: a Survey of the Films of 2001*. 21st ed (Farmington Hills, MI: Thomson/Gale, 2002), pp. 170–171.

45. *Ghost World* Blu-Ray, "Art as Dialogue: Thora Birch, Scarlett Johansson, Illeana Douglas," Criterion Collection, 2017.

46. *Ghost World*, "Art as Dialogue."

47. *Ghost World*, Commentary, Criterion Collection, 2017.

48. A.O. Scott, www.nytimes.com, September 1, 2001.

49. Christopher Orr, www.theatlantic.com, September 18, 2014.

50. Roger Ebert, www.rogerebert.com, November 2, 2001.

51. "Commentary Joel and Ethan Coen," *The Man Who Wasn't There*. DVD. USA Films, 2002.

52. Atchison, "Girl with the Golden Touch," p. 104.

53. Roger Ebert, www.rogerebert.com, July 17, 2002.

54. David Putman, www.thefrightfile.com, July 18, 2002.

55. Noah Gittell, "Scarlett Johansson's Vanishing Act," www.theatlantic.com, July 28, 2014.

Chapter 3

1. Berardinelli, www.reelviews.net, September 2003.

2. Peter Rainer, http://nymag.com, September 15, 2003.

3. Christy Lemire/AP, *News Journal* [Wilmington, DE], October 3, 2003, p. 10.

4. Edward Guthmann, www.sfgate.com. September 12, 2003.

5. Wade Major, www.boxoffice.com, November 2003.

6. Colapinto, "Girl with a Career on Fire," *Elle*, June 2004, p. 168.

7. Charlie Rose, "Sofia Coppola," https:///charlierose.com/videos/13710, September 18, 2003.

8. Marlow Stern, "Sofia Coppola Discusses 'Lost in Translation' on Its 10th Anniversary," www.thedailybeast.com, September 12, 2013.

9. Lane, "Her Again," p. 58.

10. Jimmy So, "Scarlett Johansson Is an Alien Seductress in 'Under the Skin,'" www.thedailybeast.com, April 3, 2014.

11. Charlie Rose, "Sofia Coppola," https://charlierose.com/videos/13710, September 18, 2003.

12. Lucy Bolton, *Film and Female Consciousness: Irigaray, Cinema and Thinking Women* (Houndmills, Basingstoke, Hampshire, England: Palgrave Macmillan 2011), p. 95.

13. Bolton, p. 96.

14. Bolton, p. 108.

15. Bolton, p. 109.

16. Bolton, p. 109.

17. Bolton, p. 116.

18. Bolton, p. 120.

19. Brown, "The Smart Bomb," p. 124.

20. Paul Julian Smith, "Tokyo Drifters," *Sight & Sound*, January 2004, pp. 13–14.

21. Stephen Rebello, "Scarlett Woman," *Movieline's Hollywood Life* (February 2004), p. 54.

22. Colapinto, "Girl with a Career on Fire," p. 164.

23. Kizis, "Bright Young Thing," p. 190.
24. Atchison, "Girl with the Golden Touch," p. 102.
25. Atchison, "Girl with the Golden Touch," p. 104.
26. Mark Olsen, "Sofia Coppola: Cool and the Gang," *Sight & Sound*, January 2004, p. 15.
27. "Scarlett Johansson Talks Working with Bill Murray in 'Lost in Translation' and How the Film Changed Her Life," www.howardstern.com, March 27, 2017.
28. In a conversation between Kelly, Charlotte and John, "Charlotte's expression is one of disdainful, humorous detachment, which progresses towards disgust: she makes no attempt to join in, and looks upon the conversation as a ridiculous spectacle." Bolton, p. 107.

Chapter 4

1. Alan Riding, *New York Times*, December 9, 2003.
2. Elvis Mitchell, *New York Times*, December 12, 2003.
3. *People*, January 26, 2004, p. 27.
4. Atchison, "Girl with the Golden Touch," p. 102.
5. Colapinto, "Girl with a Career on Fire," p. 16.
6. Bhattacharya, "Scarlett in Bloom," p. 85.
7. Rebello, "Scarlett Woman," p. 107.
8. *Charlie Rose,* https://charlierose.com.videos, December 12, 2003. There was a not well regarded 1958 version of the Herman Wouk novel featuring Natalie Wood and Gene Kelly. Although Johansson said her status allowed her to ask studios if she could do this or that, this *Marjorie Morningstar* never came to fruition. In movie parlance, the "It Girl" began appropriately enough with Clara Bow in 1927's *It*.
9. Atchison, "Girl with the Golden Touch," p. 100.
10. Keith Uhlich, Slantmagazine.com, January 29, 2004.
11. A.O. Scott, *New York Times*, January 30, 2004.
12. Allison Benedikt, http://metromix.chicagotribune.com, February 17, 2004.
13. *The Perfect Score* DVD. Special Features: "Making the Perfect Score," Hollywood, CA, www.paramount.com/homeentertainment, 2004.
14. YouTube. BAFTA Awards. London: British Academy of Film and Television Arts, February 15, 2004.
15. Atchison, "Girl with the Golden Touch," p. 100.
16. Atchison, "Girl with the Golden Touch," p. 102.
17. Gunnar Rehlin, "Love Scarlett," p. 52.
18. Bhattacharya, "Scarlett in Bloom," p. 84.
19. Logan Hill, "Scarlett 2.0," *Glamour*, May 2014, p. 225.
20. Gunnar Rehlin, "Love Scarlett," *Scandinavian Traveler*, March 2016, p. 48. Perhaps she considered *Eight Legged Freaks* comedic science fiction—or had forgotten about it altogether.
21. Stephen Rebello, "Scarlett Woman," February 2004, p. 54.
22. Rebello, "Scarlett Woman," p. 54.
23. Rebello, "Scarlett Woman," p. 107.
24. Kaplan, "More than a Pretty Face," *Parade*, March 11, 2007, p. 7.
25. Kaplan, "More than a Pretty Face," p. 8.
26. Kaplan, "More than a Pretty Face," p. 8.
27. Kaplan, "More than a Pretty Face," p. 8.
28. Joseph Hooper, *Elle*, November 2007, p. 329.
29. Amy Cooper, "Morsel: Scarlett Johansson Photograph Causes a Stir at Woollahra's Hotel Centennial," *Sydney Morning Herald*, November 15, 2014, https://www.smh.com.au.
30. Email from Megan Sullivan, General Manager, Hotel Centennial (Woollahra, NSW), October 30, 2018.
31. Derek Elley, http://Variety.com, September 19, 2004.
32. Claudia Puig, www.usatoday.com, February 2, 2006.
33. Stephen Holden, *New York Times*, February 3, 2006.
34. Mick LaSalle, www.ssfgate.com, February 3, 2006.
35. Liz Braun, http://jam.canoe.ca, February 17, 2006.
36. Rebello, p. 105.
37. Manohla Dargis, *New York Times*, December 29, 2004.
38. *People*, January 17, 2005, p. 33.
39. Ryan Lambie, Simon Brew, "The Top 25 Underappreciated Films of 2004," www.denofgeek.com, January 9, 2014.
40. Colapinto, "Girl with a Career on Fire," *Elle*, June 2004, p. 168.
41. *In Good Company* DVD. Universal City, CA: Universal Studios, 2005.
42. Paul Weitz, *In Good Company* DVD extras, Universal City, CA: Universal Pictures, 2005.
43. Roger Ebert, www.rogerebert.com, January 13, 2005.
44. Peter Travers, www.rollingstone.com, January 2, 2005. Posted January 6, 2005.
45. Roger Ebert, http://rogerebert.com, January 28, 2005.
46. Roger Ebert, http://rogerebert.com, January 28, 2005.
47. Rebello, "Scarlett Woman," 105.
48. William Keck, "New Year Bright for Johansson," http://usaatoday.com, December 28, 2004.
49. Kizis, "Bright Young Thing," *Allure*, August 2005, p. 191.
50. "Cosmo News," *Cosmopolitan*, August 2008, p 39.
51. Craigh Barboza, "Another Shade of Scarlett," p. 6.
52. Barboza, "Another Shade of Scarlett," p. 7.
53. Tom Sykes, "Scarlett Johansson's Sexy Style," *Harper's Bazaar*, January 2005, p. 76.
54. Barboza, "Another Shade of Scarlett," p. 7.

55. Barboza, "Another Shade of Scarlett," p. 7.
56. "Paparazzi Makes Scarlett See Red," http://news.ninemsn.com, August 23, 2005.
57. Danielle Stein, "Sister Act," *W*, March 2008, p. 443.
58. Stein, "Sister Act," p. 443.
59. Amy Larocca, "Scarlett's in Love! (But Not with This Guy)," p. 239.
60. Jane Gordon, "'Of Course I've Got a BIG E G O G O—And All Actors Think They're THE ONE," *Daily Mail*, December 21, 2013, p. 22.
61. Hannah Yasharoff, "Scarlett Johansson Slams Paparazzi for Chase: 'Just a Waiting Game' Until Someone Gets Killed," www.usatoday.com, April 9, 2019.
62. Chip Brown, "The Smart Bomb," *Elle*, January 2006, p. 124.
63. Dan Collins, www.cbs.news.com, February 7, 2006.
64. ANI. "Scarlett Johansson Is Ready to Strip on Screen," http://in.news.yahoo.com, December 14, 2006.
65. "Sexy Scarlett's Nude Ban," http://www.news24.com, April 4, 2007. For the above average British exploitation film *House of Whipcord* (1974), star-victim Penny Irving said, "I read the script, believed in the film and agreed to strip where necessary because I thought it was an integral part of the story." This confession was found in the *House of Whipcord* pressbook. p. 3.
66. Brown, "The Smart Bomb," pp. 123–124.
67. "Scarlett Johansson Gets Her Breasts Squeezed," http://www.thesuperficial.com, January 17, 2006.
68. mark, "Scarlett Breaks Silence About the Grope," http://gawker.com, March 2, 2006.
69. Dan MacMedan, "Scarlet [sic] Johansson Wasn't Amused by Red Carpet Groping," http://usatoday.printthis.clickability.com, March 3, 2006.
70. "*In Touch* Names Scarlett Johansson as Having the Best Rack," http://socialitelife.com, June 15, 2006.
71. Anthony Breznican, "Lohan, Johansson Grow into New Roles," www.usatoday.com, July 10, 2005. As the years passed, Lohan got herself into a peck of trouble *Socializing* while Johansson kept her nose to the wheel, learning the craft while churning out film after film. As the second decade of the new century passed, Johansson appeared in a string of interesting, innovative and exciting movies.
72. *Financial Times*, September 14, 2006, p. 10.
73. Dana Stevens, www.slate.com, September 14, 2006.
74. Jeff Simon, https://buffalonews.com.
75. David Germain/Associated Press, *News Journal* [Wilmington, DE], September 15, 2006, p. 4.
76. Colin Covert, *Star Tribune* [Minneapolis, MN], September 15, 2006.
77. Joe Morgenstern, *Wall Street Journal* [*Weekend Journal*], September 15, 2006, p. W1.
78. Christopher Borrelli, *The Blade* [OH], September 19, 2006.
79. Stephen Pizzello, "Darkest Noir," *American Cinematographer*, September 2006, p. 47.
80. A.O. Scott, *New York Times*, October 20, 2006.
81. David Germain/Associated Press, *News Journal* [Wilmington, DE], October 20, 2006, p. 4.
82. Peter Travers, *Rolling Stone*, October 20, 2006.
83. Colin Covert, *Star Tribune* [Minneapolis, MN], October 20, 2006.
84. John Keenan, *Omaha World-Herald*, October 21, 2006.
85. *People*, October 30, 2006, p. 33.
86. *Financial Times*, November 9, 2006, p. 12.
87. Kate Meyers, "Scarlett in Wonderland," *InStyle*, October 2006, p. 159.
88. Meyers, "Scarlett in Wonderland," p. 164.
89. Amy Larocca, "Scarlett's in Love! (But Not with This Guy)," p. 239.
90. A.J. Jacobs, "Lips, Kidneys & All: What's Not to Love About the Sexiest Woman Alive?," *Esquire*, November 2006, pp. 138–139.
91. A.J. Jacobs, "Lips, Kidneys & All," p. 140.
92. "First Annual 'Celebrity Nad's' Awards Announced," http://biz.yahoo.com, March 1, 2007.
93. "Actor Scarlett Johansson Visits India and Sri Lanka; Commits to Helping End Poverty," www.oxfam.org.uk, February 27, 2007.
94. "Johansson Misses Oscars for Charity Work," www.teenhollywood.com, February 28, 2007.
95. Loulla-May Eleftheriou-Smith, "Scarlett Johansson Has No Regrets Quitting Oxfam for Sodastream Ad Campaign," https://www.independent.co.uk, March 16, 2014.

Chapter 5

1. Sheri Linden, *Boxoffice*, July 2005, pp. 52, 68.
2. A.O. Scott, *New York Times*, December 28, 2005.
3. Peter Bradshaw, www.guardian.co.uk, January 6, 2006.
4. Leah Rozen, *People*, January 30, 2006, p. 33.
5. Derrick Bang, www.davisenterprise.com, March 1, 2006.
6. Simon Garfield, "Why I Love London," www.theguardian.com, August 8, 2004.
7. Barboza, "Another Shade of Scarlett," p. 7.
8. Harlan Jacobson, "Manhattan Transfer," *Film Comment*, January-February 2006, pp. 48–49.
9. Roger Ebert, www.rogerebert.com, July 27, 2006.
10. Borrelli, *The Blade* [OH], July 28, 2006.
11. Dargis, *New York Times*, July 28, 2006.
12. *People*, August 7, 2006, p. 34.
13. Charlotte Sinclair, "Ethics Girl," *Vogue* [UK], October 2006, p. 315.
14. "Woody Allen's 2006 Scoop on Dvd in February," www.cineoutsider.com, January 13, 2015.
15. Stephen Hunt, www.washingtonpost.com, July 28, 2006.
16. Roger Ebert, *Hamilton Spectator* [Canada], August 15, 2008.

17. Renee Montagne, *Morning Edition* [NPR], August 15, 2008.
18. Dargis, *New York Times*, August 15, 2008, p. E1.
19. Lane, "Her Again," p. 59.
20. Brooke Hauser, "Frankly Scarlett," *Allure*, December 2008, p. 224.
21. Carole Cadwalladr, "Scarlett Johansson Interview: 'I Would Way Rather Not Have Middle Ground,'" www.theguardian.com, March 16, 2014.
22. "Spotlight," *Daily Local News*, September 5, 2019, p. 2.
23. "Dylan Farrow Slams Scarlett Johansson," www.femalefirst.co.uk, September 6, 2019.
24. Gwilym Mumford, "Diane Keaton: 'Woody Allen Is My Friend and I Continue to Believe Him,'" www.theguardian.com, January 30, 2018.
25. Peter Biskind, "A Study in Scarlett," *Vanity Fair*, December 2011, p. 198.
26. George Gurley, "Scarlett's Web," *Marie Claire* (May 2013): 168.
27. Mick LaSalle, www.sfgate.com, August 15, 2008.

Chapter 6

1. Charlotte Sinclair, "Ethics Girl," *Vogue* [UK], October 2006, p.15.
2. Stanley, "Vogue: Point of View," *Vogue* (April 2007): 325.
3. "Stiller, Johansson Named Hasty Pudding's Man and Woman of the Year," http://news.harvard.edu/gazette, January 29, 2007.
4. Scott Malone, "Scarlett Johansson Leads Irreverent Harvard Parade," www.reuters.com, February 15, 2007.
5. Nancy Rabinowitz, http://news.yahoo.com, February 16, 2007.
6. "Justin & Scarlett Get Steamy in New Video," http://kdka.com/entertainment, February 15, 2007.
7. "Playboy's 25 Sexiest Celebrities," *Playboy*, March 2007, p. 108.
8. "Scarlett Johansson Dreads Looking an Old Hag!," www.newkerala.com, March 28, 2007.
9. "It's Official: Scarlett Johansson Has the World's Sexiest Body," www.dailymail.co.uk, April 11, 2007.
10. www.askmen.com, April 10, 2007.
11. Kaplan, "More than a Pretty Face," p. 6.
12. Kaplan, "More than a Pretty Face," p. 7.
13. Kaplan, "More than a Pretty Face," p. 7.
14. Kaplan, "More than a Pretty Face," p. 8.
15. Alessandra Stanley, "Scarlett Letters," *Vogue*, April 2007, pp. 323–331.
16. Joseph Hooper, *Elle*, November 2007, p. 330.
17. Roger Ebert, www.rogerebert.com, August 23, 2007.
18. Meghan Peters, "Diary of a Doormat: 'Nanny Diaries' Role Doesn't Fit Johansson," *Seattle Post-Intelligencer*, August 23, 2007.
19. Borrelli, *Blade* [OH], August 24, 2007.
20. Christy Lemire/Associated Press, *News-Journal* [Wilmington, DE], August 24, 2007, p. 4.
21. Colin Covert, *Star Tribune* [Minneapolis], August 24, 2007.
22. Shari Springer Berman, "Life at the Top as Seen from the Bottom: the Making of the Nanny Diaries," *The Nanny Diaries* DVD, Santa Monica, CA: Weinstein Company and Blockbuster, 2007.
23. Chris Evans, "Life at the Top as Seen from the Bottom: the Making of the Nanny Diaries," *The Nanny Diaries* DVD, Santa Monica, CA: Weinstein Company and Blockbuster, 2007.
24. David Denby, www.newyorker.com, August 27, 2007.
25. "Scarlett Johansson and Dave Sitek Premiere Tom Waits Tribute," www.stereogum.com, February 13, 2008.
26. NME, "The Jesus and Mary Chain Team Up with Scarlett Johansson," www.nme.com, April 28, 2007.
27. Nanciann Cherry, *The Blade*, February 29, 2008.
28. Roger Ebert, www.rogerebert.com, February 28, 2008.
29. Michael Machosky, *Pittsburgh Tribune Review*, February 29, 2008.
30. Sukhdev Sandhu, http://www.telegraph.com.uk, March 7, 2008.
31. Alessandra Stanley, "Vogue: Point of View," pp. 326–327.
32. Joseph Hooper, "Scarlett Fever," *Elle*, November 2007, pp. 329–330.
33. Hooper, "Scarlett Fever," p. 330.
34. Danielle Stein, "Sister Act," p. 439.
35. Stein, "Sister Act," p. 442.
36. Stein, "Sister Act," p. 442.
37. Stein, "Sister Act," p. 443.
38. "Cosmo News," *Cosmopolitan*, August 2008, p. 40.
39. Roger Ebert, www.rogerebert.com, December 23, 2008.
40. A.O. Scott, *New York Times*, December 24, 2008.
41. Peter Hartlaub, *San Francisco Chronicle*, December 25, 2008.
42. Brooke Hauser, "Frankly Scarlett," *Allure*, December 2008, p. 224.
43. Liza Hamm, "Just Married!," *People*, October 13, 2008, p. 76.
44. "I've Finally Found My Soul Mate," *Cosmopolitan*, UK ed., January 2009, pp. 49–50.
45. "I've Finally Found My Soul Mate," *Cosmopolitan*, UK ed., January 2009, p. 52.
46. Larocca, "Scarlett's in Love! (But Not with This Guy)," p. 239.
47. Larocca, "Scarlett's in Love! (But Not with This Guy)," p. 239.
48. Dargis, *New York Times*, February 5, 2009.
49. Peter Bradshaw, www.theguardian.com, February 5, 2009.
50. Mick LaSalle, www.sfgate.com, February 6, 2009.
51. "Cosmo News," *Cosmopolitan*, August 2008, p. 40.

52. Larocca, "Scarlett's in Love! (But Not with This Guy)," p. 239.
53. Brooke Hauser, "Miss Scarlett," p. 258.
54. Peter Biskind, "A Study in Scarlett," p. 202.
55. Larocca, "Scarlett's in Love! (But Not with This Guy)," p. 186.
56. Michael Musto, "Can Scarlett Johansson Act?" http://blogs.villagevoice.com, January 26, 2010.
57. Ben Brantley, *New York Times*, January 25, 2010.
58. Biskind, "A Study in Scarlett,", p. 199.
59. Biskind, "A Study in Scarlett," p. 202.
60. Adam Sachs, "Babe: Scarlett Johansson," *Gq* (December 2010), p. 305.
61. "The December Cover Story of *Vanity Fair* Shot in Philadelphia at the Elkins Estate by Famed Photographer Mario Sorrenti," www.uwishunu.com, November 9, 2011.
62. Maya Oppenheim, "Scarlett Johansson Addresses Her 'Devastating' Nude Photo Hacking," https://independent.co.uk, March 28, 2017.
63. Aaron Gell, "Scarlett Fever," *Cosmopolitan*, January 2012, p. 27.
64. David McKenzie, CNN, YouTube, September 24, 2011.
65. Biskind, "A Study in Scarlett," p. 257.
66. Betsy Sharkey, *Los Angeles Times*, http://latimes.com, December 23, 2011.
67. *New Zealand Herald*, December 24, 2011.
68. Michael Smith, *Tulsa World*, December 24, 2011.
69. Biskind, "A Study in Scarlett," p. 202.
70. Gell, "Scarlett Fever," p. 26.
71. Gell, "Scarlett Fever," p. 26.
72. Lili Anolik, "A(nother) Study in Scarlett," *Vanity Fair*, May 2014, p. 144.
73. Claude Brodesser-Akner, "Carey Mulligan Now the Front-Runner to Play Daisy in Baz Luhrmann's *Great Gatsby*," www.vulture.com, November 12, 2010.
74. Tom Sykes, "Scarlett Johansson's Sexy Style," *Harper's Bazaar*, January 2005, p. 74.
75. Biskind, "A Study in Scarlett," p. 199.
76. Allie Merriam, "Scarlett Johansson Hits the Red Carpet Without Her New Man," www.popsugar.com.au/celebrity.
77. "Johansson, Washington Get Germany's Golden Camera Awards as Best Actors," *The Blade* [Toledo, OH], www.toledoblade.com, February 5, 2012.
78. Roger Ebert, www.rogerebert.com, November 20, 2012.
79. Dargis, *New York Times*, November 22, 2012.
80. Mary Pols, *Time*, December 3, 2012, p. 60.
81. Barbara Vancheri, *Pittsburgh Post-Gazette*, December 14, 2012.
82. Lane, "Her Again," p. 63.
83. Scarlett Johansson, "The Cast," *Hitchcock* Blu-Ray, Beverly Hills, CA: Twentieth Century Fox Home Entertainment, 2013.
84. Jean-Paul Goude, "Hitchcock Heroine," *V Magazine*, Winter 2012/13, p.68.
85. Goude, "Hitchcock Heroine," p.68.
86. Lynn Hirschberg, "Time Is on Their Side: Four Actresses Inhabit Four Decades of Fashion," *W*, November 2012, p. 298.
87. Dargis, *New York Times*, September 26, 2013.
88. David Edelstein, *Fresh Air* (NPR), September 27, 2013.
89. Owen Gleiberman, *Entertainment Weekly*, October 4, 2013, p. 46.
90. Chris Vetter, *Leader-Telegram* [Eau Claire, WI], October 16, 2013.
91. George Gurley, "Scarlett's Web," *Marie Claire* (May 2013), p. 170.
92. Gurley, p. 170.
93. Gurley, p. 170.
94. Aronofsky, "Scarlett," p. 108.
95. Jane Gordon, "Of Course I've Got a BIG E G O G O and All Actors Think They're THE ONE," *Daily Mail*, December 21, 2013, 5 pages.

Chapter 7

1. Owen Gleiberman, *Entertainment Weekly*, April 11, 2014, p. 38. *Captain America: the Winter Soldier* gave her a meatier role. Nevertheless, the powers-that-be at Marvel hemmed and hawed over a standalone Black Widow sojourn. The excuse: there were too many projects in the pipeline ahead of her. This wouldn't be rectified until *Black Widow* (2021).
2. Kirk Baird, *The Blade* [OH], May 6, 2010.
3. Carol Cling, *Las Vegas Review-Journal*, May 7, 2010.
4. Larocca, "Scarlett's in Love! (But Not with This Guy)," p. 186.
5. Simon Dumenco, "Beyond the Bombshell," *InStyle*, May 2010, p. 306.
6. Dumenco, "Beyond the Bombshell," p. 309.
7. "Scarlett Johansson Provides a Window into Black Widow," *Life Story: Movie Magic Collector's Edition*, 2015, p. 29.
8. Chris Heath, "All Eyes on Scarlett," *Vanity Fair Awards Extra!*, 2019, p. 45.
9. Lynn Hirschberg, "Nobody's Baby," *W*, March 2015, p. 352.
10. Christy Lemire, *Ap Top News Package*, April 23, 2012.
11. Kenneth Turan, *Los Angeles Times*, May 3, 2012.
12. A.O. Scott, *New York Times*, May 3, 2012.
13. Tony Norman, *Pittsburgh Post-Gazette*, May 4, 2012.
14. Gunnar Rehlin, "Love Scarlett," p. 50.
15. Chris Heath, "All Eyes on Scarlett," p. 45.
16. Daniel D. Snyder, "Scarlett Johansson Has the Most Human Moment in 'The Avengers,'" www.theatlantic.com, May 7, 2012.
17. Robbie Collin, *Telegraph* [UK], www.telegraph.co.uk, March 27, 2014.
18. Odie Henderson, www.rogerebert.com, April 3, 2014.
19. Ann Hornaday, *Washington Post*, www.washingtonpost.com, April 3, 2014.

20. Owen Gleiberman, *Entertainment Weekly*, April 11, 2014, p. 38.
21. Saba Hamedy, "*Captain America* Posts Blockbuster Numbers in Opening Weekend," http://articles.latimes.com, April 6, 2014.
22. George Gurley, "Scarlett's Web," p. 168.
23. Gurley, "Scarlett's Web," pp. 168, 170.
24. Logan Hill, "Scarlett 2.0," *Glamour*, May 2014, p. 225.
25. Nathan Poppe, *Daily Oklahoman*, April 29, 2015.
26. Kenneth Turan, *Los Angeles Times*, April 29, 2015.
27. Dargis, *New York Times*, April 30, 2015.
28. Tony Norman, *Pittsburgh Post-Gazette*, April 30, 2015.
29. "Scarlett Johansson Provides a Window into Black Widow," *Life Story: Movie Magic Collector's Edition*, 2015, p. 28.
30. "Avengers: Age of Ultron's Scarlett Johansson on Filming While Pregnant: 'I'm Very Fortunate There's a Team Around,'" https://nationalpost.com, May 1, 2015.
31. Adam Holmes, "Scarlett Johansson Thinks Black Widow and Hulk's Romance 'Wasn't Meant to Be,'" www.cinemablend.com, September 6, 2019.
32. Adam Chitwood, "Black Widow Movie: Scarlett Johansson and Kevin Feige Have Discussed a Series of Films," http://collider.com, April 15, 2015.
33. Rafer Guzman, *Newsday* [Melville, NY], May 4, 2016.
34. Andrew Gaug, *St. Joseph News-Press* [MO], May 5, 2016.
35. Lindsey Bahr/Associated Press, *News Journal* [Wilmington, DE], May 6, 2016, p. 3HR.
36. Chris Nashawaty, ew.com, April 26, 2016.
37. Anthony Breznican, "Captain America: Civil War Star Scarlett Johansson on the Scrutiny of Black Widow," http://ew.com, December 3, 2015.
38. Corey Chichizola, "The Insane Amount of Money Scarlett Johansson Might Be Making for the Black Widow Movie," www.cinemablend.com, January 20, 2018.
39. Corey Chichizola, "How the Russo Brothers Feel About Marvel's Black Widow Movie," www.cinemablend.com, January 23, 2018.
40. Owen Gleiberman, *Variety*, April 24, 2018.
41. Brian Truitt, *Usa Today Life*, April 26, 2018, p. D1.
42. Mark Meszoros/News-Herald, *Daily Local News* [West Chester, PA], April 27, 2018, Entertainment, p. 3.
43. Will Ashton, "That Time Scarlett Johansson Accidentally Flashed Her Private Parts on a Plane," www.cinemablend.com, April 25, 2018.
44. Sean O'Connell, "What Captain America Has Been Doing Since the End of Civil War," www.cinemablend.com, March 16, 2018.
45. Gina McIntyre, "The Soldier and the Spy," *The Ultimate Guide to the Avengers*," Tampa, FL: Entertainment Weekly Books, 2018.
46. Leah Greenblatt, *Entertainment Weekly*, Summer Movie Preview 2019, pp. 68–69.
47. Brian Tallerico, www.rogerebert.com, April 24, 2019.
48. Peter Travers, www.rollingstone.com, April 24, 2019.
49. Molly Freeman, https://screenrant.com, April 26, 2019.
50. Simran Hans, www.theguardian.com, April 27, 2019.
51. Anthony Lane, "Leaps and Bounds," *The New Yorker*, May 6, 2019, p. 73.
52. She associated that name with pop stars and found it tacky, kind of violent, and insulting. Logan Hill, "Scarlett 2.0," *Glamour*, May 2014, p. 225.
53. Andrea Mandell and Brian Truitt, "Scarlett Johansson Plots (Secret) Future for Back Widow: 'I've Worked to Get Here,'" www.usatoday.com, April 24, 2019.
54. Anthony Breznican, "*Avengers: Endgame* Secrets Revealed," *Entertainment Weekly*, May 17/24, 2019, pp. 16–17.
55. Rebecca Keegan, "The Season of Scarlett Johansson: Two Hot Films, Her Marvel Future, Woody Allen and a Pick for President," www.hollywoodreporter.com, September 4, 2019.
56. Kathryn Romeyn, "Scarlett Johansson's 'Avengers' Workout: How to Get a Black Widow Body," www.hollywoodreporter.com, April 26, 2019. See also: Bridget March, "Scarlett Johansson Fasted for 12 Hours a Day and Trained Like an Olympic Athlete for Avengers: Endgame," *Harper's Bazaar*, www.harpersbazaar.com, April 25, 2019.
57. Eleni Roussos, *Avengers: Endgame: the Art of Marvel Studios*, New York: Marvel Worldwide, Inc., 2019, p. 32.
58. *Avengers: Endgame* Blu-Ray. Burbank, CA: Buena Vista Home Entertainment, 2019.
59. Nick Evans, "What a Black Widow Movie Should Explore, According to Scarlett Johansson," www.cinemablend.com, March 16, 2018.
60. Nick Evans, "What a Black Widow Movie Should Explore," www.cinemablend.com, March 16, 2018.
61. "'Black Widow' Standalone Film Finds a Director & Is Reportedly a Sequel," https://theplaylist.net, July 12, 2018.
62. "Scarlett Johansson Ushers in the Mcu'S Female Future with 'Black Widow': 'It's Pretty Explosive'" (Exclusive), *Entertainment Tonight*, www.etonline.com, July 20, 2019.
63. Rebecca Keegan, "The Season of Scarlett Johansson: Two Hot Films, Her Marvel Future, Woody Allen and a Pick for President," www.hollywoodreporter.com, September 4, 2019.

Chapter 8

1. Tom Chiarella, "Scarlett Johansson Is the Sexiest Woman Alive 2013," *Esquire*, November 2013, p. 122.
2. Chiarella, *Esquire*, p. 128.
3. Chiarella, *Esquire*, November 2013, p. 129.
4. Jean-Paul Goude, "Hitchcock Heroine," *V Magazine*, Winter 2012/13, p. 68.

5. Ben Brantley, *New York Times*, January 17, 2013.
6. ABC New Radio, "Anthony Mackie: Why Scarlett Johansson Will Be a Great Mom," https://abcnews.go.com, April 3, 2014.
7. Gina Carbone, "Anthony Mackie Hated Falcon's Avengers Death Scene, Here's His Hilarious Alternate Ending," www.cinemablend.com, February 3, 2019.
8. "Scarjo's Engaged Too!," *People*, September 23, 2013, p. 23.
9. Paul Chi, "Scarlett in Love!," *People*, February 3, 2014, p. 76.
10. Jada Yuan, "A Woman in Full," *Cosmopolitan*, May 2016, p. 162.
11. Logan Hill, *Glamour*, May 2014, p. 220. This goal was achieved with the remake of *The Jungle Book* (2016), in which she voiced the snake Kaa and sang "Trust in Me."
12. Bruce Horovitz, "Sodastream's Super Bowl Spot Gets Rejected—Again," www.usatoday.com, January 24, 2014.
13. Zayda Rivera, "Scarjo's Sodastream Super Bowl Ad Banned," www.nydailynews.com, January 29, 2014.
14. Carole Cadwalladr, "Scarlett Johansson Interview," www.theguardian.com, March 16, 2014.
15. Zev Chafets, "Pepsico's Sodastream Purchase Is Sweet News for Israelis," www.bloomberg.com, August 22, 2018.
16. Anthony Lane, "Her Again," p. 57.
17. Lili Anolik, "A(nother) Study in Scarlett," *Vanity Fair*, May 2014, p. 196.
18. Anolik, "A(nother) Study in Scarlett," p. 144.
19. Logan Hill, "Scarlett 2.0," *Glamour*, May 2014, p. 220.
20. Gary Goldstein, www.latimes.com, May 8, 2014.
21. Jessica Herndon/Associated Press, *News Journal* [Wilmington, DE], May 23, 2014, p. 6.
22. Jyoti Sharma Bawa, *Hindustan Times*, June 20, 2014.
23. Brooke Hauser, "Miss Scarlett," p. 258.
24. Barbara Walters, "The 10 Most Fascinating People of 2014," ABC TV, December 15, 2014.
25. Walters, "The 10 Most Fascinating People of 2014," ABC TV, December 15, 2014.
26. "Oscars 2015: the Daily Beast's Picks, from Scarlett Johansson to 'Boyhood,'" www.thedailybeast.com, January 6, 2015.
27. Mike Reyes, "Scarlett Johansson's Ghost in the Shell Isn't Happening Any Time Soon," www.cinemablend.com, January 15, 2015.
28. Alyssa Toomey, "Awkward! John Travolta Gives Scarlett Johansson a Smooch … and She Responds with Side Eye: Pics!," www.eonline.com, February 22, 2015.
29. Associated Press, "Scarlett Johansson Defends John Travolta: Nothing 'Creepy of Inappropriate' About Oscars Kiss," www.billboard.com, February 26, 2015.
30. Karen Valby, "Let's Kick Through the Glass Ceiling. Now," *Entertainment Weekly*, August 15, 2014, p. 14.
31. Anthony Breznican, "Captain America: Civil War Star Scarlett Johansson on the Scrutiny of Black Widow," http://ew.com, December 3, 2015.
32. *Taranaki Daily News*, June 2, 2015, p. A12.
33. "Celebrity 100," *Forbes*, July 20, 2015, p. 82.
34. Hauser, "Miss Scarlett," p. 256.
35. Brian Truitt, *Usa Today*, [Wilmington, DE *News Journal*], Feb. 5, 2016, p. 3HR.
36. Leah Greenblatt, *Entertainment Weekly*, February 12, 2016, p. 49.
37. Stephanie Zacharek, *Time*, February 15, 2016, pp. 49–50.
38. Dan Jolin, *Empire*, https://www.empireonline.com, February 29, 2016.
39. *Hail, Caesar!* Bonus Features, "The Stars Align," Blu-Ray, Universal City, CA: Universal Pictures Home Entertainment, 2016.
40. *Hail, Caesar!* Bonus Features, "An Era of Glamour," Blu-Ray, Universal City, CA: Universal Pictures Home Entertainment, 2016.
41. Tabi Jackson Gee, "Man Makes Robot Which Looks Like Scarlett Johansson—Why Do We Keep Making Creepy Female Bots?" www.telegraph.co.uk, April 8, 2016.
42. Benjamin Lee, "Scarlett Johansson Now Highest Grossing Female Star of All Time," www.theguardian.com, June 29, 2016.
43. Canada Newswire, "Scarlett Johansson Shoots Selfies with Fans at Huawei P9 Fans Club Party Event," *Canada Newswire*, November 17, 2016.
44. "Scarlett Johansson Pleased by 'Female Energy' on Set," *Brampton Guardian* [Ontario]. December 6, 2016.
45. M.B. Roberts, "Photos: See Scarlett Johansson, Chris Evans and Others on Star-Studded Uso Holiday Tour," https://parade.com, December 20, 2016.
46. Caitlin Shuda, "Scarlett Johansson Helps Wisconsin Rapids Girl Fight Cancer," *Ap Regional State Report—Wisconsin*, January 14, 2017.
47. Sessums, 2006, p. 196.
48. Danielle Stein, "Sister Act," p. 443. Who could have foreseen a greater emergency eight years hence?
49. Jeffrey Ressner, "Actress Has a Crush on Obama," www.politico.com, June 10, 2008.
50. Jada Yuan, "A Woman in Full," *Cosmopolitan*, May 2016, p. 165.
51. Jennifer Drysdale, "Madonna, Scarlett Johansson and America Ferrera Deliver Powerful Speeches at Women's March on Washington," www.yahoo.com, January 21, 2017.
52. Anne Helen Petersen, "Scarlett Johansson Means Business," *Cosmopolitan* (July 2017), p. 100.
53. Petersen, p. 101.
54. Hauser, "Miss Scarlett," p. 258.
55. John Carucci/Associated Press, "Scarlett Johansson, Post Breakup, Resurfaces for a Gala," *Ap Regional State Report—New York*, February 9, 2017.
56. Joyce Chen, "Scarlett Johansson Gives Major Sass on the Oscars 2017 Red Carpet During

Interview: 'What a Ridiculous Question,'" www.usmagazine.com, February 27, 2017.

57. Josh Horowitz, "Scarlett Johansson—Oscars 2017," *Mtv News*, February 26, 2017.

58. Vanessa Thorpe, "Scarlett Johansson, Charismatic Queen of Science Fiction," www.theguardian.com, March 25, 2017.

59. Jenna Amatulli, "'Complicit' Is the Word of the Year, According to Dictionary.Com," https://www.huffingtonpost.com, November 27, 2017.

60. "Scarlett Johansson Talks Working with Bill Murray in 'Lost in Translation' and How the Film Changed Her Life," www.howardstern.com, March 27, 2017.

61. Kara Cutruzzula, "Scarlett Johansson Finds Ivanka Trump 'Old Fashioned, Uninspired, and Cowardly.'" https://womenintheworld.com, April 6, 2017.

62. Owen Gleiberman, *Variety*, June 14, 2017.

63. David Rooney, www.hollywoodreporter.com, June 14, 2017.

64. Dargis, *New York Times*, June 15, 2017.

65. Leah Greenblatt, *Entertainment Weekly*, June 23, 2017, p. 51.

66. Derek Libbey, "Scarlett Johansson May Kill a Stripper in the Hard-R Comedy *Move That Body*," www.cinemablend, December 16, 2015.

67. Hauser, "Miss Scarlett," p. 258.

68. Jada Yuan, "A Woman in Full," *Cosmopolitan*, May 2016, p. 165.

69. Anne Helen Petersen, "Scarlett Johansson Means Business," p. 100.

70. *Rough Night: "Killer Cast Featurette*," Blu-Ray, Culver City, CA: Columbia Pictures, 2017.

71. BWW News Desk, "Photo Flash: Scarlett Johansson's Our Town Raises $500k for Puerto Rico Relief," www.broadwayworld.com, November 7, 2017.

72. YouTube, January 20, 2018.

73. Rebecca Keegan, "The Season of Scarlett Johansson: Two Hot Films, Her Marvel Future, Woody Allen and a Pick for President," www.hollywoodreporter.com, September 4, 2019.

74. Matt Donnelly, "Scarlett Johansson Leaves Manager Rick Yorn After 2 Decades," www.thewrap.com, March 29, 2018.

75. Maeve McDermott, *Usa Today*, June 28, 2018.

76. Jordan Crucchiota, "Scarlett Johansson Issues Statement About Rub & Tug Casting Backlash," www.vulture.com, July 3, 2018.

77. "Trans Actors Praise Scarlett Johansson's Withdrawal from 'Rub & Tug,'" www.out.com, July 16, 2018.

78. Ryan Scott, "Scarlett Johansson's Exit," https://movieweb.com, July 17, 2018.

79. Mike Fleming, Jr., "Bart & Fleming: the Danger in the 'Rub & Tug's Shaming of Scarlett Johansson & the Disney Banishment of James Gunn," *Deadline*, https://deadline.com, July 25, 2018.

80. Chris Heath, "All Eyes on Scarlett," *Vanity Fair Awards Extra!*, 2019, p. 45.

81. Gaby Wood, "Beyond Borders," *Vogue*, April 2019, pp. 127–141, 196–197.

82. Antoinette Bueno, "Scarlett Johansson Taken to Police Station After Paparazzi Overpower Her Security," www.etonline.com, April 9, 2019.

83. Kristin M. Hall, "Ap Exclusive: Scarlett Johansson and Colin Jost Are Engaged," www.apnews.com, May 19, 2019.

84. Rebecca Keegan, "The Season of Scarlett Johansson: Two Hot Films, Her Marvel Future, Woody Allen and a Pick for President," www.hollywoodreporter.com, September 4, 2019.

85. Tatijana Shoan and David Salle, "Scarlett," *As If*, Issue No 15 (2019), p. 144.

86. Shoan and Salle, p. 151.

87. Carla Herreria, "Scarlett Johansson Defends Her Right to Play Any Person, Tree or Animal," www.huffpost.com, July 14, 2019. See also: Rosemary Rossi and Umberto Gonzalez, "Scarlett Johansson: My Casting Comments Were 'Edited for Click Bait,' 'Taken Out of Context,'" www.thewrap.com, July 14, 2019.

88. Gabriella Geisinger, www.digitalspy.com, January 11, 2019.

89. Nicholas Barber, www.bbc.com, October 7, 2019.

90. Peter Travers, *Rolling Stone*, October 16, 2009.

91. Brian Truitt, *Usa Today Life*, October 18, 2019, pp. 1D, 4D.

92. Sarah El-Mahmoud, "Scarlett Johansson Was Worried About How Taika Waititi's Hitler Movie Jojo Rabbit Would Fare at Disney," www.cinemablend.com, September 4, 2019.

93. Eric Eisenberg, "Where Scarlett Johansson Found Inspiration for Her Vivacious Jojo Rabbit Character," www.cinemablend.com, October 17, 2019.

94. Heath, "All Eyes on Scarlett," p. 40.

95. Heath, "All Eyes on Scarlett," p. 46.

96. "Mom Lifts 'Jojo Rabbit' Above Satire," *Usa Today Life*, September 16, 2019, p. 2D.

97. Andrea Mandell, "Johansson Begins a Fresh Chapter with 'Jojo Rabbit,'" *Usa Today Life*, October 17, 2019, p. 4D.

98. Jon Frosch, *Hollywood Reporter*, www.hollywoodreporter.com, September 6, 2019.

99. Peter Travers, *Rolling Stone*, November 2019, p. 90.

100. Sean O'Connell, www.cinemablend.com/reviews, November 11, 2019.

101. "These Film-Fest Faves Are on the Rise," *Usa Today Life*, September 16, 2019, p. 3D.

102. Paul Wilson, "Final Cut: Showbiz Divorcee Noah Baumbach's New Film Is About a Showbiz Divorce," *Esquire*, August 2019, pp. 79–80.

103. Rebecca Keegan, "The Season of Scarlett Johansson: Two Hot Films, Her Marvel Future, Woody Allen and a Pick for President," www.hollywoodreporter.com, September 4, 2019.

104. Keegan, "The Season of Scarlett Johansson."

105. Paul Wilson, "Final Cut: Showbiz Divorcee Noah Baumbach's New Film Is About a Showbiz Divorce," *Esquire*, August 2019, p. 83.

Chapter 9

1. David Germain/Associated Press, *Daily Local News Weekender*, July 22, 2005, p. 4.
2. A.O. Scott, *New York Times*, July 22, 2005.
3. Tom Long, *Detroit News/News Journal 55 hours* [Wilmington, DE], July 22, 2005, p. 8.
4. Copley News Service, *Daily Local News* [West Chester, PA], August 3, 2005, p. 2.
5. Tom Sykes, "Scarlett Johansson's Sexy Style," *Harper's Bazaar*, January 2005, p. 74.
6. http://news.yahoo.com, July 18, 2005.
7. Barboza, "Another Shade of Scarlett," p. 7.
8. Barboza, "Another Shade of Scarlett," p. 7.
9. Barboza, "Another Shade of Scarlett," p. 7.
10. Barboza, "Another Shade of Scarlett," p. 6.
11. Daniel Fierman, "Attack of the Clones," *Entertainment Weekly*, July 22, 2005, p. 26.]
12. Kizis, "Bright Young Thing," *Allure*, August 2005, p. 189.
13. Edward Jay Epstein, "The End of Originality: Or, Why Michael Bay's the *Island* Failed at the Box Office," www.slate.com, February 6, 2006.
14. Chris Nashawaty, *Entertainment Weekly*, December 20, 2013, p. 48.
15. Jessica Zack, *Sydney Morning Herald*, January 2, 2014.
16. Joe Williams, *St. Louis Post-Dispatch*, January 9, 2014.
17. Jessica Herndon/Associated Press, *News Journal* [Wilmington, DE], January 10, 2014, p. 4.
18. Matthew Dallas, *Manawatu Standard* [New Zealand], March 6, 2014, p. 13.
19. *Entertainment Weekly*, January 10, 2014, p. 11.
20. Aronofsky, "Scarlett," p. 108.
21. Aronofsky, "Scarlett," p. 112.
22. Paul Chi, "Scarlett's in Love!," *People*, February 3, 2014, p. 76.
23. *Her* Press Conference after *Her* world premiere at the 51st New York Film Festival, Lincoln Center, NY, YouTube, October 13, 2013.
24. David Maltz, "Spike Jonze Talks What's Real and What's a Relationship with *Her*," www.washingtonpost.com, December 20, 2013.
25. Ann-Christine Diaz, "Celebrated Creative Pair Goes to the Movies with Scarlett Johansson," *Advertising Age*, April 14, 2014, p 39.
26. Todd Cunningham, "Scarlett Johansson's 'Under the Skin' First Film in 25 Years to Premiere at Ace Hotel's Historic Theater," www.thewrap.com, March 24, 2014.
27. Cunningham, March 24, 2014.
28. Steve Chagollan "Downtown L.A.'s Ace Hotel Hosts 'Under the Skin' at United Artists Theater," https://Variety.com, March 26, 2014.
29. Robbie Collin, www.telegraph.com.uk, March 13, 2014.
30. Mark Kermode, www.theguardian.com, March 16, 2014.
31. Alonso Duralde, www.thewrap.com, April 2, 2014.
32. Matt Zoller Seitz, www.rogerebert.com, April 4, 2014.
33. David Michael McFarlane, www.huffingtonpost, April 7, 2014.
34. Franco Freassetti, *Films in Review,* http://filmsinreview, April 10, 2014.
35. Victoria Alexander, *Films in Review,* http://filmsinreview, April 16, 2014.
36. Chris Nashawaty, "When Movie Stars Act Weird," *Entertainment Weekly,* April 11, 2014, pp. 48–49.
37. Jimmy So, "Scarlett Johansson Is an Alien Seductress in 'Under the Skin,'" www.thedailybeast.com, April 13, 2014.
38. Steven Rea, *Philadelphia Inquirer*, April 18, 2014.
39. Joe Gross, *Austin-American Statesman*, www.accessatlanta.com, April 19, 2014.
40. Richard Roeper, "Richard Roeper at the Movies," *Chronicle Herald* [Halifax, NS], May 29, 2014.
41. Australian Associated Press, "Mail Online," www.dailymail.com.uk, May 19, 2014.
42. Jeff T. Dick, *Library Journal*, http://reviews.libraryjournal.com/2014/09/media/video/controversia…
43. Jordan Zakarin, "Jonathan Glazer on Struggles with Scarlett Johansson's 'Under the Skin' and 'Suspecting Everything You Do Is Bad,'" www.thewrap.com, April 14, 2014.
44. Jonathan Glazer, "Casting" Extras, *Under the Skin* DVD, Santa Monica, CA: Lions Gate Entertainment, 2014.
45. Gunnar Rehlin, "Love Scarlett," *Scandinavian Traveler*, March 2016, p. 50.
46. Michael Rothman, "How Scarlett Johansson Really Felt About Filming Nude Scenes," https://abcnews.go.com, April 1, 2014.
47. Lynn Hirschberg, "Nobody's Baby," *W*, March 2015, p. 359.
48. David Salle, "Scarlett," *As If*, Issue No 15, 2019, p. 149.
49. Elizabeth Day, "How Scarlett Johansson Helped Me Challenge Disfigurement Stigma," www.theguardian.com, April 12, 2014.
50. Carole Cadwalladr, "Scarlett Johansson Interview," www.theguardian.com, March 16, 2014.
51. Jimmy So, www.thedailybeast.com, April 3, 2014.
52. Gittell, "Scarlett Johansson's Vanishing Act."
53. Todd Cunningham, "Scarlett Johansson Scores Twice at Box Office as 'Under the Skin' Tops Limited Releases," www.thewrap.com, April 6, 2014.
54. *Under the Skin*, Special Features. "The Making of Under the Skin," Santa Monica, CA: Lions Gate Entertainment Inc., 2014.
55. Anne Thompson, "Why Jonathan Glazer's 'Under the Skin' Took a Decade to Make (Videos)," www.indiewire.com, October 23, 2014; Playlist Staff, http://blogs.indiewire.com, October 30, 2014.
56. *The Daily Beast,* www.thedailyeast.com, January 6, 2015.
57. Danny Leigh, "Under the Skin: Why Did

This Chilling Masterpiece Take a Decade?," www.theguardian.com, March 6, 2014.

58. Maureen Foster, *Alien in the Mirror: Scarlett Johansson, Jonathan Glazer and Under the Skin* (Jefferson, NC: McFarland, 2019), p. 228.

59. David Cox, *Film4*, YouTube, March 18, 2014.

60. Justin Chang, *Variety*, July 23, 2014.

61. Dargis, *New York Times*, July 25, 2014, p. C4.

62. Claudia Puig, *Usa Today*, July 25, 2014, Sec. D, p. 1.

63. It made $43,899, 340 as of July 25, 2014, according to "The Numbers," https://www.the-numbers.com/movie/Lucy. According to Vladimir Kozlov ("Scarlett Johansson's 'Lucy' Opens Strong in Russia," *Hollywood Reporter*, September 18, 2014; http://www.hollywoodreporter.com/news/scarlett-johanssons-lucy-opens-strong-733940), *Lucy* did very well in Russia seven weeks after the U.S. release, grossing $9.6 million the opening weekend, which exceeded "even the most optimistic forecasts. Besson and the film's star, Scarlett Johansson, are popular in Russia." According to "*Lucy* Rules Hollywood-Dominated Chinese Box Office," http://pro.boxoffice.com, October 28, 2014, it did swell in China, taking first place between October 20 and 26, earning $20 million in the first three days.

64. Eliana Dockterman, "Scarlett Johansson, Lucy and the Future of the Female Action Star," *Time*, July 25, 2014.

65. Gittell, "Scarlett Johansson's Vanishing Act."

66. Richard Corliss, "Movies: a Season for Women. Finally, Complex Females Flourish on Both Sides of the Camera," *Time*, December 15, 2015, p. 70.

67. Ian Haydn Smith, *Movie Star Chronicles: a Visual History of the World's Greatest Movie Stars* (Buffalo, NY: Firefly Books, 2015), pp. 271–272.

68. Richard Corliss, "Movies," *Time*, December 22, 2014, p. 142.

69. Emma Dibdin, "Evolution in the Head," *Total Film*, February 2015, p. 124.

70. Gittell, "Scarlett Johansson's Vanishing Act."

71. *Lucy*, "The Evolution of Lucy," Universal City Plaza, CA: Universal Studios Home Entertainment, Blu-Ray, 2015.

72. Edmund Douglas, *New York Daily News*, March 30, 2017.

73. Brian Truitt, *Usa Today*, March 31, 2017, p. 1D.

74. Dougal Macdonald, *Canberra City News*, March 31, 2017.

75. Ian Sandwell, "First Reviews Drop for Ghost in the Shell," *Digital Spy*, March 29, 2017.

76. Lisa Suhay, "Scarlett Johansson in 'Ghost in the Shell': No Asian Actors Available?," www.csmonitor.com, January 5, 2015.

77. Nick Romano, "Scarlett Johansson Responds to Ghost in the Shell Whitewashing Controversy," https://ew.com/movies, updated February 9, 2017.

78. Graeme Virtue, "Scarlett Johansson in Ghost in the Shell—Will Something Be Lost in Translation?," www.theguardian.com, January 6, 2015.

79. Jordan Farley, "Ghost in the Shell: Rage Against the Machine," *Total Film*, April 2017, p. 60.

80. Farley, p. 62.

81. Farley, p. 64.

82. Farley, p. 64.

83. Farley, 64.

84. David S. Cohen, *The Art of Ghost in the Shell*, p. 41. *The Art of Ghost in the Shell* (San Rafael, CA: Insight Editions, 2017), p. 41. This is a handsome coffee-table account of the film's making. One supposes the filmmakers went to this length assuming that the film would spawn a franchise and viewers would clamor for it and, perhaps, memorabilia. In fact, there were some very good—and expensive action figures of the Major available from Weta Workshop.

85. "Hard-Wired Humanity: Making Ghost in the Shell," *Ghost in the Shell* Blu-ray, Hollywood, CA: DreamWorks Pictures, 2017.

86. Cohen, p. 41.

Epilogue

1. Quigley Publishing Company, "Top Ten Money Making Stars Poll," 1915–2013. Lana Turner was #24 in 1942, #25 in 1943, #14 in 1948; Rita Hayworth was #23 in 1942, #17 in 1947, #20 in 1948, and #25 in 1953; Ava Gardner was #21 in 1954.

2. Chris Heath, "All Eyes on Scarlett," p. 46.

3. Sarah El-Mahmoud, "8 Times Scarlett Johansson Should Have Been Nominated for an Academy Award," www.cinemablend.com, June 6, 2019.

4. Heath, "All Eyes on Scarlett," p. 40.

5. Corey Chichizola, "Apparently, a Bunch of Marvel Ladies Pitched an All-Female Marvel Movie," www.cinemablend.com, November 1, 2017.

6. Justin Kroll, "Scarlett Johansson in Talks to Star in Focus Drama 'Reflective Light' (Exclusive)," https://Variety.com, October 26, 2017.

7. Rebecca Keegan, "The Season of Scarlett Johansson: Two Hot Films, Her Marvel Future, Woody Allen and a Pick for President," September 4, 2019.

Filmography

1. Lindsey Bahr/Associated Press, *News Journal 55Hrsplus* [Wilmington, DE], April 14, 2016, p. 3HR.

2. Annie Martin, "Reese Witherspoon, Scarlett Johansson Stun at 'Sing' Premiere," www.upi.com, September 12, 2016.

Bibliography

Articles

ABC News Radio. "Anthony Mackie: Why Scarlett Johansson Will Be a Great Mom." https:abcnews.go.com. April 3, 2014.

"Actor Scarlett Johansson Visits India and Sri Lanka; Commits to Helping End Poverty." www.oxfam.org.uk. March 1, 2007.

"Actress Scarlett Johansson Got Up on Stage...." http://movie.moldova.org. May 1, 2007.

Alexander, Bryan. "'Jungle Book' Has a Human Heart." *USA Today*. April 15, 2016, p. 2D.

"Angelina Jolie and Scarlett Johansson Dubbed Perfect for Playboy Cover." www.aceshowbiz.com. September 18, 2008.

ANI. "Scarlett Johansson Is Ready to Strip on Screen." http://in.news.yahoo.com. December 14, 2006.

Anolik, Lili. "A(nother) Study in Scarlett." *Vanity Fair*. May 2014, pp. 142–149, 195–196.

Aronofsky, Darren. "Scarlett." *Interview*. October 2013, pp. 102–108, 112–113, 172.

Ashton, Will. "That Time Scarlett Johansson Accidentally Flashed Her Private Parts on a Plane." www.cinemablend.com. April 25, 2018.

Associated Press. "Scarlett Johansson Defends John Travolta: Nothing 'Creepy or Inappropriate' About Oscars Kiss." www.billboard.com. February 26, 2015.

Atchison, Doug. "Girl with the Golden Touch." *MovieMaker*. Winter 2004, pp. 98–102, 104.

"Avengers: Age of Ultron's Scarlett Johansson on Filming While Pregnant: 'I'm Very Fortunate There's a Team Around,'" https://nationapost.com, May 1, 2015.

BANG Showbiz. "Johansson, Longoria, Biel Design Corsets for Charity." www.azcentral.com. October 25, 2007.

BANG Showbiz. "Scarlett Johansson Donates to Sri Lankan School." www.azcentra..com. October 18, 2007.

Barboza, Craigh. "Another Shade of Scarlett." *USA Weekend*. July 15–17, 2005, pp. 6–7.

Baxter, Joseph. "Lucy 2 Is Definitely Happening, Will Scarlett Johansson Return?" www.cinemablend.com. October 25, 2015.

Bernstein, Jacob. "Vice Turns 20 with a Big Brooklyn Party." *New York Times*. December 10, 2014.

Bhattacharya, Sanjiv. "Scarlett in Bloom." *New York*. February 16, 2004, pp. 82–87.

Billson, Anne. "How Scarlett Johansson Got Interesting." www.telegraph.co.uk. November 19, 2013.

Biskind, Peter. "A Study in Scarlett." *Vanity Fair*. December 2011, pp. 194–203, 257.

"'Black Widow' Standalone Film Finds a Director & Is Reportedly a Prequel." https:theplaylist.net. July 12, 2018.

Breznican, Anthony. "All for One." [*Avengers: Endgame*]. *Entertainment Weekly*. April 19/26, 2019, pp. 16–24.

Breznican, Anthony. "Avengers: Age of Ultron." *Entertainment Weekly*. April 17/24, 2015, pp. 32–35.

Breznican, Anthony. "Avengers: Endgame Secrets Revealed." *Entertainment Weekly*. May 17/24, 2019.

Breznican, Anthony. "Captain America: Civil War Star Scarlett Johansson on the Scrutiny of Black Widow." http://ew.com. December 3, 2015.

Breznican, Anthony. "Don Jon." *Entertainment Weekly Summer Movie Double 2013*. April 19/26, 2013, p. 82.

Breznican, Anthony. "Lohan, Johansson Grow into New Roles." www.usatoday.com. July 10, 2005.

Brodesser-Akner, Claude. "Carey Mulligan Now the Front-runner to Play Daisy in Baz Luhrmann's *Great Gatsby*." www.vulture.com. November 12, 2010.

Brown, Chip. "The Smart Bomb." *Elle*. January 2006, pp. 123–124, 128.

Bueno, Antoinette. "Scarlett Johansson Taken to Police Station After Paparazzi Overpower Her Security." www.etonline.com. April 9, 2019.

BWW News Desk. "Photo Flash: Scarlett Johansson's *Our Town* Reading Raises $500K for Puerto Rico Relief." www.broadwayworld.com. November 7, 2017.

Cadwalladr, Carole. "Scarlett Johansson Interview: 'I Would Way Rather Not Have Middle Ground.'" www.theguardian.com. March 16, 2014.

Carbone, Gina. "Anthony Mackie Hated Falcon's Avengers Death Scene, Here's His Hilarious Alternate Ending." www.cinemablend.com. February 3, 2019.

Carucci, John. "Scarlett Johansson, Post Breakup, Resurfaces for a Gala." *AP Regional State Report—New York*. February 9, 2017.

Castle, Robert. "Film Odyssey: Scarlett Johansson Gets Under Our Skin." *NJPen* (www.njpen.com). June 2, 2015.

"The Celebrity 100." *Forbes*. July 2, 2007, p. 82.

"Celebrity 100." *Forbes*. July 20, 2015, p. 82.

"The Celebrity 100: The Players Club." *Forbes*. July 3, 2006, pp. 128 [3 pages].

Chafets, Zev. "Pepsico's SodaStream Purchase Is Sweet News for Israelis." www.bloomberg.com. August 22, 2018.

Chagollan, Steve, "Downtown L.A.'s Ace Hotel Hosts 'Under the Skin' at United Artists Theater," https://variety.com, March 26, 2014.

Chen, Joyce. "Scarlett Johansson Gives Major Sass on the Oscars 2017 Red Carpet During Interview: 'What a Ridiculous Question.'" www.usmagazine.com. February 27, 2017.

Chi, Paul. "Scarlett in Love!" *People*. February 3, 2014, pp. 75–76.

Chiarella, Tom. "Scarlett Johansson Is the Sexiest Woman Alive 2013." *Esquire*. November 2013, pp. 118–122, 128–129.

Chichizola, Corey. "Apparently, a Bunch of Marvel Ladies Pitched an All-Female Marvel Movie." www.cinemablend.com. November 1, 2017.

Chichizola, Corey. "How the Russo Brothers Feel About Marvel's Black Widow Movie." www.cinemablend. January 23, 2018.

Chichizola, Corey. "The Insane Amount of Money Scarlett Johansson Might Be Making for the Black Widow Movie." www.cinemablend.com. January 20, 2018.

Chichizola, Corey. "The Russo Brothers Explain Black Widow's Endgame Story." www.cinemablend.com. May 3, 2019.

Chichizola, Corey. "Why Ghost in the Shell Failed, According to Paramount." www.cinemablend.com. Ca. April 4, 2017.

Chichizola, Corey. "Why the Black Widow Movie Still Hasn't Happened, According to Scarlett Johansson." www.cinemablend.com. February 11, 2017.

Chitwood, Adam. "Black Widow Movie: Scarlett Johansson and Kevin Feige Have Discussed a Series of Films." http://collider.com. April 15, 2015.

Cidoni, Michael. "Magazine Celebrates Women in Hollywood." www.washingtonpost.com. October 16, 2007.

"Coachella '07: Superfans and Balloon Fish Girls." www.spin.com/coachella07. April 28, 2007.

"Coen Brothers Tap Clooney, Johansson for All-star Studio Comedy." [*Hail, Caesar!*] www.chinadaily.com.cn. October 30, 2014. [1 page]

Colapinto, John. "Girl with a Career on Fire." *Elle*. June 2004, pp. 160–163, 165–167, 169.

Collin, Robbie. "*Under the Skin*: 'simply a Masterpiece.'" www.telegraph.co.uk. March 13, 2014.

Collins, Dan. "Starlets Strip for *Vanity Fair*." www.cbsnews.com. February 7, 2006.

Combs, Richard. "Does God's Jester Exist?" [Woody Allen] *Film Comment*. January-February 2006, pp. 51–52, 54.

Comita, Jenny. "Not My Type." *W*. March 2008, p. 242.

Cooper, Amy. "Morsel: Scarlett Johansson Photograph Causes a Stir at Woollahra's Hotel Centennial. *Sydney Morning Herald*. November 15, 2014. [https://www.smh.com.au]

Corliss, Richard. "Movies: A Season for Women. Finally, Complex Females Flourish on Both Sides of the Camera." *Time*. December 15, 2015, pp. 70–71.

Corliss, Richard. "Movies." *Time*. December 22, 2014, p. 142.

"Cosmo News." *Cosmopolitan*. August 2008, pp. 38–40.

Cunningham, Todd. "Scarlett Johansson Scores Twice at Box Office as 'Under the Skin' Tops Limited Releases." www.thewrap.com. April 6, 2014.

Cunningham, Todd. "Scarlett Johansson's 'Under the Skin' First Film in 25 Years to Premiere at Ace Hotel's Historic Theater." www.thewrap.com. March 24, 2014.

Cutruzzula, Kara. "Scarlett Johansson Finds Ivanka Trump 'old Fashioned, Uninspired, and Cowardly.'" https://womenintheworld.com. April 6, 2017.

Day, Bek. "Why I Wasn't Happy to Hear About ScarJo's Latest Engagement." www.whimn.com.au. May 21, 2019.

Day, Elizabeth. "How Scarlett Johansson Helped Me Challenge Disfigurement Stigma." www.theguardian.com. April 12, 2014.

Diaz, Ann-Christine. "Celebrated Creative Pair Goes to the Movies with Scarlett Johansson," *Advertising Age*. April 14, 2014, p. 39.

Dibdin, Emma. "Evolution in the Head." [*Lucy*] *Total Film*. February 2015, pp. 124–125.

Dockterman, Eliana. "Scarlett Johansson, Lucy and the Future of the Female Action Star." http://time.com. July 25, 2014.

Dresden, Hilton. "Trans Actors Praise Scarlett Johansson's Withdrawal from 'Rub & Tug.'" www.out.com. July 16, 2018.

Drysdale, Jennifer. [*Entertainment Tonight*]. "Madonna, Scarlett Johansson and America Ferrara Deliver Powerful Speeches at Women's March on Washington." www.yahoo.com. January 21, 2017.

Dumenco, Simon. "Beyond the Bombshell." *InStyle*. May 2010, pp. 301–309.

Duncan, Jody. "Captain's Orders," *Cinefex* 138, 2014.

"Dylan Farrow Slams Scarlett Johansson." www.femalefirst.co.uk. September 6, 2019.

Eisenberg, Eric. "Where Scarlett Johansson Found Inspiration for Her Vivacious Jojo Rabbit Character." www.cinemablend.com. October 17, 2019.

El-Mahmoud, Sarah. "8 Times Scarlett Johansson Should Have Been Nominated for an Academy Award." www.cinemablend.com. June 6, 2019.

El-Mahmoud, Sarah. "Scarlett Johansson Might Make More Money for the Black Widow Movie Than We Thought." www.cinemablend.com. May 1, 2019.

El-Mahmoud, Sarah. "Scarlett Johansson Was Worried About How Taika Waititi's Hitler Movie Jojo Rabbit Would Fare at Disney." www.cinemablend.com. September 4, 2019.

Epstein, Edward Jay. "The End of Originality: Or, Why Michael Bay's *The Island* Failed at the Box Office." www.slate.com. February 6, 2006.

Evans, Nick. "Scarlett Johansson Is Pushing for That All-Female Marvel Movie." www.cinemablend.com. October 15, 2019.

Evans, Nick. "What a Black Widow Movie Should Explore, According to Scarlett Johansson." www.cinemablend.com. March 16, 2018.

Farley, Jordan. "*Ghost in the Shell*: Rage Against the Machine." *Total Film*. April 2017, pp. 58–67.

FHM 100 Sexiest Women in the World 2006. Supplement to *FHM*.

Field, Christine. "Dice-Roll on 'Monopoly' Film." *New York Post*. www.nypost.com. June 18, 2007.

Fierman, Daniel. "Attack of the Clones." [*The Island*] *Entertainment Weekly*. July 22, 2005, p. 22.

"First Annual 'Celebrity Nad's' Awards." http://biz.yahoo.com. March 1, 2007.

Fischer, Paul. "Scarlett Johansson Vicky Cristina Barcelona Interview." www.girl.com.au. Ca. 2008.

Fleming, Mike, Jr., and Bart, Peter. "Bart and Fleming: The Danger in the 'Rub & Tub's Shaming of Scarlett Johansson & the Disney Banishment of James Gunn." *Deadline*. Https://deadine.com. July 25, 2018.

Freer, Ian. "Welcome Back to the Jungle." [*The Jungle Book*] *Empire*. April 2016, pp. 082–086.

Fritz, Ben. "Wonder Girls Save the Day." *Wall Street Journal*. May 5, 2016, p. D1.

Fuselier, Herman. "Stars Shine in Maurice: Studio Gets Visit from A-list Johansson." *The Daily Advertiser* [Lafayette, LA] www.theadvertiser.com. July 13, 2007.

Garamone, Jim. "Chairman, Senior Enlisted Advisor Kick Off USO Holiday Tour." https://www.defense.gov/News/Article/1020506/Chairman-senior. December 5, 2016.

Garfield, Simon. "Why I Love London." [Woody Allen] www.theguardian.com. August 8, 2004.

Garratt, Sheryl. "Scarlett Johansson and Matthew McConaughey Reunite for Dolce & Gabbana." *The Telegraph: Luxury*. www.telegraph.co.uk. November 30, 2014.

Gee, Tabi Jackson. "Man Makes Robot Which Looks Like Scarlett Johansson—Why Do We Keep Making Creepy Female Bots?" http://www.telegraph.co.uk. April 8, 2016.

Gell, Aaron. "Scarlett Fever." *Cosmopolitan*. January 2012, pp. 24–27.

Gheorghe, Adina. "Scarlett Johansson Bursting Out of Her Dress at the Golden Globe Awards." http://news.softpedia.com. January 19, 2006.

Giannini, Melissa. "Women in Hollywood: Scarlett Johansson." *Elle*. November 2019, pp. 156–159.

"Girl with a Career on Fire." *Elle*. June 2004, pp. 161–169. Preceded by two fashion photos with Nina Garcia commentary.

Gittell, Noah. "Scarlett Johansson's Vanishing Act." www.theatlantic.com. July 28, 2014.

Gordon, Jane. "'Of Course I've Got a BIG EG O G O—and All Actors Think They're the One.'" *Daily Mail*. December 21, 2013, p. 22 [5 pages].

Goude, Jean-Paul. "Hitchcock Heroine." *V Magazine*. V80/Winter 2012/13, pp. 66–69.

Green, Adam. "Stage Goddess." [*A View from the Bridge*] *Vogue*. February 2010, pp. 198–199.

Gross, Joe. "Scarlett Johansson Surprises in 'Under the Skin.'" www.accessatlanta.com. April 19, 2014.

Gurley, George. "Scarlett's Web." *Marie Claire*. May 2013, pp. 166–168.

Hall, Kristin M. "AP Exclusive: Scarlett Johansson and Colin Jost Are Engaged." www.apnews.com. May 19, 2019.

"Halle Berry, Scarlett Johansson to Present at Oscars." *Philippines News Agency*. February 8, 2017.

Hamedy, Saba. "'Captain America' Posts Blockbuster Numbers in Opening Weekend." *Los Angeles Times*, April 6, 2014.

Hamm, Liza. "Just Married!" *People*. October 13, 2008, p. 76.

Hauser, Brooke. "Frankly Scarlett," *Allure*. December 2008, p. 224.

Hauser, Brooke. "Miss Scarlett." *Marie Claire*. March 2017, pp. 254–259.

Heath, Chris. "All Eyes on Scarlett," *Vanity Fair Awards Extra!* 2019, pp. 38–47.

Herreria, Carla. "Scarlett Johansson Defends Her Right to Play Any Person, Tree or Animal." www.huffpost.com. July 14, 2019.

Hill, Logan. "Scarlett 2.0." *Glamour*. May 2014, pp. 218–225.

Hirschberg, Lynn. "Nobody's Baby." *W*. March 2015, pp. 358–363.

Hirschberg, Lynn. "Time Is on Their Side: Four Actresses Inhabit Four Decades of Fashion." *W*. November 2012, pp. 294–298 [mostly full-page photos, one each of Keira Knightley, Johansson, Mia Wasikowska, Rooney Mara].

Hochwald, Lambeth. "Welcome to the Jungle." *Parade*. April 3, 2016, pp. 10–11.

Holmes, Adam. "Did Ghost in the Shell Consider Making Scarlett Johansson Asian?" www.cinemablend.com. April 17, 2016.

Holmes, Adam. "Scarlett Johansson Thinks Black Widow and Hulk's Romance Wasn't Meant to Be." www.cinemablend.com. September 6, 2019.

Hooper, Joseph. "Scarlett Fever." *Elle*. November 2007, pp. 325–330, 370.

Horovitz, Bruce. "SodaStream's Super Bowl Spot Gets Rejected—Again." www.usatoday.com. January 24, 2014.

Horowitz, Josh. "Scarlett Johansson—Oscars 2017." *MTV News*. February 26, 2017.

"In Many Ways, Black Widow Has Been the Soul of the Avengers.

"*In Touch* Names Scarlett Johansson as Having the Best Rack." http://socialitelife.com. June 15, 2006.

"It's Maths. Scarlett Johansson Has the World's Most Perfect Body." *Taranaki Daily News*. June 2, 2015, p. A12.

"It's Official: Scarlett Johansson Has the World's Sexiest Body," www.dailymail.co.uk. April 11, 2007.

"I've Finally Found My Soul Mate." *Cosmopolitan*. U.K. ed. January 2009, pp. 48–52.

Jacobs, A. J. "Lips, Kidneys & All: What's Not to Love About the Sexiest Woman Alive." *Esquire.* November 2006, pp. 136–143.

Jacobson, Harlan. "Manhattan Transfer." [*Match Point*] *Film Comment.* January-February 2006, pp. 48–50, 52.

James, Dorothea. "Why Scarlett Johansson Was the Correct Choice for *The Jungle Book*'s Kaa." https://cdanews.com. April 16, 2016.

"Johansson Denies Crash Film Diet." The Press Association. www.google.com/hostednews/ukpress/article/ALeqM5hR14. April 14, 2009.

"Johansson Misses Oscars for Charity Work." www.teenhollywood.com. February 28, 2007.

Johnson, Hugh. "Scarlett Johansson to Star in 'Ghost in the Shell' Movie." *Denver Post* (http://blogs.denverpost.com). January 5, 2015.

Jones, Chris. "That Voice." *Esquire.* February 2005, pp. 66–71.

Kaplan, James. "More Than a Pretty Face." *Parade.* March 11, 2007, pp. 6–8.

Katz, Gregory. "Oxfam Accepts Scarlett Johansson's Resignation." *AP Top News Package.* January 30, 2014.

Keck, William. "New Year Bright for Johansson." http://www.usatoday.com/life/people/2004-12-28-johansson-main_x.htm. December 28, 2004.

Keegan, Rebecca. "The Season of Scarlett: Two Hot Films, Her Marvel Future, Woody Allen and a Pick for President." www.hollywoodreporter.com. September 4, 2019.

Kermode, Mark. "Scarlett Johansson Interview: "I Would Way Rather Not Have Middle Ground." www.theguardian.com. March 16, 2014.

Kile, Meredith B. "Scarlett Johansson Ushers in the MCU's Female Future with 'Black Widow': 'It's Pretty Explosive" (Exclusive), *Entertainment Tonight.* www.etonline.com. July 20, 2019.

Kizis, Deanna. "Bright Young Thing." *Allure.* August 2005, pp. 186–191, 195.

Koresky, Michael. "A History of Reference: Woody Allen's 'Match Point.'" www.indiewire.com. December 27, 2005.

Krause, Amanda. "Scarlett Johansson Wore a Pink Feathered Dress with a Plunging Neckline and Cutouts That Showed Off Her Tattoos." www.insider.com. February 3, 2020.

Kroll, Justin. "Scarlett Johansson in Talks to Star in Focus Drama 'Reflective Light' (Exclusive)." https://variety.com. October 26, 2017.

Lambie, Ryan, and Brew, Simon. "The Top 25 Underappreciated Films of 2004." [*In Good Company*]. www.denofgeek.com. January 9, 2014.

Lane, Anthony. "Her Again: The Unstoppable Scarlett Johansson." *New Yorker.* March 24, 2014, pp. 56–63.

Lane, John Francis. "Dawn Addams Tells About... My Life as Chaplin's Leading Lady." *Films and Filming.* August 1957, pp. 12–13, 15.

Larocca, Amy. "Scarlett's in Love! (but Not with This Guy)." *Glamour.* November 2009, pp. 182–187, 239.

Leigh, Danny. "Under the Skin: Why Did This Chilling Masterpiece Take a Decade?" www.theguardian.com. March 6, 2014.

Libbey, Dirk. "The Avenger Who Needs Their Own Solo Movie, According to Fans." www.cinemablend.com. May 3, 2016.

Libbey, Dirk. "Scarlett Johansson May Kill a Stripper in the Hard-R Comedy Movie That Body." www.cinemablend.com. December 16, 2015.

Libbey, Dirk. "Scarlett Johansson Wasn't Paid as Much as We Thought for Avengers 2." www.cinemablend.com. November 11, 2015.

Libbey, Dirk. "Why a Black Widow Movie Needs to Happen, According to the Russo Brothers." www.cinemablend.com. April 17, 2016.

Lincoln, Kevin. "How Scarlett Johansson Became Our Finest Post-Human Movie Star." www.vulture.com. April 4, 2017.

"*Lucy* Rules Hollywood-Dominated Chinese Box Office." http://pro.boxoffice.com. November 2, 2014.

MacMedan, Dan. "Scarlet [sic] Johansson Wasn't Amused by Red Carpet Groping." *USA Today.* March 3, 2006.

Malone, Scott. "Scarlett Johansson Leads Irreverent Harvard Parade," www.reuters.com. February 15, 2007.

Mandell, Andrea. "Johansson Begins a Fresh Chapter with 'Jojo Rabbit.'" *USA Today Life.* October 17, 2019, pp. 1D, 4D.

Mandell, Andrea. "Scarlett Johansson Plots (Secret) Future for Black Widow: 'I've Worked to Get Here.'" www.usatoday.com. April 24, 2019.

Mark. "Scarlett Breaks Silence About the Grope." http://gawker.com. March 2, 2006.

Martin, Annie. "Reese Witherspoon, Scarlett Johansson Stun at 'Sing' Premiere." *UPI Entertainment.* September 12, 2016.

McConnell, Donna. "Scarlett Ditches Hollywood Glamour to Work with Woody Again." *The Daily Mail.* www.dailymail.co.uk. July 10, 2007.

McConnell, Donna. "Scarlett Launches Street but Chic Sportswear Range." www.dailymail.co.uk. March 28, 2007.

McConnell, Donna. "There's Something About Scarlett." www.dailymail.co.uk. March 12, 2007.

McKenzie, David. CNN interview. YouTube. September 24, 2011.

Mellor, Jessie. "Oscars 2015: Scarlett Johansson's Haircut Causes Waves," http://metro.co.uk. February 23, 2015.

Mendelson, Scott. "In Defense of Scarlett Johansson in 'Ghost in the Shell.'" http://www.forbes.com. January 6, 2015.

Meyers, Kate. "Scarlett in Wonderland." *InStyle.* October 2006, pp. 159–162, 164–168.

Mumford, Gwilym. "Diane Keaton: 'Woody Allen Is My Friend and I Continue to Believe Him.'" www.theguardian.com. January 30, 2018.

"The Must List." *Entertainment Weekly.* January 10, 2014, p. 11. [*Don Jon* and *Her*]

Musto, Michael. "Can Scarlett Johansson Act?" http://blogs.villagevoice.com. January 26, 2010.

"Naked Truth Is Exposed on Aptly Named

Magazine." www.orlandosentinel.com. February 22, 2006.

Nashawaty, Chris. "When Movie Stars Act Weird." *Entertainment Weekly,* April 11, 2014, pp. 48–49.

"New Pad for Scarlett Johansson." *The Times of India.* http://timesofindia.com. July 27, 2007.

NME. "The Jesus and Mary Chain Team Up with Scarlett Johansson." www.nme.com. April 20, 2007.

O'Connell, Sean. "What Captain America Has Been Doing Since the End of Civil War." www.cinemablend.com. March 16, 2018.

Olsen, Mark. "Director Makes Sure His Story Gets 'Under the Skin.'" *Los Angeles Times.* April 12, 2014.

"Paparazzi Makes Scarlett See Red." http://news.ninemsn.com. July 28, 2005.

Petersen, Anne Helen. "Scarlett Johansson Means Business." *Cosmopolitan.* July 2017, pp. 100–101.

Pizzello, Stephen. "Darkest Noir." [*The Black Dahlia*] *American Cinematographer.* September 2006, pp. 32–40, 42, 44–49.

Playlist Staff. "The 25 Best Horror Films of the 21st Century So Far." http://blogs.indiewire.com. October 30, 2014.

"Q+A." *Entertainment Weekly* (Fall Movie Preview 2013): 40.

Rabinowitz, Nancy. "Hasty Crowns Johansson as Woman of Year." http://news.yahoo.com. February 22, 2007.

Rader, Dotson, and Hill, Erin. "Scarlett in Black and White." *Parade.* April 26, 2015, pp. 6–11.

Rebello, Stephen. "Scarlett Woman." *Movieline's Hollywood Life.* February 2004, pp. 50–55, 105, 107.

Rehlin, Gunnar. "Love Scarlett." *Scandinavian Traveler.* March 2016, pp. 48–50, 52.

Reinstein, Mara. "Scarlett Johansson." *Parade.* April 26, 2020.

Reyes, Mike. "Scarlett Johansson's Ghost in the Shell Isn't Happening Any Time Soon," www.cinemablend.com. January 15, 2015.

Reyes, Mike. "Scarlett Johansson's R-Rated Comedy Movie Rock That Body Is Building the Perfect Cast." www.cinemablend.com. May 3, 2016.

Rivera, Zayda. "ScarJo's SodaStream Super Bowl Ad Banned." www.nydailynews.com. January 29, 2014.

"Robert Downey, Jr. & Scarlett Johansson Make Magic." *USA Weekend.* December 24–26, 2010, p. 10.

Roberts, M. B. "Photos: See Scarlett Johansson, Chris Evans and Others on Star-Studded USO Holiday Tour." https://parade.com. December 20, 2016.

Robinson, Joanna. "Master of the Universe." *Vanity Fair* (Holiday 2017/2018): 88–103, 143–144.

Romeyn, Kathryn. "Scarlett Johansson's 'Avengers' Workout: How to Get a Black Widow Body." www.hollywoodreporter.com. April 26, 2019.

Romney, Jonathan. "Away from the Picture." [*Under the Skin* soundtrack] *Sight & Sound.* April 2014, p. 25.

Romney, Jonathan. "Unearthly Stranger." [*Under the Skin*] *Sight & Sound.* April 2014, pp. 22–24, 26–27.

Rose, Charlie. "Sofia Coppola." https://charlierose.com/videos/13710. September 18, 2003.

Rosen, Christopher. "Scarlett Johansson's 'Her' Role Might Make History at Oscars." www.huffingtonpost.com/2013/10/14/scarlett-johansson-her_n_4096897.html. October 18, 2013.

Rossi, Rosemary, and Gonzalez, Umberto. "Scarlett Johansson: My Casting Comments Were 'Edited for Click Bait,' 'Taken Out of Context.'" www.thewrap.com. July 14, 2019.

Rothman, Michael. "How Scarlett Johansson Really Felt About Doing Nude Scenes." https://abcnews.go.com. April 1, 2014.

Rothman, Michael. "Scarlett Johansson Named *Esquire's* Sexiest Woman Alive, Again." http://abcnews.go.com. October 11, 2013.

Russian, Ale. "Scarlett Johansson: My Brother, My Hero." *People.* April 6, 2020, p. 24.

Sachs, Adam. "Babe: Scarlett Johansson." *GQ* (December 2010): 305.

"SCARJO's ENGAGED TOO!" *People.* September 23, 2013, p. 23.

"Scarlett Johansson and Dave Sitek Premiere Tom Waits Tribute," www.stereogum.com, February 13, 2008.

"Scarlett Johansson and Ryan Reynolds to Embark on European Honeymoon." www.aceshowiz.com. October 10, 2008.

"Scarlett Johansson and Ryan Reynolds Wed." www.aceshowbiz.com. September 29, 2008.

"Scarlett Johansson, Chris Evans, Ray Allen and More Visit Service Members on USO Chairman's Holiday Tour." https://uso.org/stories/1939-scarlett-johansson-chris-evans-ray-allen. December 12, 2016.

"Scarlett Johansson Dreads Looking an Old Hag!" www.newkerala.com. March 28, 2007.

"Scarlett Johansson Gets Her Breasts Squeezed." http://www.thesuperficial.com. January 17, 2006.

"Scarlett Johansson in Ad Campaign for Moet & Chandon." www.mediapost.com. February 22, 2011.

"Scarlett Johansson Named Playboy's Sexiest Celebrity." www.aceshowbiz.com. February 20, 2007.

"Scarlett Johansson Pleased by 'Female Energy' on Set." *Brampton Guardian* [Ontario]. December 6, 2016.

"Scarlett Johansson Provides a Window Into Black Widow." *Life Story: Movie Magic Collector's Edition* (2015): 28–30.

"Scarlett Johansson Shoots Selfies with Fans at Huawei P9 Fans Club Party Event." *Canada Newswire.* November 17, 2016.

"Scarlett Johansson's Mucous Sells for $5,300." www.celebitchy.com. December 24, 2008.

"Scarlett Johansson's Pregnancy Won't Affect *Avengers* Script." www.chinadaily.com.cn. March 14, 2014. [1 page]

"Scary Scarlett Turns Heads with Gruesome Stunt." *The Daily Mail.* www.dailymail.co.uk. April 23, 2007.

Schleicher, Brad. "Scarlett Johansson, Jennifer

Connelly in Town for 'He's Just Not That Into You.'" www.baltimoresun.com. November 16, 2007.

Schwerdtfeger, Conner. "Scarlett Johansson Looks Intense and Gorgeous in First Ghost in the Shell Pic." www.cinemablend.com. April 17, 2016.

Schwerdtfeger, Conner. "Scarlett Johansson May Take on Gamergate in Her Next Movie, Get the Details." www.cinemablend.com. November 11, 2015.

Schwerdtfeger, Conner. "Scarlett Johansson's Ghost in the Shell Back on Track with an Exciting Hire." www.cinemablend.com. October 25, 2015.

Schwerdtfeger, Conner. "SNL Is Adding Another Woman to the Five-Timers Club." www.cinemablend. February 24, 2017.

Scott, Ryan. "Scarlett Johansson's Exit." [*Rub & Tug*]. https://movieweb.com. July 17, 2018.

Sessums, Kevin. "The World According to Scarlett." *Allure*. November 2006, pp. 192–197.

Shoan, Tatijana, and Salle, David. "Scarlett." *As If*. Issue No 15 (2019).

Shuda, Caitlin. "Scarlett Johansson Helps Wisconsin Rapids Girl Fight Cancer." *AP Regional State Report—Wisconsin*. January 14, 2017.

Sinclair, Charlotte. "Ethics Girl." *Vogue* [U.K.]. October 2006, pp. 314–323.

Sinha-Roy, Piya. "Why Wes Anderson Went to Japan." [*Isle of Dogs*] *Entertainment Weekly*. March 30, 2018. pp. 34–35.

"The Smart Bomb." *Elle*. January 2006, pp. 122–129. Preceded by one page "Taking Charge" by Nina Garcia with Johansson in Raffia dress.

Smith, Paul Julian. "Tokyo Drifters." [*Lost in Translation*] *Sight & Sound*. January 2004, pp. 12–16.

Snyder, Daniel D. "Scarlett Johansson Has the Most Human Moment in 'The Avengers.'" www.theatlantic.com. May 7, 2012.

So, Jimmy. "Scarlett Johansson Is an Alien Seductress in *Under the Skin*." www.thedailybeast.com. April 3, 2014.

Stanley, Alessandra. "Scarlett Letters." *Vogue*. April 2007, pp. 323–331.

Stein, Danielle. "Sister Act." *W*. March 2008, pp. 434, 439–443.

Stern, Marlow. "Sofia Coppola Discusses 'Lost in Translation' on Its 10th Anniversary," www.thedailybeast.com, September 12, 2013.

"Stiller, Johansson Named Hasty Pudding's Man and Woman of the Year." http://news.harvard.edu/gazette. January 29, 2007.

Stinson, Jeffrey. "Hollywood Enters the Era of Scarlett Johansson." http://usatoday.printthis.clickability.com. August 22, 2007.

"Storm of Praise for Under the Skin at Venice." www.bfi.org.uk/news-bfi/features/storm-praise-under-the-skin-venice. September 3, 2013.

"Stunning Scarlett Delivers Bombshell Glamour at Benefit." *Hellomagazine.com*. http://uk.news.yahoo.com/hello. May 7, 2007.

Suhay, Lisa. "Scarlett Johansson in 'Ghost in the Shell': No Asian Actors Available?" (+video). *Christian Science Monitor*. www.csmonitor.com. January 5, 2015.

Sykes, Tom. "Scarlett Johansson's Sexy Style." *Harper's Bazaar*. January 2005, pp. 72–77.

Thakur, Monami. "Scarlett Johansson Shares the Magic of Moet & Chandon in Heritage Campaign (Exclusive Video)." www.ibtimes.com. February 21, 2011.

"Thank You for Everything Dave! Scarlett Johansson Heaps Praise on Letterman While Promoting *Avengers: Age of Ultron*." *Daily Mail*. April 30, 2015.

"There's Only Room for One Scarlett Johansson." *Sunday Star-Times* [New Zealand]. May 18, 2014, p. B15.

"These Film-Fest Faves Are on the Rise." *USA Today*. September 16, 2019, Life, pp. 1D, 2D. [*Marriage Story*]

Thompson, Anne. "Why Jonathan Glazer's 'Under the Skin' Took a Decade to Make (VIDEOS)." www.indiewire.com. October 23, 2014.

Thorpe, Vanessa. "Scarlett Johansson, Charismatic Queen of Science Fiction." www.theguardian.com. March 25, 2017.

Toomey, Alyssa. "Awkward! John Travolta Gives Scarlett Johansson a Smooch…and She Responds with Side Eye: Pics!" www.eonline.com. February 22, 2015.

Truitt, Brian. "Coens Hail the Bygone Era of the Hollywood Fixer." *USA Today Life*. February 5, 2016, p. 6B.

Truitt, Brian. "Iron Man 2's Dynamic Duo." *USA Weekend*. April 23–25, 2010, pp. 6–7.

Truitt, Brian. "Mom Lifts 'Jojo Rabbit' Above Satire." *USA Today*. September 16, 2019, Life, p. 2D.

Valby, Karen. "Let's Kick Through the Glass Ceiling. Now." *Entertainment Weekly*. August 15, 2014, p. 14.

Veronica. "16 Reasons Why Girls Hate Scarlett Johansson (But Guys Love Her)." www.therichest.com. May 25, 2017.

Virtue, Graeme. "Scarlett Johansson in *Ghost in the Shell*—will Something Be Lost in Translation?" *The Guardian*. www.theguardian.com. January 6, 2015.

Waintal, Fabian W. "Interview Hollywood: Scarlett Johansson." *Vanidades*. June 2016, pp. 118–121. [Spanish-language Mexican magazine]

Wakeman, Gregory. "4 Huge Mistakes Scarlett Johansson's Ghost in the Shell Made." www.cinemablend. April 4, 2017.

Wakeman, Gregory. "The Soonest We'll Find Out If a Black Widow Movie Is Happening, According to Scarlett Johansson." www.cinenablelnd.com. February 27, 2017.

Wakeman, Gregory. "The Three Highest Paid Actresses of 2016 May Surprise You." www.cinemablend.com. August 23, 2016.

Wakeman, Gregory. "To 3D or Not to 3D: Buy the Right Ghost in the Shell Ticket." www.cinemablend.com. March 31, 2017.

Walsh, Niamh, and Ryan, Alexandra. "Scarlett Johansson Fans Awaiting Her…." *Mail on Sunday*. March 23, 2014, p. 16.

Weaver, Hilary. "Scarlett Johansson and Husband

Romain Dauriac Are Separated." www.vanityfair.com. January 25, 2017.

Wei, Liu. "Film Heroes Descend on Beijing." [*Captain America: The Winter Soldier*]. www.chinadaily.com.cn. April 2, 2014. [2 pages]

WENN. "Johansson Fuels *South Pacific* Rumours." http://uk.news.yahoo.com/wenn. April 16, 2007.

WENN. "Scarlett Plays It Ugly on Comedy Show." [*Saturday Night Live*] www.hollywood.com. April 23, 2007.

"What's Wrong with a Naked Woman?" www.cnn.com. February 23, 2006.

"Why Black Widow Really Won't Choose a Side in Civil War." www.cinemablend.com. December 5, 2015.

Wilson, Paul. "Final Cut: Showbiz Divorcee Noah Baumbach's New Film Is About a Showbiz Divorce." [*Marriage Story*] Esquire. August 2019.

Wood, Gaby. "Beyond Borders." *Vogue*. April 2019, pp. 127–141, 196–197.

Wood, Matt. "The 10 Highest Grossing Movie Stars of All Time." www.cinemablend.com. June 29, 2016.

Wood, Matt. "When Scarlett Johansson May Start Developing the Black Widow Movie. Www.cinemablend.com. January 13, 2018.

Wood, Matt. "Why Scarlett Johansson Works in This *Ghost in the Shell*, According to the Producer." www.cinemablend.com. July 1, 2016.

"'World's Sexiest Body' Scarlett Sports a Plump Derriere—or Is It Just Bad Shorts?" *The Daily Mail*. www.dailymail.co.uk. July 5, 2007.

Yasharoff, Hannah. "Scarlett Johansson Slams Paparazzi for Chase: 'Just a Waiting Game' Until Someone Gets Killed." www.usatoday.com. April 9, 2019.

Yuan, Jada. "A Woman in Full." *Cosmopolitan*. May 2016, pp. 160–165 (+ photos on pp. 159, 160, 163, 164).

Zakarin, Jordan. "Jonathan Glazer on Struggles with Scarlett Johansson's 'Under the Skin' and 'Suspecting Everything You Do Is Bad.'" www.thewrap.com. April 14, 2014.

Zuckerman, Esther. "What, Exactly, Makes Scarlett Johansson's Voice So Sexy?" www.refinery.com. April 17, 2016.

Books

Bailey, Jason. *The Ultimate Woody Allen Film Companion*. Minneapolis, MN: Voyageur Press, 2014.

Banks, Michelle, ed. *Magill's Cinema Annual 1999: A Survey of the Films of 1998*. 18th ed. Farmington Hills, MI: Gale, 1999.

Bolton, Lucy. *Film and Female Consciousness: Irigaray, Cinema and Thinking Women*. New York: Palgrave Macmillan, 2011. [*Lost in Translation*]

Cohen, David S. *The Art of Ghost in the Shell*. San Rafael, CA: Insight Editions, 2017.

Ehrlich, Gretel. *The Horse Whisperer: An Illustrated Companion to the Major Motion Picture*. Foreword by Robert Redford. New York: Dell Publishing, 1998.

Foster, Maureen. *Alien in the Mirror: Scarlett Johansson, Jonathan Glazer and Under the Skin*. Jefferson, NC: McFarland & Co. Publishers, 2019.

Masamune, Shirow. *The Ghost in the Shell Volume 1*. New York: Kodansha Comics, 1991.

McIntyre, Gina. "The Soldier and the Spy," *The Ultimate Guide to the Avengers*," Tampa, FL: Entertainment Weekly Books, 2018.

Newton, Michael. *Show People: A History of the Film Star*. London: Reaktion Books, 2019. Chapter 38: "Scarlett Johansson: A New Kind of Emptiness."

Roberts, Chris. *Scarlett Johansson: Portrait of a Rising Star*. London: Carlton Books, 2007.

Roussos, Eleni. *Avengers: Endgame—The Art of Marvel Studios*. New York: Marvel Worldwide, Inc., 2019.

Smith, Ian Haydn. *Movie Star Chronicles: A Visual History of the World's Greatest Movie Stars*. Buffalo, NY: Firefly Books, 2015.

Tomassini, Christine, ed. *Magill's Cinema Annual 2002: A Survey of the Films of 2001*. 21st ed. Farmington Hills, MI: Gale, 2002.

Turner, Pete. *Film Stars Don't Die in Liverpoool*. Picador, 2017, c1987. [re: Gloria Grahame]

Chapbook

Levy, Thomas Patrick. *Please Don't Leave Me Scarlett Johansson*. Blacksburg, VA: YesYes Books, 2011.

DVD Commentary

"Commentary by Billy Bob Thornton and Joel and Ethan Coen." *The Man Who Wasn't There* DVD. USA Films, 2002.

Jonathan Glazer, "Casting" Extras, *Under the Skin* DVD, Santa Monica, CA: Lions Gate Entertainment, 2014.

Scarlett Johansson, "The Cast," *Hitchcock* Blu-Ray, Beverly Hills, CA: Twentieth Century Fox Home Entertainment, 2013.

Magazines

Marvel/Topix Media Specials. *Captain America: Civil War Official Collector's Edition*. 2016.

Prince, Tom, ed. *Rise Up! the Women's Marches Around the World*. New York: Conde Nast, 2017.

Music Videos

Bad Dreams with Peter Yorn. 2018.

What Goes Around ... Comes Around with Justin Timberlake. 2007.

Radio Interview

Howard Stern. www.siriusxm.com/howard101. March 27, 2017.

Selected Television Interviews

Barbara Walters. *The 10 Most Fascinating People of 2014*. ABC TV. December 15, 2014.
Charlie Rose. https://charlierose.com.videos. December 12, 2003.
Charlie Rose. "Sofia Coppola." https://charlierose.com/videos/13710. September 18, 2003.
Finding Your Roots. PBS TV. Season 4, Episode 35: "Immigrant Nation." October 31, 2017.
Good Morning, America. March 28, 2017. [re: *Ghost in the Shell*]
The Late Late Show with Craig Ferguson. May 5, 2010. [re: *Iron Man 2*]
The Late Show with David Letterman. May 20, 1998. [re: *The Horse Whisperer*]
The Late Show with David Letterman. November 11, 2012. [re: *Hitchcock*]
The Late Show with David Letterman. April 27, 2015.
The Late Show with Stephen Colbert. September 9, 2015.
The Tonight Show with Jay Leno. January 11, 2005. [re: *A Love Song for Bobby Long*]
The Tonight Show with Jimmy Fallon. March 28, 2017.

Theatrical Programs

Cat on a Hot Tin Roof. New York: Playbill Incorporated, 2012.
A View from the Bridge. New York: Playbill Incorporated, 2010.

Websites

http://scarlett-johansson.us ("Adoring Scarlett Johansson").
www.scarlettjohansson.org.

Index

Academy Award nominations 12, 146
Academy Awards 3; 87th x; 89th xi
Academy of Motion Picture Arts and Sciences xi, 171
action set-pieces 133
Adams, Amy 175, 176, 178
Addams, Dawn vi
Adichie, Chimamanda Ngozi 158
Affleck, Ben 103
Agutter, Jenny 123
Alaska 110
Alda, Alan 168
Alexander, Jason 13
Alien in the Mirror: Scarlett Johansson, Jonathan Glazer and Under the Skin 186
Allen, Karen 146
Allen, Ray 154
Allen, Woody x, 5, 7, 69, 75, 77–91, 147, 148, 171
Almost Famous 108
Amazon 5
Amazon Prime 141
AMC Loews Lincoln Square Theater 160
AMC Marple 10, Springfield, Pennsylvania 1
AMC Neshaminy Mall 24, Pennsylvania 1
American Museum of Natural History 2018 Gala xi
An American Rhapsody 13, 28–32, 69
An American Tragedy (book) 83
The Americanization of Emily 96
amfAR (American Foundation for AIDS Research) 156
Andrews, Julie 146, 217
anime 196
Aniston, Jennifer 103
Anthony, Emjay 133, 145
"Anywhere I Lay My Head" x, 183
The Apartment 96
Aronofsky, Darren 117
Arquette, David 38
Art, Nicholas 94
The Art of Ghost in the Shell (book) 196
art of stillness 3
As You Like It 161

Asbaek, Pilou 187, 192
Ashkenazi Jews 9
Atwell, Hayley 122, 129
Auntie Mame 10
Avatar 107, 146
Avatar 2 107
The Avengers 113, 120–122, 125, 146, 149, 186
The Avengers: Age of Ultron x, 126–128, 131
Avengers canon 148
Avengers: Endgame 66, 134–138, 164, 171; world premiere xi
The Avengers: Infinity War 131–134, 136, 138, 141, 156; world premiere xi
awards talk 199

"Babe of the Year" x
Bacall, Lauren 3, 10
Badalucco, Michael 34
BAFTA 199
BAFTA Award for Best Actress ix, 54
Bagram Air Base, Afghanistan 154
Bainkamp, Hedda 9
Bala Theatre, Bala Cynwyd, Pennsylvania 1
Baldwin, Alec 90, 157
Bale, Christian 72, 75
Bana, Eric 97, 98, 99, 217
Banfalvy, Agi 28
"The Bangover" *see Franklin & Bash*
Banlaki, Kelly *see* Endresz-Banlaki, Kelly
Bansagi, Raffaella 28
Barber, Mike 57–58
Bardem, Javier ix, 88, 89, 90, 91
Barrymore, Drew 103, 104, 157
Bassinger, Kim 22
Batman (character) 102, 154
Baumbach (Noah) 169, 199
Bautista, Michael, Jr. 132
Bay, Michael 173, 174
Bayer, Samuel 93
Bean, Sean 172
Beck 182
Bedouin 142
Beginners 163
Behrendt, Greg 104

Bell, Jillian 159
Bell, Joshua 110
Bello, Maria 158
Bendell, Emily 148
Bergen, Candice 157
Berman, Shari Springer 94
Berry, Halle 92, 156
Besson (Luc) 191
Best International Actress award x
Bettany, Paul 118, 121, 126, 129
Biel, Jessica 57, 74, 111, 174
Big Brother (TV) x
Binoche, Juliette 192
Birch, Thora 32, 33
Birdman 166
Birth 187
"Bizarre Love Triangle" x
The Black Dahlia 66, 69–72, 77
Black Panther 133
The Black Swan 117
Black Widow 163, 199
Black Widow (character) xi, 6, 105, 118, 129, 131, 133, 134, 136, 137, 138, 139, 148, 195; controversial death 136; movie 156; standalone 129, 131, 136, 139; ziploc bags 148
Blow Out 72
The Blue Dahlia 72
Bluebella 148
Bluemhuber, Claudia 187
Blunt, Emily 120
Bolton, Lucy (author) 45
The Bonfire of the Vanities 72
Bonjour Tristesse 3
Bono 92
Boseman, Chadwick 129, 132
Bosworth, Kate 23
Bourdain, Anthony (author) 45
Bowie, David 72
Boys Don't Cry 182
Break Up (album) x, 105, 162
Brexit 163
British Academy of Film and Television Arts xi, 5, 171
Brolin, Josh 132, 134, 149
The Brown Bunny 182
Bruhl, Daniel 129
Bryn Mawr Film Institute 1
Buckley, Carla 199
Burrell, Ty 159
Buscemi, Steve 32, 173

237

Index

Butterfield 8 186
Byron 61

Cabaret 166
Caine, Michael x, 72
Cameron, Dove 157
Camp, Colleen 29, 30–31
Campbell, Craig 154
Capote 68
Captain America (character) 6, 102
Captain America: Civil War 129–131, 133, 138, 139
Captain America: The First Avenger 125
Captain America: The Winter Soldier 6, 113, 122–126, 141, 146, 147, 149, 171; fighting in 125
Cassavetes, John 9
Cat on a Hot Tin Roof (Broadway) x, 140–141; 1955 stage production 140; 1958 film version 140
Cat on a Hot Tin Roof (film) 186
cat woman 128
Cataldi, Angelo 3
Cavill, Henry 153
celebrity 93
celebrity grind 3
celebrity machine 13
"Celebrity 100" 148
CGI (computer-generated imagery) 118
Chairman's USO Holiday Tour xi
Chaney, Christopher 107
Changing Faces 185
Chaplin vi
charity fashion events 3
Chasing Ice 110
Chateau Marmont ix, x, 55
Che, Michael 157
Cheadle, Don 118, 129
Chef 6, 113, 141, 143–145, 171; buddy picture 145; "sleeper" 144
China 153
Christensen, Erika 51, 52
Christopher Street 11
Church, Thomas Haden 108
Church of Scientology 162
Czinkoczi, Zsuzsa 28
Clarke, Cody 19
Clarke, Jason 146
Clarkson, Patricia 88, 91
"Climb Every Mountain" 147
Clinton, Hillary Rodham 158
Clooney, George 128, 149
Close Encounters of the Third Kind 71
Clowes, David 34
Coachella Valley Music and Arts Festival 97
Coen, Ethan 36, 149, 151, 152
Coen, Joel 36, 149, 151, 152
Coleman, Oliver 97
Colonial [Theater], Phoenixville, Pennsylvania 1
Columbus, Chris 22
comedy-drama 96

The Comedy of Errors 161
Complicit (perfume) 157
computer operating system 175
Connelly, Jennifer 103, 104
Connolly, Kevin 104
Conspiracy Theory 128
The Constant Gardener 68
Cooper, Bradley 103, 104, 132
Coppola, Sofia 45, 46, 51, 54; Academy Award–winning script (*Lost in Translation*) 48
coronavirus 199
Cort Theatre 106
The Courtship of Eddie's Father 96
COVID-19 pandemic 138
Coward, Noel 57
Cox, Brian 78, 82
Crain, Jeanne 57
Crawford, Clayne 62
Creative Artists Agency 162
Crimes and Misdemeanors 81
Crossing Delancey 10
Crowe, Cameron 108, 110
Cruise, Tom 128; auditioning to date 162
Crumb 34
Cruz, Penelope 88, 89, 91, 99; Academy Award 91
Culkin, Macaulay 22
Cumberbatch, Benedict 97, 132
The Custom of the Country 5

The Daily Beast 5
Damon, Matt 107
Danish 9
Dauriac, Romain x, 141, 145, 146
David H. Koch Theater 158
Davis, Essie 49
Davis, Roman Griffin 164, 165, 166–167
Dawn of the Planet of the Apes 146
de Cadenet, Amanda 20, 22
The Deepest Secret (book) 199
Delaware 1
del Toro, Benicio 132
Democratic National Convention (2012) x, 113
de Palma, Brian 71, 77
Dern, Laura 168, 169, 171, 199
Diaz, Cameron 54
Diesel, Vin 132
Dinklage, Peter 132
DiRado, Maya 154
Disney (studio) 146, 166
Divergent 197
Dr. X 195
Dolby Theatre 133, 146, 156
Dolce and Gabbana x, 5, 113, 117
Don Jon 6, 113, 114–117, 171, 199
Douglas, Illeana 33
Downey, Robert, Jr. x, xi, 118, 120, 126, 129, 132, 134, 137, 144, 162, 164
Downs, Paul W. 159
Dreiser, Theodore 83
Dressed to Kill 72
Driver, Adam 168, 169, 199
Dukovic, Paul (photographer) 142

Dunn, Kevin 88
Dunst, Kirsten 93, 158, 186
Dushku, Eliza 120
Dylan, Bob ix

E! People's Choice Award as Female Movie Star of 2018 xi, 134
Earth vs. the Spider 40
Eastern Europe 9
Easy Virtue 57
eBay x
Eckhart, Aaron 69, 70
Eight Legged Freaks 38–40
Eisner, Will 102
El Capitan Theatre 124
Elba, Idris 131
Elkins, William L. 106
Elkins Park 106
Elstowe Manor 106
Emmy Awards xi
Endresz-Banlaki, Kelly 28
Enemy of the State 128
Esquire ix, x; Sexiest Woman Alive 140
Evans, Chris x, xi, 51, 52, 53, 94, 95, 96, 120, 125, 126, 129, 132, 154, 162
Evans, Nicholas 24
Eyes Wide Shut 116

Fall 20–22
"Falling Down" 183
The Fan 57
Fargo 17
Faris, Anna 41, 47
Farley, Chris 113
Farrow, Dylan 90
Farrow, Mia 40
fashionista 3, 163
Favreau, Jon 6, 118, 119, 120, 137, 144, 145
Feige, Kevin 129, 199
Female First (website) 93
Female Movie Star of 2018 *see E! People's Choice Award*
Ferdinando, Peter 192
Ferrera, America 155
Fey, Tina 157
FHM ix
Fiennes, Ralph 50
15th Nobel Peace Prize Concert for Martti Ahtisaari x
57th New York Film Festival 168
Film and Female Consciousness (book) 45
film premieres 3
Fincher, David 6
Finding Your Roots xi, 9
Firth, Colin 49, 50
Fishburne, Laurence 54
Five Timer Club (*Saturday Night Live*) xi
fluff 53, 198
Forbes 148
Ford, Faith 13, 14
Ford, Harrison 153
Ford, Tom 67
Foster, Barry 83

Foster, Jodie 92
Foster, Maureen 186
Fox Searchlight 166
Fox Theatre (Atlanta) 162
Franco, James 162
Franklin & Bash 106
Freaky Friday 69
Freeman, Morgan 110, 188
Frenzy 83
Frost, Robert 48
Frozen (142)
Fuoco, Nick 27, 28

Gabbana, Stefano 117
Galko, Balazs 28
Gallo, Vincent 182
Gandolfini, James 34
Garai, Romola 83
Gardos, Eva 30–31
Garland, Judy 10
Gates, Henry Louis, Jr. 9
Geddes, Barbara Bel 140
Generation Award x
Germany x
Gervasi, Sacha 112
Ghost in the Shell 6, 45, 156, 157, 162, 164, 166, 192–197; 1995 Japanese animated feature 195
Ghost Rider 74
Ghost World 32–34, 54, 199
Giamatti, Paul 94
giant spider/bug subgenre 40
Gill, Dante 163
Gillan, Karen 132, 134, 199
Girl with a Pearl Earring ix, 5, 12, 46, 49–51, 54, 146, 186, 198, 199
The Girl with the Dragon Tattoo 6
Gladiator clone 5
Glazer, Ilana 159
Glazer, Jonathan 1, 182, 183, 186, 187
Global Fund to Fight Aids, Tuberculosis, and Malaria in Africa 92
Golden Camera Awards x, 110
Golden Globe 63, 67
Golden Globe Award nominations ix
Golden Globes xi, 46
Golden Globes Awards 68
Golden Globes nomination 65, 199
Golden Ratio 148
Goldenhersh, Heather 151
Goldwyn, Tony 28, 29
Good Morning, America 157
A Good Woman 7, 55–59
Goode, Matthew 78, 82
Goodwin, Ginnifer 103, 104
Gordon-Levitt, Joseph 113, 114, 116
Gosselaar, Mark-Paul 107
GQ x
Grace, Topher 60, 65, 99
The Graduate 96
Grease 65
Great Expectations (1946) 186
The Great Gatsby 109
Greenberg, Bryan 51, 52

Greenland ice caps 110
Greenwich Village 10
Greenwich Village School 11
Gregg, Clark 60, 121
Griffith, Scarlett 155
Grillo, Frank 122, 129, 162
Guardians of the Galaxy 197
Gustav Flaubert's *Salammbo* 55

Hagerty, Julie 168
Hail, Caesar! 36, 149–153; Coen brothers romp 153
Halfon, Liane 33
Hall, Philip Baker 60
Hall, Rebecca 72, 75, 89, 91
Hamilton 156
The Hangover 160
Harlow, Jean 3
Hartley-Merrill International Screenwriting Competition 30
Hartnett, Josh 69, 70, 71, 72
Harvard Hasty Pudding Woman of the Year Award ix, 92
Hawke, Ethan 11
Hayworth, Rita 40
Headly, Glenne 114
Helgenberger, Marg 60, 157
Hemsworth, Chris x, xi, 120, 126, 131, 164
Hepburn, Audrey vi
Hepburn, Katharine 92
Her x, 6, 12, 113, 141, 142, 171, 173–179, 190, 199; Best Original Screenplay Academy Award 177
Herbie: Fully Loaded 69
Hernandez, Maximiliano 123, 162
He's Just Not That Into You 103–105
Hiddleston, Tom 120, 126, 131
Hitchcock (Alfred) 1, 83, 112, 199
Hitchcock 110–113
The Hobbit: The Battle of the Five Armies 133
Hobbs, Jeremy 77
Hoffman, Dustin 144, 145
Hoffman, Philip Seymour 68
Holland, Tom 129, 132
Hollis, Dave 125
Hollywood Film Festival 29
Hollywood glamour 5
Hollywood Walk of Fame x
Hollywoodland 71
Home Alone 22
Home Alone 3 22
Hong Kong x, 153
Hopkins, Anthony 110, 112
Horowitz, Josh 156
The Horse Whisperer ix, 11, 23–26, 46, 67, 68, 69, 147, 198, 199
Hounsou, Djimon 172
House of Whipcord 221
Huawei and Leica 153
Huawei P9 (smart phone camera) 153
Huawei P9 Fans Club Party 153
Hudson, Kate 50
Huffington, Arianna 158
Huffman, Felicity 162, 163

Hughes, John 22
Hulk (character) 6
Hungary 30
The Hunger Games 174, 197
Hunt, Helen 55, 56
Hurricane Katrina 92
Hurricane Maria 162
Hurt, William 129
husky voice 3
HYDRA 126

If Lucy Fell 19–20
The Illusionist 74
In Good Company 59–62, 65, 99, 157
In the French Style 3
In Touch 69, 76
The Incredible Shrinking Man 40
Independent Spirit Award ix, 17
"indie" films 199
indies 163
Indio, California 97
Iron Man 118, 120
Iron Man 2 6, 53, 105, 118–120, 136, 137; diet and training 119
Irving, Penny 221
Isherwood, Christopher 166
The Island 6, 66, 69, 172–174; improper marketing 174; workouts 173
Isle of Dogs 6
Israeli Arabs 142

Jackman, Hugh 72, 73, 75, 83, 84, 87
Jackson, Samuel L. 100, 102, 118, 122, 126, 153
James, Henry 58
Jameson, Jenna 67
Jean-Remy Moet's French chalet 5
Jerry Maguire 108
The Jesus & Mary Chain (band) 97
Jimmy Kimmel Live x, xi, 133, 164
Johansson, Adrian 9
Johansson, Axel Robert 9
Johansson, Christian 9
Johansson, Ejner and Hedda Bainkamp 9
Johansson, Hunter 9, 11, 158
Johansson, Karsten 9
Johansson, Rose Dorothy x, 141, 145, 147
Johansson, Scarlett Ingrid ix, 1, 3, 14, 16, 19, 23, 28, 32, 35, 38, 41, 42, 49, 51, 52, 55, 56, 60, 62, 69, 70, 72, 73, 75, 76, 78, 79, 80, 83, 84, 88, 89, 94, 95, 97, 98, 101, 103, 108, 111, 118, 119, 120, 121, 122, 123, 124, 126, 127, 129, 130, 132, 134, 135, 137, 138, 144, 150, 154, 158, 159, 165, 168, 169, 172, 176, 180, 181, 184, 185, 188, 189, 193; Academy Award events 77; activism 158; anti-George Bush, Dick Cheney and Arnold Schwarzenegger 65; Asian admirers 153; Asian

character 162, 163; attention whore 6; attracted to the irrational 140; auditions 54; awards 5, 54; Best International Actress award (Golden Camera Awards) 110; black catsuit 53; blank stare 190; body 40, 93; born 9; bosom 76; Box Office mojo status 153; Broadway, dreaming of 9; canned ham 67; car accident 65; career 198; career path 5; career trajectory 198; charity and celebrity 92; Chihuahua Maggie 99; child 3, 5; child actress 13; child star 13; city girl 11; commercials 11; compassionate 55; Danish father's lineage 9; daughter 157; diet 136; dogs 105; dream to be a voice in a Disney musical 142; early films 13; eye candy 122; false media coverage 65; family 67; fashion-plate 149; father 11, 68; favorite films 147; figure 173; 5'4" on a good day 146; friends 66; friendship 141; fundraisers 155; game 137; "game-ness" 199; *Glamour* 93; Golden Globe Best Actress nominations 54; Golden Globes 171; grandmother 10, 67, 158; grandparents 9; Grey Poupon Dijon Mustard 68; hacked x, 107; hair 105; height 5; hidden talents 76; Hollywood starlet mode 102; indie films 110; indie status 141; integrity 90; international bacon 105; Internet Movie Database 5; "It Girl" 51; jazz hands 11; Jewish, identifies as 166; lack of style in contemporary life 66; lips 173; "love making movies" 67; low profile 174; marriage to Ryan Reynolds 102; Michael Kors jumpsuit 149; mini-theatricals 5; model 6; monogamy 100; mother 9, 10, 27, 54, 55, 92, 105, 112, 136; motherhood 141; moviegoing experience 107; moviemaking 5; muscles 149; naked 195; National Football League's Super Bowl (2014) 142; nicknames 11; not politically correct 90; nudity angle 184; nude scenes 67; object of desire 109, 143; "old soul" 125; "the other" 3, 5, 6, 7, 174; *People* (magazine) 141, 217; persona 45, 142; philosophy 146; plastic surgery 93; politics 155, 157, 161; pregnant 65; privacy 107, 164; private life 3; private parts 133; product endorsement gigs 5; P.S. 41 11; public assistance 11; public school 10; raising children 107; red carpet 76; red dress 68; relationships 141; Renaissance woman 149; robotic 153; "ScarJo"
136; sense of humor 81; sex appeal 93, 173; "Sex Star of the Year" (*Playboy*) 93; "sexiest woman in the world" 40; sexy 66; shoes 156; spokesmodel 3; spokesperson 5; "sports injuries" 125; stillness 46; stunts 136; superhero pantheon 190; tattoos 105; "Ten Most Fascinating People" TV series 145; "13 going on 30" 27; throaty voice 11; throwback 55, 65; tonsils 65; top-grossing actress of all time, 149; trajectory 5; turtlenecks 113; unique cinematic persona 172; unique oeuvre 174; "very strong work ethic" 117; "voice work" 177; White House Correspondents Dinner 105; *womanness* 77; work 49, 55, 66, 198; work mode 102
Johansson, Vanessa 9
Johansson-Dauriac marriage 142
The John Gore Organization 162
Jojo Rabbit xi, 131, 141, 163, 164–168, 171, 199; costume 167; "goofy element" 168
Jolie, Angelina 3
Jones, Toby 123
Jonze, (Spike) 177, 179
Jost, Colin xi, 164
Jumanji 158
The Jungle Book 153
Jurassic Park 113, 146
Just Cause 15–16
"Just Like Honey" (song) 97

Kani, John 129
Karol, Jim 154
Katic, Stana 101
Katz, Ross 54
Kazan, Elia 9
Keaton, Diane 90
Kelly, Grace ix
Kerry, John 65
Kicking and Screaming 169
Kidman, Nicole 162
Kierkegaard 105
Kikuchi, Rinko 195
Kim, Claudia 126
King, Jaime 101
Kingdom of the Spiders 40
Kinski, Nastassja 28, 29, 30
Kirshner, Mia 69, 70
Kitano, "Beat" Takashi 192
Kitchen Confidential (book) 45
Klementieff, Pom 132, 199
Knightley, Keira 5, 67, 93
Kravitz, Zoe 159, 161
Kretschmann, Thomas 126
Kruger, Diane 174
Kubrick, Stanley 116
Kunis, Mila 107
Kusanagi, Major 195

Ladd, Alan 72
Lady Gaga x, 146–147
Lady Windermere's Fan 57
Lake, Veronica 72
Lalonde, Daniel 5
Lamarr, Hedy 186
Lambert, Scott 54
Landin, Daniel 182
Larson, Brie 114, 199
The Last Days of Disco 182
"Last Goodbye" (song) 104
The Late Late Show with Craig Ferguson 105
The Late Show with David Letterman ix, x, 26–27, 57, 67, 147–148
The Late Show with Stephen Colbert x, 136, 149, 161
Lauria, Dan 101, 102
LBI Entertainment 162
Lee Strasberg Institute 11
Leibovitz, Annie ix, x, 55, 67
Leigh, Janet 112, 187, 190
Leno, Jay x; see also *The Tonight Show with Jay Leno*
"Let It Go" (song) 142
Leto, Jared 162, 163
Letterman, David ix, 26–27
Levi, Mica 182
LGBTQ advocates 163
LGBTQ performers 163
liberal 155
Library Journal 183
Lilith 3
Lincoln Center 158
Lincoln Center Alice Tully Hall 168
Linney, Laura 94, 95
Linz, Alex 22, 27, 28
Liotta, Ray 168
Lohan, Lindsay 69, 142, 158
Long Day's Journey Into Night 128
L'Oreal 5
Loren, Sophia 65
Los Angeles Convention Center 135
Lost in Translation ix, 5, 6, 41–48, 51, 54, 68, 81, 106, 113, 117, 146, 147, 149, 156, 186, 198, 199
Louis-Dreyfus, Julia 13
Louis Vuitton ix
Louisiana 63, 96; Dockside Studio 97
A Love Song for Bobby Long ix, 5, 62–65, 92, 147
Lucy x, 90, 110, 113, 141, 146, 147, 148, 149, 153, 161, 171, 187–192, 195, 199; TV ad time 190
Lurhmann, Baz 109

Ma, Ricky 153
Macht, Gabriel 62, 63, 65, 100
Mackie, Anthony 122, 129, 132, 141
Mad Max: Fury Road 190
Madame Tussauds (New York) x
Madonna 155
Maggie the Cat (character) 140
The Magnificent Seven 197
The Man Who Wasn't There 34–38, 151
Manga 196

Manhattan 86
Manny & Lo ix, 12, 16–19, 61, 69, 198
"Maori dude" 164
Mara, Rooney 6, 175, 176, 177
Marcuse, Herbert 151
Marjorie Morningstar (book) 51
Marquand, Ross 134
Marriage Story xi, 141, 164, 168–170, 171, 198, 199
Marvel film 167
Marvel Universe 96, 118, 136; merchandising 148; movies 6
Mary Poppins 96
Match Point ix, 5, 67, 68, 78–83, 147, 199; nominated for Best Screenplay Academy Award 81
Matinee 40
Maurice, Louisiana 96; Dockside Studio 96–97
McAdams, Rachel 67
McConnaughey, Mathew x, 117
McCowen, Alec 83
McCurley, Matthew 13
McDormand, Francis 17, 34
McDowell, Malcolm 60
McGregor, Ewan 172
McKellen, Ian 54
McKenzie, Thomasin 165
McKinnon, Kate 159, 160
McQueen, Alexander 163
McShane, Ian 83, 87
Meet Me in St. Louis 10
Memento 74
Mendes (Mendez), Eva 27, 28, 101
"message" movies 163
Messina, Chris 88, 91
Met Gala *see* American Museum of Natural History 2018 Gala
#MeToo movement 195
Metropolitan Museum of Art Costume Institute Benefit Gala 4
Meyer, Breckin 106
Meyers, Jonathan Rhys 78, 80
Miles, Darius 51, 52
Miles, Vera 112
military bases in Germany, Turkey, Qatar and Afghanistan 154
Miller, Arthur 105
Miller, Frank 102
Min-sik, Choi 187
Miranda, Linn Manuel 156
Mirren, Helen 111, 112
Miss You Already 182
Mission: Impossible 72, 128
Mitzrahi, Isaac 68
models 173
Moet & Chandon champagne 5
Monroe, Marilyn vi, 3, 10, 45, 66, 93, 143; "The Girl" 45; *The Seven Year Itch* 45
"The Moon Song" 142
Moonstruck 10
Moore, Demi 159, 161
Moore, Julianne 114, 117
Moore, Stephen Campbell 55
Morganti, Al 3

Morrissey, David 97
Mortimer, Emily 78, 82
Morton, Samantha 177
Most Dangerous Game/jungle scenario 174
Mouret, Roland 3
Move That Body see *Rough Night*
MTV Movie Awards (2015) x
MTV News announcer 156
Mulligan, Carey 109
Murciano, Enrique 160
Murray, Bill 41, 45, 46, 48, 68
Musk, Elon 149
Musso and Frank Grill 54
My Brother the Pig 22, 27–28

Nad's Hair Removal ix, 77
Nam, Leonardo 51, 52
The Nanny Diaries 94–96, 125
Nantucket, film festival in 30
Napoleon 5
Nazis 166, 171
Neshaminy Mall 1
Netflix 141, 169
Network 9
New Left 151
New Order x
New York City 1
New Zealand 195
Newell, Mike 50
Newman, Paul 163
Newtown Square, Pennsylvania 1
9½ Weeks 22
1984 (book) 179, 196
Nolan, Christopher 74, 75, 77
nomination, Golden Globe 67; Screen Actors Guild, and Academy Award 164
Noonan, Tom 38
North ix, 13–15
Norton, Edward 74
Norton, Richard 196
Novak, Kim 3, 217
nudity 67
NYU's film school 11

Obama, Barack x, 105, 113, 155; campaign 158
The Octopus (character) 102
Olsen, Elizabeth 126, 129, 132
The One (perfume) 117
"The One Street of Dreams" x
Oprah (Winfrey) 149
Orwell (George) 179
The Other Boleyn Girl 5, 97–100; sex scenes 99
Our Town xi, 162
Out Magazine 163
Oxfam (Oxfam Committee for Famine Relief) 77

Pacific Rim 195
Palestinians 77, 142
Palladino, Aleksa 16, 17
Paltrow, Gwyneth 118, 121
paparazzi 3, 13, 66, 93, 164
The Parent Trap remake 69, 158
Pariseau, Marcel 164

Parker, Sarah Jessica 19
Paulson, Sarah 101, 102
Pearson, Adam 185
Pennsylvania 1
Perabo, Piper 72
The Perfect Score 5, 51–53, 125
Philadelphia 3, 106; metropolitan area 1; Ritz East 1
Phoenix, Joaquin 142, 175, 176, 177
Pitt, Brad 117
Pitt, Ingrid 5
Pitt, Michael Carmen 192
Place, Mary Kay 16
A Place in the Sun 83, 186
Planned Parenthood xi, 155; 100th Anniversary Gala 158
Playboy ix, 93
"Playboy's 25 Sexiest Celebrities" 93
Plummer, Christopher 163
Polito, Jon 34
Portman, Natalie 93, 97, 98, 99, 162
Pratt, Chris 132
pregnancy planning 155
Preminger, Otto 57
The Prestige 5, 68, 72–76
Previews of Coming Attractions 128
Princess Diana 66
Professional Children's School ix
Project Red 92
Promising Personality of 2001 ix
Psycho 112, 113
Puerto Rico 162; hurricane relief xi
Punk Chic 146
Pussycat Dolls ix

Quaid, Dennis 59, 60, 61
Queen of Science Fiction 156

racism 155
Raiders of the Lost Ark 146
Rear Window ix
Red Carpet x, 3, 156
Redford, Robert 23, 24, 26–27, 122
REDS 151
Reebok 5
Reflective Light 199
Regal Edgmont Square 10 1
Reid, Jim 97
Reiner [Rob] 15
Reinhold, Judge 27, 28
Rembrandt 51
Renner, Jeremy x, xi, 120, 129, 134, 162
Republicans 155
Requeim for a Dream 117
Resident Evil 197
Reynolds, Ryan x, 107; divorce 107
Ribisi, Giovanni 41, 47
Richard Rodgers Theater 140
Richards, Cecile 158
Rio Bravo 120
Ritter, John 13, 14

Roberts, Julia 54, 92, 157
Robertson, Azhy 168
Robinson, Edward G. 199
robot x
Rock, Chris 145
Rock That Body see *Rough Night*
Rockwell, Sam 165
Roeg, Nicolas 186
Rolling Stone 5
Rose, Charlie 45, 51
Rough Night 61, 159–162
Rourke, Mickey 22, 118
Rub & Tug 162, 164
Rudd, Paul 129, 134, 164
Ruffalo, Mark x, xi, 120, 126, 132, 134, 148, 162
Rushdie, Salman 183
Russell, Keri 146
Russell, Rosalind 10
Russell, Theresa 104
Russo, Anthony 133
Russo, Joe 133, 136
Ryan, Meg 92
Rylance, Mark 97

salary 136
Saldana, Zoë 132, 146, 199
Salle, David (artist) 164
"Samantha" operating system 175, 190
San Diego Comic-Con 139
Sanders, Rupert 195
Saturday Night Live ix, x, xi, 145, 148, 157, 160, 161, 164
Scandinavia 9
Scar-Jo 11, 177
Scarface (1983) 72
The Scarlet Lounge 55
Schaeffer, Eric 19, 20, 21, 22
Science Fiction, Fantasy and Horror Film Sequels, Series and Remakes 72
Scoop 78, 83–87
Scorsese, Martin x, 117
Screen Actors Guild xi, 171
Screen World 1959 3
Screen World 1964 3
Screen World 1965 3
Screen World 2002 ix
Seacrest, Ryan 156
Seberg, Jean 3
security detail 164
Segal, George (sculptor) 11
The Seven Samurai 197
Sevigny, Chloë 182
"Sex Star of the Year" ix
"Sexiest Woman Alive" ix, x, 76
Sexy Beast 187
Shakespeare 161
shaming Johansson 163
Shandling, Garry 118
The Shape of Water 166
Sheridan Square 10
S.H.I.E.L.D. 118, 120, 122, 125, 131
Shortland, Cate 139, 163
Shriver, Bobby 92
"silence, certain moments of" 93
silent movie 12

Simmons, Jean 186
The Simpsons x
Sin City 102
Sing 6, 153
Singles 108
Sitek, Dave 96
60th Annual Venice Film Festival Upstream Prize for Best Actress ix
Skarsgard, Stellan 120, 126
Sloan, Melanie 5, 9, 27
Slumdog Millionaire 166
"Smoothest Celebrity of the Year" ix, 77
Smulders, Cobie 122, 126
So, Jimmy 5
social activist 3
SodaStream 77, 142
Soldier in the Rain 96
Somersault 139
Sophistry 11
Sorrenti, Mario 106
The Sound of Music 146
southern New Jersey 1
Spader, James 126
Spider-Man 2 186
Spielberg, Steven 195
The Spirit 1, 27, 100–102
The Squid and the Whale 169
Stan, Sebastian 123, 129, 132
stardom 6
Stern, Howard 6, 47, 107, 157–158
Stevens, George 83
Stewart, James ix
Stiller, Ben 19
stillness see art of stillness
Strahan, Michael 157
Streep, Meryl 92
Street of Dreams 117
Strom, Bobby (celebrity trainer) 119
Sturgess, Jim 100
Subkoff, Tara 3
Summer Crossing 5
Sundance Film Festival 17
Sunset Boulevard 90
superhero movie, all female 199
superhero oeuvre 133
Superman (character) 102
Swank, Hillary 69, 70
Sweden 9
Synergy see *In Good Company*
Szabo, Klaudia 28

tabloids 10, 65, 66
Taipei 191
Tambor, Jeffrey 162, 163
Tarantula 40
Taylor, Elizabeth 65, 140, 186
Taylor-Johnson, Aaron 126
TCL Chinese Theatre 132, 137
Teen Choice Awards nomination 109
Teenage Mutant Ninja Turtles 120
"the 10 year rule" 198
Tesla electric car 149
Testino, Mario (fashion photographer) 153

This Is What Democracy Looks Like xi
Thomas, Kristin Scott 23, 97
Thompson, Tessa 199
Thor (character) 6
Thor (film) 122, 164
Thor: Ragnarok 131, 166, 199
Thornton, Billy Bob 33–36
A Thousand Clowns 96
Thrive Global 158
Timberlake, Justin ix, 92
Time's Up 162
The Tonight Show x
The Tonight Show with Jay Leno 65
The Tonight Shell with Jimmy Fallon 157
Tony Awards x, 106; presenter xi
Tony nomination 105
Toronto International Film Festival 167; The Groelsch People's Choice Award 167
Torrent, Ana 97
transgender people 163
Travers, Peter 5
Travolta, John x, 62, 63, 65, 76, 147
Tresca, Carlo 151
Trianon 5
Trudeau, Justin 158
Trump, Donald 155
Trump, Ivanka 156, 157, 158
Tsunami (India and Sri Lanka) 77
Tuccillo, Liz 104
Turner, Kathleen 3
Turner, Lana 40, 199
TV on the Radio (band) 96
12 Years a Slave 166
Twiggy 40
Twilight 182
2001: A Space Odyssey 171, 199

Ultron (character) 148
Umbers, Mark 55
Under the Skin x, 1, 6, 7, 12, 45, 76, 113, 125, 141, 146, 171, 179–187, 190, 195, 199; art house 181; Australian premiere 183; nudity angle 184; "too weird" 1; United Artists Theater (Los Angeles' Ace Hotel) 181; Venice Film Festival, boos and cheers 186; Washington, D.C. 1
Underworld 197
United Service Organizations (USO) 154
U.S. Department of Defense 154
U.S. troops overseas 154
U.S. Westerns 197
The Untouchables 72
Upper Manhattan 11
Urban Body Fitness (Atlanta) 136
USO Holiday Tour see Chairman's USO Holiday Tour

VanCamp, Emily 122
Vanity Fair ix, 106, 143, 199; cover (March 2006) ix, 5, 67, 92

Index

Venice and Toronto film festivals 164
Venice Film Festival 63, 76, 186; 70th Annual 185
Venice International Film Festival 141
Vergara, Sofia 144
Vermeer 50, 51
Very Bad Things 160
Vice Magazine x
Vicky Cristina Barcelona 75, 78, 88–91, 147, 183; Spanish shoot 90
A View from the Bridge (Broadway) x, 105–106
Violent Saturday 15
Virtual Reality Pictionary 157

Wahlberg, Mark 156
Waititi, Taika 131, 164, 166, 167; ancestry 166
Waits, Tom x, 97
Waked, Amr 188, 191
Walt Disney Studios 166
Walters, Barbara 145–146
Walthal (Windsor), Romy 28
Warsaw Ghetto 9
Washington, Denzel 110
Wayne, John 163
We Bought a Zoo 107–110, 186

Webber, Peter 50
Weekend at Bernie's 160
Weisz, Rachel 68
Weitz, Paul 61
Welcome Back, Kotter doll 65
West Bank settlements 142
West Chester, Pennsylvania 1
Wexner Center for the Arts exhibit x
Wharton, Edith 5
"What Goes Around Comes Around" (music video) ix, 92
"When the Deal Goes Down" ix
White Cargo 186
whitewashing 164, 166
Wild, Olivia 175
Wilde, Oscar 57, 58, 59
Wilder, Billy 45
Wilkinson, Tom 49, 55, 57
Willis, Bruce 13
Willy Wonka and the Chocolate Factory 10
Wilson, Owen 77
Wilton, Penelope 78, 82
Winchester, Tom 72, 74
Winslet, Kate 81
Winters, Dean 160
WIP Sports Radio 3
Wiz Khalifa 148

Woollahra's Hotel Centennial, Sydney, Australia 55
"Woman of the Year" (*Total Film*, February 2015) x
women: empowerment 163; roles for 190; working behind the scenes 154
Women in the World Summit xi, 158
Women's March (Los Angeles) 162
Women's March (Washington, D.C.) xi, 155, 158
Wong, Benedict 132
Wood, Elijah 13, 14
Wood, Natalie 13
Woolgar, Fenella 83
The World of Henry Orient 96
Worthington, Sam 146
The Wrestler 117
Wuhrer, Kari 38

Yorn, Peter x, 105, 106, 162
Yorn, Rick 105, 162

Ziegfeld Theater 172
Zeigler, Jesse 13, 14
Zsigmond, Vilmos 71
Zwigoff (Terry) 33, 34

www.ingramcontent.com/pod-product-compliance
Lightning Source LLC
Chambersburg PA
CBHW060339010526
44117CB00017B/2894